THE AGE OF RENAISSANCE AND REFORMATION

Charles G. Nauert, Jr.

UNIVERSITY PRESS OF AMERICA

LANHAM • NEW YORK • LONDON

University Press of America,™ Inc.

4720 Boston Way
Lanham, MD 20706

3 Henrietta Street
London WC2E 8LU England

Printed in the United States of America

Library of Congress Cataloging in Publication Data

Nauert, Charles Garfield, 1928–
The age of Renaissance and Reformation.

Reprint. Originally published: Hinsdale, Ill. : Dryden Press, c1977.
Includes index.
1. Renaissance. 2. Reformation. I. Title.
CB359.N38 1981 940.2 81–40034
ISBN 0–8191–1861–3 AACR2
ISBN 0–8191–1862–1 (pbk.)

All University Press of America books are produced on acid-free paper which exceeds the minimum standards set by the National Historical Publications and Records Commission.

Introduction

The age of the Renaissance and the Reformation, stretching roughly from 1300 to the end of the Thirty Years' War in 1648, used to be relatively simple to discuss. To most historical writers of the nineteenth century, the Renaissance marked the advance of European society from the primitive cultural level of the Middle Ages to the rich, creative, progressive culture of the modern world, beginning in fourteenth-century Italy and expanding geographically to non-Italian lands about 1500, when the "medieval" age ended and the "modern" age began for Europe north of the Alps. Then, in the sixteenth century, the Protestant Reformation, completing the work of the Renaissance, ended the spiritual tyranny of Rome and prepared the way (perhaps unwillingly) for the secular, scientific, progressive outlook of modern times.

Historians no longer think about the Renaissance-Reformation period in this way. Partly this is because study of the Middle Ages has vastly raised that epoch in our esteem. In particular, study of the medieval period shows clearly that the fundamental transformation of Europe from a disorganized, underdeveloped, and primitive society into a center of high civilization occurred in the central centuries of the Middle Ages (the twelfth and thirteenth centuries) and not in that later period that traditionally has been called the Renaissance.

Indeed, the period covered by the following chapters, far from being the starting point of everything modern and progressive, was an age of turmoil and disorganization, though also an age of high achievement. The great cultural triumphs of Renaissance Italy have as their social background not a new society just being born, but a long-established society caught in the grip of a crisis. The European civilization that had been born in medieval times did eventually recover: it reorganized and then utterly transformed its economic foundations, rebuilt its political institutions, and even survived the permanent loss of the ideological unity provided by the medieval Christian church. In the midst of this recovery, Renaissance Europe created brilliant new traditions in art, music, and literature, developed the secular state into the most effective governing agency in human history, and laid down the beginnings (but only the beginnings) of a new philosophical view of the universe, a new level of economic productivity, and a new competence in technology.

The student of Renaissance-Reformation history must begin by recognizing the spectacular advances made by medieval society. Then he needs to probe the depths and causes of the crisis that challenged and modified the medieval heritage. Finally, he needs to understand why the cultural leaders of the age became convinced that they were opening a new era in Western civilization, an era that they somewhat grandiosely and quite inaccurately described as a rebirth of civilization—a Renaissance, and in religious matters, a Reformation. The point is not to demonstrate how wrong these preachers of secular and religious renewal were but to understand why they thought as they did and what in fact they did accomplish. Those accomplishments demonstrate that the old historians, though wrong about much else, were quite correct in regarding the Age of the Renaissance and Reformation as one of the greatest periods in the whole history of mankind.

Contents

Chapter One

Medieval Society in Disarray

Although Europeans of the age of the Renaissance and Reformation frequently derided their medieval predecessors and talked almost as if by some miracle they had created themselves without benefit of ancestors, they owed much to the Middle Ages. That period had been profoundly original and creative. Its stupendous achievement is well summed up in the sharp contrast between the impoverished and primitive barbarian West of early post-Roman times and the rich, highly cultivated Europe of the high Middle Ages, the twelfth and thirteenth centuries. By then, the Latin West had not only pulled abreast of the great contemporary civilizations of Islam and Byzantium but had laid the foundations for the later European domination of the non-Western world, a domination that began to be established in the age of the Renaissance.

Defects of Medieval Culture

Despite its creativity, medieval civilization contained some fundamental defects that made the fourteenth and fifteenth centuries (the period of the Italian Renaissance) an age of instability, turmoil, and alienation. The crisis that became evident in the fourteenth century has even been compared to the crisis that shattered Roman society in the fourth century and led ultimately to Rome's fall. The comparison is not exact. The European civilization created in the Middle Ages did not "fall" in the fourteenth century. But many weaknesses became painfully evident, and European civilization survived only because it was flexible enough to make some fundamental modifications.

Medieval Social Change

Several weaknesses lay deep within medieval European culture. The traditional social structure and social ideology of the Middle Ages were products of the early medieval centuries, when society really did contain only three classes of men: the clergy, who prayed, the nobility, who fought and ruled, and the peasants, who toiled in fields. This feudal and manorial society was agrarian, static, and tradition-bound. But by the high Middle Ages, the archetypal medieval society of the thirteenth century that had produced St. Louis IX of France, St. Thomas Aquinas, and the great Gothic cathedrals had begun to disappear. The rise of commerce, cities, and middle-class merchants from the late eleventh century was already undermining the rural subsistence economy, the clear and stable class relationships, and even the value systems and ideologies inherited from the past. The new economic and social reality of a postmedieval age had already arrived, but old customs, attitudes, and institutions survived in a society that clung grimly to the old ways.

The clash between old and new was everywhere, and the many crises of the fourteenth and fifteenth centuries were the result of this clash. Thus, for example, the socially immobile, tradition-bound peasant village no longer functioned well, and the cause of the breakdown was not the numerous peasant rebellions (western Flanders, 1324–28; France, 1358; England, 1381) that afflicted the age but the attempts of the dominant landholding class, the nobility, to introduce far-reaching changes that would permit the nobles to cope with inflation, rising living standards, and the political and social pressure exerted by royal governments and city-dwelling merchants. Attempts to change from traditional subsistence agriculture to profit-seeking, efficient, commercial farming set the whole of peasant society in violent motion. In the profoundest sense, the real revolutionaries of the fourteenth century were not the peasants who rebelled but the noble landlords and the capitalistic merchants whose acts were undermining the old social world.

Underlying the many examples of disorder during the fourteenth and fifteenth centuries were four persistent, long-term problems for which the traditional medieval institutions could devise no effective remedies: (1) a severe economic collapse (closely linked to a catastrophic drop of population) from which recovery was slow and uneven; (2) dynastic and political crises that demonstrated the inability of even the strongest feudal monarchies to control the aristocracy and to pursue effectively the general interest of the nation; (3) a blatant secularization of the church, the greatest institution of medieval Europe, leading to widespread but generally unsuccessful agitation for drastic reforms; and (4) the undermining of both the intellectual tradition of high scholasticism and the lay tradition of chivalric culture by developments that shattered the old cultural norms without providing widely acceptable new systems of thought and literature. A strong element of gloom and pessimism runs through the culture of the later Middle Ages, and the popularity of such themes is no accident: it represents a valid expression of society that was experiencing real trouble in every area of life.

Economic Decline

The earliest and perhaps the most fundamental area of trouble was the economy. The rapid economic expansion that had made the twelfth and thirteenth centuries a period of real social and economic advance for all classes came to an abrupt halt by the early decades of the fourteenth century. One of the clearest indicators of economic difficulty was the fall or stagnation of population in most parts of fourteenth-century Europe.

Although precise data on medieval populations are scarce and hard to interpret, there is much evidence to suggest that the well-documented drop in the population of Florence from about 100,000 in the early fourteenth century to about 70,000 from the late fourteenth century throughout the rest of the Renaissance and Reformation period is typical. Certainly it is confirmed by figures for many other cities: Modena in Italy, from 22,000 in 1306 to fewer than 9,000 in 1482; Zurich in Switzerland, from 12,375 in 1350 to 4,713 in 1468; Toulouse in France from 30,000 in 1335 to about 20,000 in 1450. Figures for any national population before the nineteenth century are at best educated guesses, but estimates for England show about 3.7 million people just before the Black Death and a fall to 2.1 million in the early fifteenth century; even though growth of population resumed in the fifteenth century, England in 1555 was still a half-million short of its preplague population. Some cities, such as Antwerp in the Low Countries, or Augsburg in south Germany, and some regions, such as Catalonia in northeastern Spain, did continue to grow during the fourteenth century, but these seem to be special cases where relatively underdeveloped districts were catching up with districts that had matured earlier. Across Europe as a whole, population declined rapidly in the fourteenth century and then made only an incomplete recovery during the fifteenth. Not until late in the fifteenth century did population growth resume strongly.

The evidence for declining or stagnating population is not limited to the few city statistics and national estimates that we have. There is also indirect evidence of declining population. For example, much land of marginal fertility, which had been pressed into use during the population growth of the twelfth and thirteenth centuries, was abandoned in the fourteenth century and never again farmed. Another indirect reflection of declining population is that even though the fourteenth and fifteenth centuries experienced general monetary inflation, the prices of staple foodstuffs such as Prussian rye and English wheat declined until about 1500 not because production was greater but because there were fewer mouths to feed. Still another phenomenon that reflects smaller populations in western and central Europe is that by the fourteenth century the flood of German and Dutch peasant colonists into newly developed regions of Slavic eastern Europe came to an end. The cities of eastern Europe long remained largely Germanic in population, but rural districts that were still Slavic in 1300 have remained Slavic in population ever since.

Anticapitalistic Regulations

This shrinking population can be regarded as either a cause or an effect of the general economic decline. Probably it functioned in both ways. More clearly a cause of the economic downturn was the structural rigidity of medieval urban society, which hindered changes in products or techniques of production. The close regulation of trade and industry by guilds and by town laws was intended to prevent any one merchant or artisan from gaining an undue share of the market by producing shoddily (or more efficiently) or by taking on a larger than usual number of employees. Although this regulatory system was the product of middle-class social groups that are often described as capitalistic, it was inherently hostile to the expansive, profit-seeking spirit of true capitalism. It worked to limit production, to keep prices high, and to prevent change in the quality of products or the techniques of production. Thus it made merchants and artisans unable to respond creatively and flexibly to new economic conditions.

In a society where capitalist enterprise had long been a dynamic force leading to economic growth, the system of anticapitalistic guild regulation was probably one of the causes of the economic downturn and surely one reason why the downward trend, once it began, persisted for more than a century. The exceptions here proved the rule: where industrial and commercial expansion did continue during the late Middle Ages, as in west English woolen cloth industry, it did so because the organizing capitalists escaped the constrictive urban regulations by transferring production to rural districts. The new woolen districts developed where the region was suited for introduction of the water-powered fulling mill, which the entrenched urban producers had fought to prohibit ever since it was introduced back in the twelfth century. The urban governments (for example, the city of York in 1304) petitioned the royal government for national legislation to stamp out rural industrial production, but they never managed to get effective action; and so the west of England became a prosperous industrial area even during the period of general economic hardship.

Perhaps in part because of guild opposition to new technology that might upset vested economic interests, the fourteenth and fifteenth centuries were not a period of technological advance. Technological stagnation could even have been a direct cause of declining prosperity. This was true in most branches of the mining industry. By the fourteenth century, most of the important mining regions had been worked for so many centuries that the pits or shafts had become deep, and serious problems of shoring up passages and draining ground-water out of the workings made continued production costly, dangerous, and in some cases impossible. Not till the late fifteenth century did the development of a new technology of draining and pumping water in the mines of southern and eastern Germany bring a revival of prosperity in mining. Industrial technology also made no important new advances in the fourteenth and the first half of the fifteenth century. In the later fifteenth century, this condition began to change. The invention of printing during the 1450s gave rise to an entirely new industry. Also in the later fifteenth century, important changes in the construction and rigging of Spanish and Portuguese ships occurred, but this new maritime technology had little economic effect until the sixteenth century.

The Agrarian Problem

The economic downturn was not limited to the cities. The landowning aristocracy was hard-pressed for income in an age when most prices were rising and when living standards for the noble elite were going up, especially as the prices of most agricultural staples (the things the landlords had to sell) were declining. Thus the aristocrats tried to squeeze extra income out of their estates. Sometimes they merely cleared and farmed more land, but this method was no solution in an age of scarce labor and falling grain prices. Hence the landlords had to change their whole agricultural system, usually by abandoning general subsistence agriculture and concentrating on one cash crop for which there was an active demand. In many districts of England, for example, landlords abandoned the growing of food grains altogether and devoted their lands to production of high-quality wool, for which the traditional wool industry of Flanders and the new English woolen industry provided eager markets. Different crop adaptations were made elsewhere. Along the shores of the Baltic Sea in Poland, Prussia, Lithuania, and western Russia, fertile land and the availability of water transportation leading to the hungry cities of the Low Countries made production of bread grains (chiefly wheat and rye) the most profitable way to utilize land.

Rural Social Change

Any agricultural specialization meant abandonment of traditional medieval patterns of subsistence farming and local self-sufficiency. For the peasant community, it meant disruptive change. Centuries-old patterns of land distribution and crop rotation had to give way to introduction of new crops or, at very least, to the abandonment of subsidiary activities and direction of all efforts toward production of things that the landlord could sell at a profit. The medieval open-field system of farming was both inefficient and inflexible and often had to be broken up. The medieval peasant was also inefficient and inflexible, having no idea of any sort of farming other than what he and his ancestors had done in the past. The constant, grinding conflict of wills between landlords eager to introduce change and the sullen, stubborn peasant masses was a major reason why the later Middle Ages, when these pressures for change increased during a period of general economic difficulty, were marked by frequent peasant revolts. At its worst, the mood of the submerged rural population is demonstrated by the jacquerie, or French peasant rebellion, of 1356, when the peasants in many districts rose up without any clear political or economic goals and simply began a massacre of all persons of noble rank—men, women, and children—burning manor houses and other aristocratic property, and destroying the manorial records that provided evidence of their servile status and obligations.

The long-term social effects of these agricultural changes varied according to local economic and political conditions, but in all cases the changes were unsettling. In England, the change from grain production to sheep ranching caused landlords to seize control of commons and wastelands formerly available to the peasants as pasture, a practice known as enclosure. Where they could, landlords abolished the planting of grains altogether, evicted the tenants, and tore down whole villages. The landlords' eagerness to destroy the peasant community was caused not only by the good market for wool but also by the reduced need for labor in sheep ranching. The tenants were not a resource but a problem to be eliminated. The resultant squeezing of many English peasants off the land of their ancestors created the social problem of rootless, unemployed vagabonds. Late-medieval governments, justifiably fearful of vagabonds, brigands, and peasant revolutionaries, legislated against enclosure of lands and eviction of peasants; moralists and social critics (Sir Thomas More in his famous *Utopia*, for example) complained, but neither governments nor moralists could reverse the process.

This gradual and systematic impoverishment of many English peasants did have one positive effect which benefited English society in the long run. Precisely because so many English landlords tried to break up the traditional peasant village, the lords were often negligent in enforcing the labor services, dues, and fees their serfs owed them. Thus the agricultural changes in England had much to do with the gradual transition of the English masses from unfree serfs to free tenants. Serfdom was never abolished in England by legislation, but it dwindled away until fewer and fewer Englishmen bore the stigma of being legally unfree. Such long-term gains in social and legal status were, however, small comfort to peasants suddenly evicted from their lands and houses.

The tendency toward dissolution of the medieval manor and the release of the peasantry from personal bondage was speeded up in many parts of western Europe by the desire of many aristocratic landlords to escape the complexities of estate management by leasing their demesne lands to others. Such leaseholders found great difficulty in enforcing on the peasants all the obligations that the traditional lord had been given without question. Hence either leaseholders or the original landlord were often willing to commute the original labor obligations of the serfs into an annual payment in cash or in kind.

Such commutation of the most servile of all obligations (the obligation to render unpaid labor services) into a monetary payment speeded the transition of the peasants in western and parts of central Europe into legally free men. Although some traces of serfdom continued down to the French Revolution or after, what survived was usually a series of troublesome financial dues and social inequities rather than the full burden of personal serfdom. Thus the agricultural adaptations in late-medieval western Europe gradually transformed peasants into free men, even though these changes left them desperately poor and sometimes actually in a worsened material condition.

For the aristocratic landowners, the effects of leasing their demesne were mixed. Since many nobles lacked the keen business sense and ruthless disregard for tradition that efficient land management required, leasing their lands could save them from ultimate ruin. If the landowner took his rents in kind rather than in money or if he reserved the right to raise fees and rents at relatively short intervals, he might derive a substantial income with few administrative burdens. But if he set fees and rents in perpetuity or for many generations and, especially, if his income was set in inflation-ridden currency rather than in a share of the produce, he or his heirs might be trapped by inadequate fixed incomes in an age of inflation. Many noble families were impoverished by the effects of unwise leases and commutation arrangements. The poor nobleman, too impoverished to live off the revenues of his estate, too proud to enter business or a trade, and too improvident to abandon the showy, profligate aristocratic standard of living, became a common character in late-medieval and early-modern society. He also became a persistent source of political intrigues, military adventures, and domestic violence as he attempted by political favoritism, military service, or brigandage to stop his family's downhill slide into poverty. The nobles of the fourteenth, fifteenth, and sixteenth centuries were a disturbed and dangerous class, and the agricultural economy lay at the root of the problem.

Social Effects in Eastern Europe

The social consequences of agrarian adaptation were very different in eastern European lands like Prussia, Poland, and Russia. Whereas the western European peasantry was slowly rising to the status of free men, the rural masses of eastern Europe, who as colonists in the twelfth and thirteenth centuries had often been recruited by promises of personal freedom, were gradually being reduced to the status of serfs. In Russia, this enserfment was not completed till the eighteenth century, but throughout the East, the process was under way by the fourteenth century.

The reason for this divergent social history in the east was partly economic. The principal commercial crops were grains—wheat and rye. This cultivation, unlike the sheep raising in England, required much field labor. Since the population decline and the plague had made hired labor scarce and costly, profit-seeking landlords could not rely on wage laborers. Instead, they rigorously enforced whatever labor obligations their tenants owed and often attempted to impose new ones, either by overt violence or by legal subterfuge.

There was also an important political cause for this subjugation of eastern peasants: The eastern kings either grew weak and unable to control what the nobles did on their own estates (as in Poland) or else they rebuilt central authority on the basis of political and military support from the landed aristocracy, who received in return broad authority over their peasants (as in Prussia, especially after 1640). The eastern nobles had a free hand, as those of England and France did not, to rely on armed force and radically change the status of the peasantry by piling on new financial and labor obligations and new legal disabilities. Eastern European rural society became more "fuedal" precisely at the time when that of western Europe, even amidst the economic troubles of the fourteenth and fifteenth centuries, tended to become more "bourgeois."

Catastrophic Events: Famine and Plague

The faltering economy of fourteenth-century Europe was further shaken by several historical events that were not fundamental causes of the crisis but which marked its arrival and deepened it. The earliest of these was the great series of famines that struck almost all of Europe. Even a purely local crop failure for one year caused intense suffering among the impoverished masses of medieval Europe. Now in the second decade of the fourteenth century, almost every part of Europe experienced from three to five *consecutive* years of crop failure. The years 1315, 1316, and 1317 seem to have been the worst of the century. The cause was a remarkable run of bad weather. The misery produced by the famine was intense. A contemporary chronicler tells of hunger so desperate that corpses of executed criminals were cut down from the gallows and eaten. More credible are statistics showing that 10 percent of the population of Ypres and 5.5 percent of Bruges (two major cities in the densely populated Low Countries) died of starvation within a single year. The ill effects were not limited to those who starved: malnutrition made fourteenth-century populations more susceptible to disease.

The Black Death

An especially dramatic and destructive event in fourteenth-century Europe was the Black Death, which entered southern Europe from the Crimea in 1347 and by 1350 had spread throughout the continent. The devastation wrought by this lethal combination of bubonic plague and pneumonic plague was so great that the historian can hardly believe what the documents clearly show. These sources allow one to trace the movement of the plague across the map (1348 was the worst year for Italy and the most advanced regions of western Europe) and to spot certain regions (Milan, the Low Countries, Bohemia) which for obscure reasons were little affected. But how is the historian to believe evidence showing clearly that more than half the people of this or that region died in a period of a few weeks? And how is the historian really to comprehend the effects, both physical and psychological, of this sudden and (to the people of that age) inexplicable obliteration of most of the population?

Contemporary reports on mortality during the Black Death strain credibility; a will made at Viterbo in 1348 states that two-thirds of the people in that part of Italy died of the plague; a chronicler of the south Tyrol claims that only one-sixth of the people there survived. Historians are aware of the tendency of all medieval chroniclers to exaggerate numbers, yet occasional documents that record actual body counts—not estimates made by excited observers—suggest that in certain hard-hit localities, the number who died of plague may have been as high as chroniclers claimed. At Givry, a community of 1,800 persons in Burgundy, 615 inhabitants died of plague in a four-month period. Some estates of the bishop of Winchester in England, where 23 deaths were recorded in 1346 and 54 in 1347, had 70 deaths in 1349, the plague year. Contemporary writers who stated that two-thirds or even five-sixths of the people died may have been quite accurate concerning their own locality.

But the plague struck with puzzling unevenness, and some large regions escaped almost entirely. Modern attempts to estimate the mortality for Europe as a whole are only educated guesses. Certainly regions where 50 or 60 percent of the people died were not typical. Yet a conservative estimate covering all of England concludes that 20 percent of the English population (that is, one person in five) died of the Black Death, while other modern students have estimated the mortality for Europe as a whole at between 25 and 30 percent.

Consequences of this dreadful epidemic are hard to prove. Obviously, a disease that in a brief time killed from one-fourth to one-third of the European population was a great event, greater even than the mortality inflicted by either of our own century's world wars. But devastated populations can often revive with amazing rapidity, as demonstrated by Germany after World War II. Hence the fantastic death rate inflicted by the plague need not have had a decisive long-term effect. Numerous deaths may merely create new opportunities for the survivors, and by encouraging early marriages they may actually bring rapid recovery of population. At the village of Givry, for example, there were eighty-six marriages in 1349, the year following the plague, whereas the annual average before 1348 was twenty-five. But in the fourteenth century, though there was some economic and demographic recovery after the plague, that recovery was incomplete.

One unquestionable effect of the Black Death is that it made a contribution (but was not the basic cause) to the general and persistent decline in the population. An even less disputable effect is that bubonic plague became endemic (i.e., persistently rooted) among European populations. Although no later epidemic was so terrible as that of 1347–50, there were several major recurrences during the later fourteenth century and afterward. England, for example, suffered major recurrences in 1360–61, 1368–69, and 1374. A recurrence in 1400–1401 struck Italy and parts of the Low Countries hard. The mortality in these later visitations was usually lower than in the 1340s, but sometimes it approached that level. At Florence in 1400 and at Bruges in 1438, 28 percent of the people perished; at Pavia in 1485, some 5,000 out of a total population of 12,000 died. In many cities, serious outbreaks occurred every few years: in the fifteenth century, London had twenty recurrences, Frankfurt eighteen, and Hamburg ten. This situation continued through the sixteenth and seventeenth centuries. London had a major outbreak—its last—in 1665. Generally, plague disappeared from western Europe after about 1666 but persisted in the east until 1713. It remained frequent in European Turkey until the nineteenth century and in Asia has survived down to the present.

Why Europe was suddenly struck in the fourteenth century and why the scourge of plague disappeared in the late seventeenth century is open to debate. There was no improvement in medical treatment, though quarantine regulations and the general level of nutrition had improved by 1700. Probably more important was the displacement of the European black rat, a crucial link in the cycle of infection, by the brown rat, which does not carry the variety of flea whose bites spread the bubonic plague.

Reactions to the Plague

In any case, Europeans of the Renaissance-Reformation period knew nothing of the future disappearance of plague. They knew only the dreadful experience of seeing thousands of relatives, friends, and neighbors die of a new sickness that spread inexorably and which no doctor could either cure or prevent. They soon discovered that the disease would return again and again in a pattern that no one could predict. The economic effects were not totally negative—certainly not for survivors who demanded and got higher wages. But in general, the aftermath was painful. Parents were left without children, and children without parents. Prices of foodstuffs, and especially of labor, fluctuated wildly. There is clear evidence that the very best members of the clergy suffered great loss of life, since their duties called on them to aid the sick.

Literature from the period suggests that for some individuals, the plague posed a severe moral crisis: stories abound of parents abandoned by children and children by parents, wives by husbands and husbands by wives. Many terrified clergymen deserted their posts. Some individuals, finding that neither medical precaution nor prayer availed them, abandoned themselves to gluttony, drunkeness, and sexual promiscuity. Many from the upper classes left for their country estates or for other cities whenever they heard reports of the plague's approach. Those who could not flee infected localities pathetically sought safety through prayer or quack remedies. Less pathetic but equally revealing of frustrated impotence was the attempt to find a human conspiracy underlying the plague. Wherever there were Jewish communities, religious bigots, accusing the Jews of deliberately poisoning the water supply, massacred whole communities. Whether mass hysteria bred by the plague also contributed to eccentric religious manifestations, such as the Flagellants, and to a general rise of anticlericalism is hard to prove, but it sounds plausible. Certainly the decimation of the more dutiful clergy by plague undermined efforts at church reform.

Perhaps the historian is on shaky ground when he suggests that the psychic effect of the plague on Renaissance Europe was analogous to the effect of trauma on an individual, and that much of the aberrant behavior and depressed mentality of the fourteenth and fifteenth centuries can be called a psychic result of the Black Death. But the analogy has attracted many.

Depression and Incomplete Recovery

The plague alone does not have to explain the gloomy outlook prevalent in late-medieval Europe. The persistent economic depression that began to manifest itself in the early fourteenth century was a more fundamental cause of the gloom. Most recent economic historians now admit that the rapid agricultural, commercial, and industrial expansion of the twelfth and thirteenth centuries was over by 1300 and that in the fourteenth century there was first a period of retarded growth, then a severe depression in which businesses failed, fortunes were lost, and old economic patterns were upset, and finally a slow, faltering, partial recovery that dragged on far into the fifteenth century. Not until nearly the end of the fifteenth century did a lasting and general economic recovery begin.

The chronology of economic recession closely parallels the chronology of population decline in this period, yet even at the worst of the depression,

Europe was far richer than it had been before the economic expansion of the twelfth and thirteenth centuries. The basic structures of high medieval commerce and industry persisted at least until the opening of overseas commerce in the sixteenth century. Many wealthy and powerful individuals and families preserved their wealth, and some even made new fortunes amidst the general distress. Italy and the southern Netherlands remained the most economically advanced, the most densely populated, and the most wealthy parts of Europe. This survival of established centers of wealth and economic leadership through the age of depression is very important, as a later chapter will show. It may even constitute a significant factor in the social background of Italian Renaissance civilization.

The reality of a fourteenth-century depression is abundantly demonstrated wherever sound quantitative documentation survives. England, for example, kept unusually complete customs records, and modern studies based on these show that exports of raw wool, medieval England's principal export, declined from an annual average of 35,840 sacks in 1357–59 to an annual average of 19,359 sacks in 1392–95. The decline continued into the fifteenth century: after 1429, the annual average never rose above 10,000 sacks. It is true that part of the export decline was offset by increased output of woolen cloth in England, but this increase probably did not offset the decline in exports. In any case, the change was bad for the weavers and cloth merchants of the Low Countries, who had dominated the medieval woolen cloth industry, for they depended heavily on England for their raw material.

Decline is also evident in agriculture. Production fell and the profits of landowners declined even more sharply because the fall in population precipitated a fall in the price of food grains. The export trade in Bordeaux wines, the salt industry, and (somewhat later) the great Baltic herring fishery also declined. The mining industry declined in most of its branches.

Industrial and Business Downturn

The principal industrial product of the medieval and Renaissance-Reformation periods was woolen cloth, and most of the great towns of the Middle Ages based their prosperity on it. Here there is clear evidence of growth in new regions, such as the west of England and the northern Netherlands, but the old, established centers of woolen production were in a disastrous decline. Flanders was so socially and politically disturbed that cloth production fell and its weavers experienced unemployment and poverty that increased their revolutionary political agitation. Where textile production survived in the Low Countries, it shifted to new centers, like Antwerp in the Duchy of Brabant, where working-class agitation was less developed. In these new centers production and prosperity increased as older Flemish towns like Ypres, Bruges, and Ghent declined. Or else it avoided the cities entirely and used part-time rural laborers whose geographical isolation hindered any tendency toward working-class organization.

The other traditional center of the production of high-quality woolen cloth for international trade was northern Italy, especially the Republic of Florence. This woolen industry was in a serious slump by the later fourteenth century. The seriousness of the situation is illustrated by one of the demands of a group of working-class rebels, the Ciompi, in 1378: that the employers should guarantee employment by agreeing to produce at least 24,000 pieces of cloth per year. Since we know that in the earlier fourteenth century Florentine woolen cloth production varied from 70,000 to 80,000 pieces per year, the demand in 1378 that production be raised to 24,000 pieces clearly indicates a disastrous collapse of the city's greatest industry.

Florence was more fortunate or more resourceful than the Flemish textile towns, for it had developed other economic bases such as the worldwide trade of its merchants and an important banking industry, and in the fifteenth century, shrewd merchants like the Medici shifted much of their capital from the faltering woolen industry into the new and profitable silk industry. Even so, the misfortune of its greatest industry produced hard times and social and political stress. Even if the areas of economic growth offset the decline of old industries (and that is doubtful), such long-range compensation would be small comfort for Flemish and Italian weavers who (like space scientists and aeronautical engineers in recent America) suddenly found that patiently acquired skills were of little use when jobs were not available.

International trade also faltered in the fourteenth century, though Italian domination of the old Mediterranean routes and German domination of the Baltic–North Sea routes survived. One promising new development of the late thirteenth century, the opening of the direct overland caravan route from the Black Sea to China by adventuresome Italian merchants like Marco Polo, proved abortive. The conversion of the western Mongols to Islamic religion, and especially the destruction of the receptive Mongol dynasty of China by the antiforeign Ming dynasty in 1368, left the trade in oriental luxuries once again where it had been before mid-thirteenth century—a monopoly of the Arab merchants of Egypt and Syria. The formerly rich Italian trade with Constantinopole declined along with that great city.

For Italian businessmen the new conditions meant reduced profits on capital. In the age of growth, investors had expected returns of from 10 to 20 percent, but now returns of from 5 to 8 percent were regarded as good. This situation did not mean the destruction of Italy's great capital resources or of its economic leadership, but it meant the end of an age when new fortunes could readily be piled up. The mentality of merchants became less expansive, more defensive. These conditions led to a marked polarization of society in the economically advanced regions: in plain words, the rich got richer and the poor got poorer, a conclusion documented by the tax records of two of Renaissance Italy's greatest cities, Florence and Venice.

Onset of the Depression

The actual onset of depressed economic conditions is hard to document, but one event does dramatically mark their arrival. This is the bankruptcy of the two leading European banking houses of the early fourteenth century, the Florentine firms of Bardi and Peruzzi. These and smaller Florentine banks had extended their diversified commercial and banking activities far and wide, and were especially active in England and the Low Countries because of the trade in raw wool and woolen textiles. Since they needed governmental favor in order to trade in those lands, they began making large loans at high interest to the governments of France and England and also to the Angevin kings of Naples and other Italian despots. As Edward III of England began preparing for war on France in 1337–39, he borrowed vast sums from the Bardi and Peruzzi. When the early campaigns of the war proved indecisive (it was the Hundred Years' War), both France and England demanded more and more money, and the Italian bankers, having already lent so much and fearing repudiation of these sums, made large additional loans. The bankers were trapped, and as the hard-pressed English king became tardy in making repayments due on earlier loans, the banks' financial condition became shaky. Meanwhile, a war between Florence and Pisa and a refusal by the king of Naples to repay a large loan deepened their crisis. The banks themselves had heavy interest to pay, for they had got much of the money they lent by borrowing from wealthy investors throughout Italy. Their own credit now disappeared, and they were unable to make payments when due. In 1343 the Peruzzi and another, smaller bank failed, and not long after, the large Bardi firm also became insolvent. In December 1344, Edward III abandoned the last pretense that he would repay what he owed. These bank failures were a disaster not only for the families that controlled the banks but also for many wealthy Italians who had invested with them. The financial crisis and loss of capital were widely felt, and though the Florentine banking industry survived, the new firms that rose to prominence, such as the Medici, never had the capital resources or the scale of operations of these earlier banks.

The bankruptcies of 1343–44 in no sense *caused* the depression, but like the great stock market crash of 1929, they marked the end of any reasonable expectation of continued prosperity. Together with the outbreak of the Hundred Years' War in 1338 and the Black Death of 1348–50, they establish the mid-fourteenth century as the time when the society of medieval Europe had entered a period of economic disruption.

Many students of the Renaissance have found it disconcerting to think that "their" period coincides not with the commercial and industrial revival of Europe and the earliest foundations of modern capitalism, but with the first major setback for the revived economy. The economic recovery of Europe becomes, perhaps awkwardly, a product of the high Middle Ages and not of the "Renaissance" as in all decency it ought to have been. But unless we want to base economic and social history purely on theory, and totally disregard the evidence produced by modern research, we must admit as an established fact that Italian Renaissance culture was born during the early part of a major depression.

Some individuals, of course, still prospered even when the economy was depressed, and some whole regions enjoyed significant gains in prosperity. The regions worst hit were those that had made the greatest progress in the period of expansion, such as Flanders and northern Italy. But even in those regions, much of the old wealth survived. Venice, Florence, Milan and Genoa in Italy remained economic leaders of Europe until well into the sixteenth century. The geographical regions that did experience rapid expansion were those that were still relatively underdeveloped by 1300: Catalonia, with its great port of Barcelona; Bohemia and, to a lesser extent, the neighboring kingdoms of Poland and Hungary; and most persistently expansive of all, the commercial towns of south Germany and Switzerland, such as Nuremberg, Augsburg, Ulm, Vienna, Basel, Zurich, St. Gall, and Geneva.

Efforts to Remedy Hard Times

Faced with deteriorating business conditions, merchants often responded by banding together to offset increasing risks, to defend established markets from outside competition, and to secure from foreign governments special legal and commercial privileges.

Hanseatic League

The greatest example of such a mercantile combination is the Hanseatic League of commercial towns in northern and northwestern Germany. These German towns had dominated the important Baltic–North Sea trade route since at least the twelfth century and had established highly privileged foreign outposts from London and Bruges in the west to Bergen in the north and Novgorod in the east.

The formal Hansa or League dates only from the 1360s and was not really the creator of German predominance. Rather, it was a defensive reaction to the economic and political troubles of the fourteenth century. The definitive organization of the League was a response to the efforts of King Waldemar IV (1340–75) of Denmark to control passage through the Sound (the strait from the Baltic to the North Sea), to dominate Baltic fisheries, and to tax German merchants. The League continued because it was faced with continued threats from Denmark and from Dutch and English merchants and fishermen, and its success against these rivals depended mainly on their weakness. When in the sixteenth century the Dutch and English intruded more determinedly into the northern trade, the Hanseatic League collapsed speedily.

The same principles of cooperative action by merchants too feeble to exploit a distant and risky trade alone also appeared in England. Medieval England's chief export, raw wool, was so scarce and valuable that there was no need for active merchandising. England's role was relatively passive: all it had to do was let foreign merchants come and purchase its fleeces. For purposes of control and taxation, the government created an official corporation, the Merchants of the Staple, and gave them a monopoly of the right to export wool. When in the later fourteenth century England was trying to develop export markets for its new woolen textile industry, its economic role changed greatly. The European market was glutted with textiles, and Englishmen had to become active seekers after customers. In order to foster this new market, the English crown in 1407 chartered the Merchant Adventurers Company and gave it a monopoly of the export of English cloth and other products (except raw wool, which remained a monopoly of the Staple). Although the name "Adventurers" sounds exciting, this venture was really cautious and limited. It sought to create the new trade not through free capitalistic enterprise but by setting up a government monopoly that allowed a limited number of small merchants to control the trade in their own interest.

The Spirit of Restriction

The exploitation of commerce through leagues of cities or chartered corporations of privileged monopolists is characteristic of northern Europe in the fourteenth and fifteenth centuries. The private ownership of commercial and industrial property is deceptive, for the capitalistic spirit of creative enterprise was markedly lacking. The mentality of the mercantile combinations and of the whole period was defensive and restrictive, suited to an age of both economic uncertainty and economic growth.

Likewise the control of local commerce and industry by guilds and town regulations was antithetical to the spirit of true capitalism. Much of the social and political tension that underlay the city riots and rebellions of the fourteenth century resulted from the ruthlessness with which persons already comfortably established in a trade preserved limited opportunities for themselves and excluded men trying to rise from the lower classes. The medieval ideal of a guild, in which each young apprentice would become a journeyman laborer and each journeyman would eventually become a self-employed master craftsman, had collapsed. The existing guild masters used high initiation fees, arbitrary requirements for creation of a masterpiece, or other subterfuges to exclude all journeymen except sons and sons-in-law of masters. The dream of economic independence faded. More and more of those who completed their apprenticeships realized that they would never become independent artisans but were doomed to a lifetime as insecure employees of others. The friction between established guild masters and this emergent proletariat explains why the history of the large industrial towns of fourteenth-century Europe is punctuated by frequent working-class riots and rebellions.

The same defensive, anticapitalistic spirit appears in the regulations that the guilds imposed on the masters themselves, as noted earlier in this chapter. The true capitalist, who wanted to get rich by enlarging trade and taking a larger share for himself, was treated as an economic criminal and restrained at every turn. Such policies must have impeded renewed economic growth. Only in places where aggressive merchants found ways of getting around guild restrictions were true capitalism and renewed growth possible. In such established cities as Florence and Venice or in the dominant cities of the future, like Antwerp, Augsburg, London, and Amsterdam, the great capitalists were largely free of restraints because they either controlled the government or gained the ruler's favor. And in those places the recovery of the later fifteenth century began.

Chapter Two
An Age of Political Turmoil

Political breakdown is an obvious characteristic of the later Middle Ages and has long been recognized even by historians who never dreamed of a fundamental economic setback during the period. Wars, revolutions, and political disasters are more easily documented than economic trends, and they abounded in the fourteenth and fifteenth centuries: collapse of the German (or Holy Roman) empire and of imperial authority in Italy, the Hundred Years' War and the civil conflicts it precipitated in both France and England, Turkish conquest of the whole Balkan peninsula. Only in East-Central Europe, in Poland, Bohemia, and Hungary, was there significant political progress.

Collapse of the Medieval Empire

Political disaster struck first in Germany and Italy, both of which had been included in the great universal secular state of the Middle Ages, the Holy Roman Empire. This empire, which had been the most powerful European state of the eleventh century, was demolished by its struggles with the other universal institution of medieval Europe, the Roman Catholic Church. The death of the Emperor Frederick II in 1250, before he had either subdued the papacy or provided effectively for transmission of the imperial title to his heirs, was a catastrophe from which the Empire never recovered. Although the popes after 1250 were remarkably energetic in extirpating the whole imperial family of Hohenstaufen, they showed little interest in providing alternative governments for the imperial territories. As Niccolo Machiavelli bitterly charged two and a half centuries later, the popes would neither govern the Empire themselves nor allow anyone else to do so. Although the imperial title survived until Napoleon forced the last Holy Roman Emperor to abdicate in 1806, the post–1250 Empire provided no government at all for Italy and little enough for Germany.

The Fragmentation of Germany

The succession to the imperial title itself was in utter confusion after 1250. Although there were several claimants, none gained general recognition, and the whole period from 1250 to 1273 is known as the Interregnum (period without a king). Germany paid a terrible price for this collapse of the kingship. Already before 1250 the emperors had bartered many of their political and financial rights in return for the military support of the great nobles. Now during the Interregnum the nobility advanced further toward virtual independence on their hereditary lands. In effect, Germany dissolved into hundreds of small and medium-sized principalities, and these territorial princes and free city governments were the real rulers of most German lands and people. The later emperors and their "government" had very little *direct* authority over any German land or German citizen. Each of the small states looked out for its own interest, and no one looked out for Germany as a whole. Even the later emperors, realizing that the aristocratic electors might well refuse to let their sons succeed to the throne, concentrated on the interests of their family and on their own hereditary principalities. After the thirteenth century, German aristocrats desired election as emperor only because the imperial title might be a useful instrument for enhancement of their family and for enlargement of their hereditary principalities. In this way, for example, the relatively obscure Hapsburg family, by frequently securing election as emperor and by a brilliantly successful policy of dynastic marriages, gradually accumulated lands and titles until in the sixteenth century it emerged as the most powerful dynasty in European history.

For Germans living during and after the Interregnum, these conditions meant public disorder and personal insecurity. Constant warfare among nobles over ill-defined borders and rights of succession was a natural consequence of the loss of a strong central authority that could impose peaceful solutions. Every merchant who found himself forced to pay arbitrary tolls on roads, bridges, and rivers every few miles as he passed from one petty principality to the next might well regret his country's loss of unity. Some petty nobles openly became brigands (*Raubritter*) preying on merchants. Within the territorial principalities, citizens often lacked any legal way of securing their lives and properties against high-handed actions by local princes. Lacking a king to whom they could appeal for justice, the estates of nobles, clergy, and towns in some principalities claimed a legal right to initiate civil war against an oppressive prince. Public disorder and insecurity became so great in some regions that since neither the emperor nor the regional nobility could keep order, bands of private citizens created *Feme*, or secret courts, to bring brigands to justice. Since the merchants suffered most from the breakdown of law and order, leagues of town governments in certain districts tried to suppress brigandage and defend self-governing towns from aggression at the hands of nobles. Only behind the strong walls of cities or, at a later period within some of the middle-sized principalities that were beginning to act like small independent kingdoms (Prussia, Austria, Bavaria, for example), were the life and property of German citizens secure.

The permanent loss of territory was another heavy price Germany paid for political collapse. By the fourteenth and fifteenth centuries, the Germanic lands of Switzerland and the Netherlands had become in reality detached from the Empire, though formal recognition of their independence did not come until 1648. Greedy neighbors, especially the kings of France and the dukes of Burgundy, annexed imperial lands throughout the period 1250–1500. In Eastern Europe, the Empire itself did not lose territory, but its satellite state, the Teutonic Knights, was crushed by the king of Poland in 1410, and German expansion eastward came to a halt.

Conditions improved a little after the Interregnum ended in 1273. The western German nobles were alarmed at French annexation of imperial border regions. The towns were weary of internal disorders. Most important of all, the papacy, which had seemed quite content to leave Germany and Italy without an emperor, decided that it needed a German emperor as a counterweight to the Angevin rulers of Naples. So Pope Gregory X threatened that if the German electoral princes could not choose an emperor, he would appoint one himself. This threat led to the election of the first Hapsburg emperor in 1273, Rudolf I, a man chosen partly because he was able and widely respected, but also because he was not powerful enough to threaten the interests of any of the larger nobles. When Rudolf proved quite skillful at using his imperial title to build up his hereditary lands, the great nobles asserted their control by electing the next emperor from another noble family. By preventing a long cycle of father-to-son succession the nobles kept their monarchy not only elective but also weak.

The Fragmentation of Italy

At least Germany did have a central government and a monarchy of some sort. The other major component of the medieval empire, Italy, lacked even that. The Hohenstaufen collapse after 1250 left the peninsula without even the shadow of a central government. Though later German emperors still claimed power over Italy and actually did provide (for a price) charters confirming titles to land and to public office, they never governed any part of Italy. Italy had simply collapsed in the years after 1250 and in effect had become a mere geographical region occupied by a large number of small and middle-sized states. There were monarchies, republics, oligarchies, and dictatorships of various sorts, and not a one of them, except the papacy in central Italy, had any security for its possessions or its independence except what its military power and political skill allowed it to get and keep.

This political fragmentation and turbulence were decisive for Italian history. The emergence of small states with an active political life may well have caused the cultural creativity of Renaissance Italy, much as the somewhat similar city-state life may well have stimulated the cultural vitality of ancient Greece. But Italians who lived through the period were less likely to sense the cultural benefits (if any) of this fragmentation than to experience the insecurity and violence it bred. The politics of Renaissance Italy was a mad scramble for power and territory, and every government dreaded the possibility of conquest from outside and revolution from within. During the twelfth and thirteenth centuries, most of the towns of northern and north-central Italy had thrown off outside control and had emerged as self-governing communes, republican in government but dominated by their richest citizens. During the struggles between popes and emperors, most cities divided bitterly into partisans of the popes (Guelfs) and partisans of the emperors (Ghibellines). These party hatreds, which had produced many outbreaks of civil war, survived even after the Empire had collapsed and the papacy had withdrawn to Avignon (1305–77). The age-old feud between Guelfs and Ghibellines helped to generate wars among the cities, though greed for land and commercial rivalry were even more potent causes. Militarism and aggressiveness were by no means limited to despotic states like Milan, for even a liberty-loving republic like Florence schemed constantly to conquer and annex nearby cities, such as its chief commercial rival in Tuscany, Pisa. Every city was eager to seize what it could, and no city felt safe from attack.

Internal Political Strife. This instability in relations among the Italian communes was paralleled by instability in domestic politics. Traditional party hatreds left over from the thirteenth-century struggles between popes and emperors poisoned the life of nearly every commune or at least of its leaders. Murders or formal executions of opposition leaders, confiscation of property, disqualification from office-holding (at Florence it was a crime for any person whom the Guelf party leaders labeled a Ghibelline to hold public office)—these were the consequences of political defeat.

As the polarization between rich and poor became more marked and as the competition for advantage in a sick economy became more fierce, new factional divisions arose, crossing the traditional Guelf-Ghibelline split and based on social and economic rivalries. This struggle between rich and poor, even more than rivalries between Guelfs and Ghibellines, explains why the traditional republican constitutions of most cities collapsed and were replaced by despotisms.

In the first phase of the class struggles, the division was between the *grandi* (hereditary nobility based on land, commercial wealth, and military traditions) and the *popolo* (the common people). Usually the commoners won. At Florence, for example, they confirmed their victory in 1293 by a constitutional charter that imposed permanent and hereditary disabilities on members of noble families. But the *popolo* was not economically and socially homogeneous, and everywhere the rich merchants and industrialists who had led the *popolo* devised ways of gaining effective control of the government. Since this mercantile oligarchy abused its power much as the *grandi* had, by the fourteenth century there was agitation among the lower middle class and the propertyless workers for further political reform.

During the period of 1329–82 at Florence, there actually were many concessions to the lesser guilds (i.e., to the lower middle class), who eventually gained a majority on the *signoria*, or chief executive council. But the lower middle class, then as now, feared and hated those who were socially below them even more than they hated the rich, and when the rebellion of the Ciompi (wool carders) in 1378 actually gained limited concessions for some working-class groups, the alarm of the smaller guilds was so great that in 1382 the rich merchants dared to seize power by armed force. Over the next few years, the lower-middle class guilds were reduced to their traditional minority representation in government, and of course the political gains by the working classes were permanently abolished. The seven greater guilds, dominated by a few wealthy and prominent families, in effect ruled the republic, and even the ouster of the leading Albizzi family and its replacement by the Medici family and their faction in 1434 did not constitute a fundamental change. The rich ruled Florence, but usually they made enough limited concessions to the middling elements of society that these more numerous classes remained politically loyal. The story of political and social turmoil in Florence is typical of most Italian communes in the fourteenth and fifteenth centuries, except that in most other cities the turmoil sooner or later led to a military dictatorship that took advantage of public distaste for riots and violence and seized power under the pretext of maintaining law and order. Even Florence, despite its fierce pride in its republican constitution, narrowly escaped the creation of a military dictatorship on three occasions in the fourteenth century.

The People and the Rulers. Whatever their form of constitution, all Italian Renaissance states were ruled by a governing class of wealthy and privileged families. All of these governments feared the rabble, the rank and file who owned no property and were not self-employed. These were viewed (in fact if not in theory) as potential troublemakers who had to be restrained, not as true members of the community. Italian governments also faced other groups who could not be trusted politically, notably the residents of the *contado* or surrounding countryside, who normally did not have citizen rights and were subject to systems of taxation and economic regulation deliberately designed to exploit them in the interests of the city folk. Partisans of defeated political factions, such as the Ghibellines at Florence, were also regarded as potential traitors and revolutionists.

Under such conditions of social tension, and in view of the actual frequency of conspiracies, coups d' état, riots and rebellions, no Italian government wanted to strengthen the disfranchised citizens by arming them for war. During the earlier period when the cities were gaining their independence, governments mainly relied on citizen militias, but in the fourteenth century, governments seldom mobilized their citizens. Instead they fought their wars by hiring bands of professional soldiers who owed allegiance to no state but only to their commander, or *condottiere.* These mercenary armies were almost like sovereign states, with their own laws, judicial procedures, and treasuries, but without permanent attachment to any geographical region. Their trade was simple: the use of armed violence in behalf of whoever contracted for their services, and the infliction of murder, rape, and (above all) robbery on all undefended civilian populations who did not buy them off.

In the fourteenth century, many *condottieri* and their followers were French, Spanish, German, or English soldiers of fortune. By the fifteenth century, most were Italians, and some of the smaller Italian princes hired themselves and their armies out as *condottieri.* Yet even these mercenaries, though quite willing to massacre civilian dissidents for the governments that hired them, were a political danger to their employers unless carefully watched, for they sometimes sold out to the other side and often plundered friendly populations if left unpaid. There was also some danger that a *condottiere* might try to seize the city and set up in business as a ruler.

Rise of Renaissance Despotisms. Faced with all these problems of staying in power and maintaining order and being themselves split by class and factional rivalries, the governments of early Renaissance Italy searched for cures for their political ills. Already by the thirteenth century most cities turned local administration over to a *podestá,* an annually appointed official brought in from another city in the hope that he would be free of bias arising from local family relationship or party interest. When the city government itself was badly divided, such an official might gain effective control of the government; and in the fourteenth century such a *podestá* actually became despot of the city of Ferrara. The more usual line of development from republic to despotism was through the office of *capitano del popolo,* a magistrate appointed by the guilds to defend the nonnoble citizens from the *grandi.* In many cities the *capitano del popolo* eventually led a popular uprising against the nobles, seized control of the government, and then revised the constitution. The source of his authority was always the people (that is, the guild members), and a popular assembly would be called to endorse the constitutional changes. This is precisely the way in which the Della Torre family of Milan began the creation of Italy's strongest despotism in mid-thirteenth century, only to have the dictatorship snatched from them by a family of nobles, the Visconti, who by the fourteenth century had made the office of *capitano* hereditary and had had the citizens name the ruler *dominus* (lord) of Milan. Nearly all the towns of Lombardy and the northern Papal States developed some such system.

These Italian Renaissance despotisms, unlike the feudal monarchies of contemporary Northern Europe, had no secure legal foundation and evoked little true loyalty. Hence unlike such troubled feudal monarchies as France during the Hundred Years' War, they had little recuperative power and collapsed rapidly once the despot began to slip. They rested not on law and custom but on military force and political manipulation and hence were a source of the kaleidoscopic instability of Italian Renaissance politics. What popular support they did have depended on the desire of influential classes to end internal disorders. They were acceptable because they guaranteed what more recent times have called "law and order." Although many of the despots were themselves harsh and violent men, most ordinary citizens felt more secure under their tyranny than under the turbulent republics they replaced.

Despots often seemed useful for other reasons also. They often did foster general prosperity through commercial treaties, regulation of trade, and public works projects. And being themselves often men of military background, they often flattered local pride and greed by becoming conquerors.

In one sense, the despots' attempt to expand their states through conquest represented an attempt to rise above their original position as local magistrates by acquiring territories that would belong to them personally and not to the city from which their power originated. When a republic like Venice or Florence conquered another city, the new region became subject to the government of the conquering city. But when a despot like Giangaleazzo Visconti (1385–1402) of Milan conquered a city, he ruled it independently of the Milanese city government, and so became less dependent on the local political forces that had originally brought his dynasty into power.

Often the despots also sought new titles that would not rest on consent of the people. Thus the second Visconti lord of Milan, Matteo, purchased from the money-hungry German emperor the title of imperial vicar in Lombardy, and the greatest conqueror of all the Visconti, Giangaleazzo, in 1395 again paid a Holy Roman Emperor large sums for the title duke of Milan. A ruler who called himself duke of Milan, who conquered and ruled most of the cities of Lombardy, and who contracted dynastic marriages of his family into the royal families of France and England, clearly had risen above the rank of a local magistrate put in office by the people.

"Law and Order": Despotisms versus Republics. Although the despots came into power as guarantors of law and order, it is debatable whether in the long run they provided greater security than the republics they replaced. Of course by suppressing overt political opposition and all attempts at rebellion by workers, nobles, or other dissidents, a strong despot did maintain order of a sort. But precisely because they lacked a secure foundation in constitutional law or popular sentiment, the despotisms were stable only when the despot was a ruler of great talent, a talent that his son might not inherit. The lack of a clear law of succession, and the essentially personal nature of a despot's power, meant that when he grew feeble or died, there was a scramble for power that reopened the floodgates of political turmoil. At Milan, when Giangeleazzo died unexpectedly in 1402, leaving only two small sons, his great state nearly collapsed. His relatives, his generals, and above all, the neighboring cities rushed in to seize land and power. Again in 1447, when the last Visconti duke died leaving no heir, a period of wild turmoil and general warfare throughout Italy broke out. Milan reemerged briefly as a faction-ridden republic, and eventually the ablest of the *condottieri* whom the Milanese hired to protect them, Francesco Sforza, seized the city by force and made himself duke of Milan.

Compared to the bloody and unstable record of the despotisms, the political record of the few surviving republics was not bad. Florence, the greatest and freest republic, had constant factional bickering and many riotous disorders, yet it also had long periods of relative stability. Even more impressive than the record of Florence was that of the great oligarchical republic of Venice. From the solidification of control by a closed group of rich merchant families in 1297, its constitution lasted almost unchanged for five hundred years, until Napoleon's French army overthrew the republic in 1797. Alone among the cities of Italy, Venice never experienced a successful revolution. While its political system was often harsh and repressive in dealing with internal dissent, the ruling caste was remarkably devoted to the city's welfare. Venice stood throughout the whole early modern period as the classic exception to the usual belief that a republican form of government was incompatible with order and strength.

War and Militarism. If internal disorder was the most fearsome curse of Renaissance Italian cities, war and fear of war ranked second. All cities lived in a state of tension, and during the fourteenth century many of the smaller ones were conquered by the stronger. The despots were the most persistent and systematic aggressors, though large republics like Florence and Venice had expansionist periods as well. The most famous aggressor of Renaissance Italy was Giangaleazzo Visconti (1385–1402), duke of Milan. Giangaleazzo adopted an expansionist foreign policy that may have been aimed ultimately at the conquest of all of North and Central Italy and the acquisition of a royal title. His crafty diplomacy, his conscienceless betrayals, and his ruthless violence soon made him ruler of almost all of the rich province of Lombardy. He also seized control of some of the semiindependent city despotisms that had grown up in the northern parts of the Papal States. His annexation of cities north and east of Milan, such as Verona and Padua, threatened the food supply and overland commercial lifeline of Venice.

Finally, his annexations in the Papal States and in Tuscany itself made the greatest Tuscan city, Florence, fear for its independence. By the early fifteenth century, Florence was virtually encircled and in real danger of being conquered.

Probably many Italians found the prospect of a forcible unification a welcome relief from their constant wars, and Giangaleazzo's propagandists recalled to men's minds the power and glory that ancient Rome had brought to Italy after first conquering the whole peninsula. But for the Florentines, this threat of forcible incorporation into a Visconti kingdom presented the most acute external crisis of their history. Proud of their independence and their republican political heritage, the Florentines refused to submit and led the opposition to Giangaleazzo.

Some historians believe that this rallying of the Florentines to the defense of their republic not only helped unite society behind the ruling oligarchy but also forged a union between patriotic defenders of the republic and the emergent culture of the humanists, who created an anti-Milanese propaganda that stressed the republican (rather than the imperial) side of Roman tradition and argued that both in ancient times and in the Middle Ages, Italy had flourished best as a league of free republics, while the oppressive hand of the Caesars in ancient times had cost Italy its freedom and had led to the decline of Roman power and culture.

The Five Italian Powers. Brave though the Florentine resistance was, the Republic survived mainly through a stroke of luck. In 1402, amidst his military preparations, Giangaleazzo Visconti suddenly died, and the resulting weakness of the duchy ended all fear of Milanese imperialism for a generation. The chance that nearly all of Italy would be united by conquest, if it had ever really existed, was over by 1402.

Nevertheless, the wars and annexations of the fourteenth and early fifteenth centuries did greatly simplify the political map of Italy. By mid-fifteenth century, five territorial states, three of them based on expanded cities, dominated the peninsula. These were the Republic of Venice, which now ruled a substantial mainland territory in northeastern Italy, the Duchy of Milan, which ruled most of the plain of Lombardy, the Republic of Florence, which had annexed much of Tuscany and hungered after the rest, the Papal States, which after the end of the papal schism in 1417 regained effective control of Rome and the district around it, but had to recognize the de facto independence of some of the despotisms in the northern parts of the papal territories, and the Kingdom of Naples (at some periods including Sicily), covering the southern third of the peninsula. Being feudal in organization, Naples was politically, economically, and socially less advanced than the rest of Italy, and was ruled at various periods by kings related to the royal families of France and of Aragon in Spain. Wedged in between these large states were a few small republics and a larger number of petty despotisms. They survived mainly because the larger states were so jealous of each other that no one of them was allowed to annex its smaller neighbors.

Foundations of Modern Diplomacy. The atmosphere of fear, violence, and diplomatic instability carried over into the fifteenth century. Each state maintained a costly professional army, and yet none felt secure. Hence the Italian states attempted to mitigate their insecurity by an active diplomacy. While no state could trust another absolutely, common fears and goals made it possible and even necessary for them to form alliances. Giangaleazzo Visconti carefully prepared his conquests by alliances, and the severity of his threat compelled his principal enemies, Florence and Venice, to coordinate their resistance through diplomacy.

The fifteenth-century states relied heavily on alliances for their security, and so they developed a new diplomatic practice to coordinate relations with their allies (and also to keep watch on the military power and political loyalty of those allies). This new practice was the sending of resident ambassadors to their allies. Medieval and ancient ambassadors were sent to conduct specific negotiations, but they returned home when their particular task was finished. What was new was the continuous nature of diplomatic contact between allied Italian states. This system is the precursor of the whole system of relations between sovereign states in the modern world. It spread to non-Italian regions at the end of the fifteenth century through deliberate imitation of Italian techniques.

The tightly organized Italian diplomatic situation meant that any event that affected the stability, strength, and policy of one Italian state became a matter of concern for all the rest. Thus when the death of the last Visconti duke of Milan left that throne vacant in 1447, a political problem arose not only for the Milanese but for all of Italy. All the neighboring states who had been so long exposed to Milanese aggression were determined to destroy the duchy or at very least to seize Milanese border districts and thus to hold the enemy away from their own lands. Venice in particular greedily occupied Milanese lands. In the resultant turmoil, the restored Milanese republic went under and the *condottiere* Francesco Sforza seized for himself the city he was hired to defend. The Venetians, fearful of a revived Milanese duchy, were determined to destroy Sforza; the king of Naples had a claim of his own to Milan; the French king backed the claim of his relative the duke of Orleans; the pope was bitterly hostile to Sforza; and the German emperor argued that since his predecessor had created the ducal title, he should be able to determine the succession. Thus the war that broke out over the Milanese succession in 1447 not only continued after Sforza seized power in 1450, but threatened to draw in such outside powers as France, Aragon, and the German empire.

The Search for Collective Security. Of all the Italian statesmen, none realized more keenly the dangers of continued war and foreign intervention than did Cosimo de'Medici, the wealthy merchant-banker whose political faction had controlled Florence since 1434. Florence had traditionally been the ally of republican Venice against despotic, aggressive Milan, but now Cosimo persuaded his fellow citizens to abandon this traditional alliance. He concluded that the rule of Sforza at Milan offered the only chance of ending the instability there; that to allow Venice to annex the whole Milanese state would make that city so powerful that it might become a threat to Florentine independence; and that to allow intervention by the foreign powers would be a disaster for all the Italian states. So he formed an alliance with Sforza and by the Peace of Lodi among Venice, Florence, and Milan (1454) secured the general recognition of Sforza's title to Milan.

The Peace of Lodi and the Italian League that all the major Italian states entered in 1455 marked the recognition by the Italian governments that their constant wars were undermining their own stability and were inviting foreign intervention. All members of the Italian League pledged to come to the aid of any member attacked by an Italian or foreign power. Although there were pious expressions about a crusade against the Turks, the real purpose was to end the violence and instability that had torn Italy for more than a century and to present a solid Italian opposition to any military adventures by the French, Aragonese, and Germans. This system of collective security maintained a certain balance among the Italian powers for forty years. During this period of relative calm, from 1454 to 1494, no large-scale foreign interventions did occur. When international crises did arise, most of the Italian states cooperated to restore peace and to prevent any one state from becoming so strong that it threatened the others. Imperfect and fragile though it was, the collective-security system engineered by Cosimo de'Medici seemed admirable and successful when viewed from the perspective of disaster-ridden sixteenth-century Italians.

Threats to Italian Stability. Although the collective-security agreement was a masterful bit of diplomacy, the stability of the period 1454–94 was fragile. The Italian League of 1455 did not end the jealousy and violence. The real basis of the system was a tripartite alliance of Milan, Florence, and Naples, all of which felt they had more to lose than to gain by political upheaval. Venice remained cool toward Francesco Sforza and greedy for mainland territory, but it was held in check by the triple alliance and by a naval contest with the Turks in the eastern Mediterranean. No one trusted Venice, and this fear was based on the fact that Venice was not merely one among equals, but potentially by far the strongest Italian power. The actions of some lesser Italian despots put the collective-security system to the test. For example, in the 1460s the famous *condottiere* Bartolommeo Colleoni tried to conquer for himself a principality in Northern Italy and had to be put down by force.

The worst internal threat to the system, however, came from the popes, whose religious principles made them guardians of peace but whose political interests made them the worst fomentors of unrest and war in late fifteenth-century Italy. Most of the northerly parts of the Papal States had never been under effective papal control, and during the thirteenth and fourteenth centuries, a number of virtually independent despotisms grew up in that region. The larger states of Northern Italy regarded those near their own borders as part of their own sphere of influence. The popes of the late fifteenth century, having regained effective control of the area near Rome itself, were now determined to reassert their overlordship over these outlying regions. They claimed that they were merely reclaiming powers that were rightfully theirs, but in fact their policy disrupted the status quo and alarmed not only the despots of the cities concerned but also the governments of Northern Italy. The hostility of the other states was also increased by the tendency of the popes to install their own relatives as rulers of the areas they regained.

The career of Pope Sixtus IV (1471–84) is a clear example of the ruthless egotism, the crass secularism, and the political disruptiveness of papal policy. Sixtus was determined to regain effective control of the whole Papal State and at the same time to use his control of political power and church patronage to elevate his numerous and needy relatives to princely rank. In ecclesiastical affairs, he pursued this policy by naming five of his nephews and one great-nephew as cardinals. But his political schemes were what really upset Italian statesmen. His decision in 1474 to make a favorite nephew lord of Imola, a town near the Florentine border, aroused open opposition from the new leaders of the dominant faction at Florence, Lorenzo and Giuliano de' Medici. The response of Pope Sixtus was a despicable conspiracy between the papal government and a group of Florentine exiles led by the Pazzi family to overturn Medicean control of Florence by murdering the Medici brothers.

Since church services were the only occasion when both brothers were likely to be together without a heavy bodyguard, the plan—connived at (but perhaps not known in detail) by the head of the Christian religion—was to stab them to death as they knelt in prayer at mass. Even the professional killers originally hired to do the job were religious (or superstitious) enough to balk at this sacrilege. The plot was abortive: Giuliano was killed but Lorenzo only wounded, and when the Pazzi conspirators tried to stir up the Florentines to rebel, the enraged people lynched all the conspirators they could find, including the archbishop of Pisa, a bitter enemy of the Medici.

The Pazzi Conspiracy of 1478 led to a dangerous war in which the Florentines were isolated, but late in 1479, after a few peace feelers had proved encouraging, Lorenzo de' Medici boldly sailed to the court of the pope's chief ally, King Ferrante of Naples, and made a separate peace.

A few months later, a temporary occupation of the Italian port of Otranto by the Turks so terrified all the Italian powers that even the pope made peace. The crisis was over, though Sixtus IV and his successors Innocent VIII (1484–92), Alexander VI (1492–1503), and Julius II (1503–13), continued to stir up wars and crises.

French Invasion and the Enslavement of Italy. What finally ended this period of relative calm in 1494 was the French invasion of Naples, at the invitation of Milan, to assert the French king's hereditary claim to the Neapolitan throne. There was a long history of armed intervention in Italy by the German empire, France, and the Aragonese kings of Spain, and during their constant bickering various Italian states tried to bring about such intervention in their own interest, even during the period 1454–94. So long as Florence, Milan, and Naples stuck together, they were able to discourage any large-scale meddling by outsiders, but in the early 1490s this crucial alliance broke down. Ludovico Sforza, uncle and guardian of the youthful duke of Milan, had in effect usurped political control of that state, and Milan's traditional allies, Naples and Florence, turned unfriendly. Since Venice wanted to grab Milanese land and since the papacy was also hostile, Ludovico felt politically isolated and feared a conspiracy by the other powers. In desperation, he conceived a master stroke against his enemies: to persuade the ambitious but dim-witted young King of France, Charles VIII (1483–98) to assert his hereditary claim to the crown of Naples. Faced with this threat, the unpopular King Ferrante would be so busy preparing his defenses that he would have to leave Milan alone.

Like many political schemers in later times, Ludovico assumed that the intervention he encouraged would be similar to foreign interventions in the past, limited in scale or even confined to mere threats. Confident in their political skill, Ludovico and the other Italian rulers thought that they could exploit the Italian ambitions of the Northern powers without falling victim to the incomparably greater power of those kingdoms. To their horror, they now discovered that the French and Spanish monarchies, stronger and more unified than in the past, could no longer be manipulated. In 1494 Ludovico's urgings produced what he never had thought of: a massive overland invasion of Italy by a huge French army that passed through his own lands, forced its way through neutral Florentine and papal territory, and in a few weeks of fighting occupied the whole kingdom of Naples. Suddenly the French king dominated all of Italy. Ludovico had reckoned without the romantic ambitions of the young king, the greed of French nobles for military glory and the profits of war, and the remarkable recovery of French power since the end of the Hundred Years' War in 1453.

Horrified at the implications of this total French victory, which put them all at the mercy of Charles VIII, the Italian powers at once conspired to launch a joint attack against the French. None was more eager for this league than the man most responsible for letting the French in, Ludovico, for he now had unquestioned control of Milan. He also remembered that the Duke of Orleans, heir-presumptive to the French throne, had a claim to Milan itself through his descent from a daughter of the old Visconti dukes. But the most important feature of the anti-French League of Venice was that the Italians brought in other foreign powers, the Holy Roman Emperor Maximilian I and especially King Ferdinand of Spain, who was related to the ousted King of Naples. The Italian allies were successful in the short run. Warned by his diplomatic agents at Venice, Charles VIII hastily withdrew most of his army northward (1495) and fought his way back to France before the allies could cut off his retreat. A Spanish army within a few months forced the French garrison at Naples to surrender.

But the relief that the Italians felt in 1495 was unjustified. The French were out of Naples, but the Spanish were in. For a few years, most Italian statesmen thought that Ludovico Sforza had played a clever trick by calling in the French in 1494, but in 1498, when the French claimant to Milan became king as Louis XII and opened his reign by conquering Milan and shipping Ludovico off to spend the rest of his life as a prisoner in France, the disastrous nature of French and Spanish intervention began to emerge. The constant succession of faithless leagues and alliances in subsequent years, often pledged to drive the "barbarians" from Italy, only made it more and more clear that the disunited Italians could only drive one foreign power out by calling in the aid of another.

The events of 1494–95 set the pattern for a long series of Italian wars extending down to 1559, in which it became more and more clear that in 1494 the Italians had lost control of their own destiny and that eventually either France or Spain would rule Italy. Italy became a collection of provinces ruled or dominated by foreign powers, a situation that did not change until it finally won its freedom and its unity in the nineteenth century.

The harsh realities of military power and foreign domination found clear expression in the writings of the two greatest political thinkers of the Italian Renaissance, the Florentines Niccolo Machiavelli and Francesco Guicciardini. Both writers clearly described the ruthless methods they had seen at work as Italy lost control of its own political destiny; but Machiavelli, who had been a lifelong defender of republicanism and a valuable civil servant of the reformed Florentine republic until its fall in 1512, still had some lingering hope that a wise policy based on imitation of ancient Rome might help the Italians regain control of their country.

Northern Europe: The Decline of Feudal Monarchy

While Italy entered the Renaissance age in political disarray, achieved a tenuous balance in mid-fifteenth century, and then after 1494 became the victim of France and Spain, the feudal monarchies of Northern Europe had a very different history. Europe north of the Alps also experienced political and social turmoil in the fourteenth and fifteenth centuries, but the medieval political institutions of several of those nations had deeper roots, and at the end of the turmoil the kings of France, England, and Spain rebuilt effective government on foundations laid in the Middle Ages. The history of all three countries amply illustrates the defects of feudal monarchy, yet the traditions and institutions of feudal monarchy provided the foundations for the reformed and strengthened monarchies of the late fifteenth and early sixteenth centuries.

During their period of growth, the feudal monarchies of France, England, and some of the Spanish states had created a structure of laws and institutions that could govern the country without the constant intervention of their kings. But over any extended period, medieval feudal monarchies functioned well only when headed by an able and dedicated king who could impose his will on the independent-minded, highly privileged, and habitually violent aristocracy. When the king was weak and the nobles were unruly, feudal monarchy provided very bad government. Even strong feudal monarchs were subject to many restrictions. They could not tax their subjects without their consent, which was rarely given except in great emergencies. They had to respect the established privileges ("liberties," as they were then called) of the nobles, the church corporations, and the chartered towns. In France, even after the strong reigns of the thirteenth century, the king had little real power in certain parts of his kingdom. The greatest vassals, such as the count of Flanders or the duke of Brittany, were almost independent rulers, and they alone could collect taxes, administer justice, and raise troops in their regions. Worst of all, the duke of Guienne was simultaneously king of England, and while he reluctantly acknowledged himself the French king's vassal for his large and valuable holdings in France, his position as a sovereign ruler across the Channel made him almost impossible to control.

The French Dynastic Crisis

The last great king of medieval France was Philip IV (1285–1314), called "The Fair" or "the Handsome." One of the secrets of success for the French Capetian dynasty had been a matter of good fortune: each king before his death had a grown son ready to take over. That was how the monarchy had through the centuries become hereditary. But none of Philip's three sons succeeded in begetting a male heir. When the first, Louis X, died in 1316, the French nobility refused to accept his daughter as their queen and preferred to acknowledge his younger brother. But when the last of the brothers died in 1328, the Capetian royal family was extinct in the male line. The nobles in 1316 had hunted out of old law books an early "Salic Law," which they interpreted as excluding a woman from the succession. Now in 1328, the question arose whether a male claimant could inherit the throne if his royal descent was through the female line. This claimant was young King Edward III (1327–77) of England, son of a daughter of King Philip IV and the closest male relative of the three latest kings. Edward III made a formal claim to the French throne, but the nobles wanted no foreign king, and the highest court ruled that only descendants through the male line could inherit the throne. Thus the French in 1328 accepted as king a distant cousin of the recent monarchs, Philip, count of Valois.

Philip VI (1328–50), the first of the Valois dynasty, was a reasonably able man. But having come out of the higher nobility himself, and having got the throne largely because the great nobles preferred him ahead of foreign claimants, he could hardly be expected to keep those nobles in line. The hardest to control was Edward III of England, a vassal of France for his great Duchy of Guienne in southwestern France. Edward believed that he had a better title to the French throne than Philip VI, and only after long delay did he come to France and publicly acknowledge himself Philip's vassal.

The real source of friction, however, was not Edward's claim to France, but his unwillingness to tolerate the busy meddling of French royal officials within his French duchy. During the weak reign of Edward III's father, French officials had scored many political successes in Guienne by a combination of bumptious interference and threats of war. Experience had shown that the English would back down rather than fight. The whole practice of having a sovereign king become vassal of another king for part of his lands was one of the many anomalies of feudalism. Logically, either Edward III should have given up his French fiefs, or Philip VI should have renounced his sovereignty over Guienne, but the one solution would have robbed Edward of valuable lands that were his by law, and the other would have amounted to a dismemberment of France.

The Hundred Years' War

As French interference in Guienne became increasingly troublesome, Edward III began deliberately to plan a war. He expected it to be short. It has since come to be known as the Hundred Years' War (1337–1453). The fourteenth century was an age of dynastic and aristocratic politics, and in a very real sense Edward III's personal motives were the "cause" of the Hundred Years' War. Yet not even a medieval king could undertake and sustain a major war without the backing of important groups in his country.

There were causes of the war other than Edward III's desire for full sovereignty over Guienne. More than a century of frequent wars had created a flourishing tradition of hatred between the French and the English. The French persistently backed Scotland in its struggle to avoid being subordinated to England. The English regularly encouraged separatist movements in the rich and powerful County of Flanders. The seafaring populations on the two sides of the Channel frequently resorted to violence against each other. Bloody fights between fishermen and merchantmen at sea were followed by raids to plunder towns on the opposite shore. Merchants and fishermen did not dictate the king's foreign policy, but they did pay the war taxes, and their spokesmen in Parliament or the Estates General had to give consent. There were also vested economic interests that might find Edward's war attractive. English wine merchants who dominated the trade in Bordeaux wines and wool merchants who profited from exports of wool to the industrial towns of Flanders tended to sympathize with their king's anti-French policies in both Guienne and Flanders.

Aristocratic Pressure for War. The greatest force working for the outbreak and prolongation of war was the aristocracy on both sides. The nobles were by profession a military caste. From warfare they sought not only personal glory but also some very tangible advantages: ransom of captives, booty from invaded territories, military commands, and both administrative appointments and landed estates in conquered districts. In an age when general inflation, rising labor costs, and falling farm profits made it impossible to live aristocratically from the revenues of their landed estates, the nobles could find no other socially acceptable occupation than war. Thus as a class they favored war as both honorable and profitable, and they were precisely the social class among whom kings constantly lived. Thus the aristocratic royal courts gave to royal policy a persistent bias in favor of war. Young Edward III shared fully the militaristic outlook of his nobles.

The French officials who goaded Edward into action doubtlessly thought that war was a possibility. It was a risk they ran gladly, for past wars had been confined to a few raids back and forth across the border of Guienne, and the French had more often gained than lost territory. But this time the French got more than they bargained for. Instead of a war of skirmishes, Edward III systematically prepared a crushing attack at the heartland of northern France, and since his small land of fewer than three million inhabitants could hardly expect to overwhelm medieval Europe's most powerful country with its twelve million people, he created a vast network of alliances, paying cash on the line to all princes and nobles of the Low Countries and western Germany who would join his assault. He shrewdly applied economic pressure on Flanders, cutting off wool exports and hence creating a social and political revolution led by unemployed woolen weavers who forced their country to adopt a pro-English policy.

Both sides expected the war to be speedily decided by a great battle between armored knights. What they got instead was a war of attrition. In

1339, Edward's army marched through northern France, burning crops and villages, but unable to take any fortified city or to seek out and destroy the French army.

There were two great and decisive battles in the first long phase of the Hundred Years' War (1337–80), yet they really decided little. At Crécy in 1346 and again at Poitiers in 1356, much smaller English armies were cut off and forced to fight the famous heavy cavalry of French nobles. In both cases, the English in their plight abandoned proper medieval reliance on massed cavalry charges and depended on nonnoble footsoldiers armed with the longbow. In both battles, the slow-moving French cavalrymen charging uphill into a storm of arrows were slaughtered by the hundreds. After Poitiers, the flower of the French nobility lay dead on the field, King John II (1350–64) of France and many of his highest officials were prisoners of war, and the glorious military tradition of the French chivalry was disgraced by its double defeats, and still more by the cowardice of many knights who ran away.

Nevertheless, though they had won two smashing victories, the English had not won the war. John II finally secured his release by signing a treaty (1360) in which he did cede Guienne to Edward III in full sovereignty. But the huge section of France that Edward got (nearly one-third of the country) was more than he could control. Although English armies could ravage the French countryside almost at will, they lacked the manpower, equipment, and money needed to take fortified towns or even to control the large territories added to Guienne in 1360. The limits of England's power became clear during the reign of the ablest of the Valois kings of France, Charles V (1364–80), under whom there was a considerable resurgence of French power.

Despite this temporary recovery, the Hundred Years' War was a devastating experience for France. The English tactical system made it a war of attrition, in which the brutal ravaging of the French countryside was the price exacted for the French refusal to submit. While people in fortified towns were fairly secure, the lives and properties of the rural population bore the brunt of the war. The military system used by both sides magnified the brutality inherent in war, for the rank and file were mercenaries whose main expectation was not the wages they were promised but the booty they could strip from the countryside. Murder, rape, and extortion were the real trade of these soldiers. Hence even during the frequent periods of truce, the pillaging of the countryside continued.

Precisely what such conditions meant to the people of France is easy to imagine but hard to document in a systematic way. We do know that at some periods the countryside in northern France was so devastated that the English armies could not find forage for their horses and had to carry along their own fodder. There are scattered statistics showing that some districts experienced great declines in population, in the revenues of landowners, and in agricultural production. The pillaging was fearsome enough that French provincial assemblies sometimes paid ransom to military contingents in order to be spared from their raids. And of course there is literary evidence: complaints by contemporary poets, chroniclers, and preachers about the desolation of the land and the sufferings of the people. Even making allowance for exaggerations, conditions must have been bad.

Collapse of the French Monarchy. At least as bad as the physical destruction was the failure of the French government and ruling classes in face of the crisis. The people found their rulers constantly increasing old taxes, devising new ones to pay for the war, and yet failing to provide effective protection from the invaders. Political discontent came to a head after the capture of King John II at Poitiers in 1356. The capture of the king created a constitutional crisis in which the nation turned to its representative assembly, the Estates General, then meeting at Paris. The dauphin (heir to the throne) Charles and other spokesmen for the royal family demanded authority to levy new taxes, but the Third Estate, made up of representatives of the towns, no longer trusted the honesty or the competence of the ruling classes. Hence they refused to vote any more taxes until dishonest and incompetent officials were weeded out of the administration, until certain legal and administrative reforms were enacted, and until the dauphin had agreed to govern with the aid of a council elected by the Estates, and to summon the Estates into session regularly in future.

These remarkably precocious constitutional demands would have given the French legislature a degree of power that even the more developed English Parliament did not obtain for several centuries. They were voiced chiefly by the provost for the Paris merchants, Étienne Marcel, and were backed by the Parisian mob. But Dauphin Charles managed to avoid making a clear commitment to most of the demands, and from London the captive king repudiated the concessions his son did make. What especially helped the old ruling classes regain control was that the reformers themselves were disunited. Representatives of the clergy and nobility, and even some of the Third Estate, were alarmed by the radicalism of Marcel and his Parisian followers. The dauphin escaped from Paris, transferred the next session of the Estates to a provincial town, and rallied the conservative elements to defend France from the Paris rabble as well as from the English.

The Jacquerie of 1358. A quite independent event, a savage uprising of peasants suffering from hunger and from the depredations of English and French soldiers, intensified the isolation of the radical reformers at Paris. This rebellion of 1358, called the Jacquerie, from the traditional nickname for the French peasant, Jacques Bonhomme, was an uprising of the oppressed classes against the aristocracy that for centuries had exploited them. Noble families were plundered and even butchered. Manorial records of peasant obligations were burned. In some places, workingmen from the towns joined the rebels. But the French nobles, while unable to defend the people from the English, were more than a match for the untrained, ill-equipped bands of peasants. Hence the rebellion was short-lived: it began in May and was suppressed by late June. More than twenty thousand peasants were killed, others deliberately maimed, and peasant-owned crops, buildings, and livestock destroyed. Financial burdens were stringently reimposed or even increased.

Étienne Marcel made some attempts to cooperate with the peasants, and suspicion that he intended to deliver Paris to them or to the English was the probable cause of his mysterious murder. The citizens of Paris then opened their gates to the dauphin, and the one great attempt to impose legislative control on the medieval French government had collapsed.

The Threat from the Great Nobles. The French monarchy even in the crisis of 1356–58 had succeeded in handling both a peasant rebellion and an attempt by the urban bourgeoisie to establish legislative control over the executive. It was far less successful in controlling the feudal nobility. Despite their humiliating defeats by the English, the nobles were still the prime possessors of military power and landed wealth. Even the growth of royal administrative control over their local governments in most parts of France had not destroyed their political power, for in France (and England, too) the greatest nobles now staked a claim to control the central administration as hereditary advisers of the king.

Relying not only on their wealth and power but also on their social prestige and often on their blood relationship to the royal family, an inner group of court nobles emerged as contenders for control of the government of both warring nations. These nobles followed two logically incompatible but politically interrelated policies. On the one hand, like the nobles of the early Middle Ages, they attempted to organize virtual subkingdoms where their control was unchallenged and where the king and his officials had little real power. On the other hand, they tried to secure for themselves and their henchmen control of key appointments in the royal administration. They regarded high office and membership on the royal council as a privilege of their caste and thought it oppressive for the king to appoint nonnoble officials merely because these men were more efficient and more loyal. Of course the great nobles used control of office, when they got it, to turn royal policy to their own political and financial advantage. At a time when most nobles could not afford to live nobly off the revenues of their estates, the profits of high office made the difference between affluence and impoverishment.

The Rise of Burgundy. The kings of fourteenth-century England and France, far from controlling these tendencies among the higher nobility, fostered their wealth and power though never able to satisfy their greed. A sort of supernobility—the king's brothers, uncles, and cousins—emerged as serious rivals to the king's personal control of government. In France, the Valois kings' folly of granting *appanages* (large, semiindependent principalities) to younger sons made this situation especially serious. It was a reversal of the long process whereby the great medieval kings had slowly brought more and more of the large territorial fiefs under royal control.

The clearest example of this political folly was the creation of the great Burgundian state by the chivalrous but politically inept King John II. In 1364, wishing to reward his younger son Philip the Bold for saving his life in battle, King John conferred on him the large and valuable duchy of Burgundy in eastern France. The king also secured for Philip the Franche-Comté of Burgundy on the German side of the border and negotiated for him a splendid marriage with the heiress of the count of Flanders, ruler of the richest and most industrialized region in Northern Europe. On this foundation Philip the Bold and later dukes of Burgundy built up a huge principality lying on both sides of the Franco-German border. It included not only French and imperial Burgundy but also most of what is now Belgium and the Netherlands.

By mid-fifteenth century, Burgundy had become a great European power in its own right, and its last duke dreamed of pinching off the parts of eastern France and western Germany that separated Burgundy from the Low Countries, and even of proclaiming himself a king. His lands would then have stretched from the mouth of the Rhine River to the Swiss border. Yet while they were building this great rival state, the dukes of Burgundy were always peers of France, close relatives of the king, and avid participants in the scramble for power, lands, and patronage in Fance.

Factional Struggles in France. Under John II's able successor Charles V, the danger posed by Burgundy remained latent. But the disastrous reign of Charles VI (1380–1422) is the clearest example of how feudal monarchies collapsed under a weak king. Charles VI came to the throne as a minor. When he took personal control in 1388, he brought some of the best of his father's ministers back into office, though the king's ambitious younger brother, the duke of Orleans, and his uncles, the dukes of Anjou, Berry, and Burgundy, had too much influence, which they used in their personal interest. Suddenly, in 1392, the young king suffered the first period of an intermittent but totally disabling insanity that, during its attacks, left him unable to transact any business. Even during his increasingly short periods of lucidity, Charles VI was unable to control policy. Direction of affairs, and physical possession of the king's person, became a matter of dispute among his queen, his greedy and ambitious uncles, and his brother, the duke of Orleans. Each contender used power, when he had it, for his personal ends, Orleans to pursue territorial ambitions in Italy, Burgundy to strengthen his great new duchy, and all of them to secure gifts of crown lands, to control patronage in the interests of their own political friends, and to exalt their own power. Under this government by rapacious and self-serving courtiers, the general interest of France was neglected.

Still worse, there was simply not enough wealth and power to satisfy the boundless greed of the great dukes and their friends. The duke of Orleans and the duke of Burgundy became heads of bitterly opposed factions, each seeking to monopolize government office. This rivalry passed from court intrigue to violence and murder (both a duke of Orleans and a duke of Burgundy were assassinated, each leaving his successor pledged to revenge). By 1411 there was open civil war between a faction led by Burgundy and a faction led by the count of Armagnac, son-in-law of Orleans. This contest was so bitter, and the nobles' sense of national loyalty so weak, that when the English reopened the Hundred Years' War in 1415, the duke of Burgundy first tacitly cooperated and then actively aided the invaders.

Dynastic Crisis in England

Fortunately for France, the English monarchy after 1392 was only a little less decrepit than the French. In England, too, the basic problem was the crown's inability to control the higher nobility, especially those closely related to the monarch. Edward III's wars in France had magnified the self-importance and military power of the nobles, many of whom had formed private armies which they hired out to the king in periods of war, but which they also used at home to conduct their personal feuds. In his later years, Edward III became prematurely senile, leaving control of government to a bickering group of low-born bureaucrats whom the nobles resented, to his various mistresses and their relatives, and to his own greedy and disputatious sons. There were frequent political crises, domestic violence, a great peasant rebellion, and finally a total breakdown of the English monarchy during Edward's declining years. The royal princes greedily appropriated crown lands and monies for themselves. The struggle was complicated by the growing importance of Parliament in an age when the crown was constantly begging it for money, but the real struggle was not between crown and Parliament but among the various aristocratic factions, who learned how to manipulate Parliamentary complaints to their own advantage.

The factiousness and violence of Edward III's later years grew worse when his grandson Richard II (1377–99) mounted the throne as a boy of ten. The king's uncles struggled for control of the council of regency. Richard II grew up an ambitious and even rather able young man, and in 1397 staged a royal coup d'état that left him great personal power. But his heavy-handed meddling in matters of justice and local government and his heavy taxation stirred up resentment. His arbitrary confiscation of the rich inheritance of his young cousin, Henry, duke of Lancaster, provided the opposition with a leader and also aroused resentment among the great landowning aristocrats. While the exiled Duke Henry raised troops on the Continent and plotted with discontented English nobles, the young king did not even know that he was in political trouble.

As soon as King Richard personally led an army to suppress a revolt in Ireland, Lancaster landed in England with a small army, proclaiming that he had come only to claim his lawful inheritance as duke. So many disaffected nobles rallied to him, however, that when Richard II came hurrying back from Ireland, Lancaster arrested him, forced him to sign an act of abdication, and a few months later had him secretly murdered. In the meantime, Henry summoned a Parliament and in its presence laid claim to the throne.

The fictitious genealogy he put forward and the assent of Parliament did not conceal the fact that Henry IV (1399–1413) was a usurper. The greatest and richest of the nobles had in fact murdered the king and seized the throne for himself. With such a shaky title, Henry IV could hardly be expected to curtail the power of the great barons whose backing had ensured the success of his rebellion. Thus the reforms he had demanded as a critic of Richard II's government were impossible for him to consider as king, since many of them would harm the interests of pro-Lancastrian nobles.

The Plight of the People. While the English kings and high nobles were keeping the government in turmoil and furnishing rich plot material for the playwright Shakespeare to use two centuries later in his history plays, the consequences for the life of ordinary people were grim. The heavy tax demands were a burden on an undeveloped nation not habituated to paying taxes at all, and the methods of collection were both wasteful and regressive. In the Middle Ages, rents, dues, and fees were paid constantly, but taxes were only an emergency measure. The tax levies were all the more resented in the period after 1360, when they no longer produced military victories. Furthermore, a Parliament dominated by high clergy, nobles, wealthy non-noble landowners, and spokesmen for the wealthy classes of the towns naturally loaded most of the tax burden on those who were unrepresented and least able to pay, the peasants and the lower classes of the towns. In 1377, 1379, and 1380, Parliament granted the crown a poll tax that fell most heavily on the poor.

English Peasants' Rebellion. The unjust poll tax of 1380 was the most immediate cause of the one great outburst by the submerged classes of fourteenth-century England, the Peasants' Rebellion of 1381. Other causes were resentment at attempts to freeze wages in the interests of employers and increasing peasant resentment against the many onerous survivals of serfdom. Active preaching of vague notions of Christian communism and social egalitarianism by heretical or unruly clergymen may have played a role also: at least some of the spokesmen for the rebels were members of the lower clergy.

The rebellion began spontaneously in various localities when efforts were made to collect the poll tax. The rebels had other demands, including abolition of serfdom and confiscation of part of the vast wealth of the Church, but the key demand was for abandonment of the poll tax and punishment of the young king's evil advisers. The ruling classes suppressed the rebellion without great difficulty, though they had some anxious moments when a sympathetic alderman opened the gates and let one band of rebels occupy London. Young King Richard II (then aged fourteen) bravely exposed himself to the mob, cleverly offered to carry through the needed reforms, and then blandly broke his promises after the rebels had dispersed.

Though the rebellion was short (mostly in May and June of 1381), and led to few evident changes, it does show that the turmoil among the ruling classes had reverberations lower down in the social scale. In one sense, fourteenth-century Englishmen were fortunate. Though mulcted by unfair and corrupt rulers and oppressed by armed nobles, the people of the countryside were spared the kind of devastation their own troops were inflicting on France.

What England shared with France was the inability of the royal government to control the great nobles. Court politics mattered little to ordinary folk, but other results of aristocratic predominance struck closer to home. All the great nobles and some of the lesser ones raised private armies they used not only in the French campaigns but also to prosecute family feuds and maintain their personal interest at home. Nobles with private armies peddled protection much like modern racketeers. They expected their weaker neighbors to join their armed bands and to vote with them at elections. They ruthlessly seized other men's lands and used their armed ruffians to intimidate judges and juries. When the interests of two great nobles clashed, armed conflicts and protracted feuds resulted. The most important victims of injustice and violence were not the peasants or urban workers, but substantial landowning families of middling rank. This internal turmoil reached its worst during the Wars of the Roses (1455–85).

Henry V and the Conquest of France. After the first Lancastrian usurper, Henry IV, died in 1413, his son Henry V (1413–22) turned from a princely playboy into a hard-driving militarist. Driven by a vision of himself as a great conquerer, Henry V reopened the dormant Hundred Years' War in 1415. Unlike Edward III, he not only claimed the French throne but seriously attempted to conquer it. He opened his campaign in France at Agincourt in 1415 with another smashing victory of his English archers over French knights, but his actual plan of operations was very different from that of Edward III. Taking advantage of the new artillery and of the distraction of the French by civil war between the factions of Burgundy and Armagnac, he systematically besieged and captured town after town in Normandy. Then in 1419 the new duke of Burgundy, seeking revenge for the murder of his father, openly joined the English. Henry V and Burgundy captured the French king and queen, occupied all of northern France, and then prevailed on the mad King Charles VI to sign the Treaty of Troyes (1420). Here Charles VI declared (falsely) that his son and heir, Dauphin Charles, was illegitimate. He acknowledged Henry V as the next king of France after his own death and sealed the arrangement by giving Henry his daughter Catherine in marriage. Since Henry and his ally Duke Philip the Good of Burgundy controlled all of northern France, plus the duchy of Guienne in the southwest, for the first time the English claim to the French royal title seemed about to become a reality. Only in the south and central parts of France did the Dauphin Charles and the leaders of the Armagnac faction provide any armed resistance. In effect, France seemed about to be partitioned.

Yet Henry V never wore the crown of France, and the Burgundian duchy never quite completed its evolution into an independent kingdom. In part, accidental circumstances foiled the English dream. Henry V suddenly fell ill and died in the flower of young manhood (31 August 1422). The feeble old French king, Charles VI, died less than two months later. By the terms of the treaty of 1420, both crowns then passed to the son of Henry V by his marriage to Princess Catherine of France. But this son, Henry VI (1422–61), was only eight months old when his father died. Councils of regency, dominated by the king's uncles, had to administer both realms. A council of regency was a poor substitute for an effective king. Furthermore, English success in France depended on the cooperation of the duke of Burgundy and his faction.

A second accidental factor in the collapse of English control of France was the character of Henry VI himself. He grew up a weak, indecisive man. Then in the face of political and military disasters in France, Henry in 1453 suffered the first attack of a periodic insanity that rendered him unable to transact business, strikingly like his French grandfather, Charles VI.

Resurgent French Patriotism. A more basic cause of the ultimate failure of the English was a decisive change within the French nation. A century and more of frequent English invasions not only had created an ingrained hatred of the English but also had heightened the national consciousness of the French. Domination by the English became less and less acceptable. Except in Guienne, where they had ruled for centuries, the English found the conquered population unfriendly. By the mid-1420s it was painfully clear that only the small English army and the cooperation of the Burgundian faction kept Henry VI's administration in control. Even the aristocratic allies who had collaborated with the invaders became unreliable. This stirring of French patriotism needed only a leader to transform it into a national uprising. The man who ought to have offered such leadership, the disinherited son of Charles VI, seemed unfit to give it. Although Charles VII (1422–

61) had proclaimed himself king and had organized an administration in the provincial town of Bourges, he was indecisive and weak. He probably doubted his own right to the throne, since both of his parents had declared him illegitimate.

Hence the necessary leadership had to come from the people themselves, in the person of Joan of Arc, a simple peasant girl who suddenly appeared at Charles's court in 1429 and declared that God had instructed her by visions to save the French nation. She persuaded the dubious French leaders to give her an army, with which she broke the English siege of Orleans, led Charles VII to the ancient coronation city of Rheims to be crowned, and gained the military initiative for the French. In town after town of northern France, the people drove out the English and Burgundian garrisons and acknowledged Charles VII. Joan herself was eventually captured and burned by the English as a heretic and sorceress in May of 1431. Charles VII did not even attempt to bargain for her release.

Nevertheless, Joan had turned the tide of the war, and the generals who had served under her continued the fight. As the military tide began to turn against the invaders, more and more of their French allies began to remember their French nationality and came to terms with Charles VII. The greatest step came in 1435, when Duke Philip the Good of Burgundy pardoned Charles VII for his complicity in his father's murder. Philip's charitable forgiveness was aided by the King's acceptance of the harsh bargain he drove. He received his French fiefs in full sovereignty and henceforth owed no feudal obligations for them while at the same time he retained his privileges as a peer of France and a prince of the blood royal. This grant of full independence was a bitter pill for the French, since an independent Burgundy was a dangerous rival. But the military advantage seemed worth the price.

The small English army, once deprived of Burgundian aid, was no longer sufficient to hold down the French. Town by town and castle by castle, the French retook their land. Finally, in October of 1453, Bordeaux, the capital of Guienne, the only region where English rule had any popular support, fell. There was never a formal peace treaty, but the Hundred Years' War was over. Of all its enormous holdings in France, England retained only the fortified port of Calais on the Channel coast.

War's Effects on Other States. The political and social turmoil that almost destroyed France affected the other powers involved in the Hundred Years' War. The rich and industrialized county of Flanders was torn repeatedly by struggles between rich and poor and by other struggles between those who favored French control and those who favored a pro-English independence. The province remained torn by frequent riots and rebellions until it fell into the firm hands of the Burgundian dukes in 1384. Burgundy itself by the early fifteenth century had risen to great-power status, and the last independent duke, Charles the Rash (1467–77) grasped eagerly for the French lands and the royal title that would have completed the territorial unity and the dynastic legitimacy of his state. But he reached too far, too fast, and his death in battle against the Swiss left the inheritance to his daughter Mary, who was unable to hold it all together. Even so, the bulk of the Burgundian state passed into the hands of Mary's Hapsburg husband, later the Emperor Maximilian I, and became the foundation for the rise of the Hapsburgs to be the most powerful dynasty of sixteenth-century Europe.

Wars of the Roses in England. Finally, the English also felt the results of protracted war. The weak reign of Henry VI not only made possible the French victory but also set loose the anarchical tendencies of the great barons at home. While the nobles with their private armies terrorized the countryside, the royal council and the Parliament were paralyzed by factional disputes. A few political leaders began to realize that the French war was fruitless and worked for peace, but the dream of glorious and profitable conquest remained popular. The administration led by the duke of Somerset came under attack because of its efforts to negotiate a peace and then got the blame for the final defeat in 1453. Richard, duke of York, led the prowar party.

The factional struggle was all the more dangerous because of the shaky legal foundations of the Lancastrian claim to the throne. Through his mother's family, York had a better claim than did Henry VI. This dynastic crisis came to a head in 1453, when King Henry suffered the first of his intermittent attacks of insanity. In the resultant struggle for control, open civil war (War of the Roses) between Yorkist and Lancastrian factions of the nobility broke out in 1455, though York did not claim the throne till 1460. In 1461 his son defeated the Lancastrians, forced Henry VI and his family to flee to Scotland, and ascended the throne as King Edward IV (1461–83).

The events after 1461 are a tangled web of court intrigues, betrayals of trust, and occasional civil war. Although Edward IV provided twelve years of relatively good government, the Wars of the Roses were not yet over. The dethronement and murder of Edward IV's young son by his uncle Richard III (1483–85) split apart the Yorkist faction and enabled a distant relative of the Lancastrians, Henry Tudor, to reopen the struggle and seize power after killing Richard III in battle. Henry Tudor's reign (1485–1509) marks not only the end of civil war and baronial violence, but also an important reassertion of royal authority.

The Wars of the Roses themselves were intermittent and were seldom more than skirmishes. The masses of Englishmen were uninvolved, and the nobles and their mercenary armies did the fighting. But the collapse of royal power removed the last effective restraints on the violence and rank injustice of the nobles, and the pillaging that went with civil war inflicted on the English at least some of the suffering that their armies had inflicted on the French.

Feudal Anarchy in Other Lands

France and England were the greatest feudal monarchies of the Middle Ages, and their political troubles are the best examples of the breakdown of feudal monarchy and the anarchical tendencies of the feudal aristocracy. Other countries showed similar tendencies. Spain did not become a single monarchy until 1479, but in the two constituent kingdoms that then came together, Castile and Aragon, the fourteenth and fifteenth centuries were a period of turmoil. The Aragonese nobles imposed many restraints on royal authority. In Castile the monarchy was somewhat stronger constitutionally but was even more disturbed by disputed successions and civil wars among factions of nobles. From mid-fifteenth century until the unification of the two countries through the inheritance of their thrones by Queen Isabella and King Ferdinand, both Castile and Aragon experienced a generation of civil war. The independent kingdom of Portugal had disorders in the fourteenth century but was relatively stable in the fifteenth century. Naples and Sicily in Italy, which were feudal in government and associated dynastically with Aragon, also experienced disputed successions and baronial insubordination.

The record of royal failure and feudal anarchy, plus the collapse of effective central government in Germany and Italy, makes the fourteenth and fifteenth centuries seem an age of unmitigated political disaster. In reality, many of the positive gains made by the feudal monarchies during the twelfth and thirteenth centuries, such as central administrative, fiscal, and judicial agencies, survived through the time of troubles. Royal officials and judges in every country persistently tried to fit together the central governmental machinery. Even at the worst periods, the various European peoples knew that the monarchy was their only hope, and a residual loyalty to the monarchy was the main force that held the nations together.

For some states, the fourteenth and fifteenth centuries were actual periods of advance. In Germany, though the central government was decrepit, the larger territorial states eventually became new bases of political authority, though most of these developments occurred only after the Reformation. The most stable political force in pre-Reformation Germany was the large group of virtually independent towns in southern and western Germany. Whatever security they achieved, however, did not extend far beyond their walls. The Burgundian state was strong, stable, and well ruled from the late fourteenth century to the death of Charles the Rash in 1477. The Swiss, also, were powerful. Indeed, if their central government had not been so feeble, their great military strength might have made them a major European power. Instead, they became a recruiting ground for the mercenary armies of other governments.

The Eastern Monarchies

The most brilliant political successes of the fourteenth and fifteenth centuries, except perhaps for Burgundy, occurred in the three large monarchies of Eastern Europe, Poland, Bohemia, and Hungary, which had close dynastic links to each other. King Wenceslas II (1278–1305) of Bohemia united all three crowns, but Hungary and Poland threw off the control of his successors. The second king of the new Luxemburg dynasty of Bohemia, Charles IV (1346–78), made Bohemia the base for his acquisition of the German imperial title. Under him Prague became an important political and cultural center, and a new sense of Czech nationality grew up, challenging the traditional domination of the country by German merchants and churchmen.

Poland experienced a period of power and territorial expansion after the Polish nobles arranged for the marriage of their Queen Hedwig to the Grand Duke Jagiello of Lithuania, ruler of the last important pagan nationality in Europe. Jagiello (or Ladislas II, to use his baptismal name) ruled the combined Polish-Lithuanian state from 1386 to 1434. To the west and north, he inflicted a great defeat on the aggressive German crusading principality, the Teutonic Knights, in 1410. To the east and south, he expanded at the expense of Muscovy and of the Tartar khans who had dominated Russia since the thirteenth century, pushing the Polish border as far as the Black Sea.

Hungary also had some periods of great strength, and under King Matthias I Corvinus (1458–90) even conquered substantial parts of Bohemia and Austria.

Yet in all three eastern monarchies, royal power (and with it, national power) was insecure. The right of the nobles to determine succession to the throne became well established and was deliberately used to limit royal power. In 1457 the Bohemian Estates elected a man who had not a drop of royal blood in his veins and who was thus under the thumb of the nobles. In 1492 the Polish nobles deliberately elected a younger rather than an elder son of the late king, mainly in order to weaken the hereditary principle. Even the greatest of the Eastern kings had to bargain away their powers in order to get aristocratic support.

Above all, the nobles of Eastern Europe received a free hand in dealing with the peasants on their estates. The Eastern European peasantry, which formerly had been the freest in Europe, was deprived of personal freedom and economic and social status, in large part by brutal violence. The representative institutions of all three kingdoms developed considerable control over taxation, lawmaking, and administration, just as their counterparts in

England and Aragon were doing. But unlike the Western states, the Eastern kingdoms did not experience a decisive reassertion of royal authority in the later fifteenth century. The long-term result of this exaltation of the nobles was the weakening not of the king alone, but of the whole nation. Hungary and Bohemia came under foreign domination in the following century, and Poland became increasingly the puppet and victim of its greedy neighbors until in the later eighteenth century the three strongest ones divided up Poland and wiped it off the map of Europe.

Ottoman Conquest of the Balkans. East-Central Europe at least had periods of power and glory. Farther south and east, the fourteenth, fifteenth, and early sixteenth centuries produced unmitigated disaster. The great military and cultural bulwark of Eastern Christendom, the Byzantine empire, never really recovered from its loss of central Anatolia to the Seljuk Turks in the eleventh century and its conquest by the misdirected Fourth Crusade in 1204. The Italian merchant cities, the kings of Serbia, and various Western European soldiers of fortune grabbed lands from the faltering empire. But the greatest danger came from the Ottoman Turks.

Taking advantage of the Byzantines' habit of employing foreign mercenaries in their own dynastic civil wars, a band of Turks in 1354 seized the city of Gallipoli on the European shore. From this beginning, Turkish occupation of the Balkan peninsula advanced rapidly. The Turkish sultan Murad I moved his capital to Adrianople on the European side in 1365. In 1389 the Turks crushed the kingdom of Serbia, which had taken much land from the Byzantines but could not hold on to it. By the time of the death of Sultan Bayezid I in 1402, the Turks held nearly the whole Balkan peninsula. The Byzantine emperor retained only a small area around Constantinople itself and a few scattered portions of European Greece.

Byzantine appeals for help from their fellow Christians produced one large crusade that ended in disastrous defeat at Nicopolis in 1396, when the brave but undisciplined Western knights showed that they were as futile against the Turks as against the English archers. More effective action against the Turks came from the kings of Hungary, Bohemia, and Poland, who had good reason to fear that they might be the next victims of Turkish expansion. In 1453 an ambitious young sultan, Mohammed II, stormed the isolated capital at Constantinople and brought the Byzantine empire to an end.

Turkish expansion also pushed into the Greek-speaking islands of the eastern Mediterranean, which the Venetians and other Italian cities had ruled. There was danger even farther west. In 1480 the Turks briefly occupied the Italian port of Otranto. Turkish fleets cooperated with the pirates of the Barbary Coast to threaten European ships in the western Mediterranean. In 1517 the Turks conquered Egypt, and in 1526 they destroyed the Hungarian kingdom and occupied all but the western third of the country.

In 1529 they besieged the lower Austrian capital of Vienna, and throughout the period there was fear of a major Turkish invasion of southeastern Germany or Bohemia. Turkey remained the ruler of the Balkan countries until the rise of nationalist independence movements in the nineteenth century.

The Political Record

The total political record of Europe in the fourteenth and fifteenth centuries was not a happy one, though in some fortunate countries (France, England, and Spain) there was a significant improvement in the later fifteenth century. Even such positive developments as the origin and growth of parliamentary institutions was not an unmixed blessing, for this development was associated with the excessive power of the aristocracy. As the irreversible triumph of aristocracy over the crown in Germany, Poland, and Hungary shows, the nobles and the parliaments they used as forums for their opposition could destroy royal power but were themselves unfit to rule. Permanent aristocratic predominance was the most direct cause of the political disintegration and foreign domination of those nations.

Chapter Three

The Waning of Medieval Church and Culture

Thoughtful Europeans living in the fourteenth and fifteenth centuries were acutely aware of the disastrous character of their political experience. The internal turmoil of the Christian nations and the frequent wars among them seemed all the more fearsome when viewed in the light of Turkish expansion in the Mediterranean and in Southeastern Europe. Yet no institutional breakdown of the period troubled contemporaries more than the decline of the greatest institution of the Middle Ages, the Christian Church. In theory, the Church had become a rationally organized hierarchy with all effective authority restricted to the ordained clergy and with clerical power flowing from the pope, vicar of Christ, through the various ranks, down eventually to the parish level. In one sense, the bureaucratic centralization of the Church during the twelfth and thirteenth centuries transformed the theoretical primacy of the pope as bishop of Rome into an absolute monarchical control.

Hierarchy and Corruption

The realities of power in the late medieval Church were very different from the theory. In practice, the hierarchy did not have effective control over all of the Church. In particular, the exemption of many monasteries and all the mendicant frairs from control of the bishops greatly weakened the ability of the bishops to impose discipline on clergy and laity alike. Where the right to appoint a parish priest had been transferred to a monastery that was exempt from the local bishop's control the monastery usually insisted that the bishop had no further right to supervise the affairs of that parish. An even greater threat to discipline was the inability of bishops and parish priests to prevent mendicant friars from preaching, hearing confessions, granting absolution, imposing penances, distributing the sacraments, and (above all, perhaps) collecting money among the laity. How could a parish priest or a bishop effectively control his flock when friars claiming exempt status wandered through a district and freely granted absolution from sins on terms easier than those offered by the parish priest?

A further derangement of discipline stemmed from the success of kings and nobles in maintaining their control of Church patronage despite the repeated efforts of medieval reformers to forbid it. Many bishops, abbots, and rectors of well-endowed parishes were in fact appointed by kings, nobles, and other laymen. Indeed, the right to appoint the holder of a valuable Church office was itself a piece of property that could be bought, sold, mortgaged, gambled for, or even (horror of horrors!) possessed by a woman. All this was contrary to the canonical rules for Church appointments, but it was nevertheless very real. Although pious lay patrons often made admirable appointments, kings and nobles all too often used their appointive powers to name persons who were unfit and legally unqualified merely because some personal, political, or family interest would be served. This system of patronage was a major cause of the low caliber of the higher clergy in the Middle Ages.

The Plight of the Reformers

Would-be reformers were faced with the power of patrons who had no intention of renouncing traditional and valuable privileges. At the same time, they faced the spiritual authority of higher clergy, from the popes on down, who had granted exemptions and dispensations that authorized such unlawful practices. The reformer attacking abuses often found himself in the position of attacking the spiritual authority of the pope, bishop, or other official who had permitted the abuses. To conduct such an attack without seeming to become a heretical rebel against recognized authority was a ticklish business. Even if he had started with no intention of undermining Church doctrines, the late-medieval reformer often wound up becoming a heretic or at least seeming to be one.

The problem, quite simply, was that once a clever scoundrel was installed in high Church office, he could use the spiritual and legal privileges of his office as a shield for his corrupt actions and as a sword to strike down his critics on charges that they were heretics. The classic example was the way in which the most corrupt of all the Renaissance popes, Alexander VI, in 1497 placed the outspoken Florentine reformer Girolamo Savonarola in the position of seeming a rebel against papal authority. The excommunication of Savonarola by the pope weakened the hold of the reforming friar on many of his Florentine followers and prepared the way for his execution on charges of heresy. Behind a wall of legal privileges, corrupt popes and bishops defended themselves with relentless determination.

The Guilt of the Roman Curia

Although lay patrons who abused their appointive powers were to blame for corruption as much as popes and bishops, corruption at Rome was the key to corruption everywhere. The popes alone were not to blame for the evil condition of the Church, but until the popes used their authority systematically to back the cause of reform, there could be no general improvement. Unfortunately, as the papacy had become more and more powerful in the High Middle Ages, it attracted ambitious and unspiritual hangers-on who made the papal Curia, even as early as the thirteenth century, notorious for its moral corruption, its worldliness, and its greed for money and power. Even the popes themselves had difficulty controlling the Church when their policies ran counter to the interests of the curial bureaucrats. Silent but effective bureaucratic obstruction was seconded at times by open defiance from the College of Cardinals. Much like the secular nobility in the monarchies of the same period, these great princes of the Church often insisted that the pope must rule in constant consultation with them. The cardinals themselves often represented the interests of the secular powers from which they had come, and the political intrigues of Renaissance Italy constantly spilled over into factional struggles in the Consistory. In 1515, for example, Pope Leo X discovered that five of the cardinals were implicated in a plot to murder him and choose a pope who better suited their interests.

This constant tug-of-war for power at Rome is the only excuse for the scandalous nepotism—appointment of close relatives to office—of the medieval and Renaissance papacy. By naming his own relatives to the College of Cardinals and to high administrative positions, the pope could build up his own faction, which left him less isolated in the complex world of curial politics.

Corrupt Popes of the High Renaissance

The situation reached its worst with the popes of the High Renaissance. Sixtus IV (1471–84) had been a friar with few political connections before his election and hence desperately needed reliable supporters at Rome. He also had a large and needy group of relatives whom he wished to promote to wealth and high social status. Five of his nephews quickly became cardinals, and a sixth became a bishop. Other nephews married into the ruling families of Naples, Urbino, and Milan, and the son of one of his nieces became a sixth family member of the College of Cardinals. Only one of these relatives thus raised to wealth and power, the future Pope Julius II, was a man of great talents. Several of the relatives openly led dissolute lives. This unsavory pack of papal relations was responsible for involving the papacy in the Pazzi Conspiracy, that disreputable plot to murder Lorenzo and Giuliano de' Medici at mass and seize control of Florence. The next pope, Innocent VIII (1484–92), was less politically aggressive, but he was the first to acknowledge his own sons and daughters openly and use their marriages as pawns in the game of papal diplomacy.

Then came Pope Alexander VI (1492–1503) a depraved scoundrel who bribed his way to the papal throne, used his spiritual authority to free his daughter Lucrezia Borgia to contract new marriages useful in papal politics, and allowed his brutal son Cesare Borgia to undertake the violent creation of a hereditary Borgia within the papal territories. The sexual incontinence of the pope himself was not, as in the case of Innocent VIII, a matter of his youthful past, and the families of his mistresses also were rewarded with Church offices. Alessandro Farnese, brother of one of these women, became a cardinal at twenty-five solely because of his sister's relationship with the pope. After Alexander, Pope Julius II (1503–13) was something of an improvement. He was utterly secular in outlook, but he did struggle to retrieve for the papacy the lands that the Borgias and other princely families had filched, though he did so by making himself the worst warmonger of his generation.

With leadership like this, it is hardly surprising that the moral tone of the whole papal curia became corrupt. At the top of Roman society was a cardinalate, many of whose members were younger sons of Italian ruling families, accustomed to luxury and sensing no calling to a religious life. Young men who became cardinals at twenty-four and twenty-five, even at seventeen and fifteen years of age, accustomed to self-indulgence, and loaded down with valuable Church offices that demanded no work but yielded great incomes, set the tone of Roman society with their costly mistresses, reckless gambling, and lavish households. The lesser fry aped the manners of the great. The curia attracted the same crowd of hangers-on who clustered about the secular courts of Europe—ranging from jugglers, pickpockets, pimps, and prostitutes at one extreme to the finest artists, poets, and musicians of Renaissance Italy at the other. Rome became famous throughout Europe for the higher cultural aspect of its court, but it also became infamous for its vices.

Effects of Moral Corruption

More important historically than the existence of corruption at Rome (for who outside of Italy knew much about these matters?) was the effect that such leaders had on the administration of the Church. The financial requirements of all this luxury compelled everyone, from the pope on down, to be constantly on the alert for new sources of revenue. Church offices were given not only for reasons of politics and personal favoritism but also for cash on the line. There was at least a taint of bribery in several papal elections of the period, and several cardinals sold their votes to Rodrigo

Borgia, richest of the cardinals, so that he could become Pope Alexander VI.

The whole papal bureaucracy became shot through with corruption. Judges in the papal courts took bribes. Administrative officials—who in any case had a claim to fees for issuing papal confirmations of appointments, dispensations from canon law on matters of marriage, eligibility to hold Church office, and other favors—took bribes to approve petitions that should have been rejected. A few officials, knowing how to draw up documents in proper legal form, even developed a thriving sideline in forged charters. In 1489, Pope Innocent VIII discovered that officials had been forging charters which purportedly authorized priests to keep concubines, and one which authorized priests in Norway to say mass without wine (which was expensive there). On this occasion two of the guilty forgers were executed.

But dishonest practices only a little less flagrant not only went unpunished but even became the basis of many officials' incomes. In the sixteenth century, the market value of curial offices that could be purchased went down whenever it seemed probable that the reform faction would win the upper hand. And the income that came into the papal treasury from the abuse of papal authority to authorize unlawful practices became so crucial to financial solvency that sixteenth-century treasury officials warned that reform of abuses would cause the bankruptcy of the whole papal administration. A curial administration that profited so greatly from abuses could not help but have doubts about the wisdom and feasibility of reforms.

Pluralism and Nonresidence. The same spirit of worldliness that prevailed at Rome also disturbed the various local branches of the Church. Here again, the great political power and the vast incomes that went with many Church offices attracted men who entered the Church not to serve religion but to make careers. Such bishops, abbots, and parish priests were interested in the income and the power, not the duty. Hence despite Church laws which strictly forbade anyone to hold more than one appointment involving pastoral care of souls, ambitious clerics collected great numbers of appointments which they held simultaneously, if necessary securing papal dispensations from Rome to override the laws they broke.

This abuse, pluralism, led almost of necessity to another abuse, nonresidence. Clearly a priest who was simultaneously pastor of two parishes could not give full time to both jobs. Indeed, the sort of clergyman who collected benefices (Church incomes) without limit very often made no effort to do his duties at all. He lived at Rome, at the court of his king, at a comfortable resort town, or in a fashionable city far from his parish. At best, he found some impoverished clergyman who lacked the connections needed to get a profitable office and hired that man for a pittance to carry out the pastoral duties that went with the benefice. Such substitutes, or curates, chosen with no consideration for their talents or competence, often provided inferior pastoral care. Sometimes, if he could get away with it, the titular benefice-holder pocketed all the revenues and refused even to hire a substitute.

Some extreme examples show how far pluralism could go. The French Cardinal d'Estouteville, who had royal backing in getting high appointments, was at one time archbishop of Rouen, bishop of three other dioceses, abbot of four abbeys, and prior of three priories. From these appointments he derived a princely income, which he probably needed, since he resided in none of his bishoprics but spent all his active career in Italy, looking out for the political interests of his king and no doubt angling for other benefices. At a lower level, many parish priests were pluralists many times over. In the late thirteenth century, one English pastor simultaneously held twenty-nine benefices, of which twenty-four involved pastoral care of souls. He was not only a pluralist but a nonresident. Since he had never bothered to be ordained a priest, he could not have performed the duties in a single one of his benefices even if he had been physically present. He merely took the money.

The practice of neglecting to be ordained as priest or consecrated as bishop was not at all uncommon, and this was how (with the help of papal dispensations) boys as young as eleven years old could become bishops. Such clerical adventurers of course sold and swapped their offices frequently in order to move up the ecclesiastical ladder, or get offices closer to home, or for other reasons. There were even professional brokers, who arranged exchanges of benefices for a fee.

The Lower Clergy. These vast accumulations of offices were of course available only to a favored few, men who usually came from the aristocratic classes. Priests who lacked influence could often get a benefice if they managed to secure a university education. If they didn't have a university education, they became curates replacing nonresident clerical aristocrats, or they took charge of impoverished parishes that no one wanted, otherwise they scratched out a living by teaching school, acting as chaplains to persons of wealth, or engaging in some secular occupation.

Since there were no seminaries to prepare young men for the priesthood, and since many bishops would ordain almost anyone who requested it, a huge proletariat of underemployed, uneducated priests arose, recruited from the lower classes and totally unfit to raise their parishioners above the level of popular ignorance, worldliness, and superstition. Thus the lower clergy became notorious for their ignorance, their personal coarseness and barbarism, and their inability to give spiritual leadership. Since they themselves received little income, they pieced together a living from the fees they demanded for every religious service they rendered or from engaging in part-time side occupations as innkeepers, shopkeepers, farmers, peddlers, or (if they were literate) secretaries to local persons of wealth. Their own coarseness of life and language, their drunkenness, violence, and incontinence, and above all their determination in wringing money out of the laity, all explain why the clergy were widely despised. Cut off from leadership by the non-resident bishops who ought to have supervised and trained them, they were sunken in poverty and ignorance. The lower clergy as a class failed to give spiritual guidance.

Clerical Aristocrats. The personal lives of the higher clergy in Northern Europe were not, as a whole, quite so openly scandalous as at Rome. But the same spirit of grasping for power and income infected the prelates of Northern Europe. Being largely recruited from the aristocracy, accustomed to the profligate expenditures and personal luxury typical of their own families, and having obtained their offices through family influence, the higher clergy did not provide effective leadership for the Church. Commonly they lived at royal courts and participated in the amusements of the nobility. They did not ride in tournaments, but they drank heavily, danced, gambled, hunted, and (perhaps less often and less openly than at Rome) chased women. They often lived in scandalous luxury and immorality. John van Heinsberg, bishop of Liège (1419–55), openly used his large revenues to provide for the future of the eighteen illegitimate children he acknowledged. His successor, Louis de Bourbon (in office, 1456–82), became bishop at age seventeen and waited thirteen years before he first said mass in his cathedral. Such Church leadership, devoted to its own pleasures and careers, and almost totally innocent of a sense of duty, could hardly be expected to see the need for reforms.

The religious orders of monks, friars, and nuns, which had been a major source of reform agitation at many times through the Middle Ages, shared the general decline. Abbacies, priories, and other valuable administrative offices were often held by persons who did not even belong to the religious order. In some cases they were even held by laymen who did nothing but collect the revenues. Lacking firm control from within and often being exempt from the jurisdiction of local bishops, the religious houses sometimes degenerated into notorious dens of vice. More frequently, the problem was not gross immorality but spiritual mediocrity. Positions in monasteries and nunneries were useful places where influential families could dump excess sons and daughters, assuring them a comfortable and sheltered existence in which the old requirements of self-denial were forgotten or loosely enforced. In many religious houses, only recruits of noble rank were welcome. The numbers of persons who entered the monastic life declined markedly in the later Middle Ages, and many religious communities were gradually becoming extinct long before the Protestant Reformation destroyed them.

What Corruption Did to the Church

Not all clergy at any level were grossly corrupt. Most performed their duties in a perfunctory but uninspired way, and some performed marvels of spiritual leadership. In itself, the presence of sinners among the clergy, even at or near the top, was not particularly significant. Orthodox reformers always insisted that they were attacking the sinners among the hierarchy, not the Church or the hierarchy themselves, and the Church never claimed that its leadership was unable to sin. Obviously, however, such flagrant and repeated violations of even the most elementary standards of moral decency could not help but bring the whole institution into disrepute. Anticlericalism —that is, hostility to the clergy as a class—was widespread, even (or especially) among very religious people.

But what really made the corruption serious was the ability of corrupt clergymen to shelter themselves behind the vast legal privileges of their order and hence not only to escape punishment but even in many cases to discredit or destroy their critics. The case of Savonarola, who began by denouncing the worldliness of the people and the injustices of Pope Alexander VI, but who ended by defying a formal sentence of excommunication and then by being burned at the stake as a heretic, underlines the plight of the reformer.

Despite their latent anticlericalism, the masses of Europeans were generally still devoted to the teachings and the authority of the institutional Church. The reformer who got trapped into the role of rebel against authority would sooner or later be isolated and hence easily destroyed. Because of this situation, reform often seemed unattainable. A reformer either had to abandon his agitation or had to run the risk of being destroyed, and the legal powers that ought to have enabled the hierarchy to step in and reform the Church were commonly used to block reforms and silence would-be reformers. Those who worked within the system for reforms seemed doomed to achieve at most very limited, local, and temporary gains. Only when Martin Luther successfully put forth a new ideology that undermined the authority of the hierarchy did it become possible for a reformer to defy the authorities with impunity.

Declining Respect for the Papacy

The external history of the Church as an institution contributed greatly to the rising level of discontent and to loss of respect for the ecclesiastical authority. Part of the problem was simply that over-frequent appeals to ecclesiastical authority in the long run undermined respect for that authority. When the popes first began making use of spiritual penalties like excommunication and interdict as instruments in what was essentially a political struggle for power in Italy, those penalties had great moral effect. The German bishops of the Emperor Henry IV in the late eleventh century quickly abandoned their support of their ruler in the face of papal threats. But as later popes repeatedly used spiritual penalties for political goals, the impact of papal sentences of excommunication and interdict grew less: people became cynical. The theories of papal political overlordship advanced by apologists for Rome continued to claim more and more power, but the instinctive respect for papal authority, at least in political conflicts, was being undermined.

At the very end of the thirteenth century, Pope Boniface VIII (1294–1303) set forth the papacy's claims to universal political rule in their most extreme form. His famous bull (official proclamation) *Unam sanctam* (1302) insisted bluntly that all lawful authority came to kings only through the Supreme Pontiff and flatly concluded that it was a necessary condition of salvation that all persons be obedient to the pope. Pope Boniface repeated the claim of earlier thirteenth-century popes like Innocent III that a pope had authority to depose a defiant king, to absolve the king's subjects from all oaths of loyalty, and to stir up rebellion against him. These papal claims had been repeatedly successful against German emperors of the twelfth and thirteenth centuries.

In 1301–2, however, Pope Boniface became embroiled with one of the most powerful of all the kings of France, Philip IV, "the Fair," and attempted to compel the king to back down as his predecessors had done to German emperors. But the French king was strong and determined. He and his predecessors had stimulated their nation's incipient patriotism and focused it on the monarchy, and in any case the French king claimed his crown by heredity and did not owe his crown to a body of jealous aristocratic electors as in Germany. Hence the pope's threats to depose King Philip had no effect in France—if anything, they caused the politically active classes to rally round their king. King Philip shrewdly exploited this national sentiment. Not only did Philip remain fully in control of France, but also he dared to launch an attack on the pope's person. While Boniface was at a small resort town of Anagni in September of 1303, an agent of the king led a band of mercenaries there and attempted to arrest the pope and bring him to France to be tried for heresy. The townspeople defended the aged pontiff, and Philip's troops withdrew without him, but the physical and psychological shock of the attack probably contributed to the collapse of Boniface's health, and a month later he died.

Even more remarkable than the boldness of Philip the Fair in attacking the sacred person of a pope was the eagerness of the cardinals and other curial officials to conciliate the king rather than to punish him. After a short and weak intervening pontificate, the curia caved in entirely to French diplomatic pressure in 1305, when the cardinals elected a French archbishop as the next pope, Clement V (1305–14). In the rising national sentiment of his people, the king of France had found a new ideological force that triumphed over the discredited claims of a blatantly secular papacy.

The "Babylonian Captivity" of the Papacy

The election of Pope Clement V opened a long period in which all the popes and most of the cardinals were French and in which the popes were physically absent from Italy and lived mostly at the city of Avignon, immediately across the Rhone River from France. This Avignonese period (1305–78) of the papacy, also called the "Babylonian Captivity" of the Church in memory of the exile of the ancient Hebrews, seriously undermined the prestige of the popes. None of these popes intended to transfer the papacy forever out of Rome, and each had plenty of excuses for staying at Avignon. But a church leadership so overwhelmingly French, directly contiguous to French territory, in a region thoroughly French in culture, could hardly seem so international and impartial as one located at Rome, even though the popes sought to give fair treatment to England and other anti-French nations.

Furthermore, at Avignon the popes created a luxurious and worldly court, which may not have been so morally corrupt as its critics claimed but which certainly was no model of Christian living. The upper levels of the papal administration were now filled with relatives and friends of the popes, drawn from the younger sons of the French nobility, and habituated to a showy opulence that was all the more offensive because it appeared in a nontraditional setting. The papal revenues from landed estates around Rome were depleted by the disorders of fourteenth-century Italy, so in order to support its extravagant lifestyle the Curia had to devise new taxes and fees and to exploit and expand old ones with a sharp acquisitiveness that caused bitter resentment among those who paid. The Avignonese period witnessed a vast expansion of papal claims to judicial authority and rights of patronage within the Church, as curial officials seized every opportunity to magnify their power and their revenues.

The tendencies toward financial exploitation and bureaucratic centralization that had begun to emerge in the thirteenth-century Church now became highly developed. A European society that was not accustomed to brisk administration and constant tax collections resented these developments. As a group, the Avignonese popes were less morally corrupt and less solely concerned with material and political advantage than contemporary critics thought. But the best that can be said for them is that some of them were brilliant administrators. Not a one of them was a great spiritual leader.

Demands for Reform

The absence of the popes from their rightful capital, the worldliness and luxury of the curia at Avignon, and the greed of the papacy for money and power led to widespread demands for both reform and return of the papacy to Rome. Since the general condition of the Church in most parts of Christendom was disorderly and corrupt, the many local demands for reform came to be associated with the conviction (unjustified though it was) that the papacy was to blame for the evil conditions everywhere. Sinners like the poet Petrarch and holy persons like St. Catherine of Siena agitated for reform of the Church and for a return to Rome as the essential first step in that reform. Every one of the Avignonese popes had promised to bring the curia back to Rome when conditions permitted. Finally, after several false starts, in 1377 Pope Gregory XI did reestablish the Holy See in Rome.

The Great Schism of the West, 1378–1417

The next year, however, Pope Gregory died, and the papal election of 1378 produced a disputed choice that led to the existence of two rival lines of popes for more than a generation. The origins of this Great Schism of the West (1378–1417) lay in the fear of the Roman populace that the predominantly French cardinals would elect another French pope who might abandon Rome for Avignon. A large mob gathered, threatening to massacre the cardinals if they did not elect a Roman or at least an Italian. As the crowd grew more restive, the cardinals speedily chose Archbishop Prignano of Bari, who took the title Urban VI (1378–89). The cardinals attempted to make it clear that their choice was voluntary and not dictated by the mob. But Pope Urban soon showed that he was arrogant, violent, and erratic—perhaps, indeed, mentally unbalanced. Within a few weeks the cardinals slipped out of Rome one by one, and the French majority issued a formal declaration that the election was invalid because the threats from the mob had destroyed their freedom of choice. Then a few weeks later, the French majority elected one of themselves as Pope Clement VIII (1378–94).

Whether in fact the mob pressure was great enough to invalidate the first election of 1378 is still a debatable question. In any case, it is clear that Urban VI had aliented the cardinals. Even the Italian ones gave their assent to the choice of Clement VIII; Urban VI had to appoint an entirely new College of Cardinals. Driven from the vicinity of Rome by Italian backers of Urban, Clement VIII and his backers went back to Avignon. Each pope excommunicated the other and all his followers as fomentors of schism.

What had happened in 1378 was not merely a disputed election. Rather, it was the creation of two distinct institutions, each of which believed itself to be the true papacy. When Urban VI died in 1389, and when Clement VII died in 1394, each College of Cardinals naturally elected a successor. Thus the schism potentially could go on forever.

In each part of Catholic Europe, supporters of each of the popes struggled to win the loyalty of the higher clergy and especially of the secular rulers, who in fact generally decided which of the popes their subjects would acknowledge. The division was fairly even, and while some governments made earnest and sincere efforts to determine the legal rights and wrongs of the two elections of 1378, in practice the choice generally followed lines of political division. Since France backed the Avignonese line of popes, hostile England became an important backer of the Roman claimants, and, therefore, pro-French and anti-English Scotland recognized the pope at Avignon.

Effects of the Schism

Although the modern student, whatever his religious views, may find something mildly amusing in this spectacle of two elder popes, each claiming the supreme power on earth and calling down hell fire and damnation onto the opposite party, the Great Schism was no joke to pious Christians who actually experienced it. The fact that each papal curia, being desperate for money, multiplied its financial exactions, was less serious than the devastating sense of spiritual insecurity people felt. No matter how loudly each side might proclaim its righteousness, it was obvious that no one could be absolutely certain which pope represented the true line of succession stemming through the ages from St. Peter. What divine judgment would await the soul of a person who (however good his intentions) had in fact defied a true pope and fomented schism by backing a false one? Were priests ordained and bishops consecrated by the authority of a schismatic pope valid? Could sacraments received from an improperly ordained priest avail for the salvation of the soul? After all, there was no question that one of the rival popes was the true one and that the other was therefore a false schismatic, consigned together with all his supporters to eternal damnation. The whole foundation on which the security of souls rested had been demolished.

Hence from a very early date, a great clamor arose for the ending of the Schism. The monarchs of Europe acknowledged their responsibility to help find a solution, and the theological and canon law faculties of the universities produced many suggestions on how to restore unity. At first, the suggestions were relatively conservative, mainly involving either impartial legal determination of the questions arising from the 1378 election (but by whom?) or attempts at negotiation and compromise. In 1397 the kings of England, France, and Castile jointly appealed to both popes to abdicate, but neither side would yield.

The Rise of Conciliarism. Finally, all conservative efforts having failed, more and more governments and individuals came to accept a solution that had often been suggested from the start, but was at first rejected as too radical: the calling of a General Council of the whole Church, which would forcibly depose any claimant who refused to abdicate and then would elect a true pope. This idea of a General Council was also appealing because reform-minded Christians soon realized that even with the best of intentions, popes who had to plead and negotiate for recognition could not carry through the kind of interference with the vested interests of powerful kings, nobles, and prelates that a real reform would entail. A council, once assembled, might not only end the Schism but also enact legislation that would destroy the abuses and institute a thorough reform of the whole Church, "in head and members," as the popular reform slogan went. Reunification and reform came to be associated in the minds of many people, and an increasing group came to regard a General Council as the only viable way to reach both goals.

Yet there were serious obstacles in the way of the council. Whatever may have been the case in the ancient Church, the medieval Church had developed constitutionally as an absolute monarchy, with the pope holding a divinely conferred power that in no degree was subject to control by a council or by any other group of his subordinates. How could a group of underlings have any right to challenge an authority that came directly from God? After all, there was a true pope throughout the Schism; the only problem was how to decide which of the claimants he was. Another obstacle was that according to the canon law of the Western Church, no one but the pope had the power to summon a General Council. Only the pope or his appointee had a right to preside over a council and to dissolve it when he wished. And according to medieval theory, the acts of a Church council had no binding force until confirmed by the pope. In order to surmount these difficulties, thinkers would have to advance radically different theories of ecclesiastical authority. More important, such theories would have to become widely acceptable.

Conciliar Theories. The elements of such a different view of the Church were available even before the schism, notably in the radically secular thought of two important political theorists, Marsilio of Padua (ca. 1270–1350) and William of Ockham (1280-1349). Each in his own way—especially Marsilio—had been too radical for their views to be accepted, and even in the age of the Schism, people who adopted their views commonly refrained from mentioning them by name. Basically the change that had to be made was to teach that Christ had conferred power not on one man, St. Peter, and his successors the popes, but on the whole Church—that is, the entire body of believing Christians. In this view, while the papacy was still to be revered, the only justification for its existence was utility: having effective power concentrated in the pope's hands made for administrative efficiency and provided a single focus for unity. But in the present emergency, the divided papacy had ceased to discharge these functions and had in fact become an obstacle to reform and to unity. Thus the whole body of believing Christians had the right and even the duty to reassert their basic power, acting through a representative General Council. Such a council, at least under these emergency circumstances, was superior to any pope and had the power to depose all claimants, to institute reforms, and to provide for the selection of a new pope. Since the popes themselves would never call such a General Council into being, any believing Christian ("even the least old woman," as conciliar theorists often wrote) had the right to issue a summons. But the most appropriate leader would be the Holy Roman Emperor, since the emperors had convoked the great ecumenical councils of the fourth and fifth centuries.

Such conciliarist theories were flatly contradictory to the ideas of papal theorists who regarded power as belonging to the pope alone. Without the crisis caused by the Schism, the conciliarist theories were so revolutionary in their implications that they would never have had a large following. But the harsh fact of the papacy's collapse as effective ruler and unifier of Latin Christendom made the traditional papalist theories of authority untenable for anyone who was serious about ending the Schism. Hence great numbers of thinkers by the early fifteenth century came around to belief in the ultimate supremacy of a General Council, and the greatest university of the age, Paris, became and long remained a hotbed of such ideas. As the Schism dragged on, the antipapal tone of the conciliar authors became more and more open.

Councils: Pisa, Constance, and Basel. The immediate result of these intellectual changes was that the plan to call a council in defiance of both popes became widely acceptable. The earliest overt action occurred in 1408, when several cardinals from both camps, disgusted by the two popes' refusal to meet in person and negotiate a settlement, issued a joint summons for a General Council at Pisa, which opened in March 1409. Unfortunately this open rebellion of the cardinals did not have effective backing from the secular rulers of Europe. Prematurely, the Council declared both popes deposed and elected a new one. Because the members of the Council did not have universal support, they had merely added a third pope to the two already contending for the honor. This failure stimulated the Emperor Sigismund, in cooperation with most of the other secular rulers of Europe, to convoke a truly representative council whose acts would be universally recognized. Late in 1414, the emperor and the pope who derived his title from the Council of Pisa, John XXIII, jointly opened the Council in the South German town of Constance.

This Council of Constance sat from 1414 to 1418, and both its successes and its failures had a profound effect on the history of Europe in the last century before the Reformation. Its most obvious success was the restoration of unity. After complicated negotiations, all three claimants were either deposed or persuaded to abdicate. In 1417 the Council elected a new pope, Martin V, and thereby reestablished a normal papal succession. Also in the interests of unity, but not successful, was the Council's summoning of the Bohemian heretic John Huss, whom it betrayed, despite the assurances given for his safety, and burned at the stake in 1415. This action precipitated an uprising by his followers in Bohemia.

On questions of church reform, the Council was equally unsuccessful. Everybody claimed to be in favor of reform, but nobody wanted to begin the reform by abolishing those particular abuses which he and his friends profited from. In the end the task of reform was left unfinished and was turned over to the new pope, who was no more effective at reform than his predecessors had been.

In one other aspect of its work, the Council was successful, but only in the short run. This was its attempt to establish permanently the theories of conciliar supremacy and to transform the General Council into a permanent restraint on the power of the pope. Its decree *Sacrosancta* (1415) defined as a Catholic dogma belief in the supremacy of a council over every member of the Church, even a pope, and its decree *Frequens* (1417) obliged future popes to summon councils on a regular basis, at least once every ten years.

The conciliarist bid for ultimate control of the church failed. Although both Martin V and his successor Pope Eugenius IV reluctantly issued the required summons to a council, the next important assembly, the Council of Basel, which met in 1431, was unable to prevail. Once the Schism ended in 1417, most Catholics were willing to accept again the papalist view of church authority. When the radical conciliarist group got control at Basel, the result was the gradual alienation of moderate churchmen, who one by one deserted to the papal side. The last straw for moderates came when the remnant of the Council declared Pope Eugenius deposed and elected a new pope. Thus the Council made itself the fomentor of schism precisely at the time when the pope was negotiating what appeared to be a successful reunion of the Greek with the Latin church. Although the Council dragged on a shadowy existence until 1449, it had failed by 1439. With it died conciliarism as an effective movement.

Nevertheless, the radical new ideas of Church authority did not die out, and both frustrated reformers and secular rulers at odds with Rome often toyed with the idea of using a new General Council to override the pope. The popes and their supporters developed a dread of all councils as potential rivals to the constitutional position of the pope as absolute ruler of the Church. European kings, especially the French, frequently used the threat of convoking a council as a form of political blackmail against the pope. The popes' habitual fear of a council goes far to explain why Rome refused to call a council in the early Reformation, when such action might have quieted the storm raised by Martin Luther.

Late Medieval Heresies

The conciliar theorists were by no means heretics, even when they challenged the traditional position of the papacy. But there were some individuals, and even some groups, who did reject the authority of the established Church. Such movements went back into the twelfth century, and despite the violent suppression of these groups, some of them survived into and through the fourteenth and fifteenth centuries.

The Waldensian heresy of medieval Italian and French townsmen retreated into the remote valleys of the Alps, but there it survived until it merged into the later Protestant movement. Underneath the surface of a Catholic Europe, groups of Waldensians and of other small sects survived here and there, usually unnoticed but occasionally hunted down and destroyed. Indeed, some sectarian groups, in regions where spiritual movements were reinforced by social unrest, surfaced as revolutionary uprisings of peasant or working-class fanatics, often led by renegade priests who attempted to destroy the corrupt visible Church by force and thus to prepare the way for the Second Coming of Christ.

Such millenarian uprisings were frequent during the fourteenth and fifteenth centuries, though eventually all of them were bloodily suppressed. A particularly dangerous mass religious phenomenon of the period just after the Black Death was the Flagellant movement, in which hundreds of fanatics wandered about, staging not only public scourging of each other as a kind of physical purging of sin, but also bloody massacres of Jews and even of members of the Christian clergy.

Wyclif and the Lollards

Two very different but related religious movements began in the late fourteenth and early fifteenth centuries, the Lollards in England and the Hussites in Bohemia. The Lollards were the spiritual disciples of an influential scholastic theologian of Oxford, John Wyclif (1320–84). Wyclif began as a critic of the wealth and secularism of the Church in England. At first he seemed merely to be voicing the marked English antipathy to clerical wealth and the exploitation of the English Church by Avignon. In this phase, highly placed officials in government found him useful and protected him. After the Great Schism raised in clear form the question of ultimate authority in the Church, Wyclif became openly a rebel against the papacy and the whole hierarchy, against the established Catholic doctrine of transubstantiation, and against the whole medieval conception that man's salvation depends on the Church's ministration of the sacraments. Wyclif and his followers now emphasized the authority of the Bible rather than of the Church. They prepared English translations of the Bible, spread them among the people, and conducted an active preaching among the laity.

Though his deviation from orthodoxy cost him the support of his earlier patrons in the aristocracy, and though he found it expedient to withdraw from Oxford, Wyclif himself died peaceably in 1384. His younger disciples were partly forced to recant and partly forced to leave Oxford, but their preaching spread Lollard ideas through many parts of the country. The Lancastrian usurper, Henry IV, in 1401 began systematic repression of the heresy by royal authority. By the second decade of the fifteenth century, Lollardy had lost most of its university-educated leadership but survived as an underground sect right down to the time of the Reformation.

Huss and the Bohemian Hussites

While the Lollard movement was quickly driven underground and England remained resolutely Catholic until the 1530s, the movement founded by the brilliant Czech preacher John Huss (1370–1415) became a successful and open rebellion against the Roman Church. The flowering of Czech power, culture, and national self-consciousness in the later fourteenth century included a movement to reform the Church, and to a considerable degree this movement also expressed growing Czech resentment of the dominance of Germans in the upper ranks of the Bohemian clergy.

John Huss was an eloquent Czech-speaking preacher of church reform. During his student days at the flourishing University of Prague, he had been exposed to some of the books of Wyclif, even though he was more conservative than Wyclif and never thought of himself as the Englishman's disciple. Like most of the Czech masters and students at Prague, he resisted the attempts of the Germans in the university to forbid the study of Wyclif's books.

A bitter division grew, first in the university and then throughout the nation, with Huss and his followers adopting the stance of Church reformers, critics of traditional concepts of Church authority, and popular agitators. One concrete issue clearly emerged when Huss attacked the traditional practice of giving laymen only the bread in communion and reserving the cup for the clergy. His view was that since the Bible describes communion as involving both bread and wine, the Church lacks the authority to reserve the wine for the clergy. A valid communion must be made in both kinds (Latin, *sub utraque specie*). His more conservative followers were called Utraquists, because their insistence on receiving both bread and wine in communion was the only obvious way in which they differed from Catholics. His more extreme followers also wanted communion in both kinds but held more radical theological opinions and sometimes also ideas of political and social revolution.

The execution of Huss by the Council of Constance in 1415 caused a mass uprising by his followers in Bohemia, and attempts by native and foreign Catholics to suppress the heresy by force produced a national movement to defend both Czech independence and the reform of religion. Despite papal and imperial efforts to crush them through a crusade, and despite the equivocal position of their own kings, the Hussites throughout the fifteenth century maintained by force of arms their right to exist. Like later Protestantism, the Hussite heresy tended to split into sectarian groups. Nevertheless, despite their divisions, the Hussites survived as the dominant religious and military force in the nation. A century before Luther, the combination of nationalist self-assertion with agitation for Church reform had brought to an end, in this one kingdom, the medieval ideal of a single all-encompassing religion for the whole of Christendom.

Saints and Heretics

A serious problem that the more sincere Church officials faced when dealing with heretics and heretical movements was the difficulty of distinguishing between an orthodox saint and a dangerous heretic. No heretic could be more blunt and forceful in denouncing ecclesiastical corruption than were such saints as Catherine of Siena (1347–80), Birgitta of Sweden (1303–73), or Bernardino of Siena (1380–1444), all of them popular religious leaders of the fourteenth and fifteenth centuries. The reason why one religious revivalist ended by being canonized as a saint and another by being burned as a heretic depended less on what they said and did than on the way in which the authorities reacted to their activity. St. Bernardino was perhaps as brilliant and stirring a preacher as the Florentine reformer Girolamo Savonarola and just as outspoken a critic of abuses, but unlike Savonarola he never faced a situation where he either had to give up his agitation or else to defy openly the authority of the Holy See. For the aggressive, outspoken, but would-be Catholic reformer of the fifteenth century, the line between orthodoxy and heresy was hard to draw. It was all the harder when the corrupt persons whom the agitator attacked were also the authorities whom as a loyal Catholic he was obliged to obey.

Deep Piety of the Late Middle Ages

At the heart of the religious problem on the eve of the Reformation was the tension generated by the coexistence of deep religious piety and a hierarchy more preoccupied with its endowments and its powers than with its duty of giving spiritual leadership. Though nineteenth-century anticlerical historians thought otherwise, European society during the Renaissance was deeply religious. It was the confrontation between this spiritual enthusiasm and a secularized institutional Church that generated conflict.

Mysticism

The fourteenth and fifteenth centuries in Northern Europe witnessed a great flowering of mysticism, the most intensely personal form of religious experience. In the early and middle years of the fourteenth century, Rhenish Germany produced three influential mystical preachers and writers, Meister Eckhart (1260–1327), Johann Tauler (ca. 1300–1361), and Heinrich Suso (ca. 1295–1366). Though some of their heady visionary teaching sounded like pantheistic and antinomian heresy, all of them were trained theologians who tried to remain orthodox. They were also popular preachers, and the impact of their sermons on the uncultivated laity may explain why some of their followers became suspect of heresy.

More significant than this unintended inspiration of some small heretical sects, however, was the obvious freedom of the great mystics from reliance on the ministrations of the unregenerate clergy. When large parts of western Germany were laid under the interdict, and hence all religious ceremonies suspended, because of a purely political conflict between the pope and the Emperor Ludwig IV, Tauler apparently obeyed the interdict and refrained from administering the sacraments. But in his sermons he consoled his hearers by reminding them that although Holy Church had the authority to deprive them of the external sacrament, no power could take from them the ability to commune with Christ inwardly and spiritually. For such a man and his disciples, their real spiritual life had little to do with the external, material sacraments through which the medieval Church had always controlled the access of men to God. Although they still praised the Church and emphasized the holiness of its sacraments, they did not feel cut off from God just because the Church had cut them off from those sacraments. In fact, though not in intention, the spiritual life of such mystics was beyond control by the hierarchy.

Movements of Lay Piety

In many areas of Europe, deeply religious laymen were finding their way to God through paths other than those provided by the official Church. Sometimes with overtones of clear hostility to the pretensions of the clergy, and sometimes in a spirit of deep reverence for all the material aids provided by Catholic tradition, pious laymen and priests were finding their own ways to personal holiness and spiritual confidence. What seemed important was not the mechanical performance of semimagical ritual, but an inner spirit of simple, trusting faith in Christ, backed by a personal moral righteousness. In Italy such intense personal religion, emphasizing simple, undogmatic biblical faith and moral rectitude, and deemphasizing theological refinements and elaborate ceremonies, was known loosely as *evangelismo.* In Northern Europe, hundreds of cooperative lay groups, often under the influence of mystics but not usually laying claim to mystical enlightenment themselves, provided flourishing centers of religious devotion.

The most famous and influential such group was a nonmonastic community of pious laymen known as the Brethren of the Common Life, founded by the disciples of a great spiritual leader and preacher of Deventer in the Netherlands, Gerard Groote (1340–84), a man who never advanced in holy orders beyond the rank of deacon and whose license to preach was revoked the year before his death because of the hostility of the clergy whose worldliness he criticized.

Groote's own conversion from ambitious young ecclesiastical careerist to spiritual leader occurred under the influence of a latter-day disciple of the German mystics, but he himself warned his followers to avoid the dangerous speculations of the mystics. His movement was at most only semimystical: like the mystics it regarded personal religious experience as the central fact of religion, but unlike the mystics it shunned the quest for spectacular ecstasies and soaring visions. Rejecting both the spectacular claims of the mystics and the complex subtleties of the scholastic theology in which he excelled as a young man, Groote emphasized two things: (1) the essence of religion is an inward, spiritual communion with God through Christ, and (2) the only valid test of this inner experience is its outward manifestation in a life of moral rectitude and Christian service. This simple message, assigning only an auxiliary role to the trappings of Catholic ceremony and caring not a whit for the intricacies of doctrine, dominated the Brethren. Although they had affiliations with a reformed branch of the Augustinian order, the Brethren of the Common Life was not a religious order, but more like a commune of laymen and laywomen, living and working in the world but sharing their earnings communally, and seeking personal awareness of God and opportunities for Christian service.

This movement became very influential in the towns of the Netherlands and adjacent parts of Germany. Its spirit was best captured by one of the most influential religious books of all time, *The Imitation of Christ,* compiled by a member of the group, Thomas à Kempis (1380–1471). Such books, and the visible example of groups of pious laymen living in communities and rendering useful social services such as giving care and relief to paupers, widows, and orphans, conducting hostels for schoolboys, or copying books, made the whole movement a major religious force in northwestern Germany and the Netherlands. The Brethren's emphasis on personal piety and moral development was important in shaping the religious outlook of Northwestern Europe on the eve of the Reformation. In intention, the Modern Devotion, as their religious approach was called, remained Catholic in teaching and submissive to authority. Yet its emphasis on the personal or subjective aspect of religion implied a certain devaluation of basic elements in medieval Catholicism, such as correct doctrine and officially prescribed ritual or the reliance of the laity on the ceremonies and sacraments controlled by the clergy. The movement was deeply pious but essentially lay rather than clerical.

Religious Life Escapes the Church

The power and vitality of the Brotherhood of Common Life further illustrate that the spiritual life of Europeans was escaping from the institutional framework provided by medieval tradition. Except for Bohemia, the official power of Rome and the whole hierarchy was still intact on the eve of the Reformation. But in manifold ways, actual control of spiritual life had begun to slip out of the hands of the authorities, long before many people seriously considered challenging the legal position of the religious establishment. The Church was on the brink of a disastrous collapse, and yet the purblind worldlings who dominated its upper ranks still thought that they held firm control of the soul of Christendom.

Cultural Problems of the Late Middle Ages

Also in its cultural life, European society experienced signs of impending upheaval. Italy formed a special case, for there the new culture of Renaissance humanism was emerging. Elsewhere, however, the traditional forms of culture persisted but in many respects were losing their vitality. Most of the vernacular literatures (English literature is a rare exception) were in an uncreative phase, still moving within the structure of forms and themes that suited the aristocratic, chivalric society of the Middle Ages, though living now in an age when the chivalric tradition was dying.

The chivalric prose and poetry no longer reflected what society really believed, and a tone of lifeless, mindless restatement of traditional themes became dominant, often tinged with an element of cynicism. A good illustration is the contrast in mood between the first part of the popular poem *Roman de la Rose,* written early in the thirteenth century and still devoted to the medieval ideals of chivalry and courtly love, and the second part of the same poem, written late in that same century and dominated by a mordant cynicism about the noble character of knights and the honor of women. French literature, which had set the style for all of medieval Europe, was in profound decay. England was an exception, at least in the fourteenth century, partly because its own native literary tradition was just beginning and partly because of the supreme genius and wide influence of its greatest medieval poet, Geoffrey Chaucer (1340–1400), whose writings vividly reflected the life of all levels of a very diverse society. Leaving aside the works of this genius, most late medieval literature outside of Italy had real power and vitality only when it reflected protest against social, political, and religious conditions, such as *The Vision of Piers Plowman*, attributed to William Langland (ca. 1332–1400).

New Directions in Scholasticism

The scholastic tradition of the Latin-speaking intellectual classes may not properly be described as decadent, but certainly its basic direction was markedly different from the moderate rationalism of St. Thomas Aquinas and the other great figures of the mid-thirteenth century. The conflict between Christian faith and the naturalistic, nonreligious rationalism of the Aristotelian tradition had not been sucessfully resolved even by the genius of St. Thomas. The condemnation of unorthodox, rationalistic opinions issued by the Bishop of Paris in 1277 offers a convenient event from which one may date a basic change in scholastic thought. Aristotle continued to be studied—indeed, his treatises or works derived from them became the standard textbooks for university instruction in all liberal arts fields. But no longer did most scholastic thinkers agree with Aquinas's confident belief that Aristotelian rationalism, properly understood, would inevitably harmonize with Christian revelation.

Philosophy in the fourteenth and fifteenth centuries was largely dominated by the brilliant but destructive mind of William of Ockham (1280–1349). His philosophical viewpoint, known as nominalism or "the new way" in philosophy, was intensely critical of man's claim to attain certitude through reason. He and his followers seriously doubted whether man can be certain of any of the sort of broad metaphysical principles that earlier scholastics had established by reason and had combined with revealed truths in their theology. To most theologians of the fourteenth and fifteenth centuries, the use of rationalistic arguments to back up religious doctrines seemed dangerous. They preferred to base theology on authority—the authority of the Church and of the Bible—and to limit the function of reason in theology to the creation of an orderly mode of exposition and the definition of terms.

In philosophy, the Nominalists who dominated most universities were interested either in the investigation of logical implications and relationships or in the analysis and organization of data derived from sensory observation. The latter interest explains why nominalism, especially before the eclipse of Paris during the Hundred Years' War, produced much scholarship in the field of natural science. Especially in certain special areas of physical science such as astronomy and mechanics, the Paris nominalists made the first significant advance beyond the level attained by ancient Greek scientists.

William of Ockham was also a very shrewd analyst of the foundations of authority in the Church and the secular state. His analysis of the nature of political (including papal) authority emphasized the role of the community as the source of all authority, and he was a sharp critic of the theoretical claims of the papacy, whose special powers he founded not on a divine commission from God but on a series of purely historical conditions that made the development of papal authority useful (up to a point) to the Christian community.

Ockham's radical opinions on authority, which undermined the divine-right claims of the papacy, had relatively few followers except as they crept into conciliarist theory, but his rejection of high scholastic rationalism was very influential. Even quite distinct scholastic traditions, such as the Scotism derived from John Duns Scotus (1266–1308), shared many of his reservations about the certitude of metaphysical doctrines and the applicability of rational philosophy to Christian theology. Christian intellectuals of the late Middle Ages had by no means lost their faith, but they questioned seriously their own ability to base their beliefs on any foundation other than faith.

The Fine Arts

In some of the fine arts, the disintegration of the medieval tradition during the fourteenth and fifteenth centuries is evident; in others, the tradition remained sound and productive. Italy, of course, was breaking through to the new artistic style known as Renaissance. Elsewhere, however, the medieval cultural heritage persisted till about 1500, and there were only a few hints of the Renaissance tradition which emerged at the end of the fifteenth century.

Persistence of Gothic Style

In architecture and sculpture, the Gothic style which developed during the twelfth century formed the basis for all further development in Northern Europe until after 1500. The age of great architectural creativity was through by mid-thirteenth century, as was the great age of cathedral-building. Later Gothic architects still produced beautiful and imposing buildings, but the later forms, such as the French flamboyant style of the early fifteenth century or the English perpendicular style of the late fifteenth century, were mainly elaborations of the established style in which the intricate decorative patterns of Gothic almost obscured the more fundamental structural elements which were the real key to that mode of building.

"International Gothic." All of the Gothic arts in the fourteenth and fifteenth centuries catered to the luxurious tastes of the great nobles who dominated the politics of the age. Although regional variations in style of building, sculpting, and painting could still be recognized, the late fourteenth and early fifteenth centuries witnessed the spread of an elegant style that blended influences from places as far apart as England and Bohemia and which even influenced contemporary Italian painting. Hence it is called the "International Style" of Gothic.

The products of this school were intended to enhance the prestige of persons who moved in the ultrasophisticated court circles. Thus the thematic content and social outlook were quite traditionally medieval, but the products typically lacked the solemnity and power of earlier Gothic art and became precious, decorative, and refined. Since the developed Gothic building emphasized windows and provided few walls for pictures but splendid windows for the creation of pictures in stained glass, the painters of the period usually produced tiny manuscript illuminations. The manuscript miniatures in the books of religious devotion made for the French aristocracy of the late fourteenth century were works of luxurious display—not utilitarian, but assuredly major achievements in a relatively minor art form.

After the catastrophes that befell France between 1415 and 1420 and the angry withdrawal of the duke of Burgundy to his domains in Burgundy and the Netherlands in 1419, the Burgundian court replaced the French royal court as the artistic capital of Northern Europe. The Burgundian artists were mostly Netherlanders, and in both sculpture and painting they developed a style far more powerful than the International Gothic from which it derived. The chief center of advance in sculpture was the old Burgundian capital at Dijon, and the greatest of the Netherlandish sculptors who worked there was Claus Sluter (d. 1406). In his work, the tendencies toward power and realism of form that had always been present in Gothic art won out over the weakness and decorative elaboration of the International Style. Impressive as his works at Dijon are, however, Sluter still stands within the medieval tradition, quite unlike his younger Italian contemporaries.

Flemish School of Painting. The shift of Burgundian interests to the Netherlands about 1419 and the emergence of that ducal court as the great center of patronage gave rise to a new and distinctively Flemish school of painting, beginning with the work of the anonymous Master of Flémalle and of Jan van Eyck (ca. 1380–1441) and his less known older brother Hubert. This school produced works of such beauty and craftsmanship that even the fifteenth century Italians, whose own Renaissance art was then arising, admired them, bought them, and exported them to Italy. Yet the new Flemish style was still essentially medieval, while the contemporary Italian masters had created a whole new mode of expression. The Flemish works were highly realistic in their accurate depiction of minute detail. Despite this realism, despite the creation of a new technical medium (oil painting), and despite the shift from manuscript book miniatures to panel paintings as the dominant form, the Flemish artists did not create a new conception of artistic reality but still worked within the tradition of Gothic realism. Their works concentrated on fine detail rather than on a dominant unifying conception as in the great Italian Renaissance paintings. Furthermore, the Flemish artists, infinitely skilled craftsmen though they were, did not found their work on a systematic and scientific study of perspective and anatomy as did the creators of Renaissance art.

This Flemish tradition continued with the work of Rogier van der Weyden (ca. 1400–1464), Hugh van der Goes (1440–82), and Hans Memling (ca. 1430–94), and on beyond these into the early sixteenth century, when Italian Renaissance influences began to modify northern painting. But despite its achievement, Flemish art of the fifteenth century really stands as a brilliant finale to the old Gothic tradition rather than as an introduction to the new age of painting that the Italians of the same period were creating.

Music in the Late Middle Ages

The development of the other great branch of fine arts, music, is difficult to correlate with the general history of society and culture in the fourteenth and fifteenth centuries. Certainly the common pattern of a declining, uncreative medieval tradition remaining dominant through the period until rudely and successfully challenged by the radically different art of Renaissance Italy (a pattern whose essential validity for plastic art is not undermined even by the spectacular achievements of the Flemish school of painting) has no validity in the history of music.

The rise of secular and ecclesiastical polyphonic music in twelfth and thirteenth-century Europe, which corresponds chronologically with Gothic art, continued into and through the late medieval period. About 1320 the music theorist Philippe de Vitry codified and explained the music that the preceding generations had created, and this type of music is called (from the title of his treatise) *ars nova* (new art) music. Although conservative churchmen often denounced the intricate new church music because it distracted worshippers from contemplation of God and also because it used secular tunes, the style became dominant throughout fourteenth-century Latin Christendom. Its center was in France, and its greatest figure was a Frenchmen, Guillaume Machaut (ca. 1300–1371), who wrote both liturgical and secular music.

The disasters that struck France after 1415 shattered French leadership in music as well as in art. Here, too, the court of the Burgundian dukes in the Netherlands became the new center. The century from about 1420 to about 1520 was a period when a series of great composers trained in the professional choirs of the cathedrals of Flemish towns dominated European music. The first great figure of this tradition, Guillaume Dufay (ca. 1400–1474), was trained at the cathedral of Cambrai but was a truly international figure. He was influenced by medieval England's greatest composer, John

Dunstable (ca. 1390–1453), and spent much of his career under the patronage of nobles and princes in France and Italy, including the pope. A generation later, Johannes Ockeghem (ca. 1420–ca. 1495) carried this tradition even further, spending his mature years in the service of three successive French kings of the later fifteenth century.

Yet a generation later came the greatest but also the last of this unchallenged dynasty of Netherlandish composers, Joaquin des Prez (ca. 1450–1521). He also was an international figure, spending the last quarter of the fifteenth century at Milan, the papal court at Rome, and Ferrara, then directing the royal chapel of Louis XII of France, and ending his career in his native Netherlands. These three were only the greatest of a host of Flemish composers whose work pointed toward the later course of Western music, both religious and secular.

In music, at least, there seems to be a continuity of development by successive stages. Except for its concentration in the Burgundian Netherlands after the disasters that shattered the traditional French cultural and political leadership in the early fifteenth century, the musical art grew without being obviously affected by the difficult circumstances that troubled European society.

Italian Divergence from the North

In almost every other aspect of life, however (except perhaps for the paintings of the Flemish school), the culture, economy, social structure, and political institutions of Europe underwent severe stress. In this period, the Northern European nations carried on their medieval traditions and institutions, which were subject to crises and breakdowns because of the defects of the medieval heritage. The Northern peoples were unable or unwilling to break through to the new economic, political, and cultural conditions that finally emerged in the sixteenth century. Only Italy diverged fundamentally from this general pattern, because until about 1500 only Italy really experienced that complex set of cultural changes that contemporaries themselves labeled a Renaissance.

Chapter Four

Italy Searches for a Renaissance

The notion that Italy during the fourteenth, fifteenth, and early sixteenth centuries experienced a "Renaissance," or epoch-making rebirth of fine arts and learning, a notion which seems too preposterous to the modern student of medieval civilization, makes much better sense when viewed in the light of the disturbed economic, social, political, and religious history of the period 1300–1500. The idea of a Renaissance, after all, did not spring from the fevered brain of some nineteenth-century scholar, but from the minds of men who lived in the period itself. No characteristic is so typical of the Italians of the fourteenth, fifteenth, and early sixteenth centuries, and of Northern Europeans at a slightly later date, as their highly emotional rebellion against their medieval heritage and their conviction that they did indeed belong to a new age—in fact, were themselves the creators of that age.

The truth of their belief in a "Renaissance" created by their own intellectual heroism may have been purely subjective. Nevertheless, it was still a very basic conviction whose rising popularity is an index to the emergence and spread of Renaissance civilization. What makes this belief in cultural renewal important is that the cultural achievements of the new "Renaissance" civilization were so great that no student of human experience can afford to neglect them. While Renaissance culture had its weaknesses—an actual regression in the quality and originality of work in philosophy and natural science, for example—its achievements in such fields as art and literature explain why Medicean Florence (shorthand for a culture that extended beyond Florence and eventually beyond Italy) stands alongside Periclean Athens and Augustan Rome as one of the creative centers of the modern Western tradition.

An Age of Italian Cultural Leadership

During the fourteenth and fifteenth centuries the intellectual and artistic leaders of Italian society did in fact set out to reject the culture of the immediately preceding age and to create a radically new one. Whether their accomplishments in this quest ought to be called a Renaissance or not is a matter of little importance on which scholars have lavished far too much attention. But that their accomplishments marked a distinctive turning point within the history of Western civilization is beyond serious dispute. Italy became, from the early fourteenth until well into the sixteenth century, the cultural pacemaker for the whole of Europe. The age of the Renaissance could also be called "the age of Italian cultural predominance." But the Italians of the period itself thought of their achievement not merely as a distinctively national culture, but as the rebirth or rediscovery of a sort of creative power which the ancient Greeks and Romans had possessed and which (so they thought) the Middle Ages had lacked. That conviction explains why they believed that "true" civilization had been reborn in their time and also why their accomplishments had great influence on other European peoples who shared their reverence for antiquity.

Social Foundations of the Renaissance

Italy had not been a leading center of medieval civilization. Compared to France, England, or western Germany during the twelfth and thirteenth centuries, Italy seems provincial and backward. But from the lifetime of Dante (1265–1321) onward, northern and central Italy emerged as Europe's most vital center of artistic and literary creativity.

Attempts to explain the change in terms of the rise of a bourgeois society in Italy sound plausible only until they are subjected to critical analysis. Then the connections between bourgeois society and Renaissance culture become more and more complex until they almost disappear. The new culture was no simple and inevitable result of the emergence of an urbanized society dominated by rich merchant-capitalists. That new society was born during the eleventh century, and the economic power and social complexity of the Italian cities grew throughout the twelfth and thirteenth centuries, precisely the period when their artistic, literary, and intellectual life was feeble and derivative. Those economic determinists who connect the new culture of the Italian Renaissance with the capitalistic society of the Italian cities have only this one point in their favor: the new culture *was* born in a distinctively urban milieu and clearly reflects a society dominated by wealthy businessmen (or urban despots) rather than by the feudal aristocracy and clergymen whose values prevailed in the culture of the Middle Ages. But the Renaissance tradition did not originate simultaneously with the urban society or even close enough in time for the comfortable theory of a "cultural lag" to explain away the two-century gap between the rise of bourgeois society and the first appearance of the Renaissance.

A more convincing account of the social foundations of the Renaissance can be built on our preceding account of the economic, social, and political turmoil of Italian society during the fourteenth and fifteenth centuries. The capitalists of the age of expansion and prosperity during the twelfth and thirteenth centuries were not men of culture, and certainly not men of leisure. The cultural life of the cities, such as it was, was in the hands of the noble classes, the *grandi,* who often lived in the city and invested in business but whose traditions were military and feudal, just as the literature they preferred was the chivalric and courtly literature of France. But in the late thirteenth century the nonnoble classes, led by rich businessmen, gained control of many town governments and drove the *grandi* from power.

Then in the fourteenth century, something even more important happened. The economic depression and the long period of stagnation that followed it closed off the founding of new fortunes, while at the same time leaving the wealth of established rich families largely intact. Thus a quite new social condition had arisen. Gone was the relatively high degree of social mobility that had kept the business classes open to new talent and preoccupied with making money. The dominant business class changed from being a group of self-made men to being a group of men who had inherited their wealth and who had grown up in an atmosphere of wealth and luxury that they intended to preserve but which they could largely take for granted. The owners of mercantile and industrial fortunes, while not totally cut off from active business, became men of leisure to a degree undreamt of by their hard-driving, self-denying ancestors. Rich businessmen, who had always been prominent in city politics, now devoted much of their time to public affairs. Indeed, in an age when working-class agitation produced such radical movements as the rebellion of the Ciompi at Florence in 1378, effective participation in politics became a necessity for rich families who wished to defend their material interests. Alongside politics, patronage of arts and literature became a traditional activity of this class.

There may even have been a direct connection between the cultivation of the new humanistic literature and the political activity of the rich and well-born. At Florence, the principal center of the new humanistic literature, the dominant business class during the late fourteenth century adopted humanistic studies as the basis for educating its young men. Both theoretical works on education and the increasing classical and humanistic element in current political debate indicate that the reason for this educational change from mere commercial training to humanistic study was that humanistic study seemed to prepare wealthy young men for effective participation in the political life to which their wealth and social position foreordained them.

The Search for a New Culture

Even before this widespread adoption of the new culture, the rich businessmen of Florence had begun to discover a new vernacular literary culture in the writings of Dante, Petrarch, and Boccaccio and to show a predisposition toward the classical enthusiasm of the humanists. Both the new Italian literature and the old Latin literature were well adapted to the outlook of an established, educated, sophisticated, and urban ruling class. The rich townsmen of Renaissance Italy felt only limited attraction to the chivalric and courtly themes of the medieval secular literary tradition, and except for those who became professionals in the fields, they found the medical, legal, and theological writings of scholasticism far too technical for their wants.

The Attractions of Ancient Rome

The ruling classes really needed an education that would make them broadly informed and intelligent amateurs, not one that made them specialists. The main practical applications that they wanted from their education were ability to cope effectively with the realities of human existence and ability to deal with and even to manipulate other human beings. For such a goal, the strongly political and ethical bent of Roman literature, and its concentration on oratorical and rhetorical training as the best practical aid to political success, was far better adapted than was the excessively speculative and intellectual scholastic education.

To a lesser degree, the ethical, political, and rhetorical nature of humanistic studies also seemed suited to the needs of the cities that came under despotic rule: the drive toward political activism might be less than in a republic like Florence, but the largely secular and urban tone of Roman literature still made it and its modern imitators attractive in courts, which were fundamentally secular and urban. The despots, having little or no legal basis for their power, often sought to use an active patronage of the arts and letters as one way of justifying their claim that their rule rested on personal merit. The princely courts did, however, show some tendency to ape the feudal manners and literature of their Northern European contemporaries; and the new humanistic culture took its deepest root and scored its greatest triumphs in the cities where a stable, sophisticated oligarchy of rich businessmen preserved the older republican forms of the High Middle Ages, most notably in Florence.

Alienation from Tradition. The tone of the new Renaissance tradition in arts and letters was often explicitly hostile to the earlier medieval culture.

From Petrarch on through the late sixteenth century, humanist intellectuals derided scholastic and chivalric traditions. As for the artists, the word *Gothic*, which modern art historians use as a neutral label for the high artistic style of the twelfth and thirteenth centuries, was originally applied as a term of reproach, intended to suggest that the buildings, paintings, and statuary of those centuries were barbarous and worthless.

Yet this element of alienation in the Renaissance outlook was severely restricted. The humanistic literature and art of the fourteenth and fifteenth centuries were not created for a "rising middle class" or for a social group that was struggling to subvert the existing social order. Its patrons *were* the ruling class, whether the despots at places like Milan or the dominant merchant oligarchy in republics like Florence. A ruling class already fully established in power was merely groping for an educational tradition, an art, and a literature that would meet its aesthetic and practical needs. This class controlled patronage of arts and letters, and used that control to solidify its social and political predominance.

Social Position of Humanists and Artists. The humanists and the more sophisticated of the vernacular writers were fully assimilated to the ruling classes. In the despotic states, humanists were often in the employ of the despot, who used them as his propagandists, thus applying their learning and eloquence to practical political ends. In the greatest humanistic center, the Republic of Florence, the humanists themselves were mostly members of the limited group of rich families who dominated the city. Those who were of humbler social origins, such as Leonardo Bruni of Arezzo and Poggio Bracciolini, were coopted into the ruling oligarchy because of their personal merit and their services to society. Indeed, far from being a focus of resistance to the Florentine establishment, humanism provided one means by which unusually talented men of obscure origins could rise into the ruling group.

As for the artists, they originally were regarded as relatively skilled handicraft workers, far removed from the high status of the rich merchants and humanist intellectuals who ran the government. But as Renaissance art became more securely based on a theoretical and scientific foundation in anatomy and perspective, the leading painters and sculptors began to rise above the level of mere artisans. Painting itself, which had originally been regarded as a mechanic art because it involved handiwork, began to take on pretensions of being a liberal art, suitable for serious attention by men of respectable social standing. As the oligarchs and despots showered money and favor on artists of great genius, these individuals began to be members of the dominant classes, though seldom equal in status to poets and classical scholars. The artists for the first time since Antiquity shared the learning and intellectual interests of their social betters, and by the late fifteenth and early sixteenth centuries, such great masters as Leonardo da Vinci and

Michaelangelo Buonarrotti were courtiers and intellectuals of the highest order.

Although the origins of Renaissance literature, art, and humanism are obviously related to the bustling city life of Italy, that relation is complex. Certainly there was (and is) nothing inevitable about the emergence of cultural greatness. While it is probably true that a wealthy republic dominated by a fairly broad class of rich merchants was especially conducive to the development of the Renaissance, no other republic rivaled the creative power of Florence. Even Venice, which had a brilliant record in the arts and an impressive record as a center for humanist activity, developed rather tardily. Another rich republic, Genoa, though it had the wealth and the rich ruling class, achieved very little for Renaissance civilization. Perhaps the Florentines themselves were not entirely wrong in attributing their literary and artistic accomplishments to their political freedom, with all its imperfections and despite the predominance of a few wealthy families. Florence really did provide more political freedom and a broader scope for political participation than any other Italian city.

Classicism—Medieval and Renaissance

Granted that conditions made them hostile to medieval culture, it is not surprising that the intellectuals of the age should look to the classical past for guidance. All medieval men of learning were well aware that Greek and Roman Antiquity possessed an art and literature more highly developed than their own; and at each stage in the growth of medieval civilization, classical influences had played a major role; for example, the emergence of high scholasticism in the French universities of the early thirteenth century was a direct result of the recovery of Aristotle's books. Especially for the Italians, living in the homeland of Roman civilization, the appeal of their own stupendous past was irresistible.

Medieval men never had a clear conception of the distinctively modern concept of progress. When they thought of better times, they never thought of creating something new in the future. Rather, they thought of rediscovering something ancient. Although they of course realized that effective Roman political control over Western Europe had collapsed in the fifth century, medieval people had not the slightest awareness that they were living in a new epoch and that theirs was a new and clearly non-Roman civilization. They thought of themselves as living at the tag-end of Roman times. Improvement of learning, art, literature, and even government meant going back to the "good old days" of ancient Rome. In religious matters, quite similarly, reform meant returning to the pure and uncorrupted ways of the Apostolic Age, a period which corresponded almost exactly with the golden age of the Roman Empire.

Medieval "Renaissances"

Throughout the Middle Ages, cultural renewals meant restoring knowledge of the ancient Roman achievements; and modern scholars have not been wrong to apply the label *renaissance*—implying rebirth of classical influence—to each of the periods of cultural renewal in the Middle Ages: the Carolingian Renaissance, during and just after the reign of Charlemagne (768–814); the Anglo-Saxon Renaissance in the England of Alfred the Great (871–899); the Ottonian Renaissance under the German emperors Otto I, II, and III (covering the years 936–1002); and greatest of all, the "Twelfth Century Renaissance," which witnessed not only Europe's decisive shift from primitive and backward culture to a high civilization, but also a great influx of classical inspiration.

The Difference of Italian Renaissance Classicism

None of these "medieval renaissances" was the same sort of phenomenon as the culture that emerged in the fourteenth and fifteenth centuries in Italy. Some differences were obvious. Each of the medieval renaissances involved a great degree of classical influence, yet in each case, the classical revival gave way to a subsequent period of indifference. On the contrary, the classical traditions founded in the Italian Renaissance remained a dominant cultural and educational force until the late nineteenth century. Each of the medieval "renaissances" was limited to a restricted geographical area and did not spread its influence far beyond the point of origin. Quite different was the influence of the Italian Renaissance, which had spread throughout Italy by mid-fifteenth century and from late in that century exerted an irresistible and dominating influence on the art, literature, and thought of all European nations. The medieval revivals of learning were all pretty largely confined to a small group of clergymen, while the culture of Renaissance Italy was dominated by laymen and became widely diffused through all but the very lowest classes of society.

The most important difference of all, however, was the way in which students of Antiquity used elements from ancient civilization. Because they thought of themselves as still part of the classical world, medieval artists, writers, and thinkers took elements from classical sources and incorporated them freely and sometimes (as we would think) incongruously into their own works. Although classical influences were often very helpful, they were used in ways that strike us as gross distortions: Aristotle's philosophical discussion of God as the Prime Mover as if it were a discussion of the personal God of Jewish and Christian religion; literary stories about ancient heroes as if these were medieval knights; artistic representations of figures and scenes from Antiquity drawn in modern dress and architectural setting. To put it very simply, medieval men indiscriminately took and applied elements from ancient art and literature without any sensitivity to what those elements meant in their original setting.

The thinkers, writers, and artists of the Renaissance, however, approached classical works of art and literature with much greater sensitivity to what those works had meant to the people who created them. Precisely because they realized that those works reflected a civilization that no longer existed, Renaissance thinkers made a conscious attempt to understand their original meaning. Thus Renaissance artists attempted to rediscover the correct appearance of an ancient theme and were less likely to paint a Roman hero in fourteenth-century chain-mail armor. The Antique heritage was for the first time conceived as a whole, all parts of which must be understood in relation to that whole.

The Humanists, Pioneers of a New Culture

The men who created and popularized this new approach to the classical heritage were known even during the Renaissance itself as "humanists." The movement they created came to be called humanism (though not till the nineteenth century). Although in the loose and intellectually slipshod usage of the nineteenth and twentieth centuries, the modern connotations of the words *humanism*, *humanist*, and *humanistic* (implying a philosophy of life that is nonreligious or even antireligious and this-worldly) have been read back into Renaissance humanism, the humanists were in no sense the purveyors of a distinctive philosophy of life: they were not as a group any more antireligious or this-worldly than their counterparts in the Middle Ages or than other groups (scholastic philosophers for example) in their own centuries.

It is even misleading, though perhaps not quite so false, to say that humanism laid greater emphasis on man and on human dignity than had medieval intellectual traditions. The humanists were simply those who rediscovered, popularized, and explained the culture of ancient Greece and Rome, chiefly as they found it expressed in Roman and Greek literature. From the time of Cicero at least, the study of grammar, rhetoric, poetry, ethics, and history had been known as the *litterae humaniores* (today we still call them "the humanities") because the Romans regarded them as the studies most necessary for an educated man.

Humanistic versus Scholastic Ideas of Education

Such humanistic subjects were by no means regarded as the totality of human learning, though their defenders did argue that they were essential for the intellectual and moral formation of all educated people, while the other branches of learning (at that period comprising natural science, law, medicine, and theology) were pertinent only to persons training for one of the learned professions.

The "humanities" did emphasize the importance of man in one way: they were the subjects that dealt with questions of the aims and ends of human life, with practical questions of how men ought to relate to one another, and with the devices (literature and oratory) through which men living in a social setting actually translate their ideals into reality and modify the behavior of others. To the mind of the humanist, the scholastic conception of education as merely the discovery and inculcation of truth was too intellectual, and that inadequacy explained why scholastic education failed to revitalize society. Education must be a development of the total potential of man, who is not a disembodied intellect but a complex blend of body and spirit, of emotion and reason. The goal of the educator, the orator, or the statesman must be to affect the will as well as the understanding of other men. As humanists often insisted, it is less important for men to be taught the correct definition of virtue than for them to be inspired to live virtuously. Thus the humanist was above all else a master of rhetoric, the art of eloquent, effective, persuasive speech and writing. His studies were primarily literary, and they focused on the world of human relationships rather than on the world of nature or theology.

Historical Origins of the Humanists. The history of the humanists as an identifiable group in Italian society confirms this definition. Medieval Italian society, as noted earlier, was not very highly cultured, but it did produce large urban populations that had a growing need for literate people, people who could read and write letters, or who could draw up contracts and other commercial documents in proper form. Thus there emerged not only a prosperous and respected legal profession but also two semiprofessional groups, *dictatores*, or professional letter writers, and notaries, or drafters and authenticators of commercial and legal documents. The training of *dictatores* and notaries was at first wholly utilitarian—largely an instruction in the proper forms to be used—and had no implication of classical study. But many of the documents were in an ancient language, Latin, and mastery of the art of clear and effective writing would be helpful to persons whose daily work involved the practical application of those arts.

By the late thirteenth century, among the Italian merchants, lawyers, notaries, and *dictatores* there developed an interest in poetry, in history, and in broad problems of personal and social ethics. For the first time in the generation just preceding the career of Dante (1265–1321), a native Italian literature emerged. In the same period, literacy—at least in Italian and often also in Latin—became a common attainment. In one direction, these developments led to the founding of a vernacular literature, of which Dante was the first great figure.

But in another direction, the interests of these groups of lawyers and notaries, with their consciousness of Italy's Roman origins, and with their practical daily contact with the Latin language, led directly to an interest in Roman literature. To some extent, the motive was still utilitarian: careful, thoughtful study of Latin grammar and rhetoric was practical for men who lived by their skill with words. To an increasing extent, however, the growing attention to Latin literature was aesthetic. Many of the individuals of the late thirteenth and early fourteenth centuries who popularized the study of Latin language and literature had some connection with the legal or notarial professions. Even Francesco Petrarca, or Petrarch (1304–74), the first really important Italian humanist, was educated in the law though he managed to make his living from poetry.

The cultural backwardness of medieval Italy, then, came to an end through two distinct but related developments: the rise of a new tradition of literature in the Italian vernacular and the slightly later emergence of enthusiasm for ancient literature. The sources of the vernacular literature were in part foreign. Precisely because it was so backward, Italy during the twelfth and thirteenth centuries had drawn its reading matter from the courtly literature of the very different feudal society of southern France. The new vernacular poetry of the late thirteenth century still imitated the verse forms and the love themes of its French models, but instead of the rather mechanical allegories and stiff conventions of the French poems, its best works focused in a new way on the subjective reactions of the poet.

This new outlook, concentrating on the poet's self, and the development of the Tuscan dialect as a suitable medium for serious literature, reached its climax in the work of the man who is not only the first important Italian poet, but incomparably the greatest of them all, Dante Alighieri (1265–1321). Although Dante's interests were still essentially medieval, his boundless literary and intellectual power gave Italian society at once an immortal literary masterpiece and and an established, effective literary language. Within one generation, Italy had changed from a backward cultural province of medieval France to the creator of a new literary tradition that eventually shaped the literary practice and theory of every European nation.

Even in the work of Dante, a lively interest in the Latin classics was evident, though the approach to classical elements was still medieval. But the classical influence on sophisticated Italians tended to increase in the fourteenth century, and the second and third of the great founders of the vernacular literary tradition, Petrarch and his friend Giovanni Boccaccio (1313–75), were not only humanists but the two principal creators of humanism as a cultural tradition. Both men were masters of Italian language, yet each of them regarded his Latin writings, chiefly on classical themes, as the truly important part of his life's work. After the death of Petrarch and Boccaccio, the growth of enthusiasm for classical studies and for the Latin language continued at so rapid a pace that Italian vernacular literature stagnated. For a century after 1375, most Italians who had something important and serious to write wrote it in Latin.

The Humanist and World History

The truly important point about Renaissance humanism is not its enthusiasm for the classics but its new conception of history, which was the source of the overpowering new interest in the classics. As we have already seen, interest in ancient Greek and Roman culture was always present in the Middle Ages, and at some times and places, notably in France during the twelfth century, a lively study of ancient books arose and had a major impact on thought and literature. Although some important works of Latin literature were little known during the Middle Ages and became widely known only during the Renaissance, the "rediscovery" of Roman literature consisted more in a new outlook on the ancient texts than in the literal findings of books previously unknown. There were some significant new finds, but it is hard to regard this filling out of the corpus of Latin literature as truly decisive in cultural history, considering how much was already well known.

It is also true that the twelfth-century interest in Roman literature had given way during the thirteenth century to an increasingly narrow professionalism in higher education and that even university faculties of liberal arts had little time for the Latin classics, but rather hurried their students through a bare minimum of grammatical and literary training in order to focus attention on logic, the one liberal art that led directly to success in the advanced professional schools of theology, law, and medicine. To some extent, humanist attacks on the narrowness of scholastic education were justified and were in fact aimed at restoring balance in liberal arts education by devoting less time and attention to logic and more to grammar and rhetoric (that is, to Latin language and literature).

Petrarch and the "Dark Ages"

Humanism involved more than demands for minor adjustments in the university curriculum. The humanists were claiming that their mission in life was nothing less than the restoration of "true" civilization in place of the "barbarous" civilization that prevailed in their own time. Such a notion implied definite ideas of historical value, implying above all the worthlessness of the whole medieval heritage—of everything, including the Gothic cathedrals and the scholastic theological books.

These ideas of history were radically new, and as much as any set of ideas can be attributed to any one person, they were the creation of Petrarch himself. During his long and active literary career, Petrarch became convinced that ancient Greek and Roman civilization had reached the highest level ever attained by any society. But this great civilization declined during the fourth, fifth, and subsequent centuries, simultaneously with the power of the Roman empire which had protected it. Europe was flooded by Germanic barbarians whose dominance completed the almost total loss of ancient art and literature. For a thousand years thereafter, European society lived through a "Dark Age"—a term by which Petrarch meant an age that had lost the light of ancient civilization and had achieved nothing of value on its own. This worthless, barbarous civilization, characterized by Gothic architecture and scholastic thought, survived down to his own time. In his terminology, it was "modern."

Historical Discontinuity. Whereas medieval thinkers had regarded their own age as a mere extension of Roman times, Petrarch drew a sharp distinction between two separate historical periods, an "ancient" period characterized by light, by high civilization, and also by the domination of the whole world by the Italians; and a "modern" period characterized by crude barbarism, by cultural darkness, and by the degrading disunity and weakness of the Italians. At least in germ, Petrarch's thought also contained the idea of a third major period in the history of civilization, a future age of cultural revival (rebirth, or "renaissance") in which there would be a rediscovery of the sources of Greek and Roman cultural power, so that a new civilization would grow up, not identical with the ancient but inspired and guided by its best elements.

There is some evidence that Petrarch himself realized that once this new historical age had developed, it would be called "modern," and that the Dark Age lying between the old and the new ages of high civilization would seem a sort of middle period, an unhappy gap in the growth of civilization. Although Petrarch himself never used the exact phrase "Middle Ages" for that worthless age, his followers within a generation did. Indeed, not only the term "Middle Ages" but also the whole concept of distinct cultural periods in history, and the conventional and still useful division of history into ancient, medieval, and modern periods, was the invention of Petrarch and his followers, the humanists.

The modern student of history is often irritated by the wrong-headedness and unfairness of this attack on medieval civilization. We know, and even Petrarch, Boccaccio, and their followers should have known, that the Middle Ages had already attained a high level of culture. The negative attitude of the humanists toward medieval civilization was not a scientific and scholarly judgment. It can be understood only in terms of the severe breakdown in late medieval civilization. Not in a social or a political sense but certainly in a cultural sense, the Renaissance humanists were rebels against the heritage of the immediate past. The idea of medieval barbarism and Renaissance rediscovery of true civilization is indeed false concerning the

Middle Ages, but it is very profoundly true concerning the Renaissance. The denigration of the Middle Ages and the rhapsodic idealization of Antiquity were devices through which a new age of creative thinkers defined their goals and justified their abandonment of prevailing traditions.

The Usefulness of Antiquity. What the humanist rebels against medieval culture found in the Latin classics was not primarily new factual knowledge about the classical past, but a new appreciation of classical civilization as a whole. Classical Antiquity gave them a yardstick by which they could measure their own age and find it wanting, thus justifying their hostility to medieval tradition. In a more positive sense, it gave them new inspiration, confidence that a better civilization, a more wholesome society, and even a stronger Italy could be created. It also offered practical guidance in the achievement of these goals. This conviction that current problems could best be solved by conscious imitation of the ancients was a powerful force throughout Renaissance civilization. It was not confined to idealistic poets like Petrarch, but was still powerful a century and a half later in the thought of the hard-bitten and politically experienced Machiavelli, who thought that the foundering Italian society of the early sixteenth century could be saved only if it reconstructed on the Roman model everything from its basic political institutions to its manner of recruiting and arming troops.

Moral Reform. In the opinion of Renaissance humanists from Petrarch to Machiavelli and beyond, the true secret of Rome's greatness was not some trick of military organization or even of constitutional structure, but its success over a long period in producing great leaders who were truly devoted to the welfare of their city. The moral grandeur that made the best and ablest men of Rome dedicate their lives to public service rather than to amassing private fortunes or seeking private enjoyment was the key to Rome's mastery of the whole world. As the Roman ruling classes became corrupted by the desire for personal advantage in the late Republic and the Empire, both the physical power and the culture of Rome declined. The spirit that made Rome great might today be called patriotism, but the men of the Renaissance commonly called it *virtù*. For this term the modern English word *virtue*, with its connotations of straitlaced adherence to a negative and puritanical moral code governing mainly individual and private acts, is a poor equivalent. The Italian *virtù* implied "strength of character" and "public-spiritedness." It dealt more with one's ethics in public life than with private life. In order to undo the political, moral, and cultural degeneracy that humanists saw in their own society and regarded as typically medieval, what was needed was a recovery of this sense of "virtue" or public spirit—in other words, a moral reform, in the broadest sense of the word *moral*.

This emphasis on the need for a moral reorientation explains many aspects of Italian humanism that otherwise fit into no rational pattern. For example, the humanists attacked scholastic education and scholarship, dismissing these flippantly as mere trifling. They did so because they believed that scholasticism, with its cold, orderly rationalism and its apparently deliberate avoidance of literary artifice, was too narrowly intellectual, too concerned with abstract speculation about metaphysical, logical, and scientific matters, to stimulate the kind of emotional commitment to a life of virtue (that is, devotion to public service) which they felt necessary for the recovery of ancient greatness. In a similar vein, the constant stress on character formation, on the reading of Roman texts on ethics, politics, and history, and even the stress on Christian piety that marks the educational reforms of the Renaissance, are closely linked with this desire to regenerate the morals of society and to graduate young men whose outstanding trait would not be their deft mastery of logical disputation but their wholehearted devotion to the general welfare.

The Need for Eloquence. Finally, the constant harping of humanists on the need for an elegant and eloquent literary style and their apparently superficial dismissal of brilliant scholastic thinkers because they wrote inelegant and nonclassical Latin are directly related to their emphasis on moral regeneration. Eloquent form and the deliberate, artistic application of stylistic devices in speaking and writing were very important to the humanists. But this stress on eloquence, on effective use of rhetorical devices learned from ancient Roman examples, was no mere accidental peculiarity of the humanists. In order to make men virtuous, they argued, more is needed than subtle, logical argumentation. Men are not purely intellectual beings, and hence their behavior will not be revolutionized by something so coldly rational as a scholastic disquisition on virtue and political obligation. The real springs of human action are more emotional than rational. Thus the man who is being educated for a career of public service and leadership must himself be personally committed to the common good by nonrational as well as rational influences, and he must be taught to use the oratorical and literary devices that will allow him to appeal to the emotions of the people and carry them along with him. The growing conviction that humanistic study of Latin literature did in fact make men more effective at persuading their fellow citizens is precisely why in the closing fourteenth century more and more heads of Florentine families, men who themselves were more interested in political power and wealth than in intellectual matters, sought a humanistic education for their sons.

The humanists' professional skills as masters of rhetoric (the art of eloquence) were intended to be instrumental in bringing about a moral regeneration. In their opinion, humanistic studies—grammar, rhetoric, ethics, and history (which they regarded chiefly as a source of concrete illustrations of moral principles)—were to be preferred above all others mainly because they were eminently practical, dealing as they did with the study of man in his social and moral setting and with the arts of modifying human behavior through oratory and writing. The humanists from the time of Petrarch onward challenged the scholastic assumption that the main purpose of man is to understand the world of God and the world of nature. Rather, they believed, the main purpose of man is to understand and control himself and the whole complex web of relationships that bind him to other men. Thus their deliberate preference for rhetoric over philosophy, for eloquence over truth, does not mean that as a class they were "mere" rhetoricians, spineless time-servers who sold their skills to the highest bidder. Their devotion to rhetoric springs partly from their view of man as a being who is not just a disembodied intellect but much more a creature of passion and partly from their conception of themselves as moral reformers struggling to regenerate society and of moral reform itself as the key to solving the many problems of their age.

New Approach to Ancient Books. This concern with recapturing the moral power of ancient Rome affected the way in which Renaissance men approached the study of Antiquity. They were doing two things never done by medieval students of ancient culture: they regarded Antiquity as a dead civilization that could be studied as a complete (and completed) whole, and they were more interested in the total structure and dominant traits of that civilization than in the many useful bits of knowledge that thinkers throughout the Middle Ages had extracted from ancient books. The humanists thought that the medieval habit of using passages from ancient authors without concern for their original context was responsible for many distortions of those authors. Their own approach to an ancient text, and to Antiquity as a whole, struck them as new. And they were right. Their linking of this new approach to a cosmic purpose, the moral and cultural regeneration of their society, made that approach seem not only new but profoundly important.

The Cult of Fame. The humanists' ideal of regenerating the world, and opening up a whole new age of human history through "the recovery of classical antiquity" (that is, through the use of classical eloquence to recreate in modern times a sense of public morality comparable to that of Rome at her best) is linked to another humanistic trait that has elicited much attention and some amusement: their constant concern about their own fame among future generations. The humanists did seek fame. Men like Petrarch may have had some qualms about this desire, but usually they concluded, as he did, that desire for fame was a noble motive, that it had been one of the sources of patriotism and self-sacrifice among the heroes of Antiquity. The notion of fame was inseparable from the humanists' conception of themselves as the men who were initiating simultaneously a new age in history and a profound moral regeneration of modern society. In all modesty, Petrarch could hardly say, "With me there begins a third age in the history of human civilization." And yet in a very real sense, that is what he must have believed, and it was to that goal that he and his followers devoted their most serious efforts. Such men did value themselves highly, but only because they valued their purposes highly.

Some humanists did become so excessively preoccupied with the purely antiquarian and stylistic aspects of classical study that even other humanists spoke out against them. For example, the greatest Northern humanist, Erasmus (1469–1536), in his *Ciceronianus* attacked the arid, pointless stylistic classicism of certain contemporary humanists like Pietro Bembo of Venice or the French scholar Christopher Longolius. In the opinion of Erasmus, the stylistic and aesthetic element of Renaissance humanism was sound and wholesome only when it was linked to the stupendous historical mission of regenerating civilization.

Rediscovery of Classical Texts

One of the most obvious results of the growing desire to recover classical Antiquity was the attempt by Petrarch and his followers to discover unknown texts of classical authors. Humanists rummaged through the libraries of old monasteries throughout Europe, and some of them built their reputations largely on their success in finding works long forgotten. Some important discoveries occurred in Swiss and south German libraries while many Italian humanists were living in Constance during the church council that solved the Great Schism.

Poggio Bracciolini (1380–1459), a leading Florentine humanist, discovered a number of works previously unknown in Italy, such as a complete text of a major Roman treatise on rhetorical education, Quintilian's *Institutes of Oratory*, which had previously been known only in part; several orations of Cicero; the works of the poet Lucretius, the historians Tacitus and Ammianus Marcellinus, and the architectural writer Vitruvuis; the letters of Pliny the Younger; and several comedies of the playwright Plautus. So much of Latin literature had already been well known to the Middle Ages that it is hard to judge how significant such new discoveries were. But there is no denying that there were substantial gains in the knowledge of Latin literature. Certainly the humanists themselves regarded such discoveries as exciting and important.

Greek Studies. Interest in Latin literature naturally led to efforts to gain a deeper understanding by studying the Greek literature that Roman authors frequently cited. Since late Roman times, very few Western Europeans had been able to read Greek. Largely from the Arab world, medieval Christendom had become well acquainted with the works of Aristotle, which had been made available in Latin translations by the early thirteenth century. But neither the Arabs nor medieval Latin Christians showed much interest in any branches of Greek literature other than medical, scientific, and philosophical works, and in the latter field they knew little but the Aristotelian tradition. Greek lyric and epic poetry, drama, history, and rhetorical works, together with philosophical writings in the Platonic, Epicurean, and Stoic traditions, remained largely unknown except for the frequent mention of them in Latin authors. The first major humanist, Petrarch, realized the necessity of learning Greek if he were to gain a deeper understanding of Latin literature, but his attempts were in vain. Petrarch's disciple Boccaccio was a bit more successful, but none of the early humanists really mastered Greek.

In 1393, however, the Byzantine emperor sent to Venice as his ambassador a brilliant Byzantine scholar, Manuel Chrysoloras, who not only had a thorough mastery of ancient Greek literature but also was fluent in Latin, so that he could communicate effectively with the Italians. His arrival and his willingness to teach the Greek language caused great excitement. During the four years he spent in Florence, he trained a whole troop of able young Italians who became the first Latin-speaking Westerners qualified to teach, read, and translate from the Greek language. The excitement he caused is well shown by the decision of the humanist Leonardo Bruni (ca. 1370–1444) to study with him. Bruni abandoned his studies leading to the lucrative profession of law, reasoning that he could always find instruction in law, but might never again have such an opportunity to learn Greek.

The work of Chrysoloras was decisive. The men he trained carried on his work so effectively that henceforth a small but substantial number of humanists could read Greek works in the original and could prepare usable translations for the larger number who could not. The craze for discovering manuscripts of unknown classical works then extended to Greek books, and truly significant discoveries were made, far outstripping in importance the treasures discovered in Latin. Those humanists who went to Constantinople and other centers of Greek culture to perfect their Greek and hunt manuscripts were able to make remarkable finds. The most successful one, Giovanni Aurispa (1374–1450), visited Chios in 1413 and came back with works by Sophocles, Euripides, and Thucydides, all of them previously unavailable in the West. From an extended stay in Constantinople he returned with a haul of 238 manuscripts. Thus well before the Byzantine capital finally fell to the Turks in 1453, its Greek scholars had passed along to Italian humanists a knowledge not only of their language but also of most of the ancient Greek literature that is known today.

A Change of Outlook

This thorough acquaintance with the full range of Greek literature, which was far more intellectually challenging than the Latin classics, does mark one significant difference between the classical revival of the Renaissance and the several classical revivals of medieval times. Because of the addition of Greek works, the scholars of the Renaissance had a far more extensive and far more profound understanding of the classical heritage than their medieval predecessors. Yet it is still questionable whether even this influx of new classical materials marked a really decisive change in the Western cultural tradition. Far more important than the discovery of Greek language and literature was the drastic change in outlook that for the first time made Latin Christians willing to invest the time, energy, and money necessary to gain mastery of the Greek heritage. After all, knowledge of Greek language and literature had always been available at Constantinople and scores of other places in the Eastern Mediterranean. Latin Christians had been in constant contact with the Greek-speaking world ever since the commercial revival and crusades of the eleventh and twelfth centuries. Between 1204 and 1261 Western conquerors ruled Constantinople itself. Yet even during the period of Latin rule, when Italian merchants continued to flock to the Greek East and when scores of Latin churchmen passed back and forth in a vain effort to establish papal control of the Byzantine Church, very little cultural exchange occurred. Apparently in the thirteenth century the Latin Christians wanted nothing of the cultural riches of the despised Greek schismatics.

Thus at the end of the fourteenth century, what was new was not the opportunity to learn classical Greek but the desire. That desire was the result of the humanistic determination to master the whole cultural tradition of Antiquity and to apply it to the reform and regeneration of Western society and culture. When the first great teacher of Greek in the West, Chrysoloras, lectured for a time at Paris, in the midst of an intellectual world still unaffected by the Renaissance, his activity aroused no interest comparable to the enthusiasm that had greeted him among the humanists of Venice and Florence. The medieval mind was still closed to the influence of any part of ancient Greek culture except Aristotle. But the Italian intellectuals of the fifteenth century were eagerly open to that influence, precisely because of their quest for a cultural rebirth.

A further result of this new outlook was the sudden interest in Hebrew studies among humanists of the late fifteenth and early sixteenth centuries. The desire to rediscover ancient wisdom led naturally to interest in the Jewish background of Christianity, and humanists like Giovanni Pico della Mirandola (1463–94) in Italy and Johann Reuchlin (1455–1522) in Germany founded the study of Hebrew language and Jewish religious literature among Christian scholars. This tradition became very powerful in the religious scholarship of the Reformation and Counter-Reformation period.

Just as in the case of Greek, these developments are evidence of a very far-reaching intellectual change that for the first time made the scholars of Latin Europe receptive to cultural influences alien to the main stream of medieval tradition. The same sort of rabbinical scholars who introduced Pico and Reuchlin to Hebrew language and literature would have been available to Western thinkers at many earlier periods in the Middle Ages. The intellectual leaders of scholasticism did not care to expend the effort required to investigate this tradition. The men of the Renaissance, with their eagerness to find and recover ancient wisdom, did care.

Stages of Humanism. Italian Renaissance humanism, like any intellectual movement extending over a long period, passed through a number of stages of development. In its very earliest form, as in the thought of Petrarch, it was largely an intellectual's flight from harsh political and social problems. Petrarch himself was the son of a Florentine political exile, and he grew up at the papal court at Avignon, without the kind of close ties to the world of business and politics that he no doubt would have developed if his family had stayed in Florence. He was a professional man of letters, a poet, fortunate enough to secure ecclesiastical appointments that assured him a modest income without any significant duties. He viewed the hurly-burly of political bickering and the materialistic process of buying and selling as something beneath a man devoted to truth and beauty.

Although his program for regenerating society obviously had implications in the area of political life and devotion to public service, he regarded active involvement in politics as unworthy of a wise man. No doubt unrealistically, he thought that renewed contact with the great works of classical literature would somehow inspire men to achieve a personal moral reform and that in this way society would be improved through humanistic studies. Improved education and the sympathetic support of powerful persons in the Church hierarchy and in secular government were the only concrete ways he proposed to foster the cultural and moral renewal. Though not a monk, Petrarch retained from medieval monasticism the ideal of withdrawal from the temptations and distractions of everyday life and of devotion to a life of contemplating eternal truth and beauty.

This ideal of scholarly aloofness from the active world was very different from the Roman ideal of the citizen's devotion to public service. When Petrarch realized that his ideal Roman hero, Cicero, was eager to abandon his philosophical studies and go rushing into the political struggle for the late Republic, he was shocked that so wise a man should have been so eager for political power. Petrarch's attitude suggests that despite a lifetime of loving study of ancient Rome, he had never grasped the Roman ideal of civic obligation. In the late fourteenth century, some of Petrarch's younger followers at Florence were criticized for a similar rejection of their own civic duties.

The Rise of Civic Humanism. By the end of the fourteenth or the beginning of the fifteenth century, however, prominent Florentine families were increasingly likely to select humanistic educations for their sons, not in order to turn them into poets but in order to make them more effective at discharging their obligation to provide leadership for the Republic. Thus humanism entered a new "civic" phase in which its practical usefulness to those destined to political leadership was emphasized. The classical education of ancient Roman times had emphasized training in oratory (in a very broad sense, involving a total education and not just study of elocution) as the proper preparation for a career of public service. Now this alliance between humanistic study and the life of active public service reemerged. The alliance appears to have been encouraged by the political crisis of the early fifteenth century, when the aggressive Giangaleazzo Visconti, duke of Milan, threatened the independence of Florence. The skills of the humanist as diplomat, political propagandist, and civil servant suddenly appeared very useful for the defense of the Republic.

The tradition of appointing humanists to the influential position of chancellor of the republic cemented the alliance between the humanist intellectuals (most of whom in any case came from the politically dominant families) and the republic. Chancellors such as Colluccio Salutati (1330–1406) and Leonardo Bruni of Arezzo (ca. 1370–1444) effectively applied their literary skills to the defense of Florence. Both through their technical skill at drafting public documents and through their intellectual defense of the city's free status and republican form of government, they confirmed the growing conviction that humanistic study was in the public interest. Bruni in particular, in his *History of Florence*, worked out an historical ideology of republicanism, arguing that both in ancient Greece and in ancient Rome, the intellectual and social freedom of a republican constitution had made possible the brilliant cultural creativity of the ancients and that the heavy hand of despotism had led directly to the cultural decline of both Athens and Rome. The parallel with modern Italy, where the rise of self-governing city republics had preceded the cultural renaissance, and where his own city of Florence was at once the most free republic and the greatest cultural center of the age, seemed evident to Bruni, who thus linked the defense of the republic against Milanese despotism with the survival of Renaissance civilization.

In reality, humanism also flourished at despotic courts, but it is true that there was a remarkable affinity between Renaissance republicanism and the flourishing of humanistic culture. The civic humanism of figures like Bruni was consciously the ideology of republican governments in Florence and later in Venice. This turning of humanism toward support of active involvement in republican politics, in business, and in direction of the family set the tone for much humanism in the early fifteenth century and was certainly compatible with the whole Renaissance thrust toward regeneration of society. By its affirmation of the active life, the life of politics, business, and family responsibility, humanism became a secularizing (but not necessarily antireligious) ideology running counter to the contemplative, ivory-tower mood of Petrarchan humanists. To men like Bruni, a scholar who turned his back on politics, business, and the family was socially irresponsible.

The Humanist as Civil Servant. Obviously this type of humanist ideology had little appeal at the despotic courts or at the papal curia. Yet if stripped of its overt commitment to republican government, the humanist endorsement of the active life could be broadened to justify the careers of the many humanists who were employed in the service of nonrepublican governments. Despite its tendency to sympathize with republicanism, humanism always remained a highly aristocratic movement, with an eagerness to come to terms with those who held power, and with a strong element of disdain for the submerged and unenlightened classes. Humanists entered the service of princes and applied their talents to the defense of princely policies and the glorification of Italian dynasties, without many qualms about the authoritarian character of the regime being served. Just as the Florentine chancery found humanists useful at drawing up effective public documents, so the despotisms also employed humanistic chancellors. The papal curia at Rome, especially from the pontificate of Pope Nicholas V (1447–1455), founder of the Vatican Library, employed large numbers of humanists as secretaries in the various branches of papal administration, and the classical style and language of their Latin documents encouraged similar employment of humanists by the governments with which they transacted business. The arts of eloquent and persuasive speech and writing were useful to any government, republican or not, and so the most distinguished and successful humanists of the fifteenth and sixteenth centuries were hired to employ these arts in the service of their patrons. Like the lawyer, but in a broader and less technical way, the humanist was hired as an advocate, pledged to apply his professional skills to advance the interests of his employer. Actually, only a small and fortunate minority of humanists ever secured lucrative and influential posts in the chanceries of Florence, Venice, the Papacy, or the various Italian despotisms, but the existence of such careers nevertheless shows that fifteenth-century humanism had largely abandoned Petrarch's clear preference for the contemplative rather than the active life.

Humanism and Other Studies

A very different direction in fifteenth-century humanism was the transformation of humanistic literary and linguistic skills into a tool of critical analysis applicable to all branches of life. Humanism had never claimed to represent the totality of human learning, and while there was often friction between humanists and spokesmen for the established scholastic tradition of the universities, such friction often amounted to little more than competition for funds, students, and prestige. Since humanism emerged as a program of studies in a limited number of fields—grammar, rhetoric, ethics, history, and poetry—and since most of those fields already had some place in the traditional liberal arts curriculum, humanism often found a niche within the universities. Many humanists were employed as professors of grammar, rhetoric, moral philosophy, or poetry. So long as their claims merely emphasized the importance of their studies as part of a good education, they did not have much trouble. But humanism also contained the implication that *all* branches of traditional medieval learning were worthless, and that humanism offered not just a narrow spectrum of worthy studies but a general intellectual method that should dominate every branch of learning.

Lorenzo Valla and Critical Humanism. The development of this more radical conception of humanism was largely the work of the most intellectually vigorous of the fifteenth-century Italian humanists, Lorenzo Valla (1406–57). The attitude of earlier humanists toward the rediscovered ancient heritage had been emotional as much as scholarly. Though in a general way the humanists had labored to establish better texts for ancient books, their standards of textual criticism were unsystematic. Lorenzo Valla, born at Rome but exposed to the thought of Florentine scholars like Bruni at a crucial stage in his development, transformed humanistic textual editing from a haphazard comparison of manuscripts into a systematic reconstruction of texts on the basis of a scientific analysis of language and manuscript tradition. But Valla, whose powerful mind and iconoclastic personality carried him far beyond the narrow, technical limits of textual scholarship, elaborated a scientific approach to language that transformed humanism into a general intellectual method applicable to any field of learning that rested on authoritative documents from the past, as nearly all learning then did. Valla was one of the first to realize that language itself is the product of historical evolution and that a given language (Latin, for example) undergoes significant and discoverable stages of growth. This discovery of the basic principle of philology, the science of language, underlay his highly successful and influential work, *Elegances of the Latin Language* (1444), which offered later humanists a sure guide to the creation of a truly classical Latin prose style.

Valla also realized that the basic principles of linguistic analysis could be applied in a critical sense to evaluate the historical foundations of modern beliefs and institutions. The most famous example of this tendency was a work he wrote while employed by King Alfonso I of Naples. The popes since the eleventh century had claimed to be feudal overlords of Naples, and they based a good part of this claim on a document called the Donation of Constantine, which purported to be a transfer of political control over Italy and the whole Western empire to the Roman bishop and his successors. Most medieval critics of papal political ambitions had accepted the document as regrettable but genuine. Now in his tract *On the False Donation of Constantine* (1440), Valla wrote not just another attack on papal political ambitions but a brilliant and devastating criticism proving that the document could not possibly have been drawn up by the fourth-century emperor but must be a forgery written several centuries later. The most impressive parts of his proof are the historical (where he searches in vain for the sort of corroborating evidence which must have existed if the pope actually did assume political control) and the philological (where he compares the Latin vocabulary and grammatical structure of the document with the actual linguistic practice of the fourth-century imperial court). Though the attack on the papacy's political claims was devastating and the tract was later printed by Protestant foes of the papacy, the important point is not its hostility to papal policy but rather its transformation of humanistic techniques of literary and linguistic analysis into a tool for criticizing medieval traditions.

In this case the object was the political ambitions of the popes, but the method was more broadly applicable. Turning to the documents of Christian faith, Valla wrote *Notes on the New Testament,* which demonstrated the existence of serious errors in the currently used Latin translation of the Bible. Here his thought pointed toward the idea later developed by Erasmus and other sixteenth-century Biblical scholars—that all serious attempts to expound the meaning of the New Testament must go back to the original Greek text. The implication was that theologians trained in the traditional scholastic way, without command of the Greek language, were not qualified for the task they had undertaken. Valla insisted that theological science must focus on the understanding of the text of Scripture and the writings of the early church fathers—a kind of theology for which humanistic linguistic study would obviously be more useful than the traditional education. Though the trend toward greater care in the reconstruction of ancient texts continued to develop in later fifteenth-century Italian humanism, Valla's notion of humanism as a tool for criticism of medieval traditions did not really bear fruit until it came to life again, under the direct influence of Valla's books, in the work of northern humanists like Erasmus.

Decline of the Civic Ideal. The humanist emphasis on active political involvement was not very important in the thought of Lorenzo Valla, who was not a Florentine by birth. Concentration on the task of editing and expounding classical texts and on the study of style and literary form, while inseparable from humanism at every stage, nevertheless provided an alternative direction. Humanism in the later fifteenth century showed tendencies to becomes less "civic" and more academic than in the earlier part of the century. This tendency developed even in Florence, where after 1434 the Medici family held an ever more overt control of the republic. By the time of Lorenzo the Magnificent (in power 1469–92), the republican tone of society gave way to a courtly spirit. Though the political machinery of the republic continued to function, independent political action and too strident a proclamation of republican political ideals increasingly seemed pointless, if not even dangerous. Humanists and artists accordingly tended to glorify the Medicean leadership more and the republic less; and both art and literature assumed a nonpolitical, even a courtly tone.

Florentine Neoplatonism

Whether by coincidence or not, the change in Florentine political climate was contemporaneous with a shift in the dominant interests of Florentine intellectuals. In the earlier fifteenth century, interest had focused on historical, political, and social questions. When Florentine humanists discussed the ideal form of life, their tendency was to stress the active life of the citizen and family head, and they justified man's concern with mundane affairs such as politics, earning a living, and bringing up a family. But in the aristocratic circles of the "court" that centered around Lorenzo de' Medici, there was a reaction back toward affirmation of the contemplative life. Virtue came to be treated as more a private than a public matter. The recovery of the whole body of Greek literature made available the writings of Plato and his later followers the Neoplatonists, and these ancient sources encouraged the growing tendency toward a contemplative and nonpolitical ideal of life. Plato himself, with his strident hatred of democracy and his denial of real worth to material reality, provided a meaningful philosophical guide for a society where the earlier ideals of political activism and affirmation of secular values were waning.

Marsilio Ficino (1433–99)

Under the patronage of the Medici, the philosopher Marsilio Ficino (1433–99) applied his humanistic command of Greek to the preparation of a complete Latin translation of all of Plato's known works, plus Latin versions of other ancient authors who stood within the Platonic tradition. Ficino and his friends restated in humanistic form a conception of human life that might be called a reaction against the secular and materialistic values of earlier humanism. The contemplation of divine truth, not the active service of the republic, came to be their ideal of life. Their quest was for spiritual and eternal values, which they claimed to discover in the thought of a long line of ancient wise men leading down from the ancient Egyptians and Hebrews to legendary Greek heroes like Orpheus and actual Greek philosophers like Pythagoras and Plato. Indeed, they believed that divine providence had created this ancient pagan tradition as part of God's plan to prepare the ancient world for acceptance of the spiritual, other-worldly values of Christianity.

Pico and the Quest for Wisdom

The most brilliant of Ficino's younger friends, Giovanni Pico della Mirandola (1463–94), pushed this quest for ancient wisdom back into the writings of the Hebrew Old Testament, the Talmud, and the Jewish mystical books known as Cabala. His famous *Oration on the Dignity of Man* affirmed man's greatness and glory, but it based that greatness on man's ability to repudiate the material side of his life and focus all attention and energy on the spirit. Thus though the work came to be an influential expression of certain Renaissance attitudes toward man, it repudiated the earlier Florentine stress on the active life of the citizen.

"Florentine Neoplatonism," as the tradition established by Ficino and Pico is called, demonstrates the persistence of religious concerns in Renaissance culture and the continuing eagerness to find solutions to present-day problems through the rediscovery of ancient wisdom. But it also reflects the loss of political liberty, as shown in its instinctive and perhaps unconscious repudiation of the strenuous and active ideal set forth in the earlier "civic" stage of humanism. The Platonic sage, devoted to contemplation of eternal truths and to an essentially nonpolitical and even antisocial set of personal values, replaced the Roman statesman as the ideal of human life. The thought of Niccolo Machiavelli, however, who was still committed to the activist and republican values enunciated by earlier figures like Bruni, shows that at least in anti-Medicean political circles the tradition of civic humanism survived into the sixteenth century.

Educational Reform and the Renaissance

In many respects, the most influential aspect of Renaissance humanism was its reform of education. Even Petrarch saw clearly that the restoration of ancient virtue and culture depended on a thorough change in the education of the dominant classes of Italian society. From its very beginning, humanism had emphasized the study of those subjects that ever since Cicero's time had been regarded as humanistic—that is, especially suited to the nature of man. This notion of education involved a sharp rejection of medieval emphasis on logic and on speculative studies and insisted instead that education should focus attention on the subjects that dealt with human behavior—moral philosophy and history—and on the subjects that imparted the skills needed for successful modification of human behavior—grammar and rhetoric, the arts of clear and persuasive communication. We have already seen that humanists commonly filled the university professorships that dealt with such matters. But the position of humanists in the traditional universities was limited even though real. Professional education in law, medicine, and theology was the overriding goal of the medieval universities, not broad general education in the liberal arts.

Humanist Philosophy of Education

The educational philosophy of the humanists, however, repudiated such narrow professionalism. Under the influence of Roman authors like Cicero and the recently rediscovered Quintilian, education was regarded not as a professional training in some one special field, but as a wide-ranging development of the inherent capabilities of man. Above all, the subjects that concerned human behavior and the arts of eloquence needed attention, and the medium through which the goals of humanistic education were to be achieved would be study of the literary masterpieces of ancient Greece and Rome. The emphasis on Latin and Greek literature was not conceived in a restrictive sense. These two ancient literatures constituted the only known body of writings capable of exposing the student to the infinite variety of human experience—precisely the goal humanist educators sought to gain from literary study.

Another leading characteristic of humanistic educational thought was its emphasis on character building, rather than mere imparting of information and skills. The Renaissance educator stressed the value of moral considerations (and so was more likely than a medieval teacher to censor or expurgate the ancient works read in school) and was firmly in the grip of Petrarch's dream of inspiring modern youth to emulate the heroic and patriotic virtues of great Romans and Greeks. Careful attention to religious training, especially as a reinforcement and culmination of the moral principles found in the works of ancient pagan wise men, was also important. Finally, since the education was designed largely for social classes whose wealth and family prestige destined them to careers as active political and military leaders, educational theorists stressed the importance of physical training and even of military exercises.

Such theories of education were advanced in a number of works on the aims and methods of education, but the most famous was *On the Education of a Free Man* by Pietro Paolo Vergerio (1349–1428). This book, widely circulated in manuscript and frequently printed after the introduction of printing, emphasized that while a central aim of humanistic education should be the development of each man's capabilities, the ultimate goal was not the self-fulfillment of the individual but his commitment to an active career of service to the state.

A very similar statement of educational ideals, but concentrating on the ideal of human excellence rather than on the philosophy of education, was *The Book of the Courtier*, written by Count Baldassare Castiglione in the second decade of the sixteenth century though not published until 1528. The book was written not for the republican society of Florence, but for the aristocratic and courtly circles of Italian princely states. It reflects the late Quattrocento decline of zeal for republican political activism. Yet the ideal of public service—in this case, loyal service to one's prince—survives as a monarchist variation on the "civic humanism" of the Italian republics.

This restatement of the ideal of political activism in terms meaningful to the subjects of a prince made the book acceptable not only among courtiers in Italy but also at the courts of Northern Europe. Hence the book was translated into the major Western languages during the sixteenth century and became an influencial guide to court life. It has the form of a dialogue conducted at the princely court of Urbino, where a group of ladies and gentlemen attempt to define the attributes of the perfect courtier. What marks this dialogue as a typical product of aristocratic Italian Renaissance society, alongside its ideal of public service, is the importance it assigns to a broad general education, especially in the classics. The gifted amateur, not the scholarly expert, is its ideal, yet that amateur would be master of Greek as well as Latin, and would be well read in both literatures.

Renaissance Classical Schools

The dominant classes of Renaissance Italy needed new kinds of schools where the educational reforms outlined by Vergerio and implied by Castiglione could be worked out in practice. Despite some concessions to humanistic interests, the universities remained predominantly professional in orientation. Hence a new type of school grew up, the humanist classical school, whose essential purpose was to give young men a broad education in the liberal arts, based on reading of classical literature and study of classical languages. The most famous such school, one later imitated throughout Italy and then in all parts of Europe, was the one organized at the court of Gianfrancesco Gonzaga, marquis of Mantua, by Vittorino da Feltre (1378–1448). Vittorino himself was educated at the University of Padua, where humanism was relatively strong, and he also studied Greek under Guarino da Verona (1374–1460), the only other humanist schoolmaster whose fame and influence rivaled his own. After many years of study and teaching at Padua, he accepted the invitation of the Marquis of Mantua to found a court school on humanistic lines. This school would be for the children of the Marquis and his courtiers, but it would also be open to poor boys of talent whose education would open brilliant careers to them. The school of Mantua became so successful that princely families and humanists from all over Italy sent their sons to Mantua or to Guarino's similar court school at Ferrara. From such centers emerged some of the finest humanists and some of the most perceptive patrons of the next generation. Of course the princes educated at Mantua or Ferrara often founded similar humanistic schools when they became rulers on their own.

The humanistic school of Renaissance Italy, with its emphasis on a broad literary education in the Latin and Greek classics, on character formation, and on the deliberate preparation of its graduates for careers of political service and leadership, spread during the sixteenth century to Northern Europe, where the Reformation produced the Lutheran academies organized under the influence of the humanist Philip Melanchthon, the great Calvinist academy at Geneva, and the phenomenally successful Jesuit colleges, all of them clearly modeled on the theories of humanists like Vergerio and the work of practical educational reformers like Vittorino and Guarino.

Renaissance Culture and the People

Humanistic culture was essentially confined to the ruling elite of courtiers and rich merchant families. Its mood was self-consciously aristocratic, and it contained a large element of contempt (sometimes softened by pity) for the unenlightened masses. Even its republicanism meant a republican tradition where the rich were dominant, and where unskilled and propertyless workers and peasants had no voice.

The Early Vernacular Tradition

Yet Renaissance culture, even Renaissance literature, had its more popular side as well. The transition of Italy from being a cultural backwater to being the leader of European culture began in the late thirteenth and early fourteenth centuries before the rise of Renaissance humanism. Dante, the first great literary figure of Italy, wrote his chief work, *The Divine Comedy*, in Italian, and despite his own aristocratic rank and outlook, the poem reflected the intellectual and political life of the Florentine people so well that it became highly popular.

The second great figure of Italian vernacular literature, Petrarch, was also the founding father of humanism. His vernacular poems are far more suited to the elegant, courtly societies in which he resided than to the matter-of-fact outlook of Florentine businessmen and artisans. Nevertheless, his highly personal and subjective love poetry had an appeal far beyond the circles of his humanist followers. Although he never became quite the folk hero that Dante did, he was revered as the city's second great poet.

The third great figure of fourteenth-century Florentine literature, Giovanni Boccaccio (1313–75), was also a humanist and did much to spread Petrarchan humanism among the educated classes of the city. Yet his principal work, the *Decameron*, was in the vernacular. While its artistic form may be the product of Renaissance culture, the themes of the stories reflect the interests of the Florentine populace, dealing with satirical attacks on corrupt clergymen, humorous treatment of human oddities, and stories of marital infidelity. This plot material is popular, traditional, and medieval, and the *Decameron* itself was a popular work.

Revival of Italian Literature. There is apparently much truth in the traditional belief that the craze for classical humanism proved harmful to this flourishing tradition of vernacular literature. Certainly little of importance was produced in Italian-language poetry in the last half of the fourteenth and the first half of the fifteenth century. Yet the Florentine people—and even many intellectuals—still revered the great works of Dante, Petrarch, and Boccaccio, and attempts by extreme humanists to question the value of this literature were given prompt rebuttal.

By the second half of the fifteenth century, there was a major revival of the vernacular. Especially in the circle of Lorenzo de' Medici, Italian reemerged as a vehicle for serious literary work. Lorenzo himself, who was a lyric poet of considerable ability, set the style for both secular and religious poetry in the vernacular. The humanist Angelo Poliziano also produced elegant Italian poems. A generation later, Pietro Bembo, a Venetian cleric who was one of the leaders of Ciceronian purism in Latin, adopted the Florentine Petrarchan tradition and language for his elegant Italian poetry. This reemergence of Petrarchan vernacular poetry, with its highly refined sentiment and its technical mastery of intricate verse forms, was an important part of the cultural heritage Renaissance Italy gave to the Western literary tradition. Both the themes and the verse forms of French, Spanish, and English Renaissance literature of the sixteenth and early seventeenth centuries show conscious imitation of such Italian models as Petrarch, Lorenzo de' Medici, Poliziano, and Bembo.

Popular literature of a less aristocratic sort was often based on themes derived from medieval French chivalric poetry. As Florentine society itself became more openly dominated by a sophisticated prince like Lorenzo de' Medici, popular poems about the deeds of heroic knights like Orlando (in French, Roland) began to furnish material for the vernacular works of Italian courtiers. The first important Florentine poet to adapt such material for consciously humorous verse was Luigi Pulci (1432–84), author of *Morgante Maggiore.* A member of Lorenzo's circle of friends, he delighted in making fun of the heavy solemnity of some of the court humanists. Chivalric themes of medieval French origin were treated more seriously in the poem *Orlando innamorato* (*Roland in Love*) by Matteo Boiardo (1441–94), a courtier at the refined court of the dukes of Ferrara, where humanistic classical interests and medieval chivalric interests both were fashionable. Far more important was a later sequel to this poem written by Ludovico Ariosto (1474–1533), *Orlando furioso* (*Roland's Insanity*). Even later in the sixteenth century, the poet Torquato Tasso (1544–95) achieved another blending of Renaissance artistic form with a medieval theme, again at the court of Ferrara. His *Jerusalem Delivered* was an epic of the Crusades. The refined artistic taste of Italian Renaissance literature thus was able to take over popular themes of medieval origin and to transform them into major literary works that influenced all sixteenth-century literatures.

Popular Influence of Literature. How far this vernacular literature influenced the masses of Florence, Ferrara, or other cities is hard to determine. While the elegant, refined, and sophisticated tone and intricate verse forms were probably over the heads of lower-middle-class persons and workers, the popular origin of the narrative themes must have made this poetry widely comprehensible to the many Italian city folk who were literate but had no pretensions to intellectual sophistication. Indeed, even a widespread familiarity with some of the themes of classical literature was inevitable in a society whose ruling classes were so keen on ancient studies. The public festivals and pageants of the time had many classical elements that no doubt reflected the tastes of rich patrons, but the characters and themes from classical literature and mythology seem to have been comprehensible to the public at large.

The revival of vernacular writing also involved prose. One of the principal examples of this revival, Castiglione's *Book of the Courtier*, has been discussed above. It stated the ideals of the elite of courtiers, not of the people. Renaissance Italy produced a number of other manuals of good manners whose popularity suggests that the desire to have at least a veneer of humanistic culture and courtly manners reached down well below the ruling classes.

Machiavelli. The most brilliant example of Italian prose in the High Renaissance (the very early sixteenth century) is the works of Niccol[Machiavelli (1469–1527) on politics and history. Although Machiavelli's writings were obviously not directed to the common man, they show clearly that even after sixty years of domination by the Medici family, the Florentine republican tradition had not perished. Machiavelli's two great works, *The Prince* and *Discourses on the First Ten Books of Titus Livius*, were written in Italian and drew heavily on the author's first-hand experience as a leading Florentine diplomat and civil servant during most of the period of the restored Florentine republic (1494–1512). Yet he constantly probed the ancient heritage to discover remedies for the political sickness of early sixteenth-century Italy. His republican political preferences are obscured in *The Prince*, for in 1513 he at least seriously considered the possibility that the moral corruption of Italy made its people unfit for republican government. But the *Discourses* show clearly that even while he was trying to curry favor with the restored Medici, he regarded a balanced republican constitution, such as Rome had been and Florence perhaps still could be, as the best and most durable form of government. Cynical though he was about human nature, Machiavelli still trusted the public spirit and wisdom of the common citizens more than he did that of princes and aristocrats.

The Renaissance in Art

Many historians in the past half-century have so warmly acknowledged the creativity of the Middle Ages that they have questioned whether there was ever any real Renaissance at all. But no historian of art, where the Italian Renaissance ranks as the most brilliant period in all history, can seriously question whether there was a Renaissance. The phenomenal creativity of Renaissance Italy—led, once again, by Florence—in architecture, sculpture, and painting is the central fact in the history of modern art. Only in the past century have the visual arts really escaped the dominance of Renaissance influences.

As in many other fields of culture, Italy was relatively backward and imitative in the visual arts during the high Middle Ages. The Gothic art of the thirteenth century had considerable impact on the Italians, and yet Italian artists never wholeheartedly accepted the northern style. Because of her commmercial ties to the eastern Mediterranean, Italy also felt Byzantine artistic influence, and during the period 1204–61, when a Latin government ruled Constantinople, this tendency was reinforced. The popularity of panel paintings and frescoes, the flat, two-dimensional forms, and the concentration on traditional religious themes are all clear evidence that thirteenth-century Italian painting was under strong Byzantine influence. This thirteenth-century style of painting was called Greek—*maniera greca*—by later Italians, who regarded the sharp break with traditional painting that occurred at the beginning of the fourteenth century as the first and decisive step toward the later art of the Renaissance.

Giotto (1266–1336)

Modern art historians do not quite agree. They can see a confluence of influences from Byzantine and Gothic art in the achievement of the founder of the new style, Giotto (ca. 1266–1336), and they usually reserve the first application of the term Renaissance for the style of painting and sculpture that emerged in Florence during the second and third decades of the fifteenth century. Nevertheless, though Giotto did not rebel against Byzantine and Gothic traditions as the humanists rebelled against scholastic traditions, his paintings are radical in conception and different in appearance from the work of his predecessors, even from the style of his own master, Cimabue (1240–1302).

Renaissance Elements in Giotto's Paintings. Giotto's paintings foretell the coming Renaissance in two principal respects. First, he wholly abandoned the hieratic, flat, nonrepresentational appearance of Byzantine art and began the march toward the illusion of three-dimensional form on the two-dimensional painted surface. His figures have three-dimensional depth, and the space in the picture gives the illusion of being an extension of the real space out of which the beholder looks: one looks into, not onto, his works.

Critics speak of the "tactile value" of his paintings, by which they mean that the painting looks as if the beholder could reach in and grasp the figures. Second—and perhaps even more clearly a prelude to Renaissance art—Giotto's works are fundamentally the visual representations of an idea, and the perception of this unifying idea, not the enjoyment of a wealth of brilliantly executed details, is the essence of appreciating one of his works. Hence Giotto's paintings are dominated by a few large, simple forms whose relationships constitute the unity of the work. Details that do not contribute to this unified statement of the artist's idea are excluded. This remarkable unity through presentation of a single idea points directly toward the high Renaissance conception of a work of art. Its prominence in the work of Giotto makes his work closer to the Renaissance masters than is the work of the technically skilled and highly realistic Flemish school of a century later—precisely because for all its many virtues, the Flemish school concentrated on realistic detail and did not define the work of art as merely the visual statement of an idea.

Giotto's work, such as the remarkable frescoes he did in 1305–06 in the Arena Chapel at Padua, also shows other traits which point toward the coming Renaissance. One unmistakable characteristic is the closer relationship of the figures to the everyday life of Florentine laymen. Giotto's themes are still religious—indeed, though pagan and classical themes eventually developed in Renaissance art, they never predominated—but the treatment might be called "bourgeois" or "laic." In other words, religious themes received a treatment that made the works convincing to everyday Florentine citizens who lacked the learning or the inclination to appreciate the hieratic and ethereal qualities of medieval art.

In this pre-Renaissance society, control of patronage was not in the hands of a few clergymen as in the medieval North, but in the hands of professional and trade guilds, confraternities of pious laymen, or the secular government. The new art had to appeal to these groups. The social position that Giotto himself held also is a preview of Renaissance conditions. Although artists were still regarded as merely skilled craftsmen for a century or more after Giotto's death, the great personal fame of Giotto marked him as someone special, a major personage in society, and not just a hired hand. The later conception of the artist as a creative genius had begun to emerge. Indeed, Giotto became so influential and famous that his many disciples were trapped into becoming imitators; and for the rest of the fourteenth century, no Italian painter appeared who really advanced further.

The Florentine Artistic Revival

The new style that eventually did take up the revolutionary features of Giotto's paintings and develop them further is conventionally labeled "Renaissance" and is usually subdivided into an "Early Renaissance" or quattrocento (Italian for fifteenth century) phase, and a "High Renaissance," or "classic" phase. This new direction was overwhelmingl·· Florentine in its origins: indeed, its political, social, and ideological background is the growing patriotism and pride of the Florentines during their successful struggle against Milanese imperialism in the early fifteenth century. One expression of this local patriotism was a renewed eagerness to complete and embellish the city's cathedral. The first great achievement was the decorative bronze baptistery doors created for the cathedral by Lorenzo Ghiberti (1378–1455) as the result of his victory in a famous competition among sculptors held in 1402. This great sculptural achievement, however, is in the traditional International Gothic style, not Renaissance.

Origins of Renaissance Style

The sixteenth-century art historian Giorgia Vasari relates that one of the losers in the competition of 1402, Filippo Brunelleschi (1377–1446), left Florence in disgust after his defeat and went with a young friend, Donatello (1386–1466), to Rome in order to study ancient Roman buildings and statues at their source.

These two men were the creators of the new Renaissance style in sculpture and architecture. Donatello, the sculptor, was the greater figure, in part because although he carefully studied classical models, he was no imitator. He assimilated the basic principles of ancient sculpture into a style that was wholly his own. His stone reliefs, his marble statues, and his bronze statues like the *David* (the first free-standing nude of postclassical times) created a new era in sculpture. The freedom of Donatello's figures from their architectural background, the ability of his work to show movement, and the accurate anatomical structure of his figures were some of the principal traits he passed along to later Renaissance sculptors. Donatello began producing works in his new style about 1411 and had a very long career.

His older friend Brunelleschi based his work in architecture on careful measurement of the ancient buildings he studied. In the course of his works on drawings of these structures, he formulated the mathematical principles of linear perspective, a discovery which in time helped revolutionize painting. In 1417–19 he again entered competition against Ghiberti, this time in the architectural problem of creating the huge dome of Florence cathedral, which the Gothic architects of the late thirteenth and early fourteenth centuries had blithely specified but had not bothered to design. This time Brunelleschi won the competition, and while his great dome certainly does not look un-Gothic or contrary to the rest of the structure, its engineering principles were radically new. A strong tendency toward incorporation of antique elements is visible in his smaller buildings, of which the Pazzi family chapel is a good example. Even the most unpracticed eye can verify that the structure is not Gothic and that ancient Roman buildings exerted a strong influence on its design.

Masaccio and Quattrocento Art. The art of painting entered the new stylistic era of Early Renaissance a decade later than sculpture and architecture. But in the end, the achievement was greater than in the other two visual arts. In his short life, the Florentine painter Masaccio (1401–28) recaptured the creative tradition begun by Giotto and carried it much further. The principal traits of Renaissance painting, its mastery of the illusion of three-dimensionality and its conception of simple, direct statement of an artistic idea as the essential task of a work of art, reemerged with grandeur in the frescoes Masaccio created in the Brancacci Chapel in Florence. Masaccio advanced much further than Giotto. His human figures show a greater awareness of the anatomical structures (that is, the nude bodies) underneath the garments, and the Adam and Eve of his *Expulsion from Paradise* are striking nudes who display the artist's ability to portray both motion and emotion. The background of his works shows control of Brunelleschi's laws of linear perspective, so that the three-dimensional illusion is more striking than in Giotto. He also skillfully commanded the use of light.

Masaccio lived too brief a life to train pupils, but many of the greatest figures of the century were his disciples in the sense that they carefully studied his works, learned from them, and avowed their debt to him. No painter since Giotto had such an impact on the future direction of Italian painting. The fifty or sixty years after Masaccio's premature death produced many splendid painters, and several lines of development revived by Masaccio were advanced greatly, such as anatomical structure and perspective. Indeed, the age known as the quattrocento was perhaps too devoted to exploration and mastery of the technical side of art for its own good. This is not to say that its products were not excellent. The paintings of men like the Venetian Mantegna, the Umbrian Piero della Francesca, and the Florentine Botticelli, as well as many others, are major expressions of Renaissance culture. The work of Giovanni Bellini (ca. 1431–1516), Titian (ca. 1477–1576), and later figures like Tintoretto (1518–94) and Veronese (1528–88) created a distinctive Venetian school that eventually rivaled the Florentine in creative power.

"High Renaissance" Art. But the continuing dominance of Florence is proved by the essentially Florentine training of the three artists whose work not only dominates but almost defines the mature style known as high

Renaissance, an art so overwhelming that it hindered the further development of art in most centers except Venice because later artists felt that the ultimate perfection had been achieved, and that nothing remained for them but to imitate and admire. These three men, perhaps the three greatest figures in the historyof art, were Leonardo da Vinci (1452–1519), Michelangelo Buonarroti (1475–1564), both Florentines, and Raffaelo Sanzio (1483–1520), known in English as Raphael, an Umbrian who closely studied Florentine achievements. Their active careers virtually delimit and define the High Renaissance style. Michelangelo's long life and remarkable artistic development carried him beyond the High Renaissance period, both chronologically and stylistically, but the deaths of Leonardo and Raphael in 1519 and 1521 mark the end of the High Renaissance in art. Michelangelo's style soon thereafter underwent a drastic change, and the death of Pope Leo X in 1521 ended the directing patronage which papal Rome had provided under Pope Leo and his predecessor Julius II, the two greatest patrons of the style at its supreme moment.

The three great masters were diverse in many respects. Leonardo was a universal genius whose real interests centered in study of nature as much as in art, and whose private notebooks, if they had been published, could have led to great progress in anatomy and in certain fields of physics and engineering. Perhaps because of his preoccupation with such matters, Leonardo left many of his paintings uncompleted, and even his greatest and most famous work, *The Last Supper*, is almost a ruin because he experimented with new paints instead of sticking with the traditional and durable fresco technique. Leonardo was, nevertheless, essentially a painter, and his treatment of the atmospheric background was an important new development in that field. He also invented machines, sculpted statues, and designed buildings. In architecture, his plans and sketches are important because they show the emergence of the perfected High Renaissance style of building that achieved its first actual successes in the buildings constructed by his friend Bramante (1444–1514), the creator of the original plan for the new St. Peter's Cathedral begun at Rome under Pope Julius II.

Michelangelo was another wide-ranging genius, more a sculptor than a painter, but skilled in both fields and in architecture as well. Even more than Leonardo, perhaps, he completed the artist's rise from the status of craftsman to the status of individual genius, associating freely with popes, kings, and nobles. His early sculptures like the *David* (1501–04) mark the maturity of the idealized, classical High Renaissance style, and the marble figures he carved for the tomb of Pope Julius II at Rome and for the tombs of the Medici family at Florence would alone suffice to make him a figure of universal fame. Yet Pope Julius compelled Michelangelo to interrupt work on his tomb and paint the spectacular frescoes on the ceiling of the Sistine Chapel (1508–12), perhaps the greatest single work of High Renaissance painting. Both in his sculptures and in his paintings, Michelangelo concentrated his attention on the nude human figure, which he clearly regarded as the most challenging and significant object for the artist. His work as an architect, crowned by his redesigning of St. Peter's Cathedral after 1546, belongs to the later part of his career, when he had passed beyond the High Renaissance style.

The third of the great Renaissance artists, Raphael, was a less stormy personality and perhaps a less interesting figure, but judged simply as a painter, he was the most productive of the three despite the brevity of his career. The more important of his many Madonnas and his *School of Athens* and *Disputà* would be high on anyone's list of masterpieces of the period.

Behind all the diversity of these three creative geniuses, there are common traits that form the distinctive notes of the High Renaissance in art. Perhaps most important is the clarity with which they accepted and developed the idea, created by Giotto and Masaccio, that every work of art should be unified by the purpose of visually stating a single great idea and that all decorative detail that does not contribute to this purpose should be suppressed. As Michelangelo himself clearly said, this conception of a work of art is what separates Renaissance art from the realism of Flemish art, whose works are by comparison cluttered and lacking in clear emphasis.

The second trait is that all three masters continued, perfected, and even transcended the Renaissance desire for a three-dimensional illusion of reality. The art of the High Renaissance is not a literal presentation of reality, but an idealized and universalized one. Its realism is not a literal-minded reality of detail, but a reality that rests on the conceptual unity of the work.

These two traits were far more definitive in the creation of the style than such matters as perfection of technique, treatment of nonreligious and pagan themes (which never prevailed over the traditional religious ones), or even the visual expression of ideas taken from the thought of Florentine humanists and Neoplatonic philosophers, though such ideas are obvious in the work of artists like Botticelli and Michelangelo.

Instability of the High Renaissance. But precisely because the High Renaissance style rested on conceptual unity and a nonliteral idea of three-dimensional form, it was an unstable and fragile thing. The externals of the style, such as the technical skill in reproducing three-dimensional forms, movement, and emotion, could now be mastered by any competent pupil, but the classical harmony of figures and mood, and the conceptual unity, were matters of instinctive judgment that no one could teach. Even in the work of Michelangelo, his own constant groping after a more satisfying conception of humanity led to a collapse of the calm order of his earlier works. The emotional turbulence and startling forms of such later paintings as *The Last Judgment* (1534–41) mark the emergence of a style that had abandoned the harmony and balance of High Renaissance and that, in the hands of lesser artists, would become so idiosyncratic or "mannered" that it might well be regarded as a decline from the high achievement of the Renaissance.

The "Courtly Renaissance" and Cultural Regression

The shift in the tone of Renaissance art and humanism from the rather literal-minded art of the politically activist "civic" ideal of the early fifteenth century to the glittering "courtly" atmosphere of the late fifteenth century might well be regarded as retrogressive, if not in art (where the Medicean and Milanese courts prepared the way for the glories of the High Renaissance style) then more plausibly in the case of humanism and literature. The ideal of active political struggle for the Florentine republic was watered down to the more neutral ideal of education for service to any regime, even that of a prince or a pope. The technical and academic side of classical humanism posed no political or social threat to any vested interest, and the radical implications of humanism as a device for critical analysis of modern beliefs and institutions were carefully ignored by later Italian disciples of Valla, who saw only the literary, textual, and stylistic implications of his work.

Also tending back toward an outlook that might be called "medieval" was the Neoplatonic preoccupation with the soul, the quest for immortality, and the repudiation of the political and material values of earlier Florentine life. The early quattrocento exalted man (though not thereby intending to attack religion) in a more true and natural way than did the Neoplatonism of Ficino and Pico, because it elaborated a social conception of virtue rather than an individual quest for personal sanctification of the material, active life and deliberate choice of a life of contemplation. Yet this "regressive" tendency that emerged in Italy late in the fifteenth century was dictated by the political and social changes of the time: the waning of the republican tradition in Florence and the passing of leadership in patronage from a rather broad group of well-to-do citizens to a group of sophisticated and aristocratic courts.

Chapter Five

The Renaissance in the North

The shift from republican civic culture to courtly humanistic culture, which is well expressed in the refined, courtly ideal of man stated in Castiglione's *Book of the Courtier* and against which only a few old-fashioned republican idealists like Machiavelli vainly protested, probably was one key to the relatively sudden spread of Italian Renaissance culture to non-Italian lands at the end of the fifteenth and the beginning of the sixteenth centuries. Many northerners in the late fourteenth and early fifteenth centuries had become interested in Italian humanism. Until almost 1500, Northern art remained little influenced by Italian, and the leading political and intellectual groups of Northern Europe supported a culture dominated by the chivalric and scholastic traditions of the Middle Ages, not by classical humanism or by the quest for a cultural rebirth.

Yet at least some of the forces that opened Italy to the new culture were also at work in Northern Europe. Probably the divorce of humanistic culture from its civic and republican social background, and its modification into a culture suitable for the courtiers of the Renaissance despots in the closing decades of the fifteenth century, explains why it became exportable to a degree never before known. To the courtly, aristocratic, and clerical society of Northern Europe, the courtly, elegant and spiritual culture of the late quattrocento had a greater relevance than the republican, bourgeois, and secular culture of the early Renaissance. Again, Castiglione's *Courtier* is a symbol of the new situation, for its transformation of humanism into a general ideal of public service (without the republican context), of refined and sophisticated manners, and of individual merit based on learning and morals, became highly popular among the courtiers and social climbers of Northern Europe as they molded a new ideal of aristocratic life to replace the chivalric ideal of the Middle Ages. Humanistic education became the education of a gentleman; and this situation prevailed throughout Europe until well into the nineteenth century.

Northern Europe's Contacts with Italy

The French invasion of Italy in 1494 is the event conventionally used as a symbol of the new contact between Renaissance Italy and the North, but it was only an occasion for the change in Northern culture, not the cause. Cultural contact between North and South was neither rare nor novel in 1494. Even since the early fourteenth century, students from Northern Europe frequently crossed the Alps to enroll in Italian universities. They came not to study humanistic subjects but to enroll in the faculties of medicine and law, which were the best in Europe. But such students could not avoid some contact with the prevailing enthusiasm for classical studies among their Italian fellow-students, and many graduates who returned north and built successful careers used their wealth and social prestige to pursue classical studies, long before humanistic study became fashionable in their homelands. The papal curia at Rome was another center that attracted northerners who might reside there for extended periods and might pick up the growing interest in Antiquity. Then, too, large numbers of wealthy and cultivated Italians lived in Northern Europe, both as merchants and as high clergymen, and their interest in humanistic studies often influenced the friends they made in those regions. The world of learning, in that Latin-speaking, Latin-reading age, was far more truly international than at any later period. Especially from the 1470s, when a great printing industry was born at Venice, Italian books (mainly those in Latin) spread Renaissance ideas far beyond the peninsula itself.

All these mechanisms of cultural contact had long existed and tended to grow more powerful. The addition of large numbers of French soldiers, including the king and the high aristocracy, to the number of persons who marveled at the wealth and refined elegance of the Italians further stimulated interest in Renaissance art, scholarship, and literature.

Northern Sources of the Renaissance

The North itself would never have accepted Renaissance culture if that culture had not suited its needs. The reorganized, powerful monarchies of the late fifteenth and early sixteenth centuries needed a new ideal for their servants and courtiers, and the emphasis on public service, on personal merit, and on learning provided an attractive substitute for the traditional manners of the unlettered, unruly, and discredited feudal classes. The new ideal contained enough emphasis on social class and military prowess to make it credible to a society where the hereditary nobility still counted for much. For the kings, it offered the added advantage of servants who were refined and cultivated, and who would wield the pen as well as the sword for their master.

In addition to the monarchs and their courts, other important groups in the North also found humanistic culture attractive. The powerful, self-confident merchant oligarchies that governed the important towns, especially the prospering towns of the Rhine Valley and of south Germany, found in humanism a cultural ideal far more suited to the needs and prejudices of urban magnates than were the chivalric and scholastic traditions of the Middle Ages. The large group of would-be Church reformers found the characteristic Renaissance repudiation of the recent past and the desire to return to the original sources quite attractive, for the Roman past included the apostolic and early patristic age, when the Church was still pure and uncorrupted.

The few and relatively isolated enthusiasts for Italian humanism in the early and middle years of the fifteenth century, such as Humphrey, Duke of Gloucester (uncle of King Henry VI of England), and Nicholas of Cusa, German church reformer who became a cardinal and narrowly missed being elected pope, left few disciples and were probably less important for the growth of a Northern Renaissance than were a number of influential teachers of Latin grammar and rhetoric in Northern universities and town Latin schools. The humanism that grew up in the North was not a mere copy of the Italian culture, but a grafting of Italian elements into a cultural tradition that varied from country to country. Obviously, for example, Germans or even Frenchmen could not revere the ancient Romans as their ancestors in quite the same sense that Italians could.

What did develop everywhere was a revulsion against the heritage of the immediate past (often more open and violent than in Italy because scholastic traditions and a clerical spirit had much greater strength in the North), and the conscious adoption of an idealized Greek and Roman Antiquity as the model for reforming literature, education, and the whole ideal of the educated man. Even more than in Italy, Northern humanists enthusiastically looked to the apostolic and patristic age of the Church as a valuable part of the ancient heritage they sought to restore. This emphasis on ancient Christianity, combined with the widespread movements of lay piety that flourished in the lower Rhine Valley and other parts of Northern Europe, explains why humanism north of the Alps directed much of its reformist activity toward reform of the Church and deepening of personal religious experience.

Humanism in Northern Europe

Germany became the first home of a native Northern Humanism. Rudolf Agricola (1444–85) spent a decade studying in Italy and spread his interest in Latin and Greek in the secondary schools of several Dutch towns and in the University of Heidelberg. One of his pupils, Alexander Hegius, became headmaster of the important school at Deventer in the Netherlands in 1483 and increased the importance of classical literature in the curriculum. This school trained many of the next generation of German and Dutch humanists.

Centers of Humanist Influence

The arts faculties of the universities, just as in Italy a century before, also provided a reasonably favorable atmosphere for a limited expansion of the classical content of higher education, though the basic structure of scholastic education remained intact. Not only in Germany but also in such centers of scholastic tradition as Oxford, Cambridge, and Paris, humanists achieved a subordinate but significant role before 1500—sometimes Italian professors who found employment in the North, such as Erasmus's friend Fausto Andrelini, and sometimes northerners trained in Italy, such as William Grocyn at Oxford and Robert Gaguin at Paris. These early humanists were themselves usually cautious, conservative men, who admired classical learning and desired to regenerate civilization but had no suspicion that the latter aim might alarm theologians or other influential groups in the educational establishment.

Another place where Northern Humanism took root was in the prospering towns of south Germany and the Rhineland, extending all the way north to the Low Countries. Augsburg, Nuremberg, Strasbourg, and Basel produced important humanists, and the closed oligarchies that ruled those towns favored humanistic education for their sons in a way reminiscent of the Florentine oligarchs of the late fourteenth and early fifteenth centuries. Somewhat later, the royal courts of Northern Europe became important centers for the encouragement of humanism; and such major rulers of the early sixteenth century as the Emperor Maximilian I (1493–1519), Henry VIII of England (1509–47), and Francis I of France (1515–47) prided themselves on their appreciation of the new culture.

These kings regularly used the graduates of humanistic schools in support of their political goals. The emperor Maximilian I was the first Northern ruler to realize how the humanists could be employed as propagandists to mobilize the resurgent national sentiment of the German educated classes in support of his many political schemes. By the early sixteenth century, humanists like the Latin poet Conrad Celtis (1459–1508) had created little circles of humanist readers and writers throughout western and southern Germany and had founded a tradition of frequent correspondence and mutual assistance among these groups, so that the humanists constituted an articulate group worthy of careful cultivation by the emperor.

With few exceptions, the literary products of such humanistic circles had little lasting importance, though the growing appreciation of classical literary form and linguistic precision had an immensely beneficial effect on the Northern vernaculars, making them far more effective media for serious literary expression than they had been in the Middle Ages. But the Latin-writing humanists, though inordinately admired at the time, included only two authors whose works had lasting literary importance, the English lawyer-humanist, Sir Thomas More (1478–1535), and his close friend, the Dutch humanist Desiderius Erasmus (1469–1536). More's *Utopia* and Erasmus' *Praise of Folly* and *Familiar Colloquies* have a literary quality seldom reached by Neo-Latin books.

"Christian Humanism" and Church Reform

Humanism had a profound impact on Northern European civilization, not only for its formative influence on vernacular languages and literatures but also because of its crucial role in the movement for reform of the Church. The term *Christian humanism* is often applied to describe that part of the Northern Humanist movement that made reform of the Church the principal focus of its agitation for a "revival of Antiquity." Christian Humanism blended the moralistic element already prominent in Italian humanism with the intense personal piety of Northern religious reformers of the fourteenth and fifteenth centuries, especially that of the *Devotio Moderna.* From humanistic love for the ancient past the movement took its general concept of reform through a return to Antiquity, in this case the spirit and practice of the early Church. From the same source it took its careful study of ancient pagan literature, especially of the moralists and historians, as the foundation for a rational morality. From Italian Renaissance Neoplatonists it drew reinforcement of its own tendency to emphasize spiritual rather than material goals in life. And in its greatest figure, Erasmus, it rediscovered the deeply radical potential of Lorenzo Valla's critical humanism and began to apply this solvent analytical tool to the critical evaluation of traditional beliefs and practices.

Religious Ideals

Its positive religious ideal, as best expressed by Erasmus in his *Enchiridion* and some of his *Colloquies,* was the view that real religion is not a matter of formal, intellectualized affirmation of complex dogmas, but a simple, personal acceptance of Christ as one's savior and a sincere effort to lead a righteous life. It intended to reject neither the essential dogmas of Catholic faith nor the authorized rituals of Catholic piety, but it did tend to minimize almost to the vanishing point the list of essential dogmas and rituals. It was aggressively hostile to all religious traditions that made man's salvation depend on external, mechanical, magical acts rather than on personal, inward faith and moral uprightness.

A New Approach to the Bible

The basic scheme of applying humanistic literary and linguistic techniques to gain a deeper understanding of the documents of Christian faith (especially the Bible but also the writings of the early Church fathers) was largely the invention of a pious English cleric who visited Renaissance Italy, John Colet (ca. 1466–1519). He was not a profound humanistic scholar (he had, for example, no command of Greek), but he had a remarkably clear-headed grasp of the humanist insistence on interpreting a literary text in its historical setting and of attributing to any particular passage only the meaning justified by the original context of that passage. He now began applying this humanist technique to the explanation of the Bible. Despite Colet's orthodoxy and piety, this practice contained theological dynamite, for this way of reading the Bible implied a total rejection of the exegetical method of the scholastic theologians, who treated excerpts from Scripture and from various authoritative writers with an almost total unconcern for what the words had meant in their original setting. Thus while Colet was no theologian, his method of reading and understanding the Bible implied that much of the textual foundation of scholastic theology was unsound.

Here is a good example of how humanism as a general intellectual method inevitably led from study of the humanistic subjects where it originated into implicit or explicit attacks on traditional scholarship in quite different subjects, such as theology or law. If these subjects rested on certain authoritative texts (the Bible for theology, the Code of Justinian for law), then the humanist inevitably would claim that at the starting point of theological or juridical science, in the critical evaluation of texts and the determination of their meaning, the principles of humanistic philology and textual analysis must govern.

Schemes of Practical Reform. John Colet and his English disciples, of whom the greatest and most famous was Sir Thomas More, hoped to revitalize faith and reform the Church through two main courses of action. First, they worked for a humanist educational reform that would indoctrinate the future ruling class of England with the humanistic learning, the moral character, and the personal piety that formed their ideal. Second, they expected their ruler, the young, intelligent, and friendly Henry VIII (1509–47), to provide royal leadership for Church reform, using his influence and especially his control of Church patronage to provide an educated, pious, and righteous hierarchy for the Church in England. Unfortunately for them, Henry VIII cared more for his personal power than for reform of the Church. Although he did eventually pose as a Church reformer, his real goal was to magnify his own power and glory. While many humanists loyally served him, the noblest, bravest, and clearest-headed of Colet's disciples, Thomas More, eventually defied royal authority and died a martyr's death in witness to his firm belief in Christian unity and in the freedom of the Church from political control.

Erasmus of Rotterdam (1469–1536)

The greatest of all the Northern humanists, Desiderius Erasmus of Rotterdam, has been mentioned several times already, for no discussion of Christian humanism is possible without discussing the beliefs, hopes, and actions of this internationally famous scholar. The illegitimate son of a Dutch priest, Erasmus received a good start in classical studies in the famous town school at Deventer. Though he later criticized his early education, his own conception of sound religion was close kin to the personal piety and moralism of the Devotio Moderna, the Dutch religious movement that had influenced several of his teachers. After being orphaned, he and his brother were railroaded into a monastery by their guardian, but Erasmus managed to continue his classical studies and eventually to get himself sent to Paris for theological training. He pieced out his insecure financial aid by tutoring wealthier students and came in touch with the early humanists at Paris. Soon he was known as a skilled Latin stylist and a promising young man of letters, but he had no real sense of his life's work until a visit to England brought him into touch with Colet and his circle.

Biblical Humanism. From Colet Erasmus took his idea of Biblical humanism, that is, the application of humanist scholarly tools to get a clearer understanding of the heroic spirit and pure practice of the early Christian Church, as an essential first step toward reform of the church in modern times. But if he were to devote his life to this rediscovery of Christian origins, he must master Greek, the original language of the New Testament.

What completed his personal definition of this program of recovering Christian Antiquity was his discovery of Valla's *Annotations on the New Testament.* From this book, which he edited and published in 1505, Erasmus got a clearer idea of how to apply humanist linguistic and textual techniques to the critical evaluation of the sources of Christianity. Also, he found confirmation of his belief that the traditional Latin Bible was defective and that any serious study of the Scriptures must go back to the Greek text. The ultimate product of this Biblical scholarship was the famous edition of the Greek New Testament which he published in 1516, accompanied by a new Latin translation and by notes. This work, despite its many defects, was the first Greek text of the New Testament actually made available to scholars, and it had a great impact on religious scholarship, being welcomed by some as a new light on divine truth and denounced by others as a reckless and subversive attack on Catholic tradition. Erasmus seconded his work on the New Testament by a series of important editions and Latin translations of the writings of early leaders of the Church.

His Popular Works. Although this scholarly editorial work, together with similar textual research on ancient pagan authors, occupied the bulk of Erasmus's time, his fame rested also on more popular works (though still written in Latin) that set forth his ideas on true, spiritual religion and castigated the abuses in contemporary religion. In a serious vein, his *Enchiridion* (1503) set forth a pattern of Christian piety in which the inner spirit, rather than formalized, external acts, constitutes the essence of true religion. This same view of religion underlies his most famous book, the satirical *Praise of Folly* (1509), which has many harsh things to say about the vain and worldly popes, prelates, theologians, and monks of that age.

Perhaps even more influential because of its use as a school manual of Latin conversation was the collection of dialogues called familiar *Colloquies* (1519 and after), which dealt with many subjects, but mainly with the contrast between sound and unsound religion. Erasmus himself was neither a teacher nor a statesman, but a professional writer and scholar, and his popular writings made him the universally acknowledged leader of Northern humanists, as well as the most famous spokesman of all those who struggled for a humanist-inspired religious reform within the traditional Roman Catholic Church.

The shattering of Christian unity after 1517, and the unbearable pressures of those who wanted him to endorse Luther and share the leadership of the Reformation and those who wanted him to condemn the new heretics flatly and issue a blanket endorsement of the Church as it then was, darkened the later years of Erasmus. Although he finally made an open break with Luther, Erasmus maintained his agitation for reform of religion, though he became less reckless in what he said about the old Church. Thus he came under attack from extremists on both sides of the Reformation.

Erasmus actually was remarkably consistent in his demands for reform. He had no desire to replace the narrow dogmatism of bigoted Catholics with the narrow dogmatism of bigoted Lutherans. He had no intention of separating himself from the ancient institutional Church. What he did wish was to inspire all Christians to put aside dogmatic intricacies and meaningless formalism, and to develop a personal closeness to God, and then to live righteous and servicable lives that harmonized with their avowed beliefs.

Other Biblical Humanists

Similar to Erasmus's desire to recover the Greek sources of Christianity, but less widely popular, was the effort of the illustrious German lawyer and humanist Johann Reuchlin (1455–1522) to probe the ancient Hebrew sources. Reuchlin not only produced textbooks for the study of Hebrew language but also investigated Jewish religious books, chiefly the Cabalistic writings, which he thought would help the Christian faith.

A similar eagerness to study classical and Christian Antiquity and thus to stimulate Church reform grew up in France, where the scholar Jacques Lefèvre d'Étaples (1450?–1536) returned from Italy eager to apply humanistic techniques to the study of Aristotle, the chief authority of scholastic education. But Lefèvre was also a deeply religious person, attracted by the otherworldly spirit of the Florentine Neoplatonists. Soon he turned to the Bible, concentrating like Colet and Erasmus on the task of elucidating the simple, literal meaning of the New Testament and brusquely dismissing the results of centuries of intricate scholastic Biblical exegesis as either incorrect or beside the point.

Lefèvre was in many ways a rather cautious and conservative Church reformer. The kind of practical reform he clearly could endorse was the work of his disciple and patron Bishop Guillaume Briconnet in the diocese of Meaux, using the lawful episcopal authority to force the clergy to do their jobs, to restrict the encouragement of materialistic and superstitious religious observances, and to provide for systematic preaching, religious instruction, and moral supervision in all his parishes. But by the early 1520s, when this reform got under way, such practices seemed too "Lutheran" for the conservatives to endure, and the reformers at Meaux were discredited by the fact that some of Lefèvre's younger friends adopted Lutheran beliefs and eventually fled into exile in Germany.

The French "evangelical" reformers also had the sympathy of the sister of King Francis I, Marguerite, duchess of Angoulême, and occasionally of the king himself. But like Henry VIII in England, Francis I was more interested in his own power than in thoroughgoing reform of the Church, and the followers of Lefèvre faced frequent persecution by conservatives who classed them as Lutherans. So long as they waited for the king to take the lead, they waited in vain; and except for their scholarly publications and their encouragement of classical education, the French humanists had little to show for their reform efforts.

Church Reform in Spain

In terms of practical accomplishment, the most successful reformers were the Spanish, largely because they had the immense power and prestige of royal authority behind a reform program that was not solely humanistic, but was rather a shrewd and successful blend of humanistic techniques with more traditional and more conservative reforms.

Two individuals, neither of them a humanist, were instrumental in a reform program that left Spain with the best-disciplined church in all of Christendom. One of them was the great Queen Isabella. Her contribution was crucial, for she consistently used her control of Church appointments not to flatter great noble families and to reward royal servants, as in most other countries, but to provide effective leadership for the Church. More directly involved in conceiving and executing the reform was her father confessor, Ximenes de Cisneros (1436–1517), a brilliant man who abandoned a successful career as an ecclesiastical politician to work out his personal salvation in a Franciscan monastery, but who was dragged back into worldly affairs in 1492 when Queen Isabella appointed him her confessor. He used his control of the queen's conscience to exert royal influence in behalf of reform.

Though Ximenes became a cardinal of the Roman Church, archbishop of Toledo, and head of the powerful Spanish Inquisition, he was essentially an austere friar devoted to spiritual matters. Hence much of his reform activity, such as compelling the various orders, monasteries, and cathedral chapters to conform to the rigorous, ascetic manner of living demanded by their vows, was conservative and traditional. Likewise the least attractive and most notorious aspect of the Spanish Church, its brutal use of the Inquisition to extirpate the large Jewish and Moslem communities and to terrorize their converted descendants, had no relation to Renaissance humanism but was, in fact, contrary to most humanists' distaste for persecution. This policy was motivated largely by a political desire to establish the new Spanish nation on an ideological foundation of Catholic orthodoxy.

Cardinal Ximenes and Humanist Education. Cardinal Ximenes had lived at the papal curia in Rome and was aware of the possible utility of humanistic education. His goal was to provide a new kind of leadership for the Spanish Church, chiefly by raising the caliber of men appointed as bishops. Since Ximenes constantly advised the king and queen on such appointments, his influence over more than two decades led to much improvement. Effective, hard-working, dedicated bishops had the power to influence all levels of the Church, both lay and clerical.

But if this reform of the episcopate were to last, it was important to provide a dependable supply of clerical leaders for the future. So Cardinal Ximenes became an educational reformer, chiefly by founding not just a new university, but a new kind of university. The University of Alcalá, which he founded, was intended to educate the religious leaders of the next generation. In organizing it, Ximenes deliberately drew upon humanist theory and practice. The aim of this university was not merely the imparting of professional skills but the formation of virtuous character grounded in earnest Christian piety. In the interests of this goal, the university was divided into small colleges so that the intellectual, moral, and religious development of the students could be effectively watched and directed. One of the colleges was even to be a trilingual college, giving the instruction in classical Latin, Greek, and Hebrew that humanists like Erasmus (who had many Spanish admirers) regarded as essential for any sound Biblical theology. There was to be no medical school and only a limited attention to law, for the university was to be a trainer of future bishops, not a trainer of men headed for secular careers.

Although the reform of the Spanish Church was humanistic only in part, it had a more immediate practical effect than the humanistic reform proposals in other nations. The Spanish Church entered the Reformation crisis with the best-educated and most sincerely devoted body of bishops in any Catholic nation. Because of this able leadership and because of the popular spiritual revival they both encouraged and disciplined, the Church in Spain was the only large national branch of the whole Catholic Church that did not collapse in the face of the Protestant challenge.

Opposition to Humanist Reformers

Although the Christian humanists of the early sixteenth century were earnest and able men, with no desire for the destruction of Catholic unity or faith, many leading churchmen and laymen regarded them with hostility. The humanists' harsh repudiation of beliefs and practices widely followed and, still more, their bitter repudiation of the medieval cultural and religious heritage made them suspect. They often seemed flippant, irreverent, and recklessly destructive.

Certain influential groups in the religious and educational establishment had particular reason to fear and resent them. As we have noted earlier, even though humanism, strictly defined, dealt with a limited group of subjects, its techniques when it was conceived as a method of inquiry were applicable to nearly every field of study. A canon lawyer who suddenly was told that the Donation of Constantine was a forgery, a civil lawyer who was told that some revered medieval legal commentator had misunderstood a section of the Roman law, or a theologian who was told that a biblical passage he was using in a proof was a mistranslation of the original Greek, knew well that humanism might intrude into his own special field. Though he never said it in so many words, Erasmus obviously believed that a scholastic theologian who had spent half a lifetime earning his university doctorate in theology was utterly incompetent to theologize unless he also learned to understand the Greek New Testament. Of all the scholastic vested-interest groups, the friars and monks were the most likely to be antihumanist, since they were powerful in the theological faculties and also since the Erasmian religious ideal implicitly denied the traditional superiority of their way of life.

So long as the humanists were confined to relatively uninfluential posts in the faculties of liberal arts and in secondary schools, the conservative Catholics were not greatly alarmed. Like all large institutions (like modern universities as well), the medieval university knew how to contain and at the same time limit dissent and conflict within itself and also how to discredit the occasional individual who refused to conform to the traditional proprieties. Furthermore, the friars within the university were the most effective popular preachers, and they sometimes used their sermons to scandalize the faithful and bring public pressure to bear on anyone they regarded as dangerous. Where the traditional religious inquisition still had power or where a modernized substitute had been created, as in Spain, the friars also controlled this tribunal and on occasion could ruthlessly play the double role of accusers and judges.

Growth of Humanist Influence

In the early sixteenth century, two developments occurred that threatened the traditional system of thought control. As the fashion for Italian culture spread among the royal courts and urban oligarchies of Northern Europe, the principal humanists secured direct access to the rulers of nations and cities. Erasmus is the best but not the only example. He corresponded with popes, cardinals, bishops, emperors, kings, secular nobles, and town councillors. Both in person and by letter he promoted his program of humanist reform. The pope, the Emperor Charles V, the king of England, and the king of France contended for the honor of being his patron and having him reside at their court. Such a person could, of course, be opposed, criticized, even accused of impiety and heresy, but he could not be silenced, and he could not be dealt with quietly within the confines of polite academic society.

The Power of the Press. Even more important than the social prestige of the humanists, and in large part underlying it, was their increasingly effective use of the printing press—a relatively new and very potent force—to mold public opinion. When the printing press was first perfected in western Germany during the 1450s, it was chiefly used to print Church servicebooks, Bibles, tracts of religious edification, chivalric romances, university and school textbooks, texts of classical authors, and serious humanistic works about Antiquity. But in the early sixteenth century, the small tract or pamphlet, cheaply printed in great numbers, and sold at a low price, began to emerge as a new weapon in the hands of persons who wanted to appeal to public opinion over the heads of university faculties, religious orders, or other constituted authorities.

The authorities saw the danger and acted to control the press, but except for works injurious to political authority, that control was not very effective until mid-sixteenth century. The friars' near-monopoly over the pulpit no longer implied control of public opinion. Among the literate upper and middle classes of the towns, among the teachers, lawyers, and even many of the ordinary parish clergy, the humanists spread their ideas by short, inexpensive, widely circulated, and highly popular tracts. Contested issues in Church reform, university education, and scholarship no longer were kept from the wider reading public, or no longer reached them only when some friar preached a sermon denouncing a certain individual or belief as dangerous to the faith. The conflicts of the early sixteenth century were fought out in the forum of public opinion, and to an even greater extent the conflicts of the Protestant Reformation a short generation later were argued before the public. The humanists and those Protestants who had mastered humanist techniques were far abler contenders in this new forum of the printed word than were the defenders of tradition.

The most famous pre-Reformation example of how the scales of power had shifted was an ugly controversy that broke out in 1510 over the opposition of the German humanist Johann Reuchlin to the attempt by a fanatical Jewish convert to Christianity, Johann Pfefferkorn, to have all Jewish books burned. Pfefferkorn had the backing of the German Dominicans, of the conservative theological faculty of the University of Cologne, and of many influential individuals. Reuchlin, who was consulted because of his mastery of Hebrew, opposed the plan, partly because he feared it would thwart his desire for Christian theologians to understand the Jewish background of their faith and partly because of the blatant injustice of Pfefferkorn's plan to seize the property of quiet, peaceable people who (whatever their religious errors) had rights under the imperial law which he as a lawyer felt bound to uphold.

An exchange of scurrilous, vituperative (and vernacular) pamphlets between Reuchlin and Pfefferkorn led to the lodging of a formal complaint by the chief inquisitor, the Dominican Jacob van Hochstraten, against Reuchlin's pamphlet *Augenspiegel* on the grounds that it was intemperate, offensive to pious persons, and too sympathetic to the Jews. Reuchlin had both legal ability and influential friends, and the case was fought before many jurisdictions, up to and including the papal curia, from 1510 to 1520. Hochstraten finally won on a second appeal to Rome, but Reuchlin was not destroyed by his enemies, and his final loss involved only a formal retraction and the obligation to pay the court costs.

What really made the case significant, however, was that although at first few other humanists cared to defend the Jews, in time a considerable number of them concluded (wrongly, perhaps) that the Dominican attack was really directed at the whole humanist enterprise of recovering the Greek and Hebrew texts of Scripture. A group of hotheads anonymously wrote and published a slanderous attack on the theologians and Dominicans of Cologne in the form of a collection of coarse, ungrammatical, and unflattering Latin letters that purported to be written *against* Reuchlin by friends of the inquisitor Hochstraten, though actually they were written *for* Reuchlin by his self-appointed defenders. This work, *The Letters of Obscure Men*, written mainly by the humanists Crotus Rubianus and Ulrich von Hutten, was a literary bombshell. It did worse than attack the Cologne friars and theologians: it made them a laughingstock by presenting them as a pack of morally depraved, incompetent, and unlearned nincompoops. The bitterness of the attack (which embarrassed the conservative Reuchlin) and the popularity it had in Germany both expressed and helped to cause a growing loss of respect for Church and university authorities.

The Dangers of Humanism

Whether humanism could have produced really effective Church reform without the agonies of religious separation, persecution, and war that the Protestant Reformation set loose has been much debated. In Spain, it helped in a successful reform, but direction of the reform was not in humanist hands. Even though all of the major humanists remained within the Catholic Church at the time of the Reformation, many of their younger disciples concluded that the Protestant way, not the humanist way, was the only effective plan of reform.

Perhaps, therefore, the conservative critics were not entirely wrong. The whole humanist program of scrapping more than a thousand years of historical development as an aberration of the Dark Ages and of accepting only the practice and belief of the early Church as found in the Bible, may well have been incompatible with the Catholic principles of Church authority and historical development. The humanists were disrespectful of tradition, and they wrote many things against Church ceremonies, fasting, pilgrimages, and the monastic orders that seemed quite as destructive as attacks made by the Lutheran heretics. Those humanists who were converted to Protestantism often broke with Catholic belief and practice far more sharply than Luther, no doubt because once they had renounced the authority of Rome, their humanistic desire for a total return to the ways of the Apostolic Church impelled them toward a radical rejection of all beliefs and practices, no matter how venerable, that the Bible did not prove to have existed in the age of the Apostles.

Furthermore, the Erasmian tradition, and even the Catholic Devotio Moderna that was the source of its underlying spiritual outlook, emphasized so greatly the inner life of the soul that it tended to give a highly subjective and rationalistic account of the effects of religious sacraments, prayers, and ceremonies, explaining away all the semimagical and miraculous element of religion and explaining religious experience exclusively as a mental process, almost as a modern nonreligious psychologist might do. The revolutionary implications of the humanist views of return to the past and concentration on inner spirituality may never have been intended, but they were implicitly present all along.

Northern Renaissance Art

A pilgrimage to Italy to study classical languages and literature under Italian humanists became one of the proprieties of sixteenth-century Northern humanism. Rudolf Agricola, John Colet, Lefèvre d'Étaples, and Erasmus himself had all done it, and clearly they had learned much from Italian classical scholarship. A similar pilgrimage to Italy became fashionable for Northern European artists. Northern art through the end of the fifteenth century continued to be dominated by the spirit and the style of the Flemish school. Though works of this school exported to Italy exerted some influence on the development of Italian painting, the Flemings showed little reciprocal interest in the epoch-making developments of Early Renaissance art. There was a growth of artistic skill and achievement in other parts of Northern Europe, especially in Germany, late in the fifteenth century, but even this art, though more open to Italian influences, stood within the Northern tradition developed in Flanders. The printing of engravings of works of art helped to break down local isolation and to increase interest in what the Italians had been doing, and late in the fifteenth and early in the sixteenth century, a number of Northern artists did visit Italy, inspect some of the Italian masterpieces, and incorporate certain Italianate elements in paintings that were still essentially non-Renaissance in conception and technique. This Germanic art produced many respectable works, and one truly great painter, Matthias Grünewald (ca. 1475–1528), whose greatest work, the Isenheim Altarpiece, is typically Northern in its mood and surface appearance. Yet careful analysis reveals a sense of movement, a vigor of bodily form, and a unity of conception that suggest Italian Renaissance influence.

Albrecht Dürer

The development of a stronger influence by Italian Renaissance art in Northern Europe is bound up with the career of Grünewald's more famous contemporary, Albrecht Dürer (1471–1528). A native of the rich and powerful south German town of Nuremberg, which had strong commercial links with northern Italy, and a friend of Nuremberg's influential humanists, Dürer visited Italy as a youth and also spent the whole period 1505–07 living in Venice and studying Italian art. Although he did not surrender his own individuality, Dürer consciously adopted the Renaissance. He not only mastered Italian advances in perspective and anatomy but composed treatises of his own on the theory of art, something that the artist-craftsmen of the North would never have thought to do. He self-consciously cultivated his own artistic personality, executing a number of remarkable self-portraits and keeping a diary and a series of notebooks. He gained his widest fame from woodcuts and engravings that were printed and then sold widely throughout Europe. In religion he was a supporter of Erasmian reform and a sympathizer with Luther. He tried in his later works to develop an austere style suitable for the art of a reformed Christianity, represented by the work

The Four Apostles, which in 1526 he presented as a gift to his native city shortly after it had become officially Lutheran.

The Protestant fear of idolatry posed a crisis for artists, and Dürer's longer-lived contemporary Lucas Cranach the Elder (1472–1553) not only had to assimilate Italian influences but also, living at Wittenberg in the heartland of Lutheran Germany, had to abandon religious for secular themes that raised no danger of idolatrous abuse. Though pagan classical themes and paintings of daily life provided some of the new material for Protestant art, the greatest success was in portrait painting. Already in the fifteenth century, Northern art had developed a psychological depth in portraiture that even the great Italian masters did not surpass. This tradition, transmuted into something new by the acquisition of Renaissance skills, is shown in the many portraits of Hans Holbein the Younger (1497–1543), who for many years was court painter to Henry VIII of England. Alongside these native Northern developments, much Italian Renaissance influence came north by direct importation of Italian works and even Italian artists. The kings of France, with their great wealth and their constant military and political adventures in Italy, were especially active in this respect; and Francis I (1515–47) scored the greatest coup by enticing the aged Leonardo da Vinci to France, where he died in 1519.

The Religious Situation in 1517: Impending Revolution

On the eve of the Protestant Reformation in 1517, intellectual and religious dominance in the North had begun to pass from the hands of the feudal aristocracy, the friars, and the scholastics of the universities into the hands of humanists and artists who had learned much from the Italian Renaissance but who also had religious and intellectual attitudes that were distinctly non-Italian. Furthermore, these new intellectual leaders were beginning to discover in the printing press a way of getting their ideas across to a mass audience and so of short-circuiting the mastery that preaching friars and scholastic theologians had held for centuries over the minds and souls of Northern Europeans. Whether humanism also had the ability to carry through the spiritual and cultural reforms its leaders had conceived is open to question. Like its Italian predecessor, Northern humanism had a strongly aristocratic tendency that made it reluctant to appeal to the masses. Though Latin was of course widely understood, it is still true that the choice of Latin for all the works of Erasmus, for More's *Utopia*, even for the rabble-rousing *Letters of Obscure Men*, bespeaks a desire to confine serious discussion to an educated elite and to carry through reform over the heads of the masses.

But the emergence of Martin Luther late in 1517 as a spokesman for a new type of reform changed all of this. The age of orderly humanistic reform and of quiet discussion of matters that only learned men could comprehend came to an end. The age of turbulent mass movements, of violent social and spiritual upheavals, and of appeals to the common man in his own tongue had opened. Northern humanism doubtless prepared the way for religious revolution, though of course the blind unspirituality and gross corruption of the late-medieval Church hierarchy were more fundamental causes. But for reform pressure to be transmuted into religious revolution, something new had to be added. That was the historic contribution of Martin Luther.

Chapter Six

Reformation: Luther and the German Upheaval

The notion that the Protestant Reformation that began in 1517 marks the end of medieval history and the beginning of the modern age is still widespread, though whether it is true or not depends on the meaning assigned to that tricky word *modern.* There can be no doubt, however, that the permanent breakdown of Christian unity that was an unwanted result of the Reformation did mark an important change in the history of Europe. Heretofore, all society had been based on the acceptance of the one "true religion" by all people, and all other institutions—marriage, property, education, the state—derived their sanction from the religious ideology acknowledged by all. The Church, the institution that embodied, created, and applied the prevailing ideology, controlled many matters that modern man regards as concerns of the secular state: education, censorship of books, and regulation of marriage and of many other types of legal relationship. The practical effect of the Reformation was to demolish, or at least decisively to weaken, the control of religious officials over life.

Why the Church Collapsed

This stunning collapse of the Church, the greatest institution of the Middle Ages, was the result of two types of causes: (1) the inherent weaknesses of the pre-Reformation Church and (2) the appearance of a new reform leadership that was both willing to defy constituted authority and able to carry a large part of the European population with it.

Corruption and worldliness among the established leaders of religion, as described in an earlier chapter, were only secondary causes of the collapse. The Church failed to destroy the heresies of the sixteenth century not because it was corrupt but because it was rigid and unadaptable. Hence its leaders were unable either to remedy the serious abuses that were generating sympathy for the heretics or to suppress dissent. This rigidity had become increasingly evident during the recurrent crises that faced the Church during the last century before the Reformation. The leadership not only failed to cope with heretics but also failed to cope with the spiritual intensity and reform demands of men and women who were (or wanted to be) orthodox Catholics.

Savonarola, a Frustrated Reformer

The most dramatic such failure in the generation before the Protestant Reformation was the cause of the revivalistic Dominican preacher Girolamo Savonarola at Florence. He first rose to fame and to political influence through his eloquent sermons urging a moral regeneration of Florentine society and prophesying divine punishment for the sins of the people. These prophecies seemed to be borne out by the political catastrophe of the French invasion of Italy in 1494. During the four years of democratic political reforms that followed the ouster of the Medici rulers of the city in 1494, Savonarola became the most powerful figure in the restored republic, though he held no public office. He used his influence in favor of two goals: democratization of the government and moral and religious reform of the city. Although he did claim to be guided by divine inspiration, Savonarola certainly preached no heretical doctrines. Yet because both his reform program and his foreign policy ran counter to the interests of Pope Alexander VI (the most worldly and corrupt of the Renaissance popes), the papacy intrigued with his political enemies within Florence to destroy his influence. The eventual result was his burning on charges of heresy (23 May 1498). The destruction of Savonarola shows the great power of the Church hierarchy, but it also shows that the hierarchy could deal with an earnest and able reformer only by treating him as a rebel.

The Plight of Catholic Reformers

A similar inability to cope with Catholic reformers, except by forcing them into open rebellion and then discrediting them and destroying them on charges of heresy, lies behind the attacks that churchmen in Northern Europe were making against humanist reformers like Erasmus, Lefèvre d'Étaples, and Johann Reuchlin during the last decade before the Reformation. These reforming humanists of the North were not executed on charges of heresy, but each of them was accused. Any person who agitated vehemently, persistently, and publicly for Church reform soon discovered that the way of the reformer was dangerous and that the zealous Christian was more likely than the lukewarm one to get into trouble. The best and noblest spirits were under constant pressure to moderate or abandon their agitation for reforms they knew were desperately needed. The official Church was no longer able to make effective use of its ablest members. It could only drive them to the despair of silence or the even deeper despair of open rebellion.

Indeed, the pre-Reformation Church hierarchy should have already learned that it could no longer suppress dissident movements that had strong political backing. Rome's clumsy and two-faced attempts to suppress the heretical followers of John Huss in the kingdom of Bohemia after the burning of Huss in 1415 merely solidified Bohemian national spirit behind the heretical religious movement. While the Catholic leadership was able to keep Bohemia in a state of war and turmoil during much of the fifteenth century, it was not able to suppress the new religion. A century before the Reformation began in Germany in 1517, Bohemia had already demonstrated what a potent mix religious discontent and national sentiment could be.

Unclarity on Dogma. A further weakness of the pre-Reformation Church was the remarkable lack of clarity about many of its teachings. Such questions as the relative importance of faith and good works in the salvation of man, or the relative weight to be assigned to the authority of Scripture and the authority of Church tradition, had never been clearly defined. When Luther in 1517 taught that man is justified by faith alone or when he declared that Scripture was the sole authoritative source of Christian doctrine, he may have been teaching error, but he was not denying authoritatively defined Catholic dogma, for on those two central questions of the Reformation debate, the Church up to 1517 (and long after) had made no authoritative decision. The teaching of the Church was so unclear that it was quite possible for loyal Catholics to argue after 1517 that Luther was not wrong in his views on the justification of man.

Indeed, on the eve of the Reformation, Catholic Europe was still not entirely agreed about just who had the right to make a binding determination of the doctrines of the church. Even St. Thomas Aquinas, propapal friar though he was, had taught merely that the power to define dogma resided "chiefly" in the popes. The late-medieval conciliarists argued that the supreme power of defining true doctrine belonged only to a properly assembled General Council representing the whole Church. Already before Luther, the biblical humanists did much to popularize the idea that all doctrine must be based exclusively on Scripture. During the early debates of the Reformation, few even of the most devoted defenders of the old religion taught clearly and unequivocally that Church tradition had equal dogmatic authority alongside the words of the Bible.

Thus although (except for Bohemia) Rome's spiritual mastery seemed as complete as it had been under Pope Innocent III three centuries earlier, papal absolutism by 1500 had been seriously undermined. Many apparently sound Catholics denied unconditional papal control over dogma. Many of the doctrines that later became characteristic Protestant viewpoints seemed to many Catholics well within the bounds of orthodox teaching. And the notorious corruption and worldliness of her leaders not only at Rome but throughout Europe stimulated the growth of a sullen hostility to Rome and a deeply frustrated demand for drastic reform. This hostility and frustration were greatest not among foes of religion and the Church but among the most devoted Christians. Finally, the growing national self-consciousness of the various European peoples made the arrogant power and wealth of Rome increasingly unpalatable. There was a danger that one or more of the larger nations would follow the example of Bohemia and throw off Roman control.

That Germany eventually led the way was no surprise. Perhaps because thay lacked a strong monarchy to protect them from papal exactions, the Germans had long been known as the most antipapal, as well as the most deeply pious, people in Europe.

Luther and the Need for a New Ideology

Whether all these latent revolutionary forces would eventually have produced a religious revolution without the personal leadership and specific ideology provided by Martin Luther is perhaps a pointless question. In actual fact, the deepening religious crisis did not reach the point of revolution until Martin Luther provided the second major causative force: a new leadership.

Martin Luther proved to be one of the greatest religious leaders in human history. He did not set out to precipitate a spiritual upheaval or even to become a leader. He sought first and foremost answers to his own personal quest for assurance of salvation. He began his career within the old Church structure as a priest, theologian, and friar. Yet in the course of his own personal search for spiritual assurance, he developed (at first without even suspecting it) the one essential thing that made it possible to lead a rebellion against the traditional church. This was a new ideology. Once he had found it, and had realized to his surprise and horror that the Church hierarchy was teaching something quite different, he had found the basis for a total repudiation of the authority of the unreformed Church. This ability to make a frontal attack on the authority of the hierarchy and on the truth of traditional dogmas was the secret of his success.

Secure in his own beliefs, and firm in his rejection of Rome, Luther attacked with a power and an assurance which made him a far more formidable antagonist that any reforming humanist, even than a brilliant preacher like Savonarola. So long as reformers accepted the authority of Rome, they were trapped by their very act of acceptance and were doomed to be either silenced or destroyed. What saved Martin Luther from a similar fate was his radicalism. At a rather early stage, though at first with surprise and reluctance, he realized that he had to attack not the abuses or even the corrupt individuals, but the institution of the Church itself, its claims to authority and its ideological foundations. His own personal development as a man and as a Christian believer compelled him to maintain his conception of true religion even though all Christendom came tumbling down.

Luther's Early Development

Because his own personal development was the source of the new set of religious ideas that emboldened him to defy the authority of the church, Luther's biography is a significant part of the history of his age. He was born at Eisleben, Germany, in 1483, the son of a man who had risen from peasant origins to substantial prosperity in the iron mining and smelting industry and who, like many an ambitious father, dreamed of raising his son still higher up in society by providing him with a university education in the lucrative profession of law. Both parents were pious. Both parents were strict. But neither the piety nor the strict family discipline were unusual for the people of their class. Young Martin Luther proved to be a promising scholar, and after his graduation from the University of Erfurt with bachelor's and master's degree in liberal arts, he returned to the university in the summer of 1505 to enroll in the faculty of law.

Up to that summer, Martin Luther's career was a story of academic success and filial obedience. Yet all was not as well as it seemed. Martin was not content with his commitment to the study of law. In some way that we shall never entirely fathom, religion lay at the center of his discontent. This discontent surfaced unexpectedly in the summer of 1505 when Martin, in route back to Erfurt from a visit home, was caught in the forest by a terrible thunderstorm. In terror for his life and for his soul, he vowed that if he were spared, he would become a monk. Two weeks later he entered the strict and highly respected order of Augustinian Hermits at Erfurt. He was aged 21. His father was furious when he learned of this decision, for it meant an end to his dream of having a successful lawyer son, an end to his dream that future generations of Luthers would be established in the upper reaches of Germany society.

Luther's Problem

These outward events were only dim reflections of the turmoil deep within the soul of Martin Luther. The decision to enter the monastery was not the result of a momentary impulse. Young Luther had a "problem," a problem that modern secular scholars may attempt to define and discuss in terms of psychological conflict and maturation but that Luther and his contemporaries conceived in purely religious terms. This problem was the question of his own personal righteousness in the eyes of God. The question with which he struggled was how a person so imperfect and sinful as himself could ever appear righteous (and hence worthy of salvation) in the judgment of an all-knowing and perfect God. This does not mean that Luther was unusually sinful. Indeed, compared with most men he led an exemplary life. But he was keenly aware that even his best efforts at righteous living must seem pitifully inadequate when measured against the absolute standard of divine righteousness. Hence Luther became deeply depressed, burdened with an acute sense of sin. His early religious training had made him think of God as the stern judge who would damn man eternally for his sins. Although this medieval tradition also taught that God through Christ had extended forgiveness to man, Luther conceived that this forgiveness was available only through the institutional Church, which required each believer to perform works of piety and charity sufficient to offset sins. The unresolved question for Luther was how he could ever gain assurance that he had done enough good works to offset his guilt.

Luther's problem was not in itself unusual for deeply religious persons brought up in the religious system of late medieval Catholicism, although the pathological acuteness with which he felt the problem was uncommon. The Church itself offered many ways of achieving righteousness through acts of worship and of charity. By becoming a monk, Luther embraced the highest form of meritorious Catholic living. Once in the monastery, Luther not only accepted this pattern of living but accepted it with an uncommon stringency. Over and above what all monks performed, Luther adopted special fasts, vigils, and prayers. He denied himself even innocent and permissible comforts, such as adequate blankets in cold weather. Yet the same question constantly recurred. How could he be sure that these good works were acceptable to God and adequate to offset his sins?

Despite these inner troubles, Martin Luther made great progress within the Augustinian order. Although his monastic superior, the learned and kindly Johann Staupitz, was puzzled by Brother Martin's recurrent moods of despair, he realized that his young disciple was a man of deep religious devotion and great intellectual power. He constantly reminded Martin that God was forgiving as well as righteous, and he insistently directed him to the Bible for help. Most important of all, Staupitz decided to compel Luther to quit concentrating on his own problem by becoming actively involved in service to others. In 1508 he dispatched Luther to the Augustinian study house at the new University of Wittenberg, where he began teaching moral philosophy in the arts faculty while studying for a doctorate in theology. Staupitz then signed over to Luther his own position as professor of theology at Wittenberg.

Luther also became active in other ways. In 1510 he was one of two Augustinians sent to represent his branch of the order on official business at Rome. In 1511 he became superior of the Augustinian monastery at Wittenberg. In 1514 he joined to his professional duties the task of preaching regularly in one of the Wittenberg churches. Despite his anguish of soul,

Brother Martin Luther was becoming an important personage in his little corner of the world.

Luther's Evangelical Theology

Although his valiant quest for holiness as a monk did not solve his spiritual problems, Luther's work as a professor of theology did. His teaching duties required close study and careful public explication of various books of the Old and New Testaments. In the course of this biblical study, perhaps as early as 1514, Luther discovered the solution to the theological "problem" that had bedevilled him, the problem of how man, though a sinner, can achieve righteousness in the eyes of God. His great discovery, drawn largely from his study and teaching of the Epistles of St. Paul, was that there is no way in which man can achieve righteousness in the traditional sense of performing good works that earn him merit before God.

How, then, is man to be reconciled to God? The answer, which implied a radically different conception of God and ultimately a radically new system of theology, is that man's justification is achieved by the wholly unmerited grace of God, who for reasons known only to Himself has chosen to save man from the damnation he so richly deserves. Justification comes not through good works done by man, but through a free gift from God, for God is not only the stern and righteous judge of sinful man, but also the loving Father who sacrificed his only begotten Son on the Cross in order to atone for man's sins. Jesus Christ through his voluntary sacrifice on the Cross assumed the immense burden of human sins. Man's sinfulness does not alienate God eternally because the merits of Christ (not of man) outweigh it.

But how does man gain this unmerited grace that makes him acceptable to God? Here Luther's study of the Bible was crucial, for he found in St. Paul's Epistle to the Romans (1:17) a passage which he later called "the gates of Paradise" and which he regarded as the true essence of Christian faith: "The righteous man shall live by faith." If man is saved by faith, then he is not saved by his own works. It is likely that Luther was already teaching this interpretation of St. Paul as early as 1515 or 1516, though not till later, perhaps not until 1518 or after, did he fully comprehend its significance.

Revolutionary Consequences of the New Theology

Luther's new ideological direction had potentially revolutionary consequences. The assertion that man depends for his salvation wholly on divine grace freely given to the faithful and that no human work, not even the most apparently noble and virtuous, is able to contribute to man's eternal righteousness, utterly demolished the value of traditional religious and moral practices through which medieval Catholics hoped to gain divine favor. The whole system of sacramental grace mediated to man through the Church lost its foundation and so did the special control over man's destiny that the medieval Church had imposed through the clergy's monopoly control over the channels of sacramental grace. A natural consequence of Luther's fundamental doctrine of justification by faith alone (rather than by faith *and* works, as the church had long taught) was his denial that the clergy have special spiritual powers not granted to laymen. This was expressed in his doctrine of the priesthood of all believers. All believing Christians, he concluded, are priests, though not all are called to an active ministry.

These two basic Lutheran doctrines, justification by faith alone and the priesthood of all believers, inevitably led Luther to a practical conclusion that he reached with great difficulty, and not before the period 1518–20: that the traditional Church, far from being infallible as it claimed, was teaching false doctrine and thus was misleading souls into excruciating doubts (like Luther's own) or into a false confidence that might bring them to eternal damnation.

This false teaching in the field of doctrine, he further concluded, lay at the root of the worldliness and corruption against which humanists and other would-be reformers struggled. The Catholic doctrine of clerical authority was invented in order to excuse and justify the enslavement of Christian believers to the clergy. The ultimate corruption was neither moral nor political nor financial, but theological, for all the specific instances of outward corruption flowed inevitably from a false theology that enslaved man to a theoretically endless round of works and so in practice also enslaved him to the clergy, who imposed and profited from the system of "good" works. If only man would return to the true doctrine of salvation by his own works, then man would be free: free from agonizing doubts about the sufficiency of his own good works, free from exploitation by the corrupt, power-crazed, and money-hungry Church leaders, and free from the danger of Hell.

True Christian reformation, therefore, involved first and foremost not mere tinkering with the details of Church ceremonies but a drastic abandonment of false doctrine and a return to the true doctrine of the New Testament. Luther's conclusions about the fundamental errors of the Church in doctrine meant that in the long run, quite unlike Erasmus or even Savonarola, he was able to justify to himself and to others a total repudiation of the authority of the Church hierarchy and to conclude that Scripture alone, not the traditions and authoritative definitions of a perverted hierarchy, was the sole source of authority for Christians. Hence unlike the humanists or even such a rebellious spirit as Savonarola, he could defy the institutional Church when it tried to silence him. Justification by faith alone, the priesthood of all believers, and the sole authority of Scripture: these were the three foundations on which Luther based his eventual rejection of the old Church and his creation of his own Evangelical (i.e., Gospel-based) religion.

Although Luther may have made his fundamental breakthrough to the first (and most important) of these three doctrines as early as 1513, he only gradually concluded that the existing Church institution was corrupt beyond redemption. His stormy debates with defenders of the old way after 1517 finally made him realize that his opinions were flatly contrary to what the clergy taught and that he must repudiate their claim to authority. Prior to 1517, he was quietly working out his new theology and teaching it to his students at Wittenberg with not the slightest suspicion that it would lead him into rebellion against the Church he loved. He might well have lived and died as nothing more than a prominent local figure in a new and relatively obscure university far out in the wilds of eastern Germany. Any divergence from Catholic dogma in his teaching and preaching might have remained unnoticed forever not only by the authorities but even by himself.

Reformation Begins: The Indulgence Scandal

What transformed Luther from a quiet, reforming educator into a towering figure of world history was his decision to speak out against a scandalous traffic in indulgences that he believed to be spiritually damaging to the souls of the laymen to whom he was ministering. Indulgences were based directly on the traditional scholastic theology Luther had already privately rejected. Indulgences grew out of the medieval Church's attempts to provide pastoral direction for repentant sinners. In the teaching of the Church, a sinner who confessed to a priest and received absolution was freed at once from guilt and eternal punishment that otherwise his sin would have brought upon him, but he was still subject to temporal (that is, not eternal) punishment so that the demands of divine justice were satisfied. In other words, the justice of God required that even a forgiven sinner should not get off scot-free. This temporal punishment might ultimately take the form of the soul's being required to spend a period of time in Purgatory, a place (or a condition) of temporary punishment created for the purification of souls that were ultimately bound for Heaven but whose record of sins made it seem improper that they should enter Heaven directly. But the temporal punishment might also be partly or wholly satisfied by works of penitence undertaken during this life. Thus good works undertaken to offset past sins played an integral part in the process whereby the forgiven sinner became reconciled to God and fit to enter Heaven without having to pass a long period of suffering in Purgatory. During the age of the Crusades, the Church began granting partial or plenary (full) indulgences, or remissions of the temporal penalty, to all who would go on Crusade. Later on, similar full or partial remission of temporal penalties were granted to absolved sinners who performed other pious works, such as going on pilgrimage to a distant shrine, performing special acts of self-denial and religious devotion, or even giving money for the support of some worthy and spiritually desirable cause. This last development eventually degenerated into the granting of indulgences for cash donations for any cause the ecclesiastical authorities wished to promote, so that in fact (though never in theory) indulgences were "sold."

The granting of indulgences also was stimulated by the growth of the doctrine of a "treasury of merits." This theory taught that since Christ and the saints in their lives had acquired far more merits through good works than were necessary for their own salvation, the surplus merits constituted an unlimited treasure that the pope could transfer to the benefit of other souls.

It is important to realize that the Church clearly taught that indulgences relieved the soul only of temporal penalties. The eternal penalty—the danger of eternal damnation—was remitted freely and instantaneously in the act of confessing to a priest and receiving absolution, thus being freed of the danger of Hell, before the indulgence could have any effect in freeing his soul from Purgatory. When the pope authorized an indulgence, he claimed merely to be transferring surplus merits from the treasury of merits in order to reduce or totally eliminate the sentence in Purgatory.

Nevertheless, even at its best, the late-medieval practice of indulgences was mechanical and materialistic. It is difficult, in describing it, to avoid terminology drawn from bookkeeping, for the concept of indulgences implies that each soul has a quantitative account that it owes to God and must bring into balance either by earning merits through good works or by transferring merits from the pope's "treasury of merits" through purchase of an indulgence. The Church's practice of assigning specific terms (so many years, months, and days) to the amount of remission from Purgatory further exaggerated this materialistic tendency.

In addition to this underlying defect, the doctrine of indulgences suffered from several other weaknesses that made it vulnerable to Luther's attack. First, the subtle distinction between remission of the eternal punishment gained freely through confession and the remission of temporal punishment gained by works of penance or by purchase of an indulgence was over the heads of most laymen and even of many of the grossly untrained clergy of the time. The unenlightened might well conclude that purchase of an indulgence could remove all guilt without the need for full confession and amendment of life, even though Rome taught no such thing. Second, since the Church did teach that one could acquire indulgences for the souls of deceased friends and relatives who were presumably still in Purgatory, there was one clear case that seemed to contradict the official teaching that contrition, or sorrow for sins, confession, and absolution must preclude any application of indulgences. The theory underlying indulgences for the dead was confused and essentially incompatible with the general theory of indulgences.

Third, although officially indulgences were not "sold," it was hard to distinguish between the sale of an indulgence and the free granting of an indulgence only after a cash donation had been made. Finally, whereas indulgences originated as a pastoral device for the benefit and comfort of souls, by the sixteenth century they were distributed chiefly to raise money for the papacy and for the local ecclesiastical authorities who participated. They had became a device that the hierarchy used to raise extra money for special needs: the financing of a crusade (which might be directed not against infidel Turks or Hussite heretics but against some Italian foe of the pope), for the creation of a new university (Wittenberg itself was partly financed by revenues from indulgences), or for the building of a new church.

Background of the German Indulgence

The particular indulgence against which Martin Luther spoke out was one of the worst conceived and worst administered in the history of the Church. It originated in 1506, when Pope Julius II decided to build a splendid new St. Peter's Cathedral at Rome and proclaimed an indulgence to raise money for the project. The next pope, Leo X, renewed the indulgence, but the terms on which it was preached in Germany after 1514 provide a remarkable example of the layer upon layer of corruption that disfigured the Church. In 1513, a young princeling of the house of Hohenzollern, Albert of Brandenburg, became archbishop of Magdeburg and administrator of the bishopric of Halberstadt, even though Church law forbade a man to hold more than one bishopric, and even though at age twenty-three he was seven years below the legal minimum age to be a bishop. He legalized this double illegality by paying heavy fees to Rome for a dispensation. Then in 1514 the Archbishop of Mainz, primate of all Germany and one of the seven electoral princes who would choose the next Holy Roman Emperor, died. Albert of Brandenburg wished to acquire this powerful position without giving up his other two bishoprics.

Pope Leo X, easygoing though he was, hesitated to authorize this further illegality, but his political interests in Germany prevailed. By approving Albert's election, he would acquire the political friendship not only of the new archbishop-elector of Mainz but also of his relative the electoral prince of Brandenburg. The prospect of assuring the political support of two of the seven German electors was so attractive that Pope Leo agreed to let him keep his other two bishoprics—but only if he would pay enormous sums for a dispensation. After much haggling, the two parties agreed that Albert would pay 10,000 ducats, a veritable fortune that he raised by taking a loan from the banker Jakob Fugger. In order to make it easier for Albert to repay this huge debt, Pope Leo agreed to extend to the archdiocese of Mainz the indulgence for St. Peter's Cathedral. Secretly it was agreed that half the proceeds would go to Archbishop Albert so that he could repay the Fugger bank. Thus ultimately the gullible German laity, by purchasing letters of indulgence, would pay for the illegal acts of pope and archbishop.

Martin Luther knew nothing of these sordid financial bargains, but he did know that the indulgence was to take money out of Germany to pay for the pope's new church. Furthermore, Luther soon heard that the indulgence preachers in the nearby lands of the duke of Saxony were making sweeping claims about the spiritual benefits available. Since the aim of the whole operation was to raise large sums of money quickly, the chief indulgence preacher, the Dominican friar Johann Tetzel, conducted a highly mercenary operation that seemed to offer instant and easy forgiveness to all who bought. Tetzel played on his hearers' love for their deceased relatives in Purgatory, urging that they could instantly release their loved ones from suffering in Purgatory by purchasing an indulgence in their behalf. His drastic teaching was widely summarized in the little jingle:

> As soon as the coin in the coffer rings,
> The soul from Purgatory's fire springs.

Both as a theologian and as a parish priest, Luther felt compelled to protest against the false sense of security that these claims would breed among laymen. Other would-be reformers, such as the humanists, had criticized indulgences because of the blatant greed and the superficial, mechanical religious observance they fostered, but Luther went much further. In the light of his new theology, he concluded that the whole basis of indulgences—even ones less obviously corrupt than this one—was mistaken. Quite simply, all indulgences were worthless. The pope, Luther concluded, had no power to release souls from any obligations except those he himself had imposed. If the pope really did have the power to release all souls from Purgatory, why did he not do so at once, out of Christian charity, without demanding money first?

The Ninety-five Theses

There were many questions in Martin Luther's mind in the early fall of 1517, as he set down a list of ninety-five theological propositions or theses concerning indulgences. Although he doubtless aimed mainly at the scandalous activities of Tetzel, Luther's Ninety-five Theses questioned the theological foundations of all indulgences, including those that his own prince, the Elector Frederick of Saxony, promoted each All Saints' Day in connection with the huge collection of saints' relics he had assembled.

The Ninety-five Theses did not explicitly state the doctrine of justification by faith alone. They certainly did not constitute an attack on the pope or the traditional Church institution, for Luther in 1517 still believed that Rome had never sanctioned the false assumptions on which indulgences were based. He merely urged that theological experts like himself should discuss and debate the doctrinal foundations of indulgences so that the church authorities could clarify the doctrine and correct certain obvious abuses.

An old tradition claims that Luther on 31 October 1517 publicly posted these Ninety-five Theses on the door of the castle church at Wittenberg and so (while intending nothing more than a scholarly debate) precipitated a public uproar, but the only action of his that can be adequately documented is that on or about 31 October he sent the theses, with an accompanying letter, to Archbishop Albert of Mainz and to several other bishops, thus calling certain abuses to their attention. Archbishop Albert never responded to this cautious raising of a serious question through proper ecclesiastical channels. Instead, he instructed his court officials to prepare an order commanding Luther to remain silent about indulgences and then wrote Rome denouncing Luther and urging that he be disciplined. The one bishop who did reply warned Luther in a friendly way that his theses would get him in trouble if he pursued the matter further. Especially if it is true that Luther never even posted the Latin text of the theses for debate, he had acted with great propriety as a Catholic theologian concerned about what he regarded as an improper and unauthorized practice. He had quietly gone through channels in order to bring his concern to the attention of the authorities. For his troubles, he got from the nobly born but theologically incompetent archbishop no reply but only an attempt to use the authority of the church to silence him.

The Controversy Becomes Public. In the face of official silence, Luther next sent copies of his theses to several German theologians whom he regarded as competent. Suddenly, quite without Luther's planning it that way, the theses fell into the hands of a printer and were printed and reprinted throughout Germany. Despite their cold, academic, and unemotional form, the theses unexpectedly crystallized all the latent resentment in Germany against the Church. Not Luther alone, but Luther plus the still unfathomed power of the press, had created a national sensation. Before the end of 1517, the obscure Wittenberg theologian had become a figure of national and even international importance. The challange to indulgences had escaped the hands of the few theological experts Luther had addressed and had become the object of an agitated public turmoil that did not end till Christian unity had been shattered and the authority of the old Church in Germany had been virtually obliterated.

Aside from failing to realize that his theses would spread rapidly and would cause excitement among reform-minded Germans, Luther had made one serious miscalculation. He assumed that the Church authorities would share his desire to restrain excesses by the indulgence preachers and to clarify the theological basis of indulgences. But neither the German prelates whom he addressed nor the Roman curial officials to whom they promptly denounced Luther cared about these matters at all. They merely saw a threat to the revenues they intended to derive from the indulgence, and they regarded Luther's questions as a challenge to their authority. They consistently refused to engage in any theological discussion with Luther, public or private, and showed not the slightest sense of any pastoral responsibility toward his troubled soul. The authorities from the very first demanded two things from Luther: silence and submission. For them, the issue was not whether he was right or wrong, but only whether he would drop the issue and humbly beg pardon for his rashness in bothering them about the theological questions.

The Conflict Widens: Authority of the Church

Pope Leo X sought from the very beginning to silence Luther by invoking the authority of the Church; and it was this effort that for the first time compelled Luther to clarify his own attitude toward that authority and to work his way toward his revolutionary attack on Rome's claims, an attack he never dreamed of making at the beginning of the controversy in 1517. The pope first worked through Luther's Augustinian order to bring the monk to obedience, but without success. Then the Pope summoned Luther to appear at Rome within sixty days to answer to charges of heresy. At this point, Luther requested and got the protection of his prince, Frederick the Wise, elector of Saxony, who did not understand the theological issues but who mistrusted the kind of justice an accused and isolated German monk would get if he delivered himself into the clutches of Rome. The years 1518 and 1519 were spent in intricate negotiations, in which various papal emissaries vainly tried either to talk Luther into a public recantation or to persuade the elector to hand him over.

The Radicalization of Luther

By its refusal even to consider the theological issues and by its characteristic practice of presenting a challenger with its claim to absolute and infallible authority, the papacy was unwittingly compelling Luther to face a question he had never before seriously considered: whether the papacy's absolute power over the consciences of Christians was justified. Luther had begun his challenge convinced that he was right and that the papacy would eventually endorse his opinions. But by the end of 1519, while still convinced that he was right, he had to consider the possibility that the papacy would decide against him and even the broader possibility that the papacy was supporting false doctrine and deliberately trying to suppress the clear teaching of the Bible.

Of particular importance in defining the issues in Luther's own mind was the famous public debate he had at Leipzig in June and July of 1519 with the shrewd and learned theologian Johann Eck. Eck was a clever debater, and he compelled Luther to admit that some of his teachings were the same as doctrines for which the Council of Constance had condemned and burned the Bohemian heretic John Huss in 1415. This arduous debate against an able foe forced Luther to extend his thinking from the narrow issue of indulgences to the broader issue of the authority of the Church. He was now compelled to decide flatly that Scripture and Scripture alone was the source of all religious truth, and that neither the Roman popes, nor the whole hierarchy, nor even a council had any authority to make Church traditions or any particular interpretation of Scripture binding on all Catholics. Once he had rejected the doctrine of hierarchical authority, Luther quickly saw that the principle of priestly power over laymen and priestly monopoly over the sacraments must be rejected too.

Fortunately for Luther, during this period when he was radically reorienting his thought, he still had the protection of the elector of Saxony; and all the political and clerical authorities were preoccupied with the problem of electing a successor to the old Emperor Maximilian I and reorganizing the administration of Germany. During the year 1520, he published three short but powerful treatises that challeneged not only the traditional practice of indulgences but the whole doctrine and authority of the medieval Catholic Church. In his *Address to the Christian Nobility of the German Nation, The Babylonian Captivity of the Church,* and *On the Freedom of a Christian Man,* Luther summoned the ruling classes of Germany to compel the Church to reform, boldly rejected the doctrines of priestly power and Roman authority that had shielded the medieval clergy from control by secular rulers, and eloquently taught all Christians that their salvation depended solely on the free gift of divine grace that was available to all who had faith in Christ and that no series of external acts or good works had the slightest value in winning merit before God.

In 1517 Luther's thought had contained merely the seeds of rebellion. Only the rude collision between his deep convictions and Rome's mindless insistence on blind obedience had caused those seeds to develop into open rebellion. By 1520, however, Luther had already repudiated the essentials of medieval Catholic religion. When the papacy in 1520 finally drew up the bull *Exsurge Domine* formally condemning his heresies and declaring him excommunicated unless he retracted his errors within sixty days, Luther defiantly burned several propapal books (in retribution for public burnings of his books) and as an afterthought tossed into the flames a copy of the papal bull.

A Revolution in Popular Attitudes

Only a few years earlier, such a repudiation of Church authority and Catholic doctrine would have shocked most Germans. Now it was done to the enthusiastic cheers of the students and professors of his own university. Far beyond Wittenberg, German public opinion had rallied behind Luther and made him a public hero, even among many who ultimately refused to follow him in his break with Rome. The original source of his support was the group of influential humanists who dominated German intellectual life and who had already become outspoken critics of corruption and agitators for reform. These humanists not only criticized indulgences (though on grounds different from Luther's) but also resented the systematic exploitation of the German people by the corrupt and clever Italians who dominated the curia at Rome. Luther's increasingly open attacks on Rome appealed to many nationalistic humanists who had little understanding of his evangelical theology. Humanists also found Luther attractive because their own leaders, such as Erasmus, had long been insisting that the church must go back to its ancient origins through study of the Bible and the early Church fathers. Luther's criticism of medieval traditions and his insistence that the Bible must be the ultimate authority in religion were quite close to their views. Finally, because of the Reuchlin controversy and several lesser quarrels of the same sort, humanists tended to be suspicious of the conservative Catholic theologians and Dominican friars who led the attack on Luther. The attitude of the greatest humanist of the age, Erasmus, was typical. He carefully avoided any blanket endorsement of Luther's views but firmly and effectively opposed the conservatives' rush to silence and destroy the Wittenburg reformer. Many German humanists were even less reserved than Erasmus, and humanists were responsible for the quick translation and republication of the Ninety-five Theses.

The Printed Word

Luther's appeal, however, went far beyond the limited circle of German humanists. Their support and the political protection of the elector of Saxony gave Luther not only time to think through his own position but also time to establish a following among the German people. While the publication of the Ninety-five Theses was an accident unforeseen by Luther, the popular excitement generated by that work pointed the way to use of the printing press to appeal to broad elements of the German populace over the heads of the Church hierarchy. Luther quickly developed into a genius of the pamphlet. He had a gift for the composition of short, inexpensive tracts that set forth his religious ideas and his attacks on Rome in ways that appealed to ordinary Germans. Though profound in their ultimate implications, his three basic teachings (salvation by faith alone, the priesthood of all believers, and the authority of Scripture alone) were simple enough to be grasped in some way by great numbers of people. These three teachings demolished belief in the value of traditional Catholic piety, subservience by laymen to the Catholic clergy, and unquestioning acceptance of traditional beliefs and practices. Centuries of unvoiced resentment against clerical arrogance and against Italian dominance of the Church now welled up into an elemental revulsion against the old religion.

Social Groups Behind Luther

Alongside the humanists, the prosperous burghers of the commercial and industrial towns of western and southern Germany became deeply committed to Luther's cause. Other classes also, such as the free imperial knights, found Luther attractive, especially because he seemed to justify their hostility to the wealthy ecclesiastical princes who were their rivals for power and wealth in western Germany.

Finally, many of the larger territorial princes of Germany found in Luther's preaching a justification for their desire to increase their control over the persons and properties of their clergy. For reasons both religious and secular, many of them welcomed Luther's urging that in default of leadership by the corrupt bishops, the secular princes should undertake the reform of their Churches. The adherence of several large territorial princes was the major reason why his movement survived and grew, while the adherence of the burghers of the towns was the major reason why in a short time his movement gained a mass following at all social levels and did not become merely a creature of the princes.

In the beginning, the protection offered by Luther's own territorial prince, the elector of Saxony, explains why the Church authorities could not arrest Luther and do him to death before his writings had created an effective mass movement. At a later stage, the administrative skills and the power of the princes provided the mechanism through which the Reformation was actually transformed from a set of ideas into an effective system of Church reform. Since the territorial princes and the burghers of the self-governing towns were the two most powerful political and social forces in Germany, Luther's success in winning converts among those groups explains why most of Germany (except where the territorial princes remained resolutely Catholic) eventually went over to the Reformation.

But Luther's appeal was not restricted to the upper levels of German society. Substantial parts of every class (including the clergy) shared his national resentment of Rome, his hostility to the pretensions of the clergy, and his insistence that the Bible, and not unscriptural traditions or decisions of popes and councils, must be the ultimate authority in religion. Furthermore, although Luther himself was more concerned about false doctrine than about worldliness and corruption (regarding the latter as a mere consequence of the former), the greed, worldliness, and corruption of so many members of the clergy, and the obvious fact that clerical scoundrels often shielded themselves from correction by insisting on the privileges of the clerical order, created sympathy for Luther even among individuals who had no real understanding of his doctrines.

Luther's propaganda tracts had a popular appeal that went far lower in society than the humanists, rich burghers, and nobles. Even among the illiterate classes, some notion of his ideas spread rapidly. Although the ruling classes of the towns were in any case predisposed in his favor, their allowing Lutheran preachers to preach and introducing changes were often speeded up by fear that unless they took such steps, bands of rioting lower-class citizens would seize control of religious policy. Even among the most unenlightened and most oppressed class of all, the peasants, some notion of Luther's teaching spread, merging strangely with their latent hatred of the clergy and their half-formulated aspirations for social justice.

Many of those who supported Luther did so under serious misapprehensions. The peasants, who read into phrases like "Christian liberty" a meaning compatible with their own willingness to agitate and even to rebel for social reform and who quite missed Luther's insistence on the sanctity of constituted authority, were not the only ones. Reform-minded humanists saw in Luther's attacks on specific abuses (such as the indulgence for St. Peter's Cathedral) an endorsement of their own essentially conservative and Catholic program of reform. Not until the appearance of the three treatises in 1520 did the more perceptive of the Catholic humanists begin to realize that Luther was really repudiating Catholic doctrine and the authority of the Church. Then they began to draw back. Some of them, such as Erasmus, became open critics of Luther. But by 1520 it was already too late, for he, not they, now had the attention and devotion of the German people.

The Diet of Worms, 1521

Luther's status as a national hero was still unchallenged in 1521, when he made his famous appearance before the new Emperor Charles V at the Imperial Diet of Worms. Luther's protector, the elector of Saxony, had been insisting since 1517 that Luther must be given a fair hearing on German soil, that he must not be condemned unheard and must not be betrayed into the clutches of the Italians at Rome. Charles V could not resist the demand that Luther should be heard, even though he personally agreed with the arguments of the papal nuncio, Aleander, that a man already excommunicated by Rome ought not to be granted a hearing. Aleander himself realized that the Germans regarded Luther as a hero, not as a despised heretic. With some exaggeration, he reported home: "All Germany is in full revolt. Nine-tenths raise the war cry 'Luther!' while the watchword of the other tenth who are indifferent to Luther is 'Death to the Roman Curia!'" So the

Emperor Charles V reluctantly issued a safe-conduct calling Luther to appear before the Imperial Diet at Worms.

Luther's trip from Wittenberg to Worms was a triumphal procession. Everywhere he was hailed by large crowds and treated as a great personage. At his first hearing before the emperor, on 17 April 1521, when formally asked whether the books gathered as evidence against him were his and whether he cared to defend them or recant any, he answered yes to the first question but (to the surprise of the crowd) begged for time to consider the second. Reluctantly the emperor agreed to hear him the next day. At that time, Luther bluntly repeated his charges that Rome exercised spiritual tyranny over the Germans and concluded by stating that the doctrine for which he was challenged was not his but Christ's, though if he were shown from Scripture that he had erred, he would gladly recant. He was then asked plainly to declare whether he repudiated his books and the errors they contained. His short and eloquent reply was a decisive defiance of established religious authority:

> Since then Your Majesty and your lordships require a simple reply, I will answer without horns and without teeth. Unless I am convinced by Scripture and plain reason—I do not accept the authority of popes and councils, for they have contradicted each other—my conscience is captive to the Word of God. I cannot and will not recant anything, for to go against conscience is neither right nor safe. God help me. Amen.

After repeating this declaration in Latin for the emperor and others who did not understand German, Luther left the hall.

The following day, the youthful emperor made an eloquent declaration of his own, that he would remain loyal to the Catholic faith of his ancestors, that he would stake all his possessions, his life, and his soul upon this loyalty, that he expected his German subjects to join him in his opposition to heresy, and that although he would honor the safe-conduct he had given Luther, he would hear Luther no more. On 20 April he secured the approval of a majority of the seven electoral princes for his policy of extirpating the new heresy, though two, the elector of Saxony and the elector of the Palatinate, refused to sign the document. The imperial government now prepared an edict condemning Luther as a heretic, placing him under the imperial ban, and threatening arrest and confiscation of property to any imperial subjects who assisted him. Not until after the elector of Saxony and most of Luther's other sympathizers had left Worms in disgust did the emperor on 26 May secure the official endorsement of this Edict of Worms by the remnant of Catholic princes.

The sentence of outlawry against Luther could hardly be enforced, for he had dropped out of sight so completely that there were rumors he had been killed. In reality, the elector of Saxony had arranged for Luther to be "kidnapped" by a band of troopers who secretly carried him to the remote Wartburg Castle, where he was required to live in disguise. In his enforced exile, Luther was for a time overwhelmed by the immensity of what he had done. Eventually, however, he found solace in hard work. He tried to direct his confused followers at Wittenberg. He wrote tracts answering the charges of his Catholic enemies. And most of all, he worked on his German translation of the New Testament, which became one of his greatest legacies to the faith and the language of the German people.

Confusion at Wittenberg

While Luther was in isolation at Wartburg, his followers at Wittenberg faced the practical problem of how to translate his religious ideas into practice. Some people wanted drastic changes and wanted them all imposed at once. The more cautious and moderate, such as the young humanist Philip Melanchthon, feared that too fast a change would excite the comon people and might lead to mob violence. Besides, too drastic a change might alienate the one man whose physical protection remained essential to Luther and his movement, Elector Frederick the Wise. The "forward" party, led by the theologian Andreas Carlstadt, wanted to abolish clerical celibacy, the mass, compulsory fasting, and many other traditional practices. Carlstadt refused to wear priestly vestments for the celebration of mass, gave lay communicants the cup as well as the consecrated wafer, and omitted those portions of the ceremony that referred to it as a sacrifice. Early in 1522 Carlstadt got married. Other radical priests began urging their congregations to use violence against clergymen who opposed religious change. Luther's own Augustinian monastery at Wittenberg formally abolished itself and destroyed all pictures and statuary that might be incitements to idolatry.

Still worse, the Wittenberg radicals came under the influence of three self-proclaimed "prophets" from the notoriously radical town of Zwickau near the Bohemian border. These extremists not only demanded radical change but also claimed that the revelations that they claimed to receive by direct inspiration from God were equally as authoritative as the Bible. The activities of these fanatics finally compelled the elector to intervene. On 17 February 1522 he suspended all religious changes and ordered that the old system should be restored until the authorities had agreed upon a reform that would be imposed throughout Germany.

Luther Expels the Radicals

The danger of a direct clash between the cause of reform and the authority of the prince compelled Luther to defy the Elector's orders to remain hidden. In March of 1522 he openly returned to Wittenberg to take charge. The activities of the Zwickau "prophets" had convinced him that the Devil was trying to discredit the reform movement by getting it blamed for rash and violent acts. A few days of preaching allowed him to regain control of the reform movement and to compel the "prophets" and some of their more radical followers to leave in disgust. While they charged that Luther had sold out to the princes, he charged that their attempts to compel a radical purging of all non-Scriptural practices and to impose a precise moral supervision for all Christians were a new form of legalism and works-righteousness no better than the one they had just repudiated. As long as the true doctrine of justification—the essence of the Gospel, as he regarded it—was being preached, he was willing to allow many secondary details (whether a priest should wear vestments, for example) to be reformed gradually and to be regulated to some extent by the ruler.

The Ruler of the Knights

Luther soon faced problems with other supporters who carried his principles far beyond what he intended. While he himself was extremely respectful of established authority and had absolutely no interest in any program of social or political reforms, there were groups in German society who found in his doctrines implications that seemed favorable to their own aspirations for social and political reform. The first such group to undertake direct and violent action that it attempted to justify with Luther's doctrines was the free imperial knights, a uniquely German class of lesser nobles who ruled many tiny principalities in western Germany. In 1522, the leading professional soldier among the knights, Franz von Sickingen, aroused by Luther's defiance of the church and encouraged by the anti-Roman humanist Ulrich von Hutten, declared war on the archbishop of Trier. Sickingen hoped to conquer the rich and strategically important principality which the archbishop ruled in western Germany. Unfortunately for him the archbishop was at least as skilled a general as he was and a far abler politician. While most of the knights hesitated to join an open rebellion, the archbishop organized a league of the larger West German princes whose armies destroyed Sickingen's forces. Sickingen himself was fatally wounded. This revolt in 1522–23 ended in the confiscation of the estates of the rebellious knights and in the establishment of political control over the remainder by the larger territorial princes.

The Peasants' Revolt, 1524–25

Luther had not become deeply involved in the issues of the knights' rebellion. But charges that his doctrines would lead to political and social turmoil seemed far better founded after the great Peasants' Revolt that swept through many parts of Germany in 1524–25. Luther's own position was very clear. He consistently opposed rebellion against lawful authority, as well as any attempt to base a program of social and political reform on his religious teachings. Nevertheless, both his friends and his foes persistently misread his remarks on Christian liberty and on social injustice, concluding that his thought did imply a need to reconstruct society and might even justify the use of force.

The real source of the Peasants' Revolt of 1524–25 was not the religious ideology of Luther but a complex set of economic, political, and social changes that left the peasants in many parts of Germany bitterly discontented. The rebels were not typically the most impoverished and oppressed peasants in Germany, but they were those who felt the most insecure. Ambitious peasants who were struggling to improve their lot in life were especially likely to resent many of the surviving restrictions imposed on them because they were legally still serfs. Particularly hated were many ecclesiastical lords. Being representatives of cautious, self-protective groups of clergy, these prelates were notoriously harsh in enforcing their rights as manorial lords.

These conditions had produced many small-scale local riots and even rebellions for at least two generations before the Refomation. While the real sources of these rebellions were political, social, and economic, many of them also expressed religious discontent. Some, such as the violent outbreak at Niklashausen near Würzburg in 1476, fell under the leadership of religious fanatics who claimed divine inspiration and foretold the imminent arrival of a millennium when all clerical and political authority would disappear and all Christians would live together in a condition of social and economic equality. Such rebellions were suppressed with great ferocity, yet periodic local outbursts continued.

The great rebellion of 1524–25 was essentially a continuation of this earlier movement, but the widespread excitement over Luther's preaching made the rebellion more widespread than its precursors. To the essentially secular demands for social reform were added a few demands for reform in religion. The rebellion began as a series of spontaneous and purely local uprisings with goals varying according to local conditions. To the east in Thuringia, for example, though the uprising began without his encouragement, the radical preacher Thomas Müntzer, whom Luther had driven from Saxony, got control of the movement and voiced demands for a drastic social revolution leading toward social and economic equality, and for a bloody massacre of all godless persons (such as unconverted Catholic clergy).

In the southwestern part of Germany, Swabia, representatives from several bands of rebels drew up a relatively moderate set of demands, the Twelve Articles of the Peasants. Obviously influenced by the conservative attitude of Luther rather than by the violent fanaticism of Müntzer, this document demanded a set of very specific and limited reforms that would have brought immediate tangible benefits to the peasants. The most extreme demand of this, the largest and most influential council of peasant leaders, was for total abolition of personal serfdom and bondage. Otherwise, the articles demanded only the end of landlord disregard of traditional peasant rights and the abolition of certain arbitrary taxes and discriminatory acts. Only one of the Twelve Articles dealt with a religious issue, affirming the right of each local congregation to elect its own pastor and to have the Gospel preached freely. The men who drew up the Twelve Articles no doubt thought that they were acting in conformity with Luther's preaching. But their demands came out of the tradition of peasant resistance, not out of Luther's books.

By April of 1525, perhaps 300,000 peasants were in arms, though many parts of Germany were unaffected. Councils such as that which produced the Twelve Articles attempted to coordinate the actions of the haphazard bands of rebels, but no capable military or political leadership emerged. The early peasant successes occurred only because the ruling classes were caught unprepared. The larger princes avoided decisive confrontations and bought time through protracted negotiations, while they mobilized their forces. By April of 1525 the princes of the Swabian League in southwestern Germany were ready to take decisive action. Once the princes were armed, the suppression of the peasants was mainly a matter of conducting massacres. The rebel army in Thuringia broke and ran when the Lord failed to stop the princes' cannonballs. Great numbers of prisoners were massacred in cold blood, and known spokesmen for discontent were effectively prevented from future agitation by being blinded or having their limbs amputated.

Thus the larger German princes had effectively suppressed two armed challenges, one by the knights and the other, far more severe, by the peasants. They emerged as the effective rulers of all of Germany, except for those regions dominated by self-governing towns.

Martin Luther, however, did not emerge from the Peasants' Revolt with his reputation untouched. Since he had urged the ruling classes to be mindful of their obligation to social justice, many conservatives accused him of causing the revolt despite his constant warnings against it. Even worse for his prestige was his ferocious revulsion against the peasants at the height of their successes early in 1525. His violent pamphlet *Against the Murdering Hordes of Peasants* bluntly urged that rebellious peasants should be struck down without mercy, exactly like mad dogs. Still worse, the pamphlet came off the press only after the main peasant armies had been beaten, so that it seemed to endorse the ruthless massacres of unarmed prisoners that went on after the military power of the peasants had been broken. Luther's later admonitions for leniency came too late to have any effect. Luther was still a popular figure in Germany after 1525, but the suppression of the rebellion does mark the end of the period when he seemed to be the only spokesman for a unified German nation. The open break between Luther and the chief of the northern humanists, Erasmus, coming about the same time, further marks the waning of Luther's position as undisputed leader of all Germans.

Failure of Charles V's Policy

Nevertheless, these blows to Luther's prestige did not enable the Emperor Charles V to make good on the policy of suppressing the heresy he had announced at the Diet of Worms in 1521. Lutheranism continued to spread into district after district of Germany. Although Charles was a capable and determined man, and although he had inherited a vast agglomeration of principalities that made him the most powerful European ruler since Charlemagne, the very immensity of the territory he ruled made it difficult for him to concentrate his power in Germany and to overpower Luther and Luther's princely supporters. Charles V's high-sounded title of emperor brought him very little direct political, military, or financial power in Germany.

Immediately after the Diet of Worms, Charles had to abandon personal direction of German affairs and hasten off to Spain, where rebellion had broken out against this foreign-born king and the many Netherlanders he had put into office there. During the crucial decade of the 1920s, when Lutheranism was becoming permanently established in Germany, and when the knights, peasants, and princes of Germany were keeping their country in turmoil, Charles was tied down in Spain, patiently (and successfully) piecing together the power to control that country. Where Charles had direct political authority, as in the Low Countries, he sternly repressed heresy. But where real power was in the hands of town councils or virtually independent territorial princes, he could neither prevent those local governments from protecting the heresy nor lend any real credibility to his threat of eventual enforcement of the Edict of Worms. Even after Charles's success in Spain and a series of brilliant military victories against the French king and the pope, his threats were not enough to compel the Evangelical (pro-Lutheran) princes to abandon their new religious reforms. In the face of renewed threats of military intervention, the German Protestants in 1531 formed a direct military alliance, the League of Schmalkalden, to protect themselves from armed attack.

Princes Organize the Reformation

By the later 1520s it was clear that the larger territorial princes were the principal beneficiaries of the religious Reformation. It is true that the motivating force behind the successes of the German Reformation was the preaching, teaching, and writing of Martin Luther and the large number of able young men whom he won over and who helped him stir the consciences of the people. Yet in the aftermath of the imperial condemnation of Luther and the rebellions of the knights and the peasants, the larger territorial princes (and to a lesser extent, the town councils of the principal self-governing German cities) emerged as effective leaders of the Reformation.

Although Luther's early thought tended to favor the self-governing congregation as the basis for reorganizing the Church, the assumption of control by princes and town councils was compatible with his appeal to the Christian nobility to provide the leadership that the Catholic hierarchy had forfeited by its worldliness and corruption. The dependence of the reformers on protection from the territorial princes and town governments further strengthened the dominance of the political rulers in Lutheran Church affairs. Since Luther defined the realm of truly spiritual matters very narrowly, assigning administration of Church properties and revenues to the secular sphere, even his own theory favored control of all the institutional aspects of religion by the secular ruler.

Thus when the new Evangelical religion faced the practical question of how to effect the transition from the old religious practices to the new, the secular ruler stepped in to organize the change. In Luther's own electoral Saxony, for example, the elector in 1529 created a special visitation committee to examine religious conditions. Since both property matters and questions of religious practice were at issue, the elector named two of his civil servants and two theologians (including Luther) to conduct the investigation. The visitors were to inventory church properties, to see that salaries of teachers and preachers were paid, and to oust clergymen who would not conform to the practices authorized by the ruler (that is, both radical Protestants and recalcitrant Catholic priests). This visitation commission recommended the appointment in each province (by the elector, of course) of a superintendent who henceforth would supervise preaching, educational activity, and administration of church properties. Each superintendent was to report to the elector the names of all who resisted reform. In effect the superintendents and the visitation commission were agents of the secular prince, who thus had seized full control of the Church. Luther himself explicitly declared that this control was a temporary expedient for the difficult transitional period. In fact, however, control of the Church by the political authority became a permanent characteristic of German and Scandinavian Lutheranism.

Despite many defections, the Evangelical or Lutheran faith swept into control of most parts of Germany, except where a local ruling family was strongly and persistently hostile. Usually with the advice of Luther and other Wittenberg theologians, prince after prince and town after town defected from the old faith. Also of great importance was the decision of a number of prince-bishops and other ecclesiastical princes to convert to Protestantism, marry, and found hereditary Lutheran states. The most famous example was the decision of the Hohenzollern prince who was Grand Master of the Order of Teutonic Knights in Prussia to secularize his state.

The eventual dynastic union of this state with the lands of the senior branch of Hohenzollern in Brandenburg laid the basis for the later rise of Brandenburg-Prussia to dominance in Germany. By about 1545 all of northern and eastern Germany was officially Lutheran, and either Lutheran or Zwinglian cities and principalities were predominant in the south and southwest.

Chapter Seven

Other Reformations, Protestant and Catholic

Martin Luther and his followers had no intention of destroying the unity of the Christian world: they intended to reform the Church in doctrine and practice, not to divide it. Yet their basic principles of the rights of individual conscience and sole authority of Scripture led readily to fragmentation of the Reformation movement. In addition, there were large numbers of earnest Christians who held resolutely to the old Church, despite its obvious need for reforms. On the Protestant side, several distinct non-Lutheran traditions began to emerge within a decade of Luther's first public appearance as reformer. These other Reformation traditions inevitably functioned as rivals of the Lutheran faith.

Zwingli and the Reformed Tradition

The earliest and most significant of these rival traditions is sometimes called Zwinglianism, from the name of its first great leader Huldreych Zwingli (1484–1531), but is more generally known as the "Reformed" tradition or as Calvinism, from the name of its greatest figure. The Zwinglian or Reformed tradition was an outgrowth of the intense excitement that Luther's early activity aroused in German-speaking Switzerland. Its growth into a rival to the Evangelical or Lutheran tradition was unintentional, though ultimately the split between the two movements became deep and bitter. The reasons for the difference lay partly in the distinctive social and political conditions in the German-Swiss towns where Zwinglianism originated and partly in the outlook and character of Huldreych Zwingli himself. The most obvious and most bitterly debated difference between Lutherans and Zwinglians arose over differing interpretations of the sacrament of the altar, the eucharist. In reality, however, the split between the two main varieties of Continental Protestantism embraced many complex issues.

Zwinglian Radicalism

Zwingli was unlike Luther in two major respects. First, he was a humanist rather than a theologian. While eventually he embraced all of Luther's major doctrines, he had begun his reform career as a follower of Erasmus, and the humanistic concept of a total return to the faith and practice of the apostolic Church pushed him toward a far more radical repudiation of unscriptural practices than Luther wanted. Luther was slow to endorse changes in traditional religious ceremony and practice unless he became convinced that a particular tradition was likely to mislead the faithful into false belief. Thus he had been reluctant to imitate even his own followers in abandoning use of priestly vestments and elaborate Catholic ceremonial in the saying of mass. He early eliminated those parts of the old eucharistic service that referred to the mass as a repetition of Christ's sacrifice on the Cross, for that belief he regarded as a serious error; and his doctrine of the priesthood of all believers made him early insist that the mass should be said audibly in German so that the whole congregation could participate actively. But traditional genuflections, turnings toward the altar or toward the congregation, and (until as late as 1542) even the elevation of the bread and wine above the celebrant's head survived in his ceremonial practice.

Zwingli, however, believed that all ceremonies and practices that could not be found explicitly in the New Testament had to go. The use of special priestly robes, tending to set the minister apart from the congregation, had no Scriptural warrant and struck Zwingli as clearly implying the rejected Catholic doctrine of priestly authority. The failure of the New Testament to mention use of musical instruments or hymns as part of early Christian worship meant that Zwingli (despite his own musical talent) eliminated musical instruments and hymns from his services. Most important of all, when he faced the problem of how to transform the celebration of the "idolatrous" Catholic mass into a true eucharistic ceremony, he did not begin with the traditional ceremony and introduce limited changes. Instead, he went to the text of the Gospels and made his eucharistic service a simple reenactment of the Last Supper. The traditional altar at the east end of the church, with the priest facing away from the congregation, was replaced by a simple table. The minister stood facing the congregation and read the biblical words of institution and the prayers in German, without any of the traditional genuflections. He clearly functioned as leader of a community action rather than as a priest performing an action for the community. This conscious attempt to eliminate all traditional practices that had no Scriptural basis produced a worship service far simpler than the Lutheran. In the eyes of a follower of Zwingli, Lutheran worship was still too "popish."

The second great reason why Zwingli's reform differed from Luther's was that it grew up in a self-governing urban society with a relatively high degree of popular participation in government, rather than in the despotically ruled states of eastern and northern Germany where Luther's influence prevailed. To a much greater extent than in Lutheran regions, popular pressure rather than princely policy was the main source of the reform, which consequently tended to be less cautious and conservative. The relation of the individual to society was more clearly an issue, and from an early date the Reformed communities were more concerned than Luther with the need to bring society into conformity with religion. Reformed Protestants were more inclined than Lutherans to gain political control of the state and then to use political power to create a strict moral police and a Christian social order. Zwinglianism and its successor, Calvinism, were at one and the same time more politically activist and more puritanical than Luther's Evangelical movement.

These differences do not mean that Zwingli's major theological principles were contrary to Luther's. Though Zwingli always insisted that he had begun his reform activity independently of Luther, his early work had been largely dedicated to stimulating personal religious piety and to agitating for social reforms, especially the abolition of the profitable system of hiring out Swiss citizens as mercenary soldiers. Zwingli became a Lutheran heretic only during the course of the year 1519, after he had become cathedral preacher in the important Swiss town of Zurich. During that year as he read more and more of Luther's writings, Zwingli unconsciously shifted his message to lay more and more emphasis on the need for true evangelical (that is, Lutheran) doctrine.

Reform at Zurich

Precisely because he was both a devoted reformer and the holder of an important position as cathedral preacher, Zwingli was pulled in two directions. As a disciple of both Luther and the reforming humanists, he drew practical conclusions about reform substantially more radical than Luther himself was urging at that time. He demanded abolition of compulsory fasting, private confession, the mass, clerical celibacy, the use of images and music in church, and all sorts of elaborate ritual. His rousing sermons stirred up great popular pressure for immediate and drastic change. On the other hand, he realized that the city council feared that such changes might stir up social disorder and also might leave the city politically isolated in a sea of hostile Catholic states.

So with considerable skill, Zwingli on the one hand stirred up popular agitation for reform, so that the city government would initiate religious changes, while on the other hand he tried to restrain his more enthusiastic followers so that the council would have considerable latitude in setting the pace of innovations. By 1523 he had persuaded the government to sponsor public debates between the reforming preachers and the defenders of the old faith. During 1524, under official sponsorship but under constant pressure from the reformers, the old religious order was demolished: pictures, statues, and crucifixes were removed from the walls whitewashed (as a safeguard against idolatry); pilgrimages, processions, and other traditional observances were abolished, and the number of religious holidays reduced to four that could clearly be justified from Scripture; monasteries were abolished and their properties confiscated by the city to be reallocated to social welfare services and education. The extremely simple Zwinglian worship service, with elaborate, non-Scriptural ceremonies expunged, with Bible-reading, prayer, and the sermon forming the heart of the service, and with the eucharist transformed from the elaborate mass at an altar to a simple reenactment of the Last Supper at a communion table, was introduced during 1525. Both in doctrine and in outward form of worship, Zwingli's reforms marked a far sharper break away from traditional Catholicism than did Luther's.

From Zurich the reforms of Zwingli spread to other self-governing cities of Switzerland and nearby southwestern Germany. At the Diet of Augsburg in 1530, four important German towns refused to endorse the Lutheran Augsburg Confession and presented the emperor with a separate Reformed creed of their own. In Switzerland, the conversion of Berne, which dominated the western part of the country, and of Basel, the great cultural center with its university and its influential printing industry, placed the Zwinglian reform on a sounder footing. But the whole position of the Swiss Reformed group was badly weakened when the Catholic cantons managed to isolate Zurich politically in 1531 and destroy its army in battle. Zwingli himself was one of the casualties, and though the Catholics were not strong enough to crush Protestantism where it already prevailed, they managed to check its expansion for a number of years.

Conflicts within the Reformation

Despite their essential agreement on the central issues that divided Protestant from Catholic, the Zwinglian and Lutheran traditions became increasingly open rivals for influence in southwestern Germany. The Reformed churches deviated markedly from the Lutheran, not only in doctrine (notably in their denial of the real presence of Christ's body and blood in the sacrament of the altar) and in their plainer, simpler form of worship, but even in social policy (where they imposed a far more strict and detailed code of social and personal ethics). Perhaps from his earlier background in Erasmian humanism, Zwingli tended to deny any mysterious or magical significance of ceremonies and to regard them as nothing but divinely instituted signs of an inward, spiritual relationship between God and man. Such an attitude struck Luther and his followers as rationalistic and even irreligious, while Luther's continuing insistence on the real and physical presence of Christ's body in the eucharist struck Zwingli as superstitious, "popish," and even as conducive to idolatry. Luther regarded the Zwinglian emphasis on a detailed and puritanical moral code as a new form of works-righteousness, while Zwinglians tended to regard Lutheran rejection of their efforts to impose discipline as a sign of moral laxity. During 1527 and 1528 Luther and Zwingli published a series of increasingly sharp pamphlets in which they debated areas of disagreement, especially the question of the eucharist.

The emerging split within the reform movement horrified many religious leaders, especially the theologians of western and southwestern Germany. Men like Johannes Oecolampadius at Basel and Martin Bucer at Strasbourg admired both Luther and Zwingli, believed that the issues on which the two agreed were far more important than the areas of disagreement, and pleaded with both parties not to direct against each other the energies that ought to be employed against defenders of the old religion. Philip of Hesse, ruler of one of the most militarily exposed of the Protestant states of Germany, also emphasized the political and military dangers of Protestant disunity and finally in 1529 managed to bring the two principal leaders together at Marburg. But despite the pleas of many on both sides, unity escaped the grasp of the Protestant leaders at Marburg in 1529.

Calvin and the Spread of Reformed Protestantism

Although Lutheranism continued to advance in Germany and although it also spread to the Scandinavian countries (usually under government sponsorship), it had only limited success elsewhere in Europe. Since the Zwinglian tradition also underwent a period of stagnation after the death of Zwingli in 1531, there seemed to be a real possibility that German and German-Swiss Protestantism might be stamped out or might become nothing more than a local Germanic mutation of Christianity. Luther's thought excited lively interest throughout Europe, but it could not by itself generate mass religious movements elsewhere as it had done in Germany.

The rival Reformed tradition, however, under new leadership, grew into a dynamic force for religious, social, and political change during the second half of the sixteenth century. Reformed Protestantism swept into control of most of Switzerland, part of the Low Countries, and Scotland. It also had a predominant influence on the religious thought (though not on the forms of worship or the ecclesiastical structure) of England. For a time in the later sixteenth century it threatened to obliterate the traditional Catholic faith of France, and it made serious inroads in Poland and in Hungary.

John Calvin: Origins and Principles

The new dynamism of the Reformed wing of the Reformation was largely the work of the leader who took over the faltering movement a few years after the death of Zwingli. John Calvin (1509–64), after whom the whole Reformed tradition is often named Calvinism, was not an original religious thinker in the way that Luther was. Indeed, most of his major doctrines came from Luther, and most of the non-Lutheran innovations he accepted came indirectly from Zwingli. But if Calvin was not a great creator of new ideas, he was a great systematic thinker and also proved to be the best practical organizer the Protestant movement ever had. Perhaps Calvin's clarity of thought was a natural reaction to the incredible confusion of spiritual life among reform-minded men and women in his native France during the years when he was growing up. Early French reformers lacked the ideological clarity and the mass following that had enabled Luther and Zwingli to create powerful movements and break down the structures of the old Church. In doctrine the French Evangelicals held a vague amalgam of reform ideas selected from the writings of Luther, Erasmus, Lefèvre d'Étaples, and a number of other humanists and Protestants. Few of the Evangelicals were ready to take the crucial step of defying the authority of the Church hierarchy if it impeded their proposals for reform, and the only real plan they had for bringing about significant improvement was the forlorn hope that King Francis I would himself compel the bishops to revitalize the Church through official, lawful channels.

John Calvin's spiritual origins lay within this well-intentioned but ineffectual French Evangelical movement. The son of an ambitious professional man from Noyon in northern France, he studied at the University of Paris and then at the law schools of Montpellier and Bourges, but he also became attracted to the classical studies and religious reform ideas that prevailed among his fellow students. His father's death in 1531 left him free to abandon law and to take up the career of a humanist writer, but in the early 1530s he was still a bright young man who had not found his goal in life.

About 1533–34, however, Calvin underwent an intense personal religious crisis from which he emerged so strongly committed to Protestant belief that he resigned all the incomes he had been receiving from patronage appointments in the old Church and eventually decided to go into exile in Germany. Unlike his Evangelical friends, Calvin had decided he must repudiate the old Church just as Martin Luther had done some fifteen years earlier. But such a flat rejection of a thousand years of religious tradition required him to think through carefully just what he did believe and why. For his own benefit he had to study theology, and in a short time he became one of the century's greatest theologians and produced a theological masterpiece that was published at Basel in 1536 with the title *Institutes of the Christian Religion.* This book quickly made its young author famous.

The theology of Calvin is, on the whole, derived from beliefs Luther had already expressed. What is new is only the clarity and consistency with which all the consequences of each doctrine are worked out. Like Luther, Calvin taught justification by faith alone, and like Luther but even more clearly than Luther, Calvin taught that the saving faith comes not by any act of man but as an unmerited gift God imparts only to those persons whom he has eternally predestined for salvation.

This doctrine of predestination has often been taken to be Calvin's central doctrine, but that place of honor rightly belongs to his view of God's absolute power and majesty. Predestination is merely a consequence of the doctrine of justification by faith alone, and as such it was accepted by Luther and by nearly every sixteenth-century Protestant theologian. To Calvin and his followers, predestination was especially stressed because they regarded it as a liberating doctrine that freed true Christians from constant concern about the fate of their souls and allowed them to concentrate on the real goal of Christian life, which is not earning salvation but serving and glorifying God.

Disagreements with Lutheranism

Unfortunately for Protestant unity, Calvin did disagree with Luther on some secondary but important questions. Although he regretted the split between Luther and Zwingli over the real presence of Christ's body in the eucharist and endorsed efforts to work out a compromise solution, Calvin shared the tendency of Zwingli to regard the sacraments as external signs confirming God's promises to the faithful but not actually conferring grace in some magical and mysterious way. Moderate Lutherans like Melanchthon found Calvin's compromise position attractive, but Luther himself remained suspicious. Most later sixteenth-century Lutherans still regarded Calvin as a sacramentarian heretic no better than Zwingli.

Another point of disagreement arose from Calvin's conviction that the New Testament clearly prescribed a system of Church government which all truly reformed Churches had to adopt. This system of Church government was incompatible not only with Roman Catholic belief in the authority of popes and bishops but also with the common Lutheran (and Anglican and Zwinglian) practice of allowing the secular ruler to control the Church. Calvin of course expected a true Christian ruler to support the Church in its struggle to create a Christian society, not only by financial support but by laws requiring all citizens to attend churches and to conform to proper moral standards. But Calvin also insisted that the Church must be free to organize and govern itself in the way set forth in Scripture, to preach the Gospel, and to impose discipline by excommunicating sinners, without any restraints by the political authority.

Thus Church and State had to be separate, a modern-sounding doctrine which under sixteenth-century conditions meant that the Church must be free from state control, and sometimes came close to meaning that the Church would control the State. Luther, on the other hand, was relatively indifferent to the forms of organization adopted by the Church. Indeed, in

Sweden the new Lutheran Church retained the office of bishop. In practice, Luther went along with the creation of firm control by the State over all Church institutions so that these institutions in the long run became virtual departments of the civil government. In the long run, the rejection of such State control by the Calvinist Churches came to be one of the most distinctive characteristics that set them apart from other denominations.

Finally, the Calvinists continued the Zwinglian tendency of purging from the outward forms of worship all practices which they regarded as idolatrous or unscriptural. The use of pictures and statuary in religious devotion, the practice of genuflecting and bowing at specified points in the service, the wearing of traditional priestly robes all impressed Calvinists as dangerous remnants of popery. Since such practices did survive in Lutheran Germany and Scandinavia and in Anglican England, true Calvinists regarded those churches with suspicion.

Discipline: The Godly Community

A significant corollary of Calvin's conception of the Church as a self-governing community devoted to glorifying God was the principle of discipline. Luther had regarded religion as essentially a personal relationship between the believing individual and his God. He regarded society and government as divinely instituted but still as essentially worldly affairs, and his acute sense of man's sinfulness made him dubious about any dreams of building a perfect Christian society. Luther believed that the tendency of radical sectarians, Anabaptists, and Zwinglians to maintain a detailed and puritanical regulation of social and personal morality would lead to a back-handed reintroduction of justification by good works. Even more than Zwingli, Calvin believed that God summoned true Christians to struggle to see that God's will was done on earth. The Church had to require all of its members (even the politically and socially prominent) to conform to the religious and moral requirements commanded by God. Calvinism would struggle actively to create a godly society on earth in a way attempted by no other major Protestant group. Not even Calvin foresaw how active and even revolutionary that struggle would become.

Calvin at Geneva

Calvin's *Institutes* by 1536 had solved his personal religious problems and quickly made him a famous personage. But he still had not found his life's work. In the summer of 1536 he set out for the Protestant city of Strasbourg in far western Germany, which had a sizable French exile community. Because of war conditions he had to take a circuitous route by way of Geneva, far to the south. There, quite unexpectedly, he found his future career. When Calvin first came there on his way to Strasbourg in July of

1536, Geneva had already achieved its political independence from the duke of Savoy and had already accepted the Reformation. The struggle for civic independence had been won in the late 1520s with the aid of two nearby Swiss cantons, Berne and Fribourg. The year before Calvin's arrival, the local government, encouraged by its Protestant ally, Berne, had abolished the celebration of mass and had turned the churches over to a group of Protestant missionaries headed by the French exile Guillaume Farel. But much remained to be done before the whole population was fully won over to the new religion, and much to his surprise, the traveling Calvin found that Farel expected him to stay in Geneva to help with the Lord's work.

Although Calvin accepted very reluctantly, Geneva proved to be precisely the base of operations he needed for his dream of spreading the Reformation in France. Unlike Strasbourg, which was so thoroughly Germanic that the French exiles formed an isolated enclave, Geneva was wholly French in language and culture, yet politically independent. It was a commercial center with excellent trade connections westward into France and eastward into German-speaking Switzerland. Its trade with France provided excellent cover for the clandestine movement of Protestant missionaries and books into France.

Calvin did not see these advantages at once, but his personal leadership transformed Geneva into a major center for the diffusion of Protestant faith throughout Europe, especially in French-speaking districts. His position in Geneva was precarious for most of his career, for he was a foreign exile struggling not just for adoption of Protestant doctrines but for the creation of his own ideal of a truly reformed, sternly disciplined Christian society. The ruling classes of Geneva had not fought for their independence only to submit themselves to the moral dictates of a foreign preacher, and neither the city's ruling class nor its powerful Bernese ally had much sympathy for the notion that the Church must be free to function without governmental control, and to spy out and punish sinners no matter how socially prominent they were. Calvin and Farel were actually driven out in 1538, but by 1541, the city begged Calvin to come back. Since Farel did not return, from 1541 until his death in 1564, Calvin was the leading minister and the most influential person in the city. This is not to say, however, that he controlled it. Not until 1555 were his friends able to break the power of a powerful opposition, mainly led by wealthy old Genevan families. Even after 1555 Calvin by no means dictated policy, not even on religious matters.

Nevertheless, Calvin did have more influence in Geneva than any other Protestant preacher had in any other European community. His essential demand, that the Church should be self-governing and free to impose discipline on all classes without intervention by the government, was substantially though not perfectly met. Under his leadership, Geneva did indeed become a "godly city," famous and admired throughout Protestant Europe for its effort to create a community devoted not only to Christian doctrine but also to Christian living. Although modern people, especially in post-Calvinist societies like the United States, have often denounced this Genevan discipline as unbearably oppressive, the basic goal of compelling the individual to conform closely to community-imposed standards was not unusual in the sixteenth century, either in Protestant or in Catholic lands. Nearly all late medieval and early modern societies (and especially self-governing towns) attempted to regulate morality. What made Calvin's Geneva unusual was not the attempt at regulation but the skill at indoctrinating the whole population and at devising agencies to enforce the rules.

The heart of the discipline was the Genevan church's twelve elders, all prominent laymen chosen by the government, and each residing in one of the city's twelve administrative districts. The elders had the duty of supervising the conduct of the residents in each district. Each elder was expected to call on each family in his district at least once a year. When an elder found some moral or religious irregularity, he was to report the problem to the Consistory, a body consisting of all the elders plus all the Genevan pastors (originally five in number). This body had the power to summon individuals to answer for offenses ranging from continuation of Catholic religious observances, to failure to attend church, to committing moral offenses that ranged from adultery to dishonest trading practices to singing a dirty song in public. Though most of its members were elected by the governing councils, the Consistory was essentially an arm of the church. Hence its punishments extended no further than to admonish, to reprimand, or in extreme cases to excommunicate. But if an errant citizen proved intractable, the Consistory could also turn the wrongdoer over to the secular authority, which could impose fines, corporal punishment, exile, or even death.

All sixteenth-century people expected their governments to regulate them closely, but the system devised by Calvin was unusually pervasive even for that age. Even relatively minor infractions, such as quarreling with one's wife, attending a theatrical performance, dancing, or playing cards, might cause a person to be called before Consistory to be admonished. But what was most resented, even to the point of generating a powerful political opposition down to 1555, was the prominence of foreign-born preachers in the Consistory and, even more, Calvin's ruthless insistence that the rules must be applied not just to humble folk but also to rich and well-born citizens.

The Genevan Academy

Calvin was also important in the reform of education. He had always insisted that Christians should hold their faith knowingly, and this goal required new schools to prepare an educated Christian leadership for future generations. Calvin pressed constantly for reorganization and improvement of the city's schools. The success of the schools in producing graduates committed to Calvinist faith and Calvinist discipline was one major reason why Calvin's position in the city grew stronger after about 1555. The rising generation of political leaders had been indoctrinated by Calvinist education.

But Calvin's educational horizons far transcended the narrow limits of one small city. In 1559 he finally persuaded the government to provide funds for the Genevan Academy, an advanced humanistic school that would provide education for the sons of Genevan citizens and also a university-level education (at least in theology) for young men from all lands. In fact (though not in name) the Academy quickly became one of Europe's most distinguished universities. In effect the Academy became a theological seminary that trained Calvinist leaders from all over Europe. The success of the Academy does much to explain why Calvinist ideas and practices had a powerful influence on the religion and intellectual life of all countries where Protestantism was able to make any headway during the late sixteenth and early seventeenth century.

Even before the opening of the Academy, the Genevan Company of Pastors had begun to dispatch young men (usually natives of France) to fill posts as ministers in the growing Protestant churches of France. After the Academy had been founded, an education at Geneva and a letter of recommendation from the Genevan clergy became an almost indispensable requirement for a man who wished to become a Protestant minister in France. Thus the Academy helped make Calvinism not just a widely disseminated ideology but also an international organization, with a centralized directorate in the Genevan Company of Pastors, a leadership training center in the Academy, and a large group of obedient and effective agents scattered throughout Europe and kept constantly in touch with one another through their voluminous correspondence with Calvin and then with his successor Theodore Beza.

Provided with the leadership of men like these two, with an ideology that had a profound appeal to sixteenth-century intellectuals, and with a remarkable organizational system that combined great local autonomy with effective direction from the Genevan Company of Pastors, Calvinism became, in the second half of the sixteenth century and the first decades of the seventeenth, the most dynamic movement in Europe, with the possible exception of the reformed and revitalized Catholicism that reemerged about the same period.

Anabaptism and the Sectarian Tradition

Not long after Zwingli laid the foundations of the Reformed (later, Calvinist) movement, a third major Protestant tradition grew up as a bitter rival of the other two. Their Lutheran, Reformed, and Catholic enemies called this third group Anabaptists, or rebaptizers. There was much confusion then and for centuries afterward about just who these Anabaptists were, how they originated, and what they taught, though all other groups agreed that the new sect was blasphemous, immoral, and dangerous to the social order, and hence deserved to be suppressed without mercy. Since some of the radical sectarians who challenged Luther at Wittenberg and who then became involved in the Peasants' Revolt did oppose the administration of baptism to infants, nearly everyone confused the real Anabaptists with these groups and attributed to them the extreme revolutionary views of figures like Thomas Müntzer.

The real Anabaptist movement originated not among the lunatic fringe of revolutionaries whom Luther drove out of Wittenberg but among the most loyal and most earnest followers of Zwingli at Zurich. In the Bible-study groups that Zwingli encouraged, his own ideal of a quick and total return to the practices and faith of the early Church received enthusiastic support. But Zwingli's followers were puzzled when their leader went along with the city council's desire for limited and gradual reform. They did not appreciate, as Zwingli did, the council's fears of domestic violence and diplomatic isolation. What particularly convinced Zwingli that a gradualist approach to reform was necessary was his pastoral concern for bringing the whole population over willingly. Like Luther, Zwingli retained the medieval notion that the visible institutional Church must include all citizens, not only the perfect saints but also hypocrites, sinners, and struggling, half-converted souls who were still emotionally tied to old religious practices but who might some day be truly converted. Zwingli and Luther also had taught that the true Church may be defined as the whole body of God's predestined saints through the ages, and that as such, it had a membership known only to God. Zwingli was willing to include in the institutional Church persons whose beliefs and habits made it quite clear that they were not yet members of this select group of perfect Christians. His Church, like Luther's and like that of his successor John Calvin, would be territorial, not sectarian.

The "Gathered" Church

This was precisely the point where future Anabaptists like Zwingli's follower Conrad Grebel parted ways with him. The apostolic Church reflected in the New Testament did not embrace all of Roman society but was a band of individuals who had been personally converted and who then separated themselves from the world in order to learn and do the will of God. Zwingli's extreme followers concluded that the modern Church, like the ancient, must be a voluntary association of believing and dedicated Christians. It must exclude all who accepted false doctrines or who lived worldly lives. It must return at once to the pure belief and practice of the New Testament Church without making concessions in order to make itself acceptable to the great masses of unconverted sinners or to the city council of Zurich. Each member of this true church must have undergone a personal conversion. The sacrament of baptism was the outward sign of this inward conversion and so must be administered only to those who have been converted—that is, to mature adults who by their acceptance of baptism were proclaiming their conversion and their entry into the true Church. A baptismal ceremony performed over an uncomprehending infant was merely an empty act with no religious validity. So when these "Anabaptists" began baptizing their adult converts who had already been baptized as infants, they denied that they were repeating the sacrament. The earlier ceremony had no validity. Hence they called themselves not "Anabaptists," but "Baptists," or "Brethren."

The first "Anabaptist" baptismal ceremony occurred in a private home at Zurich in January of 1525. It was intended as an act of defiance and as the foundation of a true Church of converted believers who repudiated the false and worldly Church maintained by the city council. Although Zwingli had once inclined to Conrad Grebel's view that there was no Scriptural basis for the baptism of infants, he firmly rejected the idea of a sectarian or "gathered" Church consisting of true believers only.

Subversive Implications

This debate between Zwingli and his former disciples involved much more than abstract theories of the Church and baptism. To the governing class of sixteenth-century communities, religion was a bulwark of social and political order. A separated Anabaptist Church that by its very existence proclaimed and condemned the worldly and un-Christian character of society as a whole seemed a threat to that order, especially since the State-controlled Church was the principal means by which rulers enforced minimal standards of behavior on the violent, semibarbarian lower classes. This mechanism of social and moral discipline would collapse if the new radicals were allowed to withdraw and organize a separate church of their own. In addition, most Anabaptist leaders and the bulk of their followers did not disguise their determination to promote programs of social reform that might well throw existing society into disorder. The rulers of Zurich realized that uncontrolled sectarian churches might become focal centers for political and social agitation by the poor: the frightening violence of the Peasants' Revolt was fresh in everyone's memory.

A further cause for official opposition to the radicals was that most of them rejected not only the official Church but the secular State as well, which, being part of "the world," was inevitably the enemy of the true saints. Quite early, most Anabaptists adopted a radical pacifism, refusing to serve or defend the State in any capacity. Being members of a truthful Church, they refused to swear oaths of loyalty or of truthfulness in court cases. They forbade their own members to conduct lawsuits. Naturally they opposed the payment of tithes for the support of the false Church. Many of them opposed the common (though illegal) commercial practice of charging interest for loans, and some of them demanded the abolition of all private property and the practice of a Christian communism like that practiced in the early Church at Jerusalem (Acts 2:44–45).

These political and social implications of Anabaptism explain the violence with which governments throughout Europe persecuted the Anabaptists. The mistaken idea that their views were identical with those of violent revolutionaries like Thomas Müntzer, and that Anabaptists were the same sort of people as the rebellious peasants of 1524–25, further encouraged persecution. Almost immediately after the first rebaptisms at Zurich, the city government imposed sentences of exile on all known Anabaptists. This act of exile merely turned them into wandering missionaries. Nearly every prominent early leader of the movement either had died of disease and exposure or had died a martyr at the hands of Catholic or Protestant governments before the end of the 1520s.

Nevertheless, their success in winning converts was remarkable. Anabaptism spread throughout Switzerland, Austria, southern Germany, and in the Low Countries, mainly among restless people of humble rank. Wherever the authorities were weak or tolerant, large Anabaptist congregations emerged. When such groups subsequently faced persecution, whole congregations might migrate across great distances to regions where the authorities were less inclined to persecute, mainly eastern European countries like Moravia, Hungary, and Transylvania. Such migrating groups developed a strong internal cohesiveness, in some cases adopting Christian communism and suppressing individual property rights. In later centuries, faced with spreading persecution, such groups made further migrations into western Russia and to North and South America.

The Fanatics at Münster

Almost inevitably such an enthusiastic popular religious movement came under the influence of extreme millennialism, the imminent expectation of the Second Coming of Christ and the end of the world. Anabaptism, with its best and sanest leaders being butchered by the authorities, sometimes fell under the leadership of unbalanced fanatics whose expectation of the millennium emboldened them to take drastic steps to prepare the world for Christ's Second Coming. Millennial expectations were especially strong among Anabaptists in the Netherlands and adjacent portions of northwestern Germany. The most influential such leader was Melchior Hoffman, a former Lutheran preacher who rebelled against Luther's conservatism and who became preoccupied with trying to calculate, from the evidence he found in the Bible, the precise date of the end of the world. His calculations convinced him that 1533 was the miraculous year. He urged his followers to prepare for the end, and while some took this to mean quiet, prayerful living, others concluded that they must take revolutionary action to prepare a perfect Christian community to receive Christ the King.

Soon his disciples put his theories into practice. In 1534, two Dutch artisans, Jan Matthys of Haarlem and Jan Beuckelsz of Leyden, took advantage of political and religious unrest in the German city of Münster to lead a popular rebellion not only against the Catholic prince-bishop but also against the Lutheran city council. Claiming direct personal inspiration from God, they persuaded the victorious people to expel all godless persons (that is, all who did not profess the Anabaptist faith), to burn all books except the Bible, and to abolish private property. Münster was to become the New Jerusalem, the place where Christ would make his appearance at the fast-approaching end of the world.

After the death of Matthys, Beuckelsz—Jan van Leyden, as he now called himself—declared himself king of the city, and so great was his power that no one dared to oppose him, not even when he reestablished Old Testament polygamy and married several women. Jan killed anyone who dared to question his "revelations." As so often in European history, what had begun as a revolutionary democracy ended as a bloodthirsty despotism. The nearby princes, both Protestant and Catholic, were alarmed at this attack on such basic institutions as private property, monogamous marriage, and the family. They raised a large army that besieged the city and finally, in June of 1535, stormed the fortifications and massacred all who had aided in the defense.

Menno Simons and Anabaptist Survival

The fanatical tyranny at Münster was nearly fatal to Anabaptism. All the earlier fears about its subversive social and political implications seemed to have been confirmed, and repression became even fiercer than before. The man who saved Anabaptism by repudiating the violent tendencies and creating a pattern of close-knit community life that enabled some Anabaptist groups to escape virtually unnoticed and to remain aloof from the larger society was Menno Simons (1496–1561), after whom the largest and most influential group of surviving Anabaptists came to be called Mennonites.

Menno Simons emphasized the idea of the Church as a voluntary community of converted Christians who accepted the right of the religious community to expel sinners. Menno preached a doctrine of obedience to the secular state in all matters where its orders did not contradict Scripture. But the relation of the true Christian to the State must be passive only, for the State was fundamentally hostile to Christian values. No true Christian would hold public office, engage in warfare, or swear oaths. Mennonite Anabaptism transformed itself into a separate Christian society living within, but not being part of, the larger secular society. It was marked by strict moral requirements, systematic use of the ban to expel imperfect members, pacifism, and a submissive but profoundly alienated attitude toward the political authorities. These small, underground communities, leading simple, prayerful, and hard-working lives, tried hard to stay out of trouble with their unconverted neighbors. Though the general reputation of Anabaptism made them still feared and even persecuted, they gradually gained for themselves a niche on the fringes of the larger society.

Although Anabaptism never became a powerful, widely organized movement controlling whole nations, the basic Anabaptist idea of the Church as a voluntary association sharply set apart from the total society of false Christians was the remote ancestor of later sectarian movements like the English Baptists, Independents, and Quakers. Ultimately (though mainly for nonreligious reasons) the "gathered" or voluntary church became the typical form of religious organization in the modern world, especially in the English-speaking world.

England: Reformation by Decree

When the Reformation entered the English-speaking world, it took a form the very opposite of sectarian Protestantism. In the Continental European countries, the Reformation generally began as a popular movement for reform that the political authority then either suppressed or led and controlled. In England, on the other hand, it is broadly correct to say that the Reformation did not begin until the government of King Henry VIII (1509–47) called it into being in order to further the dynastic goals of the ruler. This is not to say that England lacked certain tendencies toward Protestantism before official religious policy changed in the late 1520s. England had an influential group of humanists who agitated for Church reform, and its active trade connections with northwestern Europe meant that the ideas of Luther and other Protestant leaders penetrated easily among the intellectual and commercial classes. Furthermore, England had a long tradition of anticlericalism and of resentment of Roman exploitation of English churches, derived in part from survivals of the native heresy of the late fourteenth and early fifteenth centuries, Lollardy. Nevertheless, only a tiny handful of Englishmen was won over to Lutheran beliefs during the first decade of the Reformation.

Under Henry VIII, there seemed little prospect of royal leadership for the Reformation. The king was personally assiduous in observing the ceremonies (though not the moral requirements) of the Church, he was actively engaged in a complex foreign policy that made it to his advantage to maintain close diplomatic ties with Rome, and he prided himself on his personal mastery of Catholic theology and even wrote (or at least signed) a treatise defending the Catholic sacraments against Luther. Furthermore, despite popular complaints about papal control of patronage in the English Church, the king in effect already controlled most of the best patronage appointments and felt little need to attack existing arrangements.

Henry VIII's Marital Troubles

Yet despite his outward piety and resolute support of Catholic dogma, Henry's policy was determined mainly by political considerations. Although he felt no desire to upset the existing arrangements which allowed him to name most of the bishops, Henry VIII did face one problem that eventually proved fatal to the traditional Catholic Church in England. This problem was both marital and dynastic. It surfaced openly in 1527, when Henry began pressing the papal curia for a divorce (in Catholic Church law, really an annulment) from his queen of many years, Catherine of Aragon. Part of the problem was that in 1527 the king had fallen passionately in love with a scheming adventuress named Anne Boleyn. But royal passions can be handled without religious revolution: all kings (including Henry) kept mistresses, and if there had not been some serious problem with Henry's first marriage, Anne Boleyn could never have insisted on becoming his wife.

This marital problem was partly legal and partly dynastic. Catherine of Aragon, daughter of Ferdinand and Isabella of Spain, had originally been married to Henry's elder brother Arthur when she was sixteen and her husband fourteen. When Prince Arthur died shortly after the marriage, King Henry VII, reluctant to lose this dynastic connection with Spain, betrothed her to his second son, the future Henry VIII. Marriage to the widow of a brother was forbidden by a well-known passage in the Bible (Leviticus 18:16) and by the canon law. But since both royal families wanted the second marriage and since Princess Catherine firmly insisted that because of his youth Prince Arthur had never consummated the first marriage, Pope Julius II granted a dispensation specifically legalizing the second.

Probably if Catherine of Aragon had successfully given birth to a brood of royal princes, the papal dispensation would have settled the matter forever. Instead, except for one sickly girl, Princess Mary, all the children born to Catherine and Henry VIII died in infancy. Since no woman had ever successfully claimed the English throne, Henry VIII had good reason to think that despite the survival of Princess Mary, he had no child who could follow him peacefully to the throne. The Tudor dynasty was still new. Henry's father had ended a generation of civil war (The Wars of the Roses, 1455–85) by military conquest, and if his son Henry VIII failed to beget a son to inherit the throne, there was danger that the country would again be torn by civil war. As his Spanish queen approached the end of her childbearing years, Henry VIII became frantically eager to have a legitimate male heir. How could he help but recall the biblical passage that forbade such a marriage as his? Was not his lack of a son and heir a divinely inflicted punishment for the sinfulness of his marriage? Did even the pope have authority to dispense from a clear command of the Bible? These doubts were encouraged by the fact that by 1527 Henry had found in Anne Boleyn a prospective mother for the race of English princes he still hoped to engender. Yet Henry's scruples of conscience were not mere hypocrisy. The real driving force behind Henry's decision to get rid of his aging queen was his need for an heir.

Negotiations with Rome

Since the king wanted release from his marriage, it became the duty of his chief government minister, the worldly but able Thomas Cardinal Wolsey, to get it for him. Marital questions were determined in the Church courts, but since a papal dispensation was involved and since Queen Catherine firmly refused to renounce her rights as queen and her daughter's right of succession to the English throne, the matter could not be settled locally by one of the compliant bishops whom the king had appointed. The pope himself either had to make the decision or authorize someone else to do so. There could be no legal flaws or ambiguities in the procedure, for the fate of a dynasty and of a nation depended on it.

Normally, the popes of the high Renaissance were accommodating in interpreting the marriage laws for the benefit of European monarchs. Within living memory, popes had terminated other royal marriages on grounds far less valid. But Pope Clement VII faced two special difficulties in granting what Henry wished. First, the original papal bull of dispensation had explicitly authorized the marriage despite all legal impediments. Thus the pope could not decree that the marriage was legally invalid unless he was willing (as he was not) to rule that his predecessor had no power to set aside a legal impediment based on the text of the Bible. Second, Queen Catherine's cause was firmly backed by the diplomatic support of her powerful nephew, Emperor Charles V. A further complication was that the emperor possessed the dominant military power in Italy and for a time during the negotiations actually held the pope prisoner. Caught awkwardly between the wills of two mighty rulers, Pope Clement stalled.

Independence from Rome. After two years of fruitless negotiation, in 1529 Henry VIII adopted a new policy that eventually led to the coming of the Reformation to England. First, he dismissed Cardinal Wolsey from office and eventually turned to two men of Protestant inclinations, Thomas Cromwell (1485–1540), who became his chief political adviser, and Thomas Cranmer (1489–1556), who became archbishop of Canterbury. Suddenly, at the court of this zealously Catholic king, Lutheran books began to circulate, and the king gave clear indications that if Rome did not do his will, he would follow the Lutheran princes' example of breaking with Rome and regulating ecclesiastical matters (including questions of marriage) independently within his own kingdom.

To strengthen his hand, Henry summoned a Parliament that during its six years of sessions (1529–35) gave its own legal endorsement to his new policy. At first Henry still tried to bargain with Rome, having Parliament pass laws authorizing him to take certain antipapal actions if he wished, and then using this new authority as a threat during negotiations. Finally, however, after Archbishop Cranmer had ruled his first marriage unlawful and had married him to Anne Boleyn, Henry secured from Parliament the passage of several laws that cut the English Church loose from Rome.

Henry's "Anglo-Catholic" Church

These Parliamentary statutes of 1533 and 1534 did not make England Protestant in religion. They merely abolished the power of a "foreign" prince, the bishop of Rome, in the English Church, and shoved the English king into the position of power once held by the pope. At first, there was no other change in doctrine, practice, or organization. But Henry's chief administrative official, Thomas Cromwell, also intended to increase the wealth of the crown. He did so by plundering the vast endowments of the English monasteries. Beginning in the summer of 1535, he sent out commissioners supposedly to report on the condition of monasteries and nunneries, but actually to dig up enough evidence of moral irregularity and financial maladministration to justify the suppression of all monasteries and the confiscation of their properties by the crown. Between 1536 and 1539, the task was accomplished.

The secret of Henry VIII's success was his skill in exploiting the tendency of the English people to regard the popes as foreign oppressors and in playing on the rising national pride of Englishmen and on their reverence for the monarchy. He avoided any doctrinal changes, which might have divided his people. Faced with a choice between loyalty to Rome and loyalty to the king, only a handful of Englishmen expressed any attachment to the ideals of Christian internationalism symbolized by the papacy. As for English Protestants, though Henry occasionally used them to foster his own schemes, he had no taste for their doctrines and through most of his reign persecuted them just as resolutely as ever.

Except for the suppression of the monasteries and the ending of judicial appeals and financial payments to Rome, there were few visible signs of change. The English bishops, nearly all of them appointed by Henry and sharing the widespread English antipathy for Rome, went along wholeheartedly, for they saw no danger that an orthodox king like Henry would ever introduce heretical doctrine. Only one bishop, John Fisher, and one great public official, Sir Thomas More, refused to support the new system. These men and a few lesser ones were easily isolated and executed. There was only one large popular uprising in favor of the old religious system, and it was limited to the backward and uninfluential northern provinces and was quickly put down (1536). The English Church during the last decade of Henry VIII's reign is often called "Anglo-Catholic," for except for its rejection of papal control, it did not depart at all from traditional Catholic belief and practice.

Pressures for Doctrinal Change

Nevertheless, there were people in England and even high up at court who sympathized with Protestant doctrine and would have introduced major changes in belief and practice if the king had allowed. In particular, Archbishop Cranmer and a few of the other bishops were attracted to the ideas of Luther and Calvin. Such persons did not dare to become openly Protestant or push too openly for doctrinal change, for the king's preferences were well known. The conservative faction, led by Bishop Stephen Gardiner, even intrigued in vain to have Cranmer arrested on charges of heresy.

The reform faction had a few victories, of which the most important was probably the authorization of an official English-language translation of the Bible. Briefly, there even seemed to be evidence of some movement toward Protestant theological views. An official statement of belief, the Ten Articles of 1536, studiously avoided use of the specifically Catholic term *transubstantiation* in its definition of the eucharist and made explicit mention of only the two sacraments (baptism and eucharist) retained by the Protestants. Yet it made no specific endorsement of any characteristically Protestant belief. Its main purpose was to propitiate the German Lutherans, with whom Henry was then negotiating a military alliance.

Three years later, when the deal with the Germans had gone sour, Henry had Parliament define the creed of the Church in the Act of Six Articles, which reaffirmed all the traditional beliefs and practices of Catholicism (except, of course, the power of the pope): transubstantiation, denial of the cup to the laity at communion, the seven sacraments, clerical celibacy, the binding nature of monastic vows, private masses for the souls of the dead, and the necessity of confession to a priest before communion. From this time forth, overt Protestants were burned for heresy, while those few Catholics who remained defiantly loyal to Rome were hanged for treason.

Nevertheless, Henry VIII failed to purge his own surroundings of sympathizers with Protestantism. Although he tried to strike a balance between religious conservatives and innovators on the council of regency he created to rule England in case he died before his son Edward was grown, he allowed Edward to be educated under the influence of his Protestant uncles. The pro-Reformation leaders were content to bide their time, while the conservative Anglo-Catholics apparently felt reassured by the traditional character of Henry's religious policy.

Edward VI: The Protestants Take Over

When Edward VI came to the throne in 1547, he was a boy of ten. First under his uncle the duke of Somerset and then under the duke of Northumberland, the Protestant group gained the upper hand and soon showed what royal control of the Church meant when the king was not a defender of Catholic orthodoxy. Parliament abolished the reactionary Act of Six Articles, provided that laymen should receive the cup when taking communion, and legalized marriage of the clergy. For the first time, English replaced Latin in Church services, and in 1549 a parliamentary Act of Uniformity required all English churches to conduct services according to the revised liturgy, the Book of Common Prayer, which Archbishop Cranmer had prepared.

The Anglo-Catholic bishops now found that their willingness to renounce Rome and accept the supremacy of Henry VIII had been a mistake. So long as Henry lived, they kept firm control over the doctrine and practice of the national Church, but now that Cranmer and his friends had the ear of the regents and of the boy-king, the conservatives were defenseless. The English universities swarmed with foreign Protestant theologians whose teaching exposed the rising generation to Protestant points of view. By 1550 the Anglo-Catholic bishops came under attack for their opposition to these changes. Several were deprived of their offices and replaced by men of Protestant sympathies, and a few were arrested. For the first time, the ordinary English churchgoer could see evident and substantial changes in the way he was directed to worship his God. For the first time also, broad elements of the population were regularly exposed to Protestant ideas disseminated from the pulpit.

The one cloud on the horizon was that King Edward was a sickly youth, not likely to live long enough to consolidate these changes or to beget a line of Protestant successors. The duke of Northumberland plotted to pass the throne to a distant cousin of Edward, Lady Jane Grey, and then to marry the new queen to his own son. But the English people would have nothing to do with such a usurpation. Parliamentary statute and the will of Henry VIII provided that if Edward VI died without children the throne should pass to Henry's daughters in order of age. Hence the mistreated daughter of Henry and the unfortunate Catherine of Aragon, Princess Mary, easily won the throne in 1553.

Queen Mary: The Catholic Reaction

Queen Mary Tudor (1553–58) was determined to undo the religious changes of her father and especially of her half-brother Edward and to bring England back not only to the Catholic faith but also to acknowledgment of papal supremacy. In pursuit of her goal, Mary executed or drove into exile the principal leaders of the Protestant faction, from Archbishop Cranmer on down. Ultimately, about three hundred persons of varying ranks were burned as heretics during her five-year reign; and the Queen received from her Protestant foes the sobriquet "Bloody Mary" by which (rather unfairly, since all religious sects persecuted their enemies) she has been known in later times. She had the cooperation of the conservative Anglo-Catholic bishops who survived from Henry VIII's time, for their experience under a Protestant monarch had shown them that only the authority of the pope (which they had willingly repudiated in 1534) provided lasting protection for the traditional religion.

Aside from a few active Protestants, the majority of Mary's subjects accepted the restoration of Catholicism willingly. Nearly all persons with high rank or political ambitions conformed. In London there was a riot when the Catholic prayers for the dead were publicly reintroduced, but London was not typical of England as a whole. Probably Parliament reflected more accurately the attitude of the nation (or at least the propertied classes). The legislative body made no trouble at all over the total repeal of the radical ecclesiastical laws of Edward VI's reign, but it obviously would have preferred to leave the schismatic and antipapal, but conservative, laws of Henry VIII on the books. There was no effective opposition to the reintroduction of the mass or to the return to medieval beliefs and practices.

At first, there was not even any vocal opposition to the queen's decision to arrest and punish the leaders of the Protestant faction. But Parliament made no move to restore papal authority until strongly pressed by the queen. Parliament also had to be put under great pressure before it would reenact the medieval laws providing the death penalty for heresy. Most important of all, the landowning classes made it brutally clear that while they were willing to have the Catholic mass, and even the pope, back they would demand clear assurances that the restoration of the Catholic faith did not involve restoration of the confiscated monastic lands, most of which had been sold or given by Henry VIII and Edward VI to landed gentlemen who wished to enlarge their estates.

In the long run, the growing severity of persecution—Archbishop Cranmer and Bishops Latimer and Ridley were among those burned—contributed to the unpopularity of Queen Mary. But the most serious complaint against her was the pro-Spanish foreign policy she adopted, especially after she married Philip II of Spain. Even so, there was no real political opposition to her rule. What really undermined her reestablishment of Catholicism was her failure to have a child, for this meant that when she died, her half-sister Elizabeth would come to the throne.

The Elizabethan Religious Settlement

Elizabeth I (1558–1603) inclined toward Protestantism, but she was no zealot. What she most wanted was a religious settlement that would keep the country united and would assure firm royal control of the Church. She created a Church system that was intermediate between the Anglo-Catholic conservatism of her father Henry and the rather extreme Protestantism of her half-brother Edward VI. Thus she refounded the national or Anglican Church, placed rather moderate but clearly Protestant men in office as bishops, and strove for a form of worship that would be essentially Protestant but would retain enough of the traditional ceremony that it would not offend tradition-minded Englishmen. Parliamentary legislation restored to the monarch the legal supremacy over the English Church and denied the authority of any foreign bishop (i.e., Rome). Another law required all churches to follow the forms of a new Book of Common Prayer based on Archbishop Cranmer's work. All clergymen and all public officials were required to swear an oath acknowledging Queen Elizabeth's power over the Church.

The laity accepted this new settlement quietly. More surprising is that while nearly all the Catholic bishops refused the oath and were suspended from office, a mere handful of the lower clergy resisted: only about two hundred out of England's nine thousand beneficed clergy refused the oath and were driven from office. In theology, the Elizabethan Church settlement was deliberately vague. The official statement of doctrine straddled the issues that divided Lutherans and Calvinists, and the forms of worship, which were the only aspect of the Reformation evident to most Englishmen, were so traditional that even persons of Catholic inclination generally conformed. The Anglican Church deliberately took broad national inclusiveness, rather than ideological purity, as its ideal. Its most famous intellectual defender, the theologian Richard Hooker, justified its practices largely by the need for unity and harmony within the community.

Catholic and Puritan Dissent. Not all Englishmen were satisfied with the Elizabethan settlement. A small minority of convinced Catholics refused to attend its services (though this exposed them to heavy fines and civil disabilities), and a somewhat larger number conformed outwardly but heard Catholic mass secretly when they could. More numerous were the Protestants who thought that Elizabeth had not gone far enough in reforming the Church and who wished to "purify" the national Church by making its ideology more clearly Calvinist and by dropping from its worship services many "popish" traditions. These "Puritans," as they came to be called, wished for a further reformation. Most of them wanted to abolish the authority of the bishops and to bring the form of Church government closer to the Presbyterian system the Calvinists had created in Scotland. Some

Puritan clergymen modified or abandoned the legally required forms of worship, and a tiny group, led by a preacher named Robert Browne, went so far as to separate themselves from the national Church and found underground Churches organized on a congregational basis. These Separatists, however, were not typical of the Puritans, most of whom stayed within the official Church and grumbled.

The vast majority of Englishmen were neither Catholics nor Puritans, but accepted the Anglican Church willingly if not exactly enthusiastically. Although Puritans were numerous, public opinion regarded the extremists among them as troublemakers. The relative unity and calm achieved by the English settlement had considerable attraction for a generation that remembered the burnings under Mary Tudor and that had only to look across the Channel to witness the results of ideological rigidity in the civil wars and massacres that devastated France and the Netherlands.

Elizabeth's Goal: Outward Conformity. Queen Elizabeth herself helped the popularity of her settlement by refusing to inquire deeply into men's religious opinions. She required outward conformity and dutiful attendance at the lawful Church services, but she made no real effort to force lay people to reveal what they thought about doctrinal matters. Puritans were persecuted, but only when they disturbed public order, departed from the prescribed forms of worship, or separated themselves from the Church. Catholics were fined for nonconformity, and Catholic priests might suffer severe penalties, even death, if caught. But only in cases where their conscience led them into political conspiracies were Catholic laymen liable to capital punishment. While fear of Catholics was destined to play a prominent role in English life from the time of the Armada crisis (1588) down until at least the eighteenth century, the source of that fear was not their numbers or their power but the possibility that they might be disloyal.

In the seventeenth century, Puritanism became dangerous to the crown. Part of the reason was the spread of Puritan sentiments among the urban middle class, the landed gentlemen, and even some families of the aristocracy—that is, the classes which dominated the Parliament. Part of the reason was political: the political intentions and conduct of the new Stuart dynasty did not inspire the sort of loving trust that Elizabeth I attracted, and the spread of dissatisfaction with royal policy on taxation, economic development, and foreign relations made many of the dissidents incline toward Puritan views in religion. The prominence of a number of Roman Catholics at the courts of James I and Charles I aroused the Protestant fears. The emergence of the High Church movement, with its emphasis on the value of precisely those things the Puritans attacked, such as the authority of bishops and the value of traditional ceremonial, made many ordinary Protestant Englishmen conclude (wrongly) that Anglicanism was being betrayed from within by men who were secretly papists at heart.

Calvinism, the International Form of Protestantism

A substantial number of the more determined Puritans looked with approval at religious developments across the border in Scotland. From the middle of the sixteenth century, Scottish Protestantism became clearly Calvinistic, and under the leadership of Calvin's disciple John Knox, the Scottish Kirk, or national Church, adopted a Presbyterian from of government and set up a Calvinist system of discipline. The Kirk became the nation's most powerful and influential institution, dethroning the famous Mary Stuart (Mary Queen of Scots) on account of her Catholic religion and her alleged implication in the murder of her husband, and jealously restraining the authority of the kings.

Calvinism elsewhere also showed its ability to create a powerful, well-organized movement in opposition to the will of the ruler. In the seventeen provinces of the Low Countries, Protestantism had seeped in from nearby Germany as early as 1523, when the government burned some Lutheran heretics; but under the firm rule of Emperor Charles V, who was hereditary prince of this region, Lutheranism never spread widely. Anabaptism penetrated the area but did not become a mass movement. But Calvinism began spreading rapidly in the Netherlandish towns during the 1550s. When the new ruler, Philip II of Spain, attempted to reorganize the Church and to make the persecution more effective, his actions aroused a storm of opposition. Philip's Church reforms seriously affected the financial and social interests of the nobility, who had controlled most Church patronage under the old system. Also, the ruler's acts in creating new laws and new tribunals for suppression of heresy seemed to be an autocratic violation of the constitutional traditions he had sworn to uphold. Not least important, the whole concept of shedding blood in the name of religion was repugnant to large numbers of Netherlanders, who in this sense were heirs to the tolerant outlook of their fellow-countryman, the humanist Erasmus. In the religious and political crisis generated by this conflict between the native leaders of the Low Countries and their Spanish-born king, Calvinism soon became the faith of a large, growing, and determined minority. The eventual result was a civil war in which the seven northern provinces came to be dominated by the Calvinist activists and eventually won their independence from Spanish rule.

A similar growth of Calvinism occurred across the border in France. Calvin's chief missionary effort was directed toward his native land, and by the 1550s, in the face of severe persecution of heretics, those reform-minded French Evangelicals who were too deeply Protestant to be frightened back into Catholicism were becoming Calvinistic. Here as in Scotland and the Netherlands, Calvinism displayed its genius for organizing and propagating itself in the face of governmental repression. By the end of the 1550s, the French Reformed Church, aided by pastors, books, and advice sent from

Geneva, was ceasing to be a clandestine movement and was openly holding worship services, seeking converts, and organizing its political supporters to work for a change of government policy. The movement, which began among university teachers and students, spread among their substantial middle-class relatives and even among the nobility. The conversion of large numbers of nobles, a caste deeply involved in politics and habituated to the use of arms, made French Calvinism a powerful political force and eventually precipitated a series of civil wars, the French Wars of Religion (1562–98).

The Reformation in Other Lands

In other parts of Europe, the Reformation either failed to penetrate deeply or else had an early growth but then lost its hold. Spain was probably the least affected of the larger European countries, partly because of the firmly Catholic policy of its rulers, partly because of the nation's remarkably deep commitment to Catholic doctrine, and partly because pre-Reformation reforms had freed the old Church from many of the scandalous abuses which in other lands alienated the population. Many Spanish intellectuals were attracted by the reform ideas of Erasmus, and among this group some of Luther's books began to circulate. But before this vague reform enthusiasm could be transmuted into genuine Protestantism, the Inquisition destroyed not only the handful of Protestant leaders but also the Erasmian humanist movement. As for the rank and file of the people, Protestant ideas rarely reached them. Spain had a vigorous spiritual life during the sixteenth century, but thanks to the earlier period of reforms, spiritual leadership remained in the hands of the Catholic clergy.

Protestantism also had relatively little appeal to the people of Italy. A number of humanist intellectuals carried their enthusiasm for reform beyond the limits of Catholic orthodoxy. Some of these became openly Protestant, though this meant that they had to go into exile. Many of these Italian exiles became theologically too radical for the Lutherans, Anglicans, and Calvinists among whom they settled. Their biblical literalism made them question even the Trinitarian creeds, and modern Unitarianism traces its origins to the work of the Italians Lelio and Fausto Sozzini, chiefly in Poland. But the Italian population as a whole remained Catholic.

The lands of Eastern Europe (except for Eastern Orthodox countries like Russia) were more deeply touched by Protestantism. Their young men often brought back Protestant ideas from years of study in Germany or other Western European countries, and Poland, Bohemia, Moravia, and Hungary all had intricate political and economic ties with Germany and the lands to the west.

While the substantial German ethnic groups settled in the cities of these countries often became Lutheran, Calvinism was the most widespread form of Protestantism in the East. The Protestant movement in Poland was weakened by the rise of anti-Trinitarian radicalism (called Socinianism from the name of its chief leader, Fausto Sozzini), and in the early seventeenth century, the Catholic King Sigismund III took advantage of sectarian divisions among the Protestants to wipe them out. The Calvinists in Hungary were more successful in preserving their movement into modern times, but after the second half of the sixteenth century, the Reformation made no more substantial gains there. Bohemia, where many of the people had abandoned Catholicism even before Luther under the influence of John Huss, was penetrated by both Lutheran and Calvinist influences and remained predominantly non-Catholic until the suppression of the country's political autonomy during and after the Thirty Years' War. Other parts of Europe were also affected by the Reformation. All of the Scandinavian countries became Lutheran under the leadership of rulers who sought to enhance their own wealth and power at the expense of the old Church.

Protestant Disunity

One persistent problem that weakened the whole Protestant movement from a very early date was its tendency to split into many hostile sects that often spent more time and energy opposing each other than trying to convert Catholics. Even within Lutheranism, there were serious divisions after Luther's death in 1546 between the moderate group led by Luther's friend Melanchthon and the "true Lutherans," who regarded any conciliatory move toward either the Calvinists or the Catholics as a betrayal of religion.

The various Calvinist churches remained relatively cooperative toward one another, though there was some conflict between those who preferred a Presbyterian form of church organization and those who favored more autonomy for the local congregation. Calvinism also tended to produce small radical offshoots, beginning with the Anabaptists in Zwingli's Zurich, continuing with the anti-Trinitarian radicals in Poland during the late sixteenth century, and reaching its peak in the incredible proliferation of sects in England during the 1640s and 1650s, after the Puritans had broken the power of the monarchy and the Anglican Church. Then Presbyterians, Congregationalists, Baptists, and Quakers—to name only the larger and more enduring groups—separated from the English Puritan tradition and became permanently established as distinct and mutually antagonistic sects. Despite the reestablishment of Anglicanism as the official state religion in 1660, English Protestantism remained divided to a degree unknown elsewhere in Europe.

Charles V's Attempt to Conquer Germany. In Germany, the original homeland of the Reformation, Protestantism survived mainly because of the failure of the Hapsburg effort to enforce the imperial edict of 1521 against Luther. The threat of armed force always lurked in the background, but Charles V was so distracted by his military and political conflicts with the Turks, the French, and the papacy that he was unable to take effective military action until 1546. Then, with the aid of the turncoat Maurice, elector of Saxony, Charles V broke the military power of the Protestant Schmalkaldic League and imposed an interim religious settlement (1548) that made a few minor concessions to the Protestants but was clearly a first step toward restoration of Catholicism throughout Germany. But the dissatisfaction of Maurice of Saxony, who had not gotten all the territorial rewards he expected, and the intrigues of the French, who did not want Charles V to consolidate his control of Germany, led him to a revival of the German Protestant opposition. The unexpected defection of Maurice of Saxony in 1552 completely overturned imperial control. The emperor was unable to regain the military upper hand. Finally, despairing of ever being able to impose his will by force, Charles V authorized his brother and designated successor as emperor, Ferdinand, to make the best settlement he could with the Lutheran princes.

Religious Peace of Augsburg (1555). The Religious Peace of Augsburg (1555) legalized the situation that had grown up de facto since 1521: each German prince had the right to determine for his own lands whether the Lutheran or Catholic faith should be legally established. While there was no guarantee of religious toleration, German citizens who found the religion established by their prince unacceptable were guaranteed the right to migrate into another province. The Peace of Augsburg helped pacify Germany by giving permanent legal recognition to the hard fact that the country was forever divided in religion. It also marked the failure of Charles V's effort to revive imperial power. Henceforth even more than in the past, the real power in Germany would be in the hands of the larger territorial princes, and the monarchy would count for little.

The greatest weaknesses of the peace settlement were that it did not resolve the issue of what happened when a Catholic ecclesiastical prince turned Protestant and tried to secularize his principality, and it did not specifically grant to the growing Calvinist denomination the same liberties it gave to the Lutherans. These weaknesses had much to do with renewed armed conflict among the religious groups during the Thirty Years' War (1618–48).

The Catholic Reformation: Survival and Recovery

Although Germany and the northern Netherlands became predominantly Protestant during the Reformation era and countries like England, Scotland, the Scandinavian kingdoms, and parts of Switzerland became overwhelmingly Protestant, millions of Europeans stayed with the Roman Catholic faith they had inherited from the Middle Ages. Some lands—Portugal, Spain, and Italy—were almost untouched by the new heresies. Others, such as Bohemia and the Austrian parts of Germany, were won back after having been virtually lost to the old religion. In yet others, after having made a promising beginning, Protestantism lost its ability to expand and either remained as a substantial minority (as in France and Hungary) or else was almost wholly obliterated (as in Poland or the southern Netherlands). The Roman Catholic Church, which in the early decades of the Reformation was so worldly, bureaucratic, and corrupt that it seemed unable even to realize that the crisis was spiritual rather than administrative, had before the end of the sixteenth century undergone a remarkable revitalization.

Pre-Reformation Origins

The reform and recovery of the Roman Catholic Church began even before the appearance of Martin Luther. Some historians prefer to speak of one great Reformation movement that gained momentum in the later fifteenth century and reached its full development in the sixteenth, though only after the Lutheran crisis shattered Christian unity and created two Reformations, one Protestant, the other Catholic. In a very real sense, the reform agitation of Erasmus and of other humanists who refused to follow Luther out of the old Church represents one significant expression of this early Catholic Reformation.

Even in the worldly Italian Church, there were clearly signs of reviving spiritual vitality. The famous attempt of the friar Savonarola to transform worldly, cultured Renaissance Florence into a puritanical Catholic republic was a spectacular example. More indicative of the future were a number of confraternities and associations of pious Italian Catholics who sought to begin reform of the Church by deepening their personal spiritual life, such as the Oratory of Divine Love, formed at Rome in 1517. This particular association was a group of intellectuals, many of whom were destined to become leaders of Catholic reform later in the century.

There were also special associations of priests who banded together to live lives of personal morality and piety while continuing to discharge (in a new and zealous spirit) their parish duties. One of the earliest and most distinguished such groups was founded in the early 1520s and known as the Theatines from the name of one of its principal leaders, Gaetano di Thiene (1480–1547), a nobleman who resigned valuable Church offices in order to devote himself to improving the moral and spiritual character of Italian parish priests. Also important was the reform and revitalization of old religious orders, such as the Capuchins, a reformed branch of the Franciscan order that devoted itself to popular preaching and ministering to the spiritual and material needs of the urban poor

The Jesuits

Several new religious orders were dedicated to reform of the Church. Of those the most important was the Society of Jesus, commonly known as the Jesuits. The founder of the group was a Spanish nobleman, Ignatius de Loyola, who started life as a professional soldier but was permanently disabled for military service in 1521. Loyola's physical suffering and his quest for a new purpose in life led him into a severe religious crisis. Eventually he decided to devote himself to religion and to become a spiritual soldier for the Church since he could no longer serve as a military soldier for the king. After returning to school to learn Latin and study theology, Loyola (though still just a layman) began preaching in the streets, a practice that caused him to be twice interrogated by the Spanish Inquisition. Loyola eventually left the Spanish universities for the traditional center of Catholic theological learning, the University of Paris. There he began to attract followers. In 1534 a few of this group took a vow to serve the Church together, and finally in 1540 they received papal authorization as a new religious order.

The leading characteristics of this Society of Jesus were two. First, they combined a vividly personal piety of almost mystical intensity with a determination not to remain fixed in the act of contemplation but to pass on to active struggle in the world for the Church. Second, they clearly and bluntly identified true Catholicism with unquestioning obedience to Rome. In addition to the usual three monastic vows of poverty, chastity, and obedience, the Jesuits took a special fourth vow of loyalty to the pope.

A prime characteristic of the new religious orders of the Catholic Reformation was their combination of religious contemplation with active work in the world. But no other order illustrates this combination so well as the Jesuits. The *Spiritual Exercises* that Loyola worked out for the devotions of his followers read much like a description of preparation for mystical union with God. But although Loyola himself claimed to have experienced visions, the goal of the *Spiritual Exercises* is not contemplation as an end in itself but contemplation as the individual's personal preparation for action in the world. The Jesuits were not a cloistered order, cut off from the world, but rather were a group of activists. They worked in the world among laymen, as missionaries in pagan lands overseas and in European areas penetrated by heresy, as teachers in colleges and universities, as confessors and advisers to laymen (especially to Catholic rulers who needed advice on their responsibilities as rulers over non-Catholic people).

The educational work of the Jesuits was especially important. Their colleges became known as the best in Europe. Jesuit schools and Jesuit missionary work were essential in the recovery of Catholicism in many parts of Europe. In many respects, they were forward-looking and progressive. But on the one crucial issue of the century, the Jesuits were unflinchingly conservative and authoritarian: loyalty to the papacy was the very hallmark of true Catholicism, and even in the face of corruption, a sound Catholic should be cautious, lest he harm the very institution he sought to reform.

Catholic Reform in Spain

Spain at the beginning of the sixteenth century was on the eve of a great spiritual revival that did produce a few mystical heretics (the *alumbrados*) and might have led to a religious upheaval if the Spanish clergy had been as corrupt and incompetent as the bishops who faced the Lutheran challenge in Germany. But the skill of Queen Isabella and Cardinal Ximenes in carrying through a Catholic reform based on the use of humanistic education to train an elite of leaders and on systematic use of royal patronage to promote well-qualified men to bishoprics had left the Spanish Church well prepared to face the storms of the sixteenth century. Hence the welling up of religious enthusiasm (expressed in a vast literature of popular devotion and in an active mystical tradition) did not lead to rebellion against authority. Instead, the Spanish hierarchy skillfully managed to control this popular religious enthusiasm and to make it work for the institutional church rather than against it. Spain showed clearly that a national Catholic Church led by bishops who were fit to provide spiritual leadership not only could survive the impulse toward reform but even could emerge stronger than ever.

Reforming Bishops

This same lesson was illustrated on a narrower scale in several dioceses of Italy. Gian Matteo Giberti (1495–1543), bishop of Verona, abandoned a promising career as a functionary of the Roman curia to go back to his diocese and perform the duties he had previously neglected. The basis of Catholic Church organization is the power of the bishop, and the worst of all the many kinds of corruption in the pre-Reformation Church was the abuse of patronage rights to appoint bishops who lacked both the ability and the will to discharge their duty of keeping clergy and laity alike faithful to their obligations. Wherever Catholicism revived in the post-1517 period, one important cause was that some bishop, instead of drawing his income and neglecting his duty, undertook the one essential task of his office, providing an orthodox Catholic leadership to his people rather than allowing that leadership to pass by default to preachers of heresy.

The Papacy and Reform

Of all the bishoprics of the world, the most important for the cause of Catholic reform was the papacy, the bishopric of Rome. The abuse of papal power to appoint unworthy persons to high office or to authorize ruinous and unlawful abuses that fostered corruption (such as pluralism and nonresidence) lay at the very heart of the Church's problem. Again and again, would-be Catholic reformers found their efforts thwarted when the abuses they were struggling to correct received shelter from a papal dispensation. Until the papacy stopped using its unlimited authority against reform and began applying that same authority to compel reform, every serious Catholic reformer would eventually be forced to abandon his efforts or to rebel against authority and thereby endanger his status as a Catholic.

What hindered the conversion of the papacy to real reform was in part the fear that since many of the abuses rested on dispensations given by the papacy, attacks on the abuses would undermine the papacy's claim to unlimited power in the Church. Even more compelling was the fact that the papacy, which had become a vast and costly bureaucracy, relied heavily on many abuses for the income that kept it from going bankrupt. Sale of administrative offices in the Curia, fees for confirmation of archbishops and bishops, letters of provision, and (above all) dispensations from the ordinary rules and laws brought in vast amounts of money. Furthermore, even in cases where a pope did try to compel reform, he soon found that like all bureaucracies, the Curia was set in its ways and slow to change. The efforts of the last non-Italian ever to be elected pope, Adrian VI (1522–23), were futile because every reform he attempted was undone by obstruction among the curial officials. The failure of Pope Adrian was due not only to the shortness of his pontificate but also to the hard fact that even the pope could not bring about reform—not even at Rome—unless he remade the whole Curia, the group of advisers and functionaries who surrounded him.

The Achievements of Paul III

The conversion of the papal institution to the cause of reform really began with the pontificate of Paul III (1534–49). His antecedents were hardly promising. He became a cardinal at the scandalously early age of twenty-five solely because his sister was mistress of the corrupt and immoral Pope Alexander VI. He himself lived an immoral, ambition-filled life for the first two decades of his career, but from about 1513 he abandoned his mistress and began showing concern for the obligations of his high office. Even in his later years, he was too inclined to favor his relatives, too inclined to allow political expediency to shape Church policy, and too inclined to let the advice of his astrologers guide his policies. Nevertheless, he clearly realized that if the papacy were to survive, it had to change its worldly ways. He also learned from the failures of Pope Adrian VI that a reforming pope would have to prepare the way carefully if his reform decrees were not to remain mere empty words.

The most famous of his reforming acts was to create a Reform Commission of eminent Catholic reformers to investigate conditions at Rome and to propose reforms. The report of this commission in 1537 was blunt: the source of all abuses was the popes' reckless abuse of their supreme authority in ways that deranged the enforcement of the laws. The report was brutally frank in describing the administrative and moral corruption that prevailed at Rome. Pope Paul adopted some, though not all, of the administrative reforms suggested by the commission. But the prestige of the reformers was hurt when the text of their report fell into the hands of German Protestants, who quickly published it as proof that their repudiation of the papacy was justified.

Of greater long-range significance for lasting reform was Pope Paul's appointment of leading Catholic reformers to the College of Cardinals. Although some of his appointments still went to members of his family and to favorites of European rulers, over the long run the men he named as cardinals were leaders of the Catholic reform movement. Because its cardinals participated in the administration of the central bureaus of the Church, and still more because they elected future popes, this domination of the cardinatate by earnest reformers had a long-term beneficial effect.

Liberal versus Conservative Reformers

By the 1530s, reform-minded Catholics were becoming sharply divided into liberal reformers, who took their inspiration from humanists like Erasmus and who saw the need for substantial changes in Catholic religious practices and even for limited concessions to the Protestants, and a group of conservative reformers, who conceived reform as essentially a twofold process of enforcing the old and long-neglected rules of the medieval church and clearly condemning the errors of the heretics. At first the Erasmian liberals seemed to have the upper hand. They dominated the Reform Commission of 1537. They successfully involved the papacy in a series of colloquies with the Lutherans at Hagenau, Worms, and Regensburg in 1540–41. Their leading spokesman, Gasparo Cardinal Contarini, the papal legate for these negotiations, went very far toward accepting the Lutheran position on justification by faith alone. When, however, both Rome and Wittenberg rejected this compromise, and when similar accords proved unattainable on other doctrines such as transubstantiation, not only Contarini but the whole group of liberal, compromise-minded reformers lost influence at Rome.

The other faction, whose chief spokesman was Cardinal Gian Pietro Caraffa, charged that Contarini and other humanistic Catholics were unsound on doctrine. The conservatives argued that the time was past for conciliation and negotiation with those who had willfully separated themselves from the true Church and that what was required was clear official condemnation of the heretical doctrines and an unequivocal demand that all who claimed to be Catholic either embrace the traditional beliefs and practices or face condemnation for heresy. As for reform, enforcement of the long-standing laws of the Church and elimination of blatant corruption were needful, but there should be no wavering on traditional religious doctrine and practice, and all should be done in submission to the authority of the pope.

Conservative Victories

The rising fortunes of the conservative Catholic reformers can be traced not only in the papal financial support of Charles V's effort to crush German Lutheranism by force in 1546 but also in institutional developments at Rome itself. In 1540 Paul III confirmed the rule of the conservative, authoritarian new Jesuit order, and in 1543 he removed the restrictions he had originally placed on the size of the order. In 1542 the same pope founded the reorganized Roman Inquisition, modeled on the national Spanish Inquisition. This institution, especially in the hands of the archconservative Cardinal Caraffa, soon destroyed the more extreme liberal Catholic reformers in Italy, arresting some and forcing prominent men like Bernardino Ochino and Peter Martyr Vermigli to avow their Protestant sympathies by fleeing north of the Alps. Caraffa regarded compromise-minded Catholics as at least as bad as open followers of Luther. He also thought it important to concentrate on arresting and punishing persons of high rank, in the belief that a few such well-publicized examples would make lesser people afraid to flirt with heresy. Later, after he became pope himself with the title Paul IV (1555–59), he continued his emphasis on repression and strict discipline.

The disciples of Erasmus, even among the cardinals, faced arrest and prosecution if they did not practice extreme caution. Paul IV also in 1559 adopted a practice that had grown up in various localities, that of compiling an Index of Forbidden Books that Catholics were forbidden to read or possess. By giving the Index papal authority, the practice of physically restricting the movement of dangerous ideas among Catholic populations was strengthened. Needless to say, not only the heretic Luther but also the liberal Catholic Erasmus appeared on the list of dangerous authors whose books were forbidden. In Spain about the same period (mid-sixteenth century), although the Spanish Inquisition was not under direct papal control, the same emphasis on repression of both heretics and liberal Catholics grew up. Spanish Erasmianism was ruthlessly destroyed.

The Council of Trent, 1545–63

The capstone of the conservative triumph came with the Council of Trent. The demand for a general council to reform the Church went well back into the Middle Ages. In general, it was antipapal and liberal-reformist in its implications, and humanist liberals and even some of the early Protestants were among the leaders in the demand. The popes and curial officials, on the other hand, feared such a council as a potential rival to papal control of the Church. Here again, Paul III represents the crucial stage of development, for while other popes had promised to call councils, he actually did so in 1542 and persisted (despite the problems caused by war between the two leading Catholic rulers) until the council actually opened in the city of Trent late in 1545.

Although conceived as a concession to liberal critics, the council was so carefully managed that it posed no challenge to papal authority. The location at Trent was technically on imperial German territory, since the emperor, the king of France, and many others warned that they would not recognize the validity of a council held in Italy. Yet Trent is on the southern slope of the Alps and hence was most accessible to Italian bishops, who were usually propapal. Thus the papacy always had a comfortable majority of votes, and the only limit on what it might order the council to do was the danger that the non-Italians might walk out. The papal legates, who by law had a right to preside, pushed through rules on voting and procedure that demolished the power of the antipapal conciliarists who had dominated the councils of the fifteenth century. Most important of all, when a conflict arose between conservatives, who wanted the council to concentrate on condemning Protestant errors, and liberals, who wanted to avoid dogmatic decisions that would end forever the hope of a negotiated reunification and who wished to concentrate on passing legislation that would compel the pope to undertake drastic disciplinary and administrative reform, the papal legates negotiated a "compromise" that was essentially a victory for the conservatives.

Two separate commissions took up dogmatic definition and disciplinary reform simultaneously. In this way, the liberals' hope of avoiding a quick repudiation of Protestant doctrine and even of persuading the Protestants to attend the council and accept its decisions (thus reunifying the Church) was thwarted. Indeed, while the Council of Trent did legislate many reforms, it left implementation largely up to the good will of the popes. During its three widely separated periods of work (1545–47, 1551–52, and 1562–63), the Council's main accomplishment was in the field of defining Catholic dogma. All the main points of dispute between Protestants and Catholics were defined in an uncompromising and clear way, and all the distinctive Protestant beliefs were bluntly condemned. At least after 1563, unlike in 1517, no Catholic had any excuse for uncertainty about what the Church's authoritative position was on the issues of the day.

The Catholic Laity: Rulers and the Masses

The Catholic solidarity in Italy, Spain, and Portugal, and the eventual recovery and reform of the old faith in the southern parts of Germany, in

France, in the southern Netherlands (modern Belgium), and in Eastern lands like Poland, Bohemia, and Hungary depended on more, however, than the work of councils, new religious orders, intellectuals, popes, and bishops. The loyalty of certain secular princes to the old religion had a decisive effect on the religious development of the lands they ruled, just as the decision of certain rulers to back the Reformation assured the triumph of the new religion in their territories. The firmness of the Hapsburgs in Austria and the Wittelsbach dynasty in Bavaria eventually brought those parts of Germany back to the Catholic faith. Sigismund III of Poland (1587–1632), aided by the Jesuits, used his royal authority to turn the tide in that country. In Spain, Charles V and his son Philip II held that country for the old faith and also eventually restored Catholic supremacy in those parts of the Low Countries that they were strong enough to hold militarily.

The work of such Catholic rulers often involved forcible suppression of Protestantism—the hunting out and burning of heretics, the stopping of Protestant preaching, and the prohibition of Protestant books. But it also involved less violent methods when the rulers did not consider violence feasible. By their ability to grant patronage and social prestige to those who shared their religion, many Catholic rulers made it clear to politically ambitious noblemen that those individuals and families who refused to be converted to Catholicism were destroying any hope they might have for the political influence, social prestige, and wealth that came from a favorable position at court. In cases where a Catholic ruler was bound by written constitutional law to respect the freedom of Protestant towns and Protestant nobles, it was still possible to interpret the guaranteed rights in a narrow, restrictive sense. Finally, in a more positive way, the Catholic ruler might encourage the growth of the old religion by measures such as giving the Jesuits control of secondary schools and universities (done by the Hapsburgs at Vienna, for example), or forbidding students from their lands to attend foreign universities where they might be exposed to heresy. By a combination of force, pressure, and encouragement, Catholic rulers in the late sixteenth and early seventeenth centuries played a crucial role in actually bringing the reforms decreed at Trent into being and in making possible the substantial successes of Catholicism in regaining lost ground.

One other factor was perhaps even more essential to the survival and recovery of Catholicism. This was the inarticulate but dogged loyalty of millions of ordinary Catholic laymen to the traditional religion. Despite the criminal negligence and corruption of its leaders, despite its lack of clarity on many crucial dogmatic issues until the Council of Trent, the Catholic faith still had a powerful appeal to earnest Christians of many classes and many nations. Spain, which was the leading Catholic nation of sixteenth-century Europe, experienced a great religious revival that (thanks in large part to the reforms) acted to strengthen the power of the Church rather than to weaken it.

Intensely personal and mystical religious experience lay behind the monastic reform work and the highly popular devotional writings of St. Teresa of Avila (1515–82) and St. John of the Cross (1542–91). The career of St. Ignatius Loyola, founder of the Jesuits, is a remarkably clear example of the fruitful interplay between deeply personal and mystical religious experience on the one hand and intensely practical work to strengthen the church on the other. Although France, riddled by Calvinist heresy and torn by religious civil wars in the late sixteenth century, was slow to follow the Spanish example, by the seventeenth century a marked revival of religious devotion had also seized upon that country. The hallmark of the popular religious revival everywhere was a union between intensely personal piety on the one hand and hard-driving practical struggle for the revival of the Church on the other.

Catholicism survived because of the reform work of popes and bishops, because of the accomplishments of the Council of Trent, because of the patient work of the Jesuits, and because of the political backing of powerful rulers. But more than all this, Catholicism survived because millions of loyal Catholics, though they might be confused by the Church's theological equivocations and though they might blush with shame about the worldliness, immorality, and incompetence of their popes, bishops, and priests, nevertheless stubbornly refused to leave an institution which they had received from their ancestors and which in their own uneloquent but firm way they sincerely believed to have been created by God for the salvation of souls.

Reduced Power of Church Leaders

The striking recovery of Catholicism in the second half of the sixteenth century, together with the tendency of Protestantism to divide into mutually antagonistic sects, meant that the end result of the Reformation was a permanent loss of religious unity for Western civilization, as well as a decided long-term weakening of the power of religion over the lives of Europeans. This does not mean that religion ceased to exert a powerful influence, but gone forever were the days when the head of the international Church, such as Pope Innocent III in the early thirteenth century, could make powerful rulers yield to his will or face the danger of being dethroned. Even in firmly Catholic lands, such as Spain, the power of Rome and of the whole Church hierarchy in relation to the power of the monarchy was far weaker than before the Reformation. A Church that had to rely on the political authority for support against heresy simply could not have the same degree of independence as a Church whose claims were accepted without question throughout Christendom. The political rulers nearly everywhere came out of the sixteenth century with vastly increased power over the Church and over all aspects of life.

Chapter Eight

The Politics of Power, 1494–1610

The kings and lesser ruling princes of Europe were the most obvious beneficiaries of the religious and institutional changes that came with the Protestant Reformation. But even before Martin Luther's rebellion, the rulers of the three great states of Western Europe—France, Spain, and England—had made important gains in power and prestige. Some modern historians even refer to them as "new monarchies," implying that the monarchies not only increased in power but became essentially a different type of political institution, quite unlike the medieval feudal monarchies from which they descended. Whether these monarchies were "new," "modern," and "absolute" is a debatable question whose answer depends largely on the precise meaning given to those very imprecise terms. What is not debatable, however, is that during the second half of the fifteenth century, the power of the central governments of France, Spain, and England was increased and reorganized and that this increase and reorganization everywhere took the form of an increase in the power of the king, at the expense of the privileged orders of late medieval society: the clergy, the self-governing towns, and (above all) the feudal nobility. In some respects, at least, these changes foreshadowed the later emergence of absolute monarchy as the predominant form of government.

Growth of Royal Power

The strengthened royal power in the Western monarchies was due partly to accidents of inheritance. Politically effective men (and women) came to the throne in France, Spain, and England. In a more profound sense, however, royal authority grew because society needed strong government after an age in which the feudal aristocracy in all three countries had run wild. The nobles' control of central government had set their class free to exploit their position as landlords, military commanders, and leading political figures in their home districts with a brutal disregard for the interests of the nonnoble classes. The feudal aristocrats so savagely exploited their own peasants that serious peasant revolts occurred, especially in the fourteenth century. Relying on their own private armies, nobles seized other men's property, conducted private warfare, and often acted the parts of brigands plundering the countryside. During the Hundred Years' War, large portions of the French nobility sold out to the English invaders and the whole class again and again demonstrated its political unreliability and its military incompetence. The record of the English nobility was equally unattractive, with disorders reaching their peak during the Wars of the Roses. At the worst periods, the kings of France, England, and the Spanish kingdoms of Castile and Aragon became little more than pawns in the hands of aristocratic factions. Since weak monarchy in every case was the most obvious cause of the nation's woes, a strengthened monarchy was the obvious solution.

The Recovery of France

France, which had fallen from being the strongest feudal state of the high Middle Ages to being the prostrate victim of its English invaders and its own disloyal nobles, was the first of the three Western monarchies to recover. Restoration of national power and pride went hand in hand with the military effort to drive the English into the sea and to compel their allies among the French nobility to return to their loyalty to France. The monarchy was crucial to this process of recovery, and every success for the nation came through a victory for the crown. Yet the institution of monarchy was more important than the person of the monarch. Charles VII (1422–61), under whom the recovery began, was a man of limited ability. Joan of Arc, not King Charles, provided inspiration for the recovery of military power and national morale that turned the tide of the war. It is, however, significant that Joan presented herself first to the king and had to receive his grudging consent before she could begin her remarkable career.

Of particular importance was the crown's skillful use of the national representative assembly, the Estates General, to endorse its policies and increase its authority. The legislative session of 1439, under the impulse of the national struggle against the English, took two steps that had long-term effects not foreseen by the representatives. First, it passed laws for the reorganization of the armed forces that laid the basis for a permanent standing army of full-time professional soldiers, recruited and controlled directly by the crown. Thus the monarchy was no longer wholly dependent on the traditional role of the aristocracy as military entrepreneurs. The new standing army was too small to conduct a major war by itself or to enable the king to rule by force against the united will of the nation. Nevertheless, it marked a significant increase in royal authority.

The second importt action of the Estates General of 1439 also ended by strengthening the monarchy. The deputies empowered the king to collect the *taille*, the most important direct property tax. There was nothing unusual about such a grant of this tax in wartime, but the crown's lawyers took advantage of the ensuing decade of costly military effort against the English in order to reimpose the tax again and again without seeking further consent from the Estates General. Thus precedents were set for the French kings' claim to collect the *taille* at any time, and at any rate, as if the Estates General of 1439 had intended to give away this power forever.

To a degree unthinkable in the Middle Ages, the crown of France gradually usurped the right to levy a direct tax on property without calling the Estates General, though the government still had to rely on provincial and local assemblies for help in apportioning and collecting the amount due. This broadened taxing power gave the French kings a financial strength never possessed by their medieval predecessors. Furthermore, the loss of control over this crucial tax by the Estates General greatly reduced the king's dependence on the Estates and was one important reason why later kings were able to dispense with the medieval custom of assembling the representatives of the whole nation.

Charles VII and his son Louis XI (1461–83) also did other things to strengthen the ruler. Louis, who was an unscrupulous but effective politician, was particularly successful in establishing his personal control over the policy-making and administrative councils handed down from earlier reigns. These agencies had become largely independent of royal control during the preceding century of royal weakness. Louis gave real power to men of low rank raised to office by his favor and wholly dependent on him for their position. He kept powerful positions out of the hands of the great dukes and counts who had taken over direction of various governmental departments in earlier reigns.

Louis knew that the great nobles were his political rivals, and he schemed to end or reduce the semi-independent rule they had gained over large portions of French territory. The expulsion of the English kings from the vast duchy of Aquitaine (Guienne) had already ended the most dangerous of these vast fiefs. In 1477, when the last duke of Burgundy died without a male heir, Louis XI claimed that under French law the duke's daughter could not inherit the French part of her father's lands and seized the duchy of Burgundy, though he was unable to prevent the new duchess from retaining her crown. When the last duke of Anjou died childless in 1481, Louis XI, who had cultivated his friendship, inherited not only his French lands but also the sunny and strategic county of Provence on the Mediterranean coast, and the duke's long-standing but unenforced claim to the kingdom of Naples in Italy. Brittany, probably the most separatist-minded of all of the French duchies, retained its semi-independence even when a female inherited it, but in 1491, when there was talk of marrying the Duchess Anne to the German prince Maximilian of Hapsburg, the young French King Charles VIII occupied Brittany by force and compelled the duchess to marry him. In time, this last of the semi-independent duchies of medieval France was incorporated into the main body of the kingdom.

Louis XI and his successors also aggressively extended their control over the local government of the major cities and towns, many of which had formerly been self-governing. The system of tax collection and administration remained vastly inefficient and corrupt when compared to modern standards. Nevertheless, Louis XI made improvements in these fields also, less by creating new methods of governing than by making sure that the traditional methods worked in the interests of the crown.

Thanks to the consolidation of power by Charles VII and Louis XI, their successors Charles VIII (1483–98), Louis XII (1498–1515), and Francis I (1515–47) had far better control of the country than their late medieval predecessors. At least as much as the kings themselves, the real architects of the increased power of the crown were ambitious royal officials who, by aggressively pushing royal claims into types of activity formerly controlled by the feudal nobility or the towns, increased the power and income not only of their royal master but also of themselves.

The Monarch as Nation-Builder

France was not the only country where increased power for the king meant increased unity and political stability for the nation. All of the early modern European nations began as loose collections of small principalities ruled by the nobles and held together (often very loosely) by the feudal relationship between the nobles and the king. The only real bond that held a medieval nation together was the monarchy. Where the monarchy perished or became irreversibly weak, as it did in thirteenth-century Germany and Italy and several centuries later in Poland, the nation eventually lost its separate existence. Monarchs built the European nations by the careful and systematic expansion of what had originally been a weak feudal overlordship. One great phase of progress in this growth occurred in the twelfth and thirteenth centuries. The fourteenth and most of the fifteenth centuries in Western Europe had been a period of reverse for the monarchies, though the basic central institutions created by the medieval kings (royal council treasury, chancery, judicial system, and representative assembly) survived and provided the foundation for the further progress of royal power during the late fifteenth and early sixteenth centuries.

The Rise of a Unified Spain

In Spain, the crucial step toward forming a united nation was a royal marriage. After the Moorish conquest in the eighth century, several small

Christian states grew up and eventually became consolidated into two monarchies, the kingdoms of Castile and Aragon. In 1469 Princess Isabella of Castile married Prince Ferdinand, heir to the kingdom of Aragon. After they had inherited their respective thrones in 1474 and 1479, a single Spanish monarchy based on their union began to emerge, though in many respects the two kingdoms remained distinct for several centuries. The eventual inheritance of both crowns in 1516 by Charles of Hapsburg, a grandson of Ferdinand and Isabella, confirmed and solidified this union.

Ferdinand and Isabella did far more than create the dynastic union through their marriage. Each was an able and hard-working ruler. They completed the reconquest of the country from the Moors by seizing the last surviving Moorish kingdom, Granada in 1492. They reorganized the fiscal, administrative, and judicial institutions, especially in Castile, where the crown was far more powerful than in Aragon. Since the earlier part of the fifteenth century had been a period of civil war and baronial insubordination in Castile, Isabella's reign began with a serious problem of brigandage in the countryside. One sign of the rulers' political skill is that instead of devising a new, costly, and possibly unconstitutional armed force to police the country, they reorganized a traditional body, the Hermandad, or league, of Castilian towns. The reorganized Santa Hermandad was still a league of towns intended to support armed forces for the suppression of brigandage, but since the crown had led the reorganization of this agency, the crown had also carefully provided that its own appointee would control the body. The Hermandad organized squadrons of archers to patrol the countryside, and it imposed summary execution on captured brigands. Within two decades it had largely eliminated brigandage from the countryside; and so in 1498 the crown disbanded it. The genius of this agency lay partly in the skillful adaptation of a traditional organization, and partly in the crown's shrewdness in arranging that while the cities bore the burden of paying, recruiting, and organizing the troops, the queen through her appointment of the head controlled the activities of the Hermandad.

The new Spanish monarchy, like its French counterpart, also realized that it needed greater revenues if it were to control the country. A policy of revoking all gifts of land from the royal estates made by the weak predecessors of Isabella greatly increased the regular revenue from the estates. In the field of taxation, the Castilian queen reorganized the *alcabala*, a very lucrative 10 percent levy on all commercial transactions, though also a great burden on the economy. Finally, more careful management of royal revenues by a ruler who insisted on enforcing her traditional rights to payments in money and services did much to make the crown strong enough to overawe the unruly Castilian nobility.

Ideological Unity and Persecution. Ferdinand and Isabella also carefully controlled the Church in their dominions. From the popes they secured an almost unlimited control over appointments to influential positions in the clergy. While they consistently used this power to bring about reforms within the Church, they also ensured that it became an important institutional and ideological support for their new political authority. In 1478 they secured papal permission to found the infamous Spanish Inquisition (the only institution except the monarchy that was common to the two Spanish kingdoms) in order to enforce ideological uniformity.

Whereas medieval Spain had been remarkably tolerant of its Jewish and Moslem minorities, the new Spain exerted great pressure for conversion and then ruthlessly employed the Inquisition to make sure that Jewish and Moslem converts did not continue to practice their old religion or to observe the distinctive social customs that set them apart from the rest of society. Finally, continuing its pursuit of a homogeneous national society, the crown in 1492 compelled all remaining Jews to be converted or to go into exile; and in 1502, despite the guarantees of toleration made when the king of Granada surrendered, a similar policy was applied to the Moors. Although these cruel measures are usually regarded as examples of religious bigotry, they also had the crassly political goal of making Spanish society homogeneous and abolishing the claim of any subgroup to exemption from royal policies. The monarchy exercised firm control over its national Church. Not even papal decrees and proclamations could be transmitted to the clergy and laity of Spain unless the crown had first given its permission.

The highly privileged Castilian nobility was unable to retain its former degree of independence. The revocation of royal land grants (most of which had gone to nobles) and the assertion of royal control over Church patronage not only increased the power of the crown but also decreased the power of the nobles. The destruction of unlicensed castles reduced the nobles' ability to resist royal policy. As in France, the rulers systematically squeezed nobles out of policy-making positions in the central administration. The noble classes had long controlled the vast properties and considerable military resources of the three great military orders formed to conduct the long campaign against the Moors. Now Queen Isabella compelled each of these to elect King Ferdinand as its head, and henceforth these positions remained in the hands of the royal family. The Castilian nobles still retained great social prestige, high command in the army, and a set of privileges ranging from minor ones like keeping their hats on in the presence of the ruler to important ones like freedom from torture in judicial proceedings and exemption from many forms of taxation. But the crown ruled the country.

Spain Becomes a Great Power. The new Spain not only survived as a single political unity but also became the greatest military power in sixteenth-century Europe. Castile was the principal focus of royal power and was more heavily burdened with taxes and other obligations than the kingdom of Aragon. Ferdinand and Isabella laid the foundations for Spain's military predominance in Europe, which lasted well into the seventeenth century. Their colonial enterprise from the time of Columbus provided a flood of gold and silver bullion from America that helped Spanish kings like the Emperor Charles V and King Philip II pay the costs of an ambitious foreign policy that no other sixteenth-century European monarchy could afford. The exaltation of royal power in Castile was the source of Spain's exaltation above all other European nations, and all this power went back to the solid foundations laid by Ferdinand and Isabella.

The Tudor Monarchy in England

Medieval England had developed the strongest and best organized of the feudal monarchies, but like France and the Spanish kingdoms, it suffered from civil war, political instability, and oppressive and violent acts by the nobility during the fourteenth and fifteenth centuries. In 1485, however, the struggle among factions of the higher nobility ended with the victory of Henry Tudor. Enthroned as King Henry VII (1485–1509), he managed to place his new dynasty firmly in power even though his own legal claim to the throne was shaky. Although in many respects he only continued practices begun by his rivals, Henry VII is usually credited with initiating the revival of royal authority and the reorganization of central government in England. Perhaps his most important services were his success in remaining on the throne despite several rebellions and his marriage to a Yorkist heiress so that their children would have through their mother a far better legal claim to the throne than Henry VII himself ever did.

But Henry VII was also a skillful politician, fully capable of getting personal control of such traditional medieval institutions as the royal council, the Exchequer, and the complex Common Law judicial system, and able also to use and yet control the national representative assembly, Parliament. When viewed from the standpoint of institutional structure and procedures, Henry VII's administration seems to be little more than a skillful and effective reorganization of medieval English government. In terms of policy, however, the first Tudor reign shows new characteristics similar to those that permitted the governments of Louis XI or Ferdinand and Isabella to grow strong.

In the field of royal finance, for example, Henry VII never achieved anything so radically unmedieval as the right to levy property taxes without legislative consent, as the French kings did with the *taille.* Furthermore, except in the shaky early years of his reign, when he faced several rebellions, he did not frequently summon Parliament and request authority to tax. Instead, he relied mainly on traditional medieval revenues: the income from royal estates, fees and payments he received as supreme overlord of the feudal system, and customs duties.

But Henry was an astute financial manager, careful to collect all that was due and slow to spend his money. Like the kings of France and Spain, he secured legislation requiring the return of royal lands extorted from his weak predecessors by aristocratic intimidation. Since he had won his throne on the field of battle, he ruled that all who fought against him were traitors, subject to the death penalty and to confiscation of all their lands. He was not interested in the death sentences he might impose but in the rich lands he might confiscate from Yorkist nobles. Although political expediency made him give pardons liberally, he was able to begin his reign by confiscating many valuable estates, and he added more lands through confiscation after each of the rebellions he overcame. Coupled with more effective administration of the royal estates, these confiscations gave the king a large income from a source that everyone admitted to be rightfully his. Henry also carefully revived and enforced his right to payments from his vassals under the feudal system. Henry reorganized the collection of customs duties, which became an important source of money. By the latter years of the reign, Henry's persistence in collecting and his notorious stinginess in spending made him able not only to finance his administration without calling on Parliament for taxes but also to accumulate a large treasury surplus. Henry was widely regarded as the richest king in Europe.

Coming to power at the end of a long period of civil war and insecurity, the first Tudor king had to provide law and order. He was remarkably successful, even though he did not have the substantial armed force his French and Spanish counterparts had. The curse of the preceding age had been the systematic use of violence and intimidation by great nobles who maintained large bands of armed retainers. Such private armies had long been illegal, but Henry VII was able to enforce the laws as earlier kings were not. Henry defined a special class of "penal offenses"—those violations by which the aristocracy had disrupted the internal peace of the realm, such as the kidnapping and forcible marriage of young heirs or heiresses, or intimidation of judges and juries.

Since juries made up of local persons had long hesitated to determine cases against the interests of powerful and unscrupulous noblemen, King Henry took such penal cases out of the regular law courts and had them tried before a special committee of his royal council. By late Tudor times this committee had developed into a highly arbitrary but effective court, the Court of Star Chamber. It did not impose the death penalty but could inflict brief imprisonment and heavy fines on persons whom it found guilty of acts that endangered the peace of the countryside. Unlike the ordinary Common Law courts, the Star Chamber heard witnesses in secret, so that humble folk would dare to testify against great nobles. It could also apply torture in the interrogation of witnesses. Although such special judicial commissions were not unprecedented, Henry's systematic use of them to crack down on unruly noblemen was new, and in 1487 he had Parliament strengthen Star

Chamber by authorizing it to compel witnesses to appear and testify by issuing writs *sub poena.* Later on, in Stuart times, this Court of Star Chamber came to be regarded as oppressive, but throughout the Tudor period the ruling classes regarded it as a useful agency to repress violent acts.

Henry Tudor also provided an effective remedy against violent crime by lesser persons. He reorganized the traditional office of justice of the peace, creating a network of courts throughout England that could deal summarily with petty crime and could refer more serious cases to higher jurisdictions. Furthermore, by staffing these local courts with unsalaried amateur judges appointed from the middling landowners, the royal government was entrusting local law and order to precisely that social class which had suffered most from the disorders of pre-Tudor times.

Similarities of the Western Monarchies

At the end of the Tudor age, Sir Francis Bacon referred to Louis XI of France, Ferdinand I of Spain, and Henry VII of England as "the three magi of kings of those ages," regarding them as the founders of the powerful Western European monarchies of his time. Certainly those three rulers did carry out any urgently needed reorganization. Just as certainly, the enhancement of royal power and the restrictions of such rival political elements as the nobility lay at the very heart of what these kings accomplished. There were marked similarities of policy, not so much because of conscious imitation as because all three faced a common problem of ending the disorders and of restraining the nobles. Three politically skillful, hard-working kings and one queen acted decisively to establish their personal control of the government and to break the stranglehold that the higher nobility had established over key government positions. The nobles had to be squeezed out of policy-making positions and replaced with the king's trusted servants. In one way or another, all three monarchies had to increase royal income and reduce the waste and inefficiency of financial administration. In all three countries, new judicial agencies grew up, usually derived from committees of the royal council and charged with the task of controlling the powerful and violent nobles. Each successful king had to devise some agency for the internal police of the country and the repression of brigandage. The English, Spanish, and French monarchies became stronger not because of royal greed for power but because enhanced royal power was beneficial to the whole society.

Political Innovation and Tradition. Whether these reformed monarchies of the late fifteenth century mark a fundamental political transition from the limited feudal monarchy of the Middle Ages to the absolute power of the century is a question on which scholars disagree. There was a medieval precedent for almost everything that rulers like Louis XI, Ferdinand the

Catholic, and Henry VII did, and there is little decisive evidence that these kings and their immediate successors ever seriously thought of themselves as above the law or as free from traditional constitutional restraints. There is some evidence of significant change in the structure of government, most notably in the administrative reorganization carried out under Henry VIII (but not in the lifetime of the first Tudor king, Henry VII) by the brilliant royal minister Thomas Cromwell. Yet the basic structure of each European government—the representative institutions, administrative councils, and judicial organization—were not creations of the "three magi" but of the great feudal monarchs of the twelfth and thirteenth centuries. Even something so apparently new as the English Court of Star Chamber or the Castilian Hermandad was merely an adaptation of practices well established in medieval tradition.

Even the notion that these kings built absolute power by persistently weakening the power of the representative institutions is more plausible than correct. Like their medieval predecessors, these early modern rulers regarded assemblies of their subjects as useful devices for certain limited purposes—as methods of enhancing royal power, not of restraining it. Hence in periods of political crisis, the kings called the Parliament, the Estates General, or the Cortes into session frequently in order to get popular authorization for new legislation or for taxes. But parliaments were never a regular part of medieval government, and when the kings had internal and foreign problems well in hand, they called their representative assemblies together only infrequently. In England, where the Parliament was in many respects already more representative and more politically useful than its counterparts on the Continent, the age of "Tudor despotism" was an age of significant growth in the importance of Parliament, not as a restraint on the monarch but as a means of strengthening royal power. Henry VIII's use of Parliamentary legislation to carry through his religious reformation, for example, did much to enhance the political importance of Parliament. Not until the seventeenth century, under a new and less politically adept dynasty, did this growth make Parliament a political rival of the crown.

Limits on Royal Power. The Western European monarchies were in many respects still far from the "absolutism" often attributed to them. On balance, the kings of the late fifteenth and sixteenth centuries were politically stronger than the royal weaklings who allowed the nobles to run wild during the fourteenth and fifteenth centuries. Yet though the new kings forced the aristocracy to obey the laws and squeezed them out of key positions in the royal administration, they by no means sought to destroy the vast hereditary privileges of nobility, such as their special position in parliamentary bodies, their exemption from most kinds of direct taxation, and their role as a class of socially dominant landowners and as a military caste. Within the reorganized royal armies, noblemen were still the only persons deemed appropriate for high command.

If the kings kept nobles out of policy-making positions at the royal court, they gladly accorded them social prestige at court and conferred on them pensions and valuable patronage positions in such profusion that important noble families became dependent on the monarch's generosity. Each king thought of himself as the principal nobleman of the realm, and even if he kept nobles out of his inner council, he was constantly subject to their political influence because they were the only class with which he associated intimately. The monarchs of the early modern age—even the monarchs of the "age of absolutism"—had no plan for abolishing the privileges of the aristocratic classes. They merely insisted that as a condition of holding those privileges, the nobles should abandon political opposition to the ruler and should become his loyal servants. With the nobility as with the corporate liberties of the towns and of the clergy, sixteenth-century kings normally intended to preserve the traditional privileges that each social rank had inherited from the medieval past. But they would not tolerate having those privileges made the basis for political opposition.

None of the monarchies of the age became orderly and efficient in the modern sense of those words. Royal financial management, even at its best, was an incredibly complex bundle of collecting and disbursing agencies that had no rational relationship with each other. Income from particular sources of revenue was assigned haphazardly to one agency or another, and if a government creditor received a pay warrant drawn on a treasurer who was without ready cash, there was seldom any way he could compel any other treasurer to honor the warrant. Many taxes or fees were not collected by royal officials at all. Instead, the right to collect a certain tax was let out to private tax contractors, who made a lump-sum payment to the treasury and then got their own reward by pocketing the difference between what they paid the crown and what they could squeeze out of the taxpayers. No government had any systematic method of budgetary planning, and when funds ran short (as they always did in wartime and often did in time of peace), the government lived from hand to mouth by taking out short-term loans at enormous rates of interest from the great bankers of Genoa, Lyons, Augsburg, and Antwerp. During the second half of the sixteenth century, both France and Spain underwent major governmental bankruptcies that made the bonds they issued to lenders virtually worthless. Repeatedly the military operations of warring powers were paralyzed by lack of ready money. In 1557, for example, after winning one of the most brilliant victories of the century, the Spanish army in Flanders sat motionless, vainly awaiting money to pay its disgruntled troops, and the food and munitions necessary for a march on Paris. This delay totally wasted the results of the great victory of St. Quentin.

Other examples of the gross inefficiency of governments include the failure of the French monarchy to establish a single national system of laws to replace the bewildering tangle of local and regional laws that grew up in the Middle Ages; the failure of the Spanish monarchs to compel the inhabitants of the Aragonese half of Spain to bear a fair share of the tax burden imposed by Spain's ambitious foreign policy and frequent wars; and the habit of English kings of allowing insiders at the royal court to get lucrative commercial and industrial monopolies and to buy crown lands at advantageous prices.

The monarchies of the age even developed a method of paying public officials at no cost to the treasury: the fee system, whereby anyone who sought justice from a royal judge or any official document from a government bureau had to pay a fee to the judge or the official, who kept the money as his own. Such a system easily and almost insensibly passed into the giving and taking of bribes. In many jurisdictions, the mark of an honest judge was not that he took no bribes but that after taking bribes from both sides, he decided the case on its merits. In sum, even the reformed and revitalized "new monarchies" were so corrupt and inefficient and were operated so much in the private interests of court favorites that the effective power of the ruler was severely limited.

Recurrent Political Weakness. Even the most powerful monarchy of the age required a reasonably able king before it functioned very well. Part of the success of kings like Louis XI, Ferdinand of Aragon, and Henry VII was due not to new institutions or new policies but to the personal qualities of the ruler. A king like Henry VII, who personally checked every page of the account books of his most trusted agents, governed well in part because he worked hard. The Tudor monarchy worked less smoothly in the closing years of Henry VIII, when the ruler's health began to fail, or under Edward VI, who was only a boy. Spain emerged as a strongly ruled kingdom and the dominant power in Europe partly because under Ferdinand and Isabella (1479–1516), Charles V (1516–56), and Philip II (1556–98), it lived for three consecutive reigns under able and hard-working rulers. In the seventeenth century, when the lethargic Philip III (1598–1621) and his still more incompetent successors sat on the throne, Spanish government quickly declined.

The persistent instability of even the reformed monarchies and their need for an able ruler was most strikingly displayed in France during the second half of the sixteenth century. The accidental death of Henry II in a tournament in 1559 left the crown successively in the hands of his three children, Francis II, Charles IX, and Henry III. The weakness of the rulers, coinciding with a rebirth of factional strife among the nobility and the peak of the Calvinist attempt to make France a Protestant nation, led to a terrible epoch of intermittent civil wars, the French Wars of Religion (1562–98). Only after the talented King Henry IV (1589–1610) took control of the country did orderly government return.

These low points in the history of the English, Spanish, and French monarchies suggest that the political repairs made by the kings of later fifteenth century were mere palliatives whose defects were partly offset by the personal ability of individual kings and by the unearned financial benefits of an expanding economy or of bonanzas like the Spanish plundering of Mexico and Peru or the confiscation of the rich monastic estates by Henry VIII of England. When the economy turned sharply downward in the early seventeenth century, when the wealth from the monastic lands had all been spent, and when the flood of gold and silver treasure from Spanish America fell off sharply after 1600, the deficiencies of the governmental systems of Western Europe became apparent. The apparently strong monarchies of England and Spain quickly ran into financial and political trouble that the new Stuart dynasty in England and the later Hapsburg kings of Spain could not solve.

The Price of Royal Power: War and Dynastic Greed

One immediate price that the Western European nations paid for the exaltation of their kings was the series of bloody and costly wars in which the rulers' selfish pursuit of dynastic interest got their peoples involved. As the English humanist Sir Thomas More pointed out in a brilliant satirical passage of his *Utopia* (1516), the strengthened monarchs were not content to confine themselves to the hard tasks of internal reform. Instead, as soon as their countries had recovered somewhat from the disasters of the late Middle Ages and had gathered some surplus in the treasury, the kings eagerly plunged into wars that involved nothing but their own quest for personal glory and dynastic aggrandizement. When in 1494 King Charles VIII of France led an army to Italy to enforce his hereditary claim to the throne of Naples, his costly expedition may have redounded to his own adolescent hunger for military glory and to the profit of the aristocrats who officered the armies and looted and administered conquered provinces, but it contributed nothing to the well-being of France. This war, and the half-century of other wars that followed from the French kings' attempts to seize Naples and Milan and to dominate Italy, merely squandered French taxes and French lives in an enterprise which sought no goal except the advantage of the Valois dynasty.

The monarchs of Western Europe were indeed the creators of the modern European nations (and had been fulfilling that task since the twelfth century), but the rulers themselves did not seek truly national goals, only dynastic goals. In the short run, the recurrent wars between the French and Spanish kings for control of Italy (1494–1559) brought disaster only to the

Italians, who lost their political independence. But in the long run, the financial strain of the wars, the kings' neglect of domestic problems, and the exaltation of certain groups of nobles through their leadership in the wars led toward political instability.

The Hapsburg Empire: A Dynastic Conglomerate

The prime example of the dynastic, rather than national, orientation of royal policy in sixteen-century Europe was the enormous Hapsburg empire which reached its greatest extent under the Emperor Charles V. This empire rested on no solid foundation of geographical and national groupings and expressed no true political community; it was the result of a remarkably successful policy of dynastic marriages. The Hapsburgs emerged in the late Middle Ages as one of several important territorial princes in Germany, with most of their lands in the region known as Austria. Hapsburgs were frequently elected as Holy Roman Emperors, but the dynasty had no great importance outside of Germany until Prince Maximilian of Hapsburg wed the richest heiress of the fifteenth century, Mary, duchess of Burgundy. This marriage brought into the Hapsburg family the great Burgundian inheritance that earlier dukes had almost built into a monarchy and included most of the Low Countries (modern Belgium and the Netherlands), plus the Free County of Burgundy and a claim on the French duchy of Burgundy, which Louis XI of France had seized in 1477.

The son of Maximilian and Mary, Philip the Handsome, married Princess Juana, daughter of Ferdinand and Isabella of Spain, and their son, Charles of Ghent, acquired the throne of Spain after the death of his maternal grandfather, King Ferdinand, in 1516. When the Emperor Maximilian died in 1519, Charles inherited the Hapsburg domains in Germany and also, despite frantic efforts by Pope Leo X and the king of France to prevent it, secured election as Holy Roman Emperor. Thus at age nineteen, young Charles V not only had the imperial title and the Hapsburg lands in Germany but also ruled the Low Countries and Spain. With the throne of Spain, furthermore, came the still untapped resources of Spanish America and the traditional claim of the Spanish kings to the kingdom of Naples, to Sicily, and to political influence throughout Italy. Other dynastic marriages during Charles V's reign brought to his family a claim on the thrones of Bohemia and Hungary. In 1580, his son Philip II successfully laid claim to the throne of Portugal.

This huge empire looked impressive on the map and made Charles V the most powerful ruler of his century. Yet it was so diverse in peoples, customs, and constitutional traditions, and so scattered across Europe that even an able ruler like Charles V had great difficulty in mobilizing its resources and coordinating its many and very diverse local governments in order to achieve major goals, such as the suppression of the German Protestants or the defense of Christendom from the Turks. The huge Hapsburg empire was not a single state with a single government, but a series of totally distinct governments, in each of which the power of the Hapsburg ruler depended on local custom. Only the accident of having a single ruler brought these diverse states together into a single unit.

In the beginning, young Charles V's administration was so dominated by the Netherlanders among whom he had grown up that other nationalities resented his rule. In the period 1521–22, Spanish resentment at the foreign character of the king and his advisers precipitated serious rebellions. Although his regents put these revolts down, Charles V had to spend most of the 1520s in Spain, reorganizing that country's government and learning its ways, instead of enforcing his policy of suppressing the Lutheran heretics in Germany. Eventually his administration of Spain was so successful that the Spanish kingdom became the main source of his power. But the price he paid was the neglect of German affairs during the whole of the 1520s and the gradual alienation of his subjects in the Low Countries as it became increasingly clear that Spain was now the center of his empire and Spaniards the ruling nationality. Under his wholly Spanish son, Philip II, this alienation grew into an open rebellion in the Netherlands.

Hapsburg-Valois Rivalry. Despite its internal problems, the Hapsburg empire under Charles V functioned as a single power in foreign relations and became a threat to the other European states. In particular the Valois kings of France, finding themselves almost totally encircled by Hapsburg-ruled lands, regarded the accumulation of territories by Charles V as an acute danger. Francis I (1515–47) and Henry II (1547–59) of France fought five wars and intrigued constantly against Charles V in their efforts to break up this overgrown empire. The principal focus of conflict was Italy, and not until the Treaty of Cateau-Cambrésis (1559) did Henry II finally concede to Charles V's son Philip II of Spain the rule of Naples and the dominance of Italy. The same implacable opposition to Hapsburg power explains why Francis I and Henry II, even when they were resolutely persecuting Protestants at home, gave money, munitions, and even open military intervention to help the German Protestant princes. The French goal was not to aid heresy but to prevent the emperor from consolidating his own power in Germany. An even clearer proof that the French kings would ally with anyone in order to break the Hapsburg power was their shocking alliance with the Turks.

The strain of the recurrent Franco-Spanish wars was felt not only by the Italians, whose lands were the principal battleground, but also by the major contending powers, France and Spain. France suffered several invasions along its northern and southern borders. Turkish pirates, tacitly encouraged by the French, ravaged the coasts of Spain. The populations of both lands paid dearly in blood and treasure for the dynastic aspirations of their rulers.

Despite this self-centered pursuit of dynastic advantage at the cost of their subjects, and also despite their aristocratic wastefulness, the kings of

France, Spain, and England held their nations together and made it possible for their people to enjoy a reasonable level of security and well-being. The monarchy in all three countries was popular, and loyalty to a tangible person, the king, was a far more vital influence than loyalty to such an abstract, ill-defined entity as the nation. The people knew that their well-being depended on the king. Even during times of turmoil, such as the French Wars of Religion (1562–98), personal loyalty to the king was the main force that held the country together and made recovery possible.

Effects of Weak Monarchy in Central and Eastern Europe

The importance of the Western European monarchs to the growth of the nations they ruled is underlined by the very different history of Central and Eastern Europe. Italy had never really had a monarchy of its own, and after the collapse of the power of the German emperors in the thirteenth century, it had developed as a collection of totally independent city-states. When the small Italian states were faced with intervention by France and then by Spain from 1494 on, they were overwhelmed by the powers that invaded them. After being fought over from 1494 to 1559, Italy came to be dominated by the Hapsburgs—first the Spanish branch and later the Austrian—right down to the middle of the nineteenth century.

Disintegration of Germany

Germany, the other half of the medieval Holy Roman Empire, retained the shadow of a national government until the French Revolution but in reality fell apart into a collection of almost independent states. The patriotic aristocrats who talked of governmental reform in the late fifteenth century were not willing to surrender their own privileges to the Hapsburg emperors. In his struggle to suppress Lutheranism in Germany, especially during and just after his victory over the Lutheran princes in the Schmalkaldic War of 1546–47, Emperor Charles V made a determined bid to strengthen his control over the territorial princes. Since he could draw on the resources of his Spanish kingdom and his lands in the Low Countries, he appeared close to becoming the actual ruler rather than merely the titular head of Germany. But the defeat of his forces by the Lutheran princes and their French allies in the early 1550s ended his dream of political power as well as his dream of religious unity. The political terms of the Religious Peace of Augsburg (1555) meant that the larger territorial princes, not the emperor, would dominate Germany and that Germany would function not as a single unity but as a collection of small and medium-sized monarchies until the nineteenth century, when the two most powerful, Austria and Prussia, struggled for control of the whole country.

Poland, Bohemia, and Hungary

The three large kingdoms that lay east of Germany—Poland, Bohemia, and Hungary—also illustrate the unhappy political fate of countries where the monarchs failed in their attempts to create a highly centralized state and where the nobility dominated the country. All three were threatened during the sixteenth century by the Turkish expansion. Hungary, in fact, was almost destroyed as an independent state at the battle of Mohacs in 1526, when two-thirds of the country fell under Turkish domination and the other third was seized by Ferdinand of Hapsburg, the brother of Charles V. The nobility in all three countries struggled to keep the monarchy elective, but their basic goal was not to control the central government themselves but to keep it so weak that they had a free hand in dealing with their own oppressed peasantry and in dominating the government of their own localities.

The success of the nobles depended partly on their control of landed wealth and partly on the power of national, provincial, and local representative assemblies that they dominated. Since high matters of national policy interested them very little, the true measure of their success is reflected in their ability to depress the masses of the peasants to the status of legally unfree serfs. Control of the legislative assemblies allowed the noble landlords to give an air of legality to this brutal destruction of peasant liberties, and one reason for keeping the monarchy weak was to prevent any possibility that the king might strengthen his position by championing the rights of the peasants.

Bohemia and Hungary drifted under increasing control of their Hapsburg kings after 1526, and the rulers were able to weaken the elective character of both crowns and even to undermine the special constitutional privileges of the Bohemian Protestants, though Bohemia remained loosely controlled until the Hapsburgs reconquered the country after the Bohemian rebellion that opened the Thirty Years' War in 1618. In Hungary, the power of the nobles remained far greater, because the crown had to have their help against the Turks. The Hungarian nobles controlled local and county government almost unchallenged until the political reorganization of the Hapsburg monarchy in 1867.

Poland, unlike Bohemia and Hungary, did not come under the rule of a foreign dynasty, though its nobles elected kings from both the French and the Swedish royal families. Though the nobility was already very strong, King Sigismund III (1587–1632) was able to play a major role in restricting the religious rights of the nobles, many of whom had become Protestants, and in the reconversion of the country to Catholicism. Local autonomy was already so strong that decisions of the national legislature were not binding on a region if the local assembly rejected them. The Polish Diet already tended to seek unanimous consent to many types of action, though the disastrous practice of *liberum veto* (that one negative vote could block a proposed law) had not yet become established. Poland was still big and militarily formidable in its own region. But the success of the nobility in keeping the monarchy weak and in retaining great power at the local level of government pointed the way to the fatal weakness of Poland in the eighteenth century, when its greedy neighbors partitioned the whole country.

The Ottoman Threat

To the east and southeast of Poland, Bohemia, and Hungary lay two large empires that were partly outside the sphere of traditional Western civilization. The Ottoman empire during the fourteenth and fifteenth centuries had already occupied most of the Balkan peninsula and had conquered Constantinople. During the sixteenth century, this militaristic state was ruled by two of its greatest sultans, Selim I (1512–20) and Suleiman the Magnificent (1520–66). These rulers defeated the Persian empire and forced it to give up the region now known as Iraq; they conquered all of Syria and Egypt (1516–17), shattered the Hungarian kingdom (1526) and occupied two-thirds of its territory, and conducted a vigorous naval campaign against Christian states in the Mediterranean.

The Ottoman empire was a major factor in European history. The fear that the Turks would break out of the Balkans entirely and occupy lands in Bohemia, southeastern Germany, and even Italy was a very real one, and defense against the Turks was a major concern of the Emperor Charles V and his son Philip II of Spain, often at the expense of their policy in other regions. In 1529 the Turks conducted a major siege of Vienna but failed to take it. During this and other periods of crisis, the imperial government had to beg the Lutheran princes for aid instead of enforcing its decrees against heresy. Even the defeat of the Turkish fleet at Lepanto by the combined fleets of Venice, the papacy, and Spain in 1571 did not permanently end the power of Turkey to threaten all neighboring states.

Russian Despotism

East of Poland lay the state of Muscovy, Christian in faith but almost as culturally alien to Western Europe as was the Ottoman empire. After the fall of Constantinople to the Turks in 1453, the Muscovite rulers assumed the title of emperor (czar) and claimed to have inherited the universal authority and the special protectorate over Orthodox Christians that the Byzantine empire claimed in the Middle Ages. Sixteenth-century Muscovy was far too weak to enforce these sweeping political claims. But under the ruthless Ivan IV (Ivan the Terrible, 1533–84), wars against the Tatars left the Russians in control of the huge Volga river basin, an acquisition that opened the way for later expansion into Siberia and all the way to the Pacific. Ivan the Terrible had much less success against states to the west—Poland and the Teutonic Knights in Livonia—but he at least foreshadowed future Russian expansion toward the Baltic Sea.

Internally, Russia was ruled as a despotism. The czars wiped out the self-governing status of the towns and established firm control over the influential and wealthy church. Ivan the Terrible realized that the boyars (the landed nobles) were the most serious threat to his power, so he engaged in a brutal policy of massacres and land confiscations with the goal of plundering the old nobility in order to strengthen himself and the new service-nobility he was creating from his personal agents. Since the new nobles desperately needed peasants to till their lands, and since the wars and massacres of the reign had depopulated many areas, Ivan helped the nobles reduce the formerly free Russian peasantry to a class of serfs bound to the soil, though this attack on the liberties of the people was not completed until the eighteenth century. Russia was already developing into the autocratically ruled, militaristic, and expansionist state that achieved great-power status during the eighteenth and nineteenth centuries. Its primitive political machinery, however, prevented rapid progress. After Ivan IV's death in 1584, his weak successor was unable to cope with the internal tensions and the hostility of neighboring states that Ivan's policies had generated.

The end of the sixteenth and the beginning of the seventeenth century are known in Russian history as the "time of troubles." Civil war among the nobility, intrigue among court factions, uprisings by oppressed peasants, and military intervention by the king of Poland nearly destroyed the country. Recovery did not begin until 1613, when Michael Romanov established his new dynasty on the throne. The early Romanovs accomplished little more than the ending of civil war and the regaining of some of the lands lost to Poland during the Time of Troubles. Not until the reign of Peter the Great (1689–1725) did Russia begin its advance toward great-power status.

War and Politics in the Later Sixteenth Century

The focus of European politics in the later sixteenth century lay outside Eastern and Central Europe. Even Germany, after the Religious Peace at Augsburg (1555), played only a limited role until the approach of the Thirty Years' War. The Hapsburg-Valois rivalry which poisoned international relations in the earlier sixteenth century continued, but after the Treaty of Cateau-Cambrésis (1559) and the outbreak of its own Wars of Religion (1562), France was no longer able to challenge Spanish domination of Italy. Spain was clearly the strongest power in Europe, with the most effective armed forces and the most broadly conceived foreign policy of the century. Spanish ships and a Spanish admiral led the Christian naval victory over the

Turks at Lepanto in 1571. In 1580, Philip II of Spain successfully enforced his claim to the vacant Portuguese throne, thus acquiring a great colonial empire second only to that of Spain. Although Philip failed in his efforts to suppress rebellion in the Netherlands and in his attempted invasion of England (1588), his combined kingdoms of Spain and Portugal retained their military and political predominance well into the seventeenth century.

Religion and Politics

The dominant force in European politics in the late sixteenth century, however, was not the persistent Franco-Spanish rivalry but a pair of revolutionary outbreaks in the two empires. These disturbances are commonly known as wars of religion, pitting Protestants against Catholics. Conflicting ideologies, however, were only one source of violence. Complex political, constitutional, and soical problems were at least equally as important. What made the wars appear predominantly religious was the way in which Calvinism in both France and the Low Countries provided potential rebels with a revolutionary leadership and an effective form of organization.

Calvinism (like all major religions of the age) did not preach a doctrine of revolution. It taught that all existing governments were divinely ordained and that all Christians must obey a lawful ruler, even if he is oppressive. A true believer would refuse to obey his ruler only if commanded to do something directly opposed to God's commands, and even then, he must passively accept his punishment and would not be justified in rebelling. Almost as an afterthought, Calvin had added that where there were constitutionally established "inferior magistrates" who had a lawful share of public authority, these persons might properly organize a resistance to tyrannical acts, though no private citizen had any such right. Such a theory, however, was not uniquely Calvinist: Luther and his followers had used a similar theory to justify the German territorial princes' opposition to the religious policies of Charles V.

Calvinism as a Revolutionary Movement. What really set Calvinism apart from other major Protestant denominations was its polity—the method it used to organize and govern its own movement. Alone among the large religious movements of the Reformation, Calvinism had consistently refused to accept control of the Church by the political authorities. Instead, it created self-governing local churches and a hierarchy of representative assemblies such as the provincial synods and the national synod that, by 1559, the French Calvinists had organized right under the noses of hostile governmental authorities. This series of self-governing institutions made the Reformed churches in Scotland, France, and the Netherlands able to organize and propagate themselves without governmental support and even in direct opposition to governmental policy, whereas the Lutheran and Anglican denominations relied on support by the government. This distinctive polity made the Calvinist churches remarkably effective instruments for organizing political (and religious) opposition groups into powerful revolutionary organizations. These organizations were not large enough to precipitate effective armed resistance on the question of religion alone, but once a political crisis had developed on a broad range of issues, the Calvinist organizations were remarkably effective at taking control of the political opposition. Even those opposition politicians who did not find Calvinist ideology attractive soon learned that the fanaticism of Calvinist extremists and the nationwide organization of the Reformed churches were tools essential to their political struggle.

Political Crisis in France. The "religious" wars in every case broke out over issues that were more secular than religious and in every case only in countries where the monarchy became weak. In France, the most immediate cause for the Wars of Religion that tore the country apart between 1562 and 1598 was the weakness of the Valois dynasty. None of the last three Valois kings, the brothers Francis II (1559–60), Charles IX (1560–74), and Henry III (1574–89) was personally fit to rule, and only Henry III lived long enough to rule as an adult. Furthermore, none of the sons of Henry II managed to beget a male heir, so that with them the Valois dynasty came to an end. Domestic politics took the form of a bitter struggle for control of government among factions of the nobility, and the bitterness became worse because one of the factions, led by the noble Guise family, was fiercely Catholic and determined to root out heresy, while the rival Bourbon faction, headed by the family next in line for the throne if the Valois family died out, was Protestant. The political bickering also involved a third faction of nobles led by the great family of Montmorency, which was divided in religion. Furthermore, complicating all politics were the efforts of the mother of the last three Valois kings, the Italian princess Catherine de Medici, to dominate the government of her weakling sons.

Although the question of whether to continue trying to destroy Calvinism through persecution was at the center of conflict, and although riots between bands of Catholic and Protestant ruffians provided the impetus that led to full-scale civil war by 1562, political rivalry for control of government was a more basic cause of conflict. What really held the noble court factions together and enabled them to enlist adherents among provincial nobles was the economic dependence of the noble class on the profits of government office. Kings Francis I and Henry II had heaped honors and gifts upon the nobility, and their wars—especially the campaigns in Italy—had opened great opportunities for the class that officered the armies and administered conquered provinces. After 1559 the profits of war were cut off. Under young Francis II (1559–60) the heads of the Guise faction, as uncles of the queen, dominated the administration and used their control of patronage to drive their political rivals from positions of power and profit and to install their own friends in office. The ousted nobles in 1560, led by the impulsive prince of Condé, formed a plot to kidnap the young king and the whole royal court and thus to control the government. This Conspiracy of Amboise was found out. Several of the leaders were executed, though Condé was too powerful and too closely related to the royal family for the Guise faction to touch him.

After the death of Francis II at age seventeen, Queen Mother Catherine de Medici was able to break Guise control of the administration. But being a woman and a foreigner, she was not able to establish her own power firmly. Catherine tried to solve the problem of rioting between Catholics and the expanding Calvinist group by a series of public religious discussions and by the granting of limited toleration. But since neither side would settle for toleration, conflict became more and more violent. The rapid conversion of large numbers of French nobles to the new religion further increased the tendency toward violence, for as men of military habits and social prestige, the nobles became the natural protectors of Huguenot (Calvinist) churches, which more and more frequently abandoned their clandestine status and openly conducted services and sought converts.

The Wars of Religion, 1562–98. An incident at Vassy in eastern France in March of 1562, when the armed retinue of the duke of Guise massacred a Huguenot congregation, marks the transition from widespread rioting to real civil war. Between 1562 and 1598, France underwent eight short outbreaks of civil war, with brief and violence-prone truces spread between. The actual military operations were confused and indecisive. Despite the role of religious hatreds, both sides relied heavily on foreign mercenaries. Each side sought intervention by ideologically sympathetic foreign powers —Catholic Spain and Protestant England—at the cost of promising away French territory to reward its rescuers. The most famous event of the wars actually came during a period of "peace"—the infamous St. Bartholomew's Day Massacre of 1572, when the queen mother abandoned her conciliatory policy and cooperated with the ultra-Catholic duke of Guise to murder the dynamic Protestant nobleman Coligny and to incite the people of Paris to massacre the Protestant nobles who had come to the city to attend an important royal wedding.

Politiques versus the Catholic League. The savage massacre of 1572 disgusted many moderate French Catholics, and long continuation of the disorders encouraged the growth of a political group whom their ultra-Catholic enemies contemptuously labeled *Politiques* because they put the political tranquility of the country ahead of the need for "true religion." Instead of moderating under the influence of the Politiques, however, the violence became worse under the last, the ablest, and the most corrupt of

Catherine de Medici's sons, Henry III (1574–89). Although Henry himself had participated in planning the St. Bartholomew's Day Massacre, once he became king, he developed a deep fear and hatred of the duke of Guise. But he was unsuccessful in rallying the moderate people of France to his leadership, partly because he lacked the energy necessary to direct a political faction, partly because his overt homosexuality caused him to be despised by the aristocracy, and most of all because his failure to beget a male heir meant that the next lawful heir to the throne would be the despised heretic, Henry of Navarre, leader of the Bourbon faction.

The prospect of a Protestant king caused a radical change in the political theory and actions of extreme French Catholics. Up to 1584, when the death of Henry's younger brother made it certain that Henry of Navarre would be the lawful heir, Calvinists had played the role of revolutionaries in French politics. After 1584, however, a new Catholic League emerged to replace one dissolved earlier by the king. Led originally by priests, professional men, and prominent Paris bourgeois, this new league became a mass organization controlled not by its titular head, the duke of Guise, but by the bigoted lower middle-class artisans of Paris.

Faced with the prospect of a heretical king and with the actual rule of a king who was willing to negotiate with the Huguenots in order to weaken the duke of Guise, the Catholic League became a revolutionary organization dedicated to the defense of the Catholic faith at any price. Led but not really controlled by Guise, the league negotiated an alliance with Philip II and in 1588, with the encouragement and financial support of the Spanish ambassador, staged an uprising at Paris that drove King Henry III from his capital. In a desperate gamble to recoup his authority, the king had both the duke of Guise and his brother the cardinal of Guise murdered, but this act merely inspired a fanatical monk to stab the king himself to death. This deed created precisely the situation the ultra-Catholics had feared: under any possible interpretation of the laws of hereditary succession, the Calvinist Henry of Navarre, head of the Bourbon family, would come to the throne as King Henry IV.

The Success of Henry IV

Members of the Catholic League had sworn that they would never accept Navarre as king. The more extreme were even willing to accept Philip II of Spain, a distant relative of the recent Valois kings, as their new ruler. Fortunately for Henry IV, several forces worked in his favor: the lack of any legally defensible claimant of French birth, the widespread feeling that the Guises had sold out to Spain, and growing tension within the Catholic League between the conservative Catholic nobles and the fanatical rabble who dominated the powerful Paris organization. The new king could not at once abandon the Huguenot party whose troops formed his chief military support, but he knew that ultimately he would have to turn Catholic. The conservative royalist Catholics known as Politiques had long been hostile to the ultra-Catholic and pro-Spanish policies of the League and the Duke of Guise. Yet they hesitated to help a Calvinist win the throne for fear that their own religion would then be persecuted, as had happened in Geneva, in the Netherlands, and even in some French towns the heretics controlled. For this group, whose political influence was growing, the conversion of Henry IV to the Catholic faith in 1593 was a great relief. Although it was obvious that political expediency was the reason for the conversion, the moderates now actively helped the new king, and except for a small group of extremists, even the members of the Catholic League began to rally to the Bourbon king. In 1594, Henry easily occupied Paris, which had been the center of resistance to him, and in 1595, the pope himself accepted Henry's conversion.

While the Catholic majority of France was rallying round the new Bourbon ruler, King Henry did all he could to heal the nation's wounds. In his famous Edict of Nantes (1598), he guaranteed full religious toleration and relatively generous rights of public worship and full civil rights to the large Huguenot minority, thus proclaiming that an ultra-Catholic policy of persecution was too costly for his exhausted country to bear. In order that the Huguenots would trust his promises, he also gave them the right to fortify and garrison a number of strategic towns in regions they controlled, so that they would feel able to resume the war if the government reneged on its promises. In handling the ultra-Catholic nobles, the king used armed forces where necessary, but he cynically realized that most of them had their price and that it was cheaper to buy them off than to reduce them to obedience by armed force. Increasingly the military operations in France lost the character of a civil war and took the form of a national war against Spain. Finally, in 1598, Henry forced the dying King Philip II of Spain to sign a treaty acknowledging Henry as king of France.

For the rest of his reign, Henry IV concentrated on two goals: (1) internal reconstruction from the ravages of civil war, involving both physical rebuilding of bridges, roads, and harbors, and governmental encouragement of agriculture, commerce, and industry, and (2) a reassertion of France's claim to be a dominant power in Europe and an effective counterweight to Spanish dominance. Henry even returned to the policy of French encouragement to the Protestant foes of Hapsburg power in Germany, and his own murder in 1610 by an unbalanced Catholic extremist was a result of his imminent preparations to begin a war against the Hapsburgs in support of the West German Protestants.

Political Unrest in the Low Countries

The "religious" wars across France's northern borders in the Low Countries were even less exclusively religious than those in France. The seventeen provinces that had been an important part of Charles V's dominions went to his Spanish son Philip II when the emperor retired in 1556. Only the person of the Hapsburg ruler and a few central institutions the Hapsburgs and their Burgundian ancestors had developed (e.g., a Council of States and a representative assembly, the Estates General) held together these provinces, each of which had its own traditional political institutions. The government of each province, as well as control of the few organs of central government, was in the hands of the wealthy merchants who dominated the towns and (still more) of the highly privileged nobility, a class that regarded high office as its hereditary right. Emperor Charles V had grown up among this nobility and understood its traditions. Although there was some resentment at his tendency to reduce provincial autonomy, he catered to the aristocrats, who trusted him personally even though they grumbled about the many distant wars on which Charles squandered the lives and money of his fellow Netherlanders.

When the utterly Spanish son of Charles V, Philip II of Spain, took control of the Low Countries, the grumbling that had met his father's policies grew into a loud protest, and ultimately to riot and revolution. Part of the problem was the foreign character of the ruler. Philip II spoke only Spanish and understood neither the languages nor the mentality of his Netherlandish subjects. As soon as the peace of 1559 with France made it possible, he hastened back to his native Spain and never again left its soil. Anti-Spanish sentiment had grown overt during the closing years of the French war. In 1556 the nobles formally charged that the war was not being fought in their interest. At the end of the war in 1559, the Estates General demanded that the Spanish garrison, which the Nherlanders had come to detest, be withdrawn.

Sources of Conflict. There were more substantial issues that set the king and his subjects at odds. Although Philip II began his reign by granting important offices on the Council of State to high nobles, and although his choice of his half-sister Margaret of Parma as governor was not unpopular, it soon became obvious that real power was not in the hands of the Council of State but in the hands of a tiny inner circle of royal servants who discussed policy in secret and were dominated by a foreign appointee, the Cardinal Granvelle.

A second bitter issue was a radical plan for reform and reorganization of the Catholic Church in the Low Countries, announced by Philip II in 1561. In many ways, the king's plan was intelligent and effective. It wiped out the unworkable crazy-quilt pattern of church organization inherited from the distant past and redrew the bounderies of bishoprics and archbishoprics so that all Netherlands parishes would be under the undisputed authority of a Netherlands bishop, with a clear chain of command extending downward from the senior archbishop through the bishops to the parish level. It even took careful account of the major cultural and linguistic division between French-speaking and Dutch-speaking regions. It provided financial support for the new bishoprics by suppressing a number of rich monasteries and reallocating their landed wealth as endowments for the bishoprics.

But judged from the tradition-dominated viewpoint of the ruling classes of the Low Countries, this Church reorganization was an act of tyranny. It totally disregarded the long-established control that certain noble families held over the patronage of certain Church offices; it neglected the provisions of the wills by which pious donors had given property to suppressed monasteries, and it followed the autocratic Spanish model by transferring control of valuable and powerful positions in the Church from the nobles to the king. The nobles and the people defined right and justice in terms of what had existed from time immemorial. They resented both the tangible loss of wealth and power they suffered and the king's arrogant disregard of tradition. The issue involved a clash between two opposing concepts of the prince's authority: the medieval ideal of a king limited by a contractual obligation to respect the traditional rights of the nobility and the other privileged groups, *versus* King Philip's new-fangled idea that his will must be supreme and that he must be free to do anything he judged expedient for society. There was also a personal basis for the conflict, since as archbishop of Malines, the unpopular Cardinal Granvelle would be head of the new system. The outcry for cancellation of the whole plan originated with the nobles but was seconded by the Protestants, who already were persecuted but who feared that the dreaded Spanish Inquisition would be extended to all parts of the Netherlands.

Indeed, fear that the reforms would increase the level of persecution was a further irritant. Philip II took a typically Spanish approach to the problem of heresy, which he regarded as socially and politically subversive and thus intended to root out by force. But even many Dutch Catholics shared the tolerant attitude of their fellow-countryman, the humanist Erasmus, that it was un-Christian to kill people for their opinions. Also, royal acts directed against heresy often seemed unconstitutional: Philip's attempt to define new classes of crimes and to create new courts by his own authority posed a threat to the traditional laws and law courts. And in a commercial society that lived on foreign trade, policies that might scare away English, German, and Scandinavian merchants would endanger the country's prosperity.

This religious situation was complicated by the rapid spread of Calvinism, which during the 1550s penetrated into such important classes as the nobility and the wealthy merchants. The Calvinists were still only a small minority, but their effective organization and their gains in membership among the politically influential classes made the issue of persecution especially acute.

"Beggars" and Rioters. Public agitation for the removal of Cardinal Granvelle, led not by Calvinists but by high-ranking nobles such as the prince of Orange, caused Philip II to dismiss that unpopular official in 1564. But the basic sources of unrest were unresolved. Agitation next focused on petitions for relaxation of the severe royal edicts against heresy and on resistance to Philip's attempts to enforce the decrees of the Council of Trent. The "Beggars," as a royal official contemptuously labeled a group of noble petitioners in 1566, were almost ruined in 1567, when bands of lower-class people aroused by Anabaptist and Calvinist attacks on the "idolatry" of the Roman Catholic Church but also enraged by high unemployment and rising food prices, broke into savage riots aimed at smashing the "idols"—the religious statuary and paintings—in the churches. This lower-class violence caused many of the crown's critics to rally to the government. Troops suppressed armed bands of radical Protestants. The great prince of Orange, who had opposed the riots but was major leader of the earlier lawful opposition, prudently left the country and went to live on his estates in Germany.

Alva's Policy of Terror. The riots so deeply compromised the opposition to royal policy that good political management might have solidified Philip's control of the provinces. Instead, however, the king of Spain sent his ablest but most brutal general, accompanied by a large army of Spaniards and Italians, to take control. This man, the duke of Alva, not only hunted down rioters but also extended his arrests so far that great numbers of Netherlanders concluded that Philip II was using the riots of 1567 as a pretext for the destruction of the region's liberties. Alva arrested and summarily executed great nobles like the count of Hoorne and the count of Egmont despite their high rank and their scrupulous abstention from all acts of opposition except peaceful petitioning. Alva imposed crushing fines on cities where riots had occurred and then jailed the municipal officials until the fines were paid. The country seemed to be thoroughly cowed, and when the prince of Orange raised a small army in Germany and attempted an invasion in 1568, there was almost no trace of support. Confident that he had the country firmly in hand, Alva summoned the Estates General and proposed that it pay his troops by levying a tax of 10 percent on all transfers of goods, a tax like the Spanish *alcabala*, which had harmful economic effects even in agrarian Spain and would cause economic chaos if applied to an advanced commercial economy like that of the Netherlands. Instead of the anticipated submission, this tax proposal met such a storm of opposition that eventually the plan fell through.

What really upset Alva's plans, however, was an unexpected military reverse. Neither the riots of 1566, nor the abortive invasion by William of Orange in 1568 can properly be called the outbreak of a true civil war. Large numbers of the "Beggar" opposition fled abroad. The seafarers among them began operating as pirates against Spanish shipping, and the English government studiously looked the other way as these "Sea Beggars" used English ports to outfit their ships and sell their plunder. In 1572, however, diplomatic pressure from Spain forced the English government to banish these pirates from English seaports. Desperate for a base, in April of 1572 the Sea Beggars surprised and captured the fortified port of Brill on the Dutch coast. In the next few months, aided by Calvinists and anti-Spanish Catholics working from within, the rebels captured most of the towns of the maritime provinces of Zeeland and Holland. William of Orange came from Germany to take command of the rebel forces, and from 1572 onward, the rebels always had substantial control of those two northern provinces.

Constitutional Issues and Religion. The prince of Orange was originally little more than a reactionary aristocrat trying to defend the special interests of his class, but by the 1570s he was firmly convinced that he was upholding the constitutional liberties of the whole country against a ruler who was undermining the constitution. Orange did not fight for the triumph of Calvinism or even for legal toleration of heretics (though he himself opposed Philip II's persecutions and eventually became a nominal Calvinist) because he realized that such aims would divide the opposition movement, which was united only on the question of defending the ancient constitution. Yet Orange also realized that his most reliable and effective supporters were the Calvinist Beggars, and while he regretted their ruthless suppression of Catholic worship in the northern provinces, he had to close his eyes to it.

For a time it seemed as if a united Netherlands fighting to defend its constitution would compel King Philip II to give in. The hated Duke of Alva was dismissed in 1573. When the Spanish army in the southern part of the country, furious at the inability of its bankrupt government to pay the troops, attacked and brutally plundered the rich city of Antwerp even though it was loyal to Philip, the local and provincial governments of the South organized for their own defense and in 1576 made an agreement with the rebels in the North and recognized Orange as commander of their troops.

The Division of the Low Countries. Mistrust of Philip II and hatred of Spain pulled the country together. But the Netherlanders had not yet developed a strong sense of national identity. The cultural and linguistic divisions that still threatened modern Belgium with civil strife weakened their unity. Most of all, the wealthy Catholic nobles and merchants who had taken control of the South were dismayed at the way in which the triumphant Calvinist minority in Holland and Zeeland had violated the rights of the Catholic majority, and feared that their own religion might be suppressed likewise. A new series of iconoclastic riots by mobs of working-class Protestants deepened these fears. In 1579 the Catholic nobles who led the southern provinces formed a special league, the Union of Arras, which negotiated a separate agreement with Philip II. The king confirmed their constitutional liberties and promised to help them reestablish the Catholic religion. In the face of these developments, the seven northern provinces controlled by the rebels formed the Union of Utrecht. Although each side claimed to speak for the whole country, in fact the Netherlands had become divided.

Dutch Independence. In 1581 the Union of Utrecht adopted the Act of Abjuration, in which they stated that by violating their constitution Philip II had broken his coronation oath and hence had forfeited his right to rule them. It was a declaration of independence, and from this time forth, the federal union of the seven northern provinces became a separate nation. Thanks to their naval control of the coastal waters and to the inability of the Spanish army to conquer the Dutch seaports, by 1609 the new nation had won its independence and compelled Spain to sign a twelve-year truce, though Spain did not formally recognize Dutch independence until the end of the Thirty Years' War in 1648. In the southern provinces, however, Philip II managed to reestablish his control, thanks to the political and military skill of his new governor, Alexander Farnese, duke of Parma. The Spanish Netherlands became solidly Catholic once more and remained firmly under the rule of the Spanish and then the Austrian Hapsburgs down to the French Revolution. In the nineteenth century it reappeared under the new name of Belgium.

The Contest between Spain and England

The emergence of England as the deadly rival of Hapsburg Spain and the chief political and military support of the Protestant rebels in France and the Netherlands was the third great political event of the age, alongside the French Wars of Religion and the Dutch rebellion. Queen Elizabeth I (1558–1603) had no desire to become a rival of Philip II, and she certainly had no desire to play the role of crusader for Protestantism abroad. At first, Philip II was at least moderately friendly, and even Elizabeth's abandonment of Catholicism and return to a separate national church that was vaguely Calvinist and firmly antipapal did not cause serious hostility.

The dominant influences in shaping Elizabeth's foreign policy were her desire for security and her fear that since Catholic Church law did not recognize her father's marriage to Anne Boleyn, foreign Catholic powers might back Catholic pretenders to her throne. At the outset of the reign, the latter danger came not from Spain, whose king recognized her title, but from Scotland and France. Young Mary Stuart, Queen of Scotland, was a Catholic princess with good claim to rule England if Elizabeth's title were invalidated; and Mary's marriage to Francis II of France and her relationship to the ultra-Catholic Guise family created the danger that France and

Scotland might conspire together to unseat Elizabeth and to restore Catholicism. Hence even though Elizabeth had no desire to aid foreign Protestants, she knew that it was to her advantage for the discontented Protestant groups in Scotland, France, and the Netherlands to keep their rulers so preoccupied that none of those three areas could become a base for an invasion of England. When the Scottish nobility rebeled against French domination and royal opposition to Calvinism in 1559, Elizabeth intervened with her navy and her army, claiming that she was merely trying to prevent the establishment of a French military base in Scotland. At a later stage of Scottish political turmoil, in 1568, when the Calvinist nobles drove Queen Mary Stuart into exile and took power in the name of her infant son James, Elizabeth refused to aid the exiled Scottish queen and kept her in protective custody for almost two decades. Elizabeth finally had Mary executed on charges of conspiring to murder her.

The outbreak of the French Wars of Religion in 1562 and of disorder in the Netherlands in 1566 provided Elizabeth with an opportunity to keep the governments of both regions so distracted that they could never attack England. Elizabeth preferred limited and secret encouragement rather than open aid to either rebellion. When she did make agreements with the rebels, she selfishly demanded financial and territorial concessions. Despite her lack of generosity and the limited scale of the help she gave, Elizabeth's help was of crucial importance to both groups of rebels.

Since Elizabeth's actions in the Netherlands were directly encouraging rebellion against Spanish rule, and since Spain was intervening in favor of the French Guise faction, these policies gradually poisoned the traditionally friendly relations between England and Spain. By 1585, Elizabeth was openly sending troops to aid the Dutch, and raids by English pirates against Spanish settlements and ships in America provided another irritant. Philip II was no mindless servant of the popes, but he did energetically play the role of defender of Catholic religion against the heretics in the Netherlands, France, and Germany and against the Turks in the Balkans and in the Mediterranean Sea, so long as this role fostered the interests of his own Hapsburg dynasty. He showed no similar desire to help English Catholics by overthrowing their heretical queen so long as the Catholic claimant to the English throne was the half-French Mary Queen of Scots. But as Mary became more desperate for Spanish aid, and hence seemed less likely to become an anti-Spanish ruler, and as English aid to the Dutch rebels became larger and more open, Philip II began considering an invasion of England. The execution of Mary in 1587 was a further encouragement to action, for now Philip II might claim the English throne for himself.

The Plan for the Armada

Philip II had begun plans for an invasion of England by 1585, but the preparations took on far greater urgency after Philip could envision himself as the logical Catholic ruler of England. The plan was for a great fleet to sail from the ports of Spain and Portugal and defeat the English navy. Then convoy barges would carry the Duke of Parma's veteran army from Flanders to England, where it seemed certain that the Spanish infantry would make short work of the English army, and where it was also hoped that English Catholics would rise up to help the invaders. Once Philip had made his final decision to attack, not even the brilliantly successful raids led by the famous commander Drake could do more than delay Spanish preparations. In July of 1588, the great Spanish Armada (fleet) set off to accomplish "the Enterprise of England." A running naval battle along the length of the English Channel in late July and early August proved that the Spanish Armada was unable to destroy the English and convoy the invading troops securely. Hence although the Spanish fleet was by no means destroyed, its commander had to give up the invasion plan and make his return to Spain by sailing around the northern coasts of Scotland and Ireland. Violent storms along those treacherous coastal waters destroyed far more Spanish ships than the English had done. Although forty-four out of the original sixty-eight ships got back to Spain, many of these were unfit for further service.

The defeat of this costly invasion attempt was a heavy blow to Spanish power, not only at sea but also in the wars in France and the Netherlands. But it certainly did not end Spain's ability to fight the heretics, nor did it even establish a clear English predominance at sea. It did mean, however, that an ambitious Spanish attempt to win in France and the Netherlands by defeating the main supporter of the rebels had failed. It meant that Spain had less chance than ever of establishing strongly Catholic and pro-Spanish governments in France and the Netherlands; and even many Catholic rulers felt relieved at the defeat of a plan that might have left the Hapsburgs directly or indirectly in control of most of Europe.

Ideological Results of Conflict

The religious tensions, international rivalries, and civil wars of sixteenth-century Europe compelled thinkers to devote much attention to basic questions of political experience, such as the relative rights of society and of individuals and subgroups within society, the relation between the centralizing innovations of rulers and the desire of society to preserve ancient laws and customs, and the foundations of international peace in a society of separate states intent on their own advantage.

Conscience and Political Obedience

The leading Protestant Reformers—Luther, Zwingli, and Calvin—dealt mainly with theological issues and only incidentally with politics. But the clash between religious innovators and political rulers raised the unavoidable questions of the rights of individual conscience and the limits of political obedience. All the major Protestant theologians agreed in teaching a doctrine of passive obedience: that Christians were bound in conscience to obey even an oppressive ruler, except in cases where he commanded a violation of a clearly stated command of God, in which cases the believer must reluctantly disobey and meekly accept the tyrant's punishment. None of the great reformers allowed a general right of resistance by individuals. All of them did, however, teach that where the laws provided for inferior magistrates (the nobles, or a representative assembly, for example) who had the right and duty to uphold the laws against an oppressive king, such authorities might organize a resistance to oppression—in extreme cases, even a revolution. This was the theoretical basis for the refusal of Protestant territorial princes and town councils in Germany to obey the emperor's orders for the suppression of Lutheranism. This theory of lawful resistance by constituted authorities also provided the theoretical basis for political and military resistance by Calvinists in Scotland, France, and the Low Countries.

Rise of Revolutionary Ideology. Thus the "modern" social and ideological force of Protestantism used the traditional and "medieval" theory of limited constitutional monarchy to justify resistance to Catholic oppressors. But Calvinist political theory soon turned more radical. Calvin's Scottish disciple John Knox cast aside the idea of passive obedience and frankly preached that where a ruler violates the will of God, the people have an inherent right of revolution. Knox emphasized obedience to divine commands more than defense of constitutional liberties in his justification of the revolutionary acts of the Scottish Calvinists.

The most important writings in defense of Protestant rebellions, however, came out in France as a response to the St. Bartholomew's Day Massacre. This bloody deed, in which the king, the queen mother, and other members of the royal family were implicated, demolished the Huguenots' earlier pretense that they were merely trying to free the king from evil advisers. The earliest important response was the *Franco-Gallia* of François Hotman, which attempted to prove both from medieval history and from philosophical analysis that the king of France received his power from the people on condition that he govern justly. If the king violates this condition and becomes a tyrant, the "inferior magistrates" (but not private citizens) may organize a rebellion. A few years later, an even more influential treatise, the anonymous *Vindicias contra tyrannos* (1579) set forth the theoretical basis for a lawful revolution against a tyrant, with special reference to situations where the ruler upholds false religion and persecutes true religion. This book teaches that the basis of political authority is a contractual agreement between the whole community and the king. If the king violates the agreement, the community may act to enforce its terms, though it must act through its constituted leaders (again, the "inferior magistrates"). Precisely this sort of political theory formed the basis of the Act of Abjuration (1581), by which the Dutch rebels repudiated Philip II's authority by accusing him of unconstitutional government.

Catholic Extremists and Tyrannicide. After the death of the last Valois heir to the French throne in 1584, when it became clear that a Protestant would succeed King Henry III, it was the turn of Catholic political theorists to find justification for the rebellious acts of the Catholic League. The same ideas of popular sovereignty, derivation of royal authority from a contract, and right of resistance to a king who violates the terms of the contract dominated Catholic tracts and pamphlets. The essential condition which the king must not violate, of course, was his obligation to uphold the true and traditional Catholic faith and to suppress heresy. Catholic extremists, however, went beyond their Calvinist predecessors by teaching that not only the inferior magistrates but even a private individual might resist and even assassinate a heretical king. This infamous theory of tyrannicide was defended in the works of the Spanish Jesuit theologian Juan de Mariana. Most Protestants of the age denounced it as a belief held by all Catholics, or at least by all Jesuits, though in fact most Catholic thinkers repudiated the idea that a single individual had the right to judge and kill the king. More typical was the opinion of the famous Jesuit Robert Bellarmine, who accepted the idea that secular political power came from the people and that the people might revoke the power of a tyrant, but who added that royal power might also be revoked by the pope, since his authority came directly from God.

In the long run, what both Calvinist and Catholic theorists accomplished was to popularize the idea that the ruler's power came from the community and hence might be revoked if the ruler seriously misused it. This theory of popular sovereignty and the right of rebellion had a great future in store for it in seventeenth-century England and eighteenth-century America and France.

Theories of Royal Absolutism: Sovereignty and Divine Right. The dominant tendency of political thought, however, was to defend the power of the monarch rather than the right of revolution. Faced with the dire consequences of civil war in France and the Netherlands, many thinkers concluded that only the unlimited power of the king could preserve the country from internal disorders and foreign attack. Hence the ideology of absolute monarchy developed mightily. In France the political group known as *Politiques* had long argued that the country could be secure only if loyalty to the king prevailed over all special interests of creed, class, or region.

The work which best expressed this viewpoint was the *Six Books of the Republic* (1576) by Jean Bodin. Bodin hammered incessantly at two themes: that in all stable political systems there must be a sovereign power—that is, an unlimited power to make and enforce law—and that in France, this sovereignty belonged to the king. Confusion about this power, and conflicting claims of various groups to a share of it, was the source of France's civil disorders. No individuals or groups in society, not even defenders of true religion, have a right to resist the sovereign's will, for resistance undermines the basis of orderly society. Bodin's principle of sovereignty was directly contrary to the medieval feudal tradition of limited royal authority.

Less secular than Bodin's theory of sovereignty was the theory of divine right of kings, especially popular because it employed the kind of biblical arguments the age favored. Catholic and Calvinist rebels had both claimed that human government was based on a merely human contract and hence that if civil government opposed the divinely created power of the true Church, the will of the Church must prevail. Royalist pamphleteers, however, argued that the source of political authority was also divine, both in the sense that God originally created the institution of monarchy and also in the sense that the action of divine providence, which decreed that this royal child should live and that one should die, that this royal heir should have children and that one should be childless, had created an indefeasible hereditary right so that in each generation one person and one person alone had the right to rule. Since the king's power came from God, no group of subordinates had a right to disobey or to rebel. The most famous writer who upheld this theory was King James VI of Scotland, who wrote several learned books about politics.

The emerging theory of absolute and unlimited power reached its most extreme form after the English Civil Wars. Thomas Hobbes in his *Leviathan* (1651) produced an uncompromising defense of the need for the sovereign's power to be totally unrestricted, concluding that no group in society has any rights except those which the sovereign chooses to grant. Although Hobbes's book is full of quotations from the Bible, the true outlines of his thought are starkly secular. Political authority comes not from God but from a contract by which the people, in order to gain relief from the anarchy of primitive life, agree with each other to surrender all their rights and powers into the hands of some designated sovereign. Since the sovereign is not a party to this contract, he is not bound by it and hence the contract creates no right of rebellion against tyranny as it would if the sovereign were regarded as one of the contracting parties. Even religion is subject to the sovereign: true religion is whatever the ruler declares it to be. This bluntly secular theory was not very popular among kings and their supporters, who preferred the less radical doctrines of divine right. Perhaps they realized that Hobbes's "sovereign" would not have to be king, but could be any agency of government that could get control. Hobbes's thought boldly states the basis on which all modern states function: that the collective will of society, expressed through its political agencies, must always prevail over the wishes of any individual or group within society. In the Middle Ages, the sovereign powers of government—the power to declare and enforce law, the war-making power, and power to judge civil disputes and criminal cases—were parceled out into many hands—the Church, the towns, and the various feudal lords. But Hobbes saw that the political developments of the sixteenth and seventeeth centuries meant that the modern state would enforce its own monopoly of these sovereign powers.

International Law and the Problem of Peace. European intellectuals and statesmen also struggled to understand how the distinct, sovereign, and utterly selfish political units that now ruled the European peoples could achieve some measure of international order and peaceful coexistence, since in both Catholic and Protestant countries the papacy's old claim to a moral supervision over international relations had collapsed.

Italy during the political crisis caused by the French and Spanish invasions first faced the harsh realities of an international politics based on power and egotism. The great Florentine political analysts Niccol[Machiavelli (1464–1527) and Francesco Guicciardini (1483–1540) did not create the violent and ethically unrestrained nature of Italian Renaissance diplomacy, nor did they really even glorify it. Machiavelli did not encourage violence, faithlessness, and evil deeds, but he sought to give useful advice to governments that wanted to survive in a world where those traits prevailed. Although his own diplomatic experience made him keenly aware that unexpected events might upset even the wisest plan, he remained hopeful that rational understanding of the selfish interests and material power of each state might give a people or a ruler a fairly good chance of avoiding ruin.

Oddly enough, the collapse of a moral basis for conducting international affairs produced a line of firmly Catholic political speculation that also admitted that the selfish interests of the sovereign states were the prime reality of political life. Jesuit thinkers like Juan de Mariana and Francisco Suarez confused the issue by reviving the medieval idea that God had given the popes a general authority to supervise the morality of international relations. Suarez is important not because of this outmoded theory but for his effort to explain how sovereign states could live together in an international community governed by law and not just by brute force and selfishness. He was pushed in this direction by the practical problem of defining how the Spanish king could have meaningful relations with non-Christian peoples in Asia and America who did not acknowledge papal power. This quest for a true international law was perhaps easier for a Protestant thinker who did not have to make allowances for papal claims, and in the treatise *On the Law of War and Peace* (1625), the Dutch jurist Hugo Grotius set forth a system of international law that began by acknowledging the existence of separate states, each seeking its own advantage, but that then attempted to set limits on the conflicts among these states by a natural law discoverable by reason. Though it is doubtful that the concept of international law ever became a dominant force in European politics, the thought of men like Suarez and Grotius did create the ideological framework within which the Western nations conducted war and peace.

Chapter Nine
Life in Early Modern Europe

The century of religious upheavals, dynastic rivalries, and wars of religion was also a century when most Europeans lived out their lives with only the dimmest awareness of the theological conflicts and high-level politics that dominate history books. The documents of the Protestant and Catholic reformations and of the many wars of the sixteenth century are numerous, and hence the history of those happenings and of the handful of kings, nobles, and public officials who acted out the great events of the age is easy to write. To discover how the nameless millions of the Reformation era lived, and what the experience of their lives meant to them, is a more arduous task. Often the records we would like to have do not exist, and many of them may never have existed, for except for entries in parish registers of baptisms, marriages, and burials (which many priests and ministers kept negligently or not at all), the typical European lived his whole life without ever performing any act that would create a permanent record.

Prosperity and Population Growth

One experience that affected most sixteenth-century Europeans was a resumption of rapid economic expansion after the severe economic decline of the fourteenth century and the stagnant economic conditions that prevailed until the late fifteenth century. France, which had undergone more than a century of agony during the Hundred Years' War, made a steady recovery after the return of internal peace in 1453 and continued to prosper until the 1560s, when the Wars of Religion caused a new and very severe decline.

After a long period of decline or stagnation in population, sixteenth-century Europe as a whole experienced rapid population growth. Germany, despite the religious and political upheavals of the century, not only overcame its earlier population losses but even grew rapidly, from about 12 million people in the late fifteenth century to about 20 million people at the end of the sixteenth century. The great peasant rebellion of 1524–25 reflected severe social unrest, but not abject misery. Parts of England, chiefly the regions that profited from the growing production of woolen textiles, which replaced raw wool as England's greatest export, had already prospered greatly during the fifteenth century. Tudor England experienced a general economic expansion, and population grew so rapidly that sixteenth-century Englishmen thought their thinly settled land to be suffering from severe overpopulation. Italy for the most part did little more than hold its own in population and wealth, and gradually—though not until the very end of the sixteenth century—it lost its traditional commercial and industrial leadership, not so much through failure to share the growth of Atlantic countries like Spain, Portugal, France, England, and the Low Countries. In the latter region, the southern province of Flanders, which had been the most economically advanced part of northern Europe in the Middle Ages, remained economically depressed, while the new prosperity and growth came first to the city of Antwerp, and then to the towns of Holland. Spain, despite her great-power status, did not share the economic advance of the sixteenth century fully, and by the latter decades of the century was experiencing severe decline in population and major economic dislocations.

Antwerp and World Trade

Most of the new prosperity of the northern and western parts of Europe was built upon commercial and industrial growth. Antwerp, the financial center of sixteenth-century Europe, became powerful in the first place because about the end of the fifteenth century, its merchants managed to persuade large numbers of English and German merchants to abandon their traditional medieval centers, such as the Flemish city of Bruges, and to make Antwerp their meeting place. Then, just before 1500, the agent in charge of merchandising the oriental spices that the king of Portugal was gaining from the new trade with India chose Antwerp as the most convenient point for distributing his wares in Northern Europe. Antwerp also prospered as a seaport, a center for warehousing, and a significant industrial center. Finally, with the active encouragement of the town government, it grew into Europe's major financial center, where the European governments raised loans to fight their many wars and where great bankers from other regions, such as the Fugger and Welser banks of the South German town of Augsburg, concentrated much of their activity of lending money, exchanging and transmitting currency, and speculating on the future prices of staple commodities like wheat, wool, and spices. When Amsterdam replaced Antwerp as Europe's chief financial center after the 1560s, it depended far more on shipping than on industrial activity for its prosperity.

Agriculture still remained important, and agricultural commodities were a major object of the speculative activity of the urban capitalists, but purely agrarian regions, such as the Baltic countries whose wheat and rye fed the populous towns of the Low Countries, had a semicolonial status and often felt exploited by the great merchants of Western Europe. Agriculture in advanced regions like the Netherlands was often innovative, for high land values and nearby markets encouraged specialized production and efforts to increase efficiency. The Low Countries were the site of some experiments with new crop rotations, but for the most part agriculture remained tradition-bound and unscientific. Where change did occur, it was not so much in technique as in reallocation of land use in order to concentrate on crops that could be sold to the urbanized regions, such as wheat and rye in eastern Germany, Poland, Prussia, and western Russia, and wool in England and Spain.

The Revival of Mining. Prosperity in Eastern Europe rested not only on export of grain to the West bu also on mining, an industry that had stagnated during the later Middle Ages but then staged a major recovery in the late fifteenth century. The mountainous parts of eastern Germany, Bohemia, Hungary, and Poland were the main centers of advance, and many fortunes, great and small, were piled up. The Fugger banking firm first grew to real importance when it abandoned its original concentration on the cloth trade and undertook to manage the potentially rich mining properties that the Hapsburg dynasty controlled in Austria. On a much smaller scale, the father of Martin Luther advanced from peasant status to the rank of a prosperous mine operator in eastern Germany. Germans dominated European mining to the extent that foreign rulers like the kings of Hungary and of England brought in German miners to open new fields or revive old ones. The recovery of mining was due partly to the better management mines received when they fell under the control of profit-seeking capitalists like the Fuggers of Augsburg and partly to technological advances, both in the timbering and draining of underground shafts and in the extraction of metals from the ores.

The Great Bankers and the Monarchs. An alliance between government and capital was a major cause of the renewed prosperity, epitomized in the spectacular rise of the Fugger family of Augsburg from being merchants dealing in cheap south German cloth to being the bankers and financial agents of the whole Hapsburg empire, rich and famous men who dared rudely but truly to remind even the great Emperor Charles V that he owed his imperial title and much of his power to the financial services of the Fugger bank. What the bankers offered the financially hardpressed governments of sixteenth-century Europe was an advance of ready cash (or a "line of credit" equally useful) needed to pay current expenses, especially in time of war. Step by step, loans from the Fugger and other south German banks had financed the dynastic aggrandizement of the Hapsburgs and their emergence as the most powerful ruling family in Europe. When Charles V won the imperial election in 1519 against frantic opposition of Pope Leo X and King Francis I of France, the main cause was the ability of the Fugger bank to finance larger bribes for the German electors than the French king could pay. All of the wars of Charles V and his son Philip II were financed by huge loans.

What the bankers got in return was not just the high interest rates of from 11 to 31 percent a year, but also valuable economic concessions. The early Hapsburgs gave security for loans by giving the Fugger bank control of the mines in the Tyrol. In 1525, being involved in a major war against France for control of Italy, Charles V leased to the Fuggers the extensive lands of the three Spanish crusading orders. Still later, when the rich plunder of Mexico and Peru and the opening of the Mexican and Bolivian silver mines had created new resources, Charles V and Philip II began pledging future shipments of precious metals from America in return for loans. When the bankers received control of mining districts, valuable farm lands, or other revenue-producing property in this way, they generally took firm command of the entire operation and greatly increased the profits. Control of capital resources like mines and land which rulers pawned as security for loans was one major foundation of the vast fortunes which the bankers piled up.

On the other hand, since the governments were chronically short of money, in the long run the bankers found that they not only failed to repay the principal of loans but also eventually proved unable to keep up the interest payments. Three times in the second half of the sixteenth century (1557, 1575, and 1596) the Spanish government suspended payments on its debts, each time causing a crisis for the bankers, who had depended on those payments to satisfy their own creditors. Most of the great south German banking companies went under, and even the great Fugger bank was much reduced and eventually was liquidated in the seventeenth century. The bankers were in an awkward position because once they had got deeply involved in financing governments, they found it necessary to keep lending more in order to protect the investments they had already made.

Mercantilism: National Economic Policy. Medieval economic life and economic regulation had been highly localized: each town and each provincial government framed policy in accord with its own interests. By the sixteenth century, however, the newly strengthened national monarchies in the Western European countries were beginning to adopt national economic policies, using trade and manufacturing regulation, production and export bounties, commercial agreements with foreign powers, and protective tariffs as their principal methods. This practice of national control of economic life (in the interest of the nation and of the royal treasury) is known as mercantilism. Though its details varied from place to place and from time to time, mercantilism always involved the active intervention of government to regulate the economy and to stimulate prosperity. Since the governments that formulated these policies usually conceived prosperity in a crudely materialistic way, as the accumulation of more and more gold and silver treasure, mercantilistic regulations generally sought to limit imports and to increase exports so that the nation would take in more treasure than it had to send out to pay for imports.

Governments tended to be suspicious of any economic activity they could not closely control, and the medieval preference for restricting major lines of trade to monopolistic associations of merchants became even stronger in the sixteenth century. Particularly when a nation entered a new trade, both merchants and rulers preferred to create a trading company and to limit participation in the new trade to its members. England, for example, had long limited the right to export woolen cloth to the members of the Merchant Adventurers' Company. When in the sixteenth century the nation's merchants opened new trade routes to Russia, to the lands encircling the Baltic Sea, and to the Levant, a special company was chartered by royal authority and given a monopoly of all trade between England and each new region. The most famous and most profitable companies created along these mercantilistic lines were the English East India Company and the Dutch East India Company (founded in 1600 and 1601, respectively).

Mercantilistic regulation early became a device of politics as well as economics. As early as the fourteenth century, the English government had manipulated the location of the staple, or outlet for raw wool exports, in order to bring pressure on foreign governments, and Philip II of Spain regularly awarded the *asiento*, or contract for import of African slaves to his American colonies, only to those nations whose governments followed pro-Spanish foreign policies.

Mercantilistic policies were also supposed to contribute to internal political stability. Governmental policies consistently encouraged the organization of the various industrial trades into guilds so that production standards, wages, and prices could be regulated. Governments everywhere carefully watched to see that guilds and town governments were in the hands of orderly, stable, and well-to-do merchants and artisans. Any attempt by apprentices, journeyman laborers, or unorganized workers to form their own associations and to bargain collectively over wages and working conditions met ferocious opposition from guild masters, municipal officials, and national governments. Strikes and riots against high prices, food shortages, and low wages were not uncommon, but they were everywhere suppressed by royal governments and by the "better sort" of townsmen, especially as these protests also often became involved with religious radicalism—for example, the iconoclastic riots that played a major role in the early stages of the Dutch rebellion. Unions and associations of workers were everywhere suppressed as revolutionary conspiracies.

Overseas Expansion and Colonization

The mercantilistic spirit of close regulation and monopoly also dominated the field of overseas expansion and colonization that was a major innovation of the late fifteenth, sixteenth, and seventeenth centuries. Although missionary zeal and yearning for adventure played an important part in motivating the Portuguese and Spanish expeditions that opened the non-European world to Europeans, the essential and costly governmental support that made exploration and colonization possible was available only because rulers became convinced that the expeditions would enhance their military power and their national wealth.

Portuguese Leadership

It was no accident that the exploration of the West African coast in the fifteenth century was the work of Portugal, a nation that had a long established tradition of land and sea conflict with the Moslem peoples of North Africa. Prince Henry of Portugal (1394–1460), the dominant figure in the early Portuguese expeditions down the African coast, first became interested in exploring Africa after he accompanied a Portuguese expedition against the Moroccan city of Ceuta in 1415. Henry apparently sought unknown Christian nations that he believed to exist in Africa and hoped would join him in a smashing attack on the Infidel, and he was also attracted by the knowledge that the Moslems of North Africa traded southward across the desert for gold, ivory, and slaves.

Just when the Portuguese conceived the idea of searching for a way around the southern tip of Africa to the spices and other luxuries of Southern and Eastern Asia is uncertain. But when Bartholomew Dias discovered the Cape of Good Hope and the way into the Indian Ocean in 1487–88, it is clear that the goal of finding a new route to the profitable oriental trade was already well established. Not until the expedition led by Vasco da Gama in 1497–99 did the Portuguese actually reach the coast of India (1498) and begin forcing their way into a trading world that the Arabs had dominated for centuries. But from 1441, when the Portuguese mariner first made contact with black Africa south of the Sahara and opened a trade in ivory, spices, slaves, and even gold, some tangible profits began to come from the expeditions.

The dream of a military alliance with Asian Christians against the Moors never worked out, but the militaristic aspect of overseas exploration re-emerged as soon as the Portuguese reached India, for they quickly realized that they would have to fight to prevent the Arabs from forcing them out of the Indian Ocean. In 1509 the brilliant commander Almeida attacked and destroyed a strong Egyptian fleet at Diu, thus establishing Portuguese naval predominance. Under his successor as governor-general, Alfonso de Albuquerque, the Portuguese seized and fortified not only Goa (1510) on the western coast of India but also Malacca (1512) on the Malay Straits and Ormux (1515) at the entry to the Persian Gulf, though their attempts to take Aden and so to control entry to the Red Sea were unsuccessful. The ruthlessness of Portuguese military enterprise in the East was matched by an equal ruthlessness in dominating the spice trade and ensuring that the crown of Portugal gained the profits from the new route.

Columbus Sails for Spain

A similar mercantilistic desire for wealth from trade with the Orient and for the discovery of Christian (or at least non-Moslem) allies against the Islamic world explains the Spanish government's willingness to finance the expedition westward across the Atlantic proposed by the Genoese mariner Christopher Columbus. Although Columbus also had idealistic goals of opening Asia to Christian missionaries and undermining the power of the Turks by organizing attacks from the Far East, he insisted on promises that he personally would gain vast wealth and political power as the reward of success. His basic plan was very simple: to reach the coast of China by sailing directly westward across the Atlantic. The Portuguese king, whom Columbus had first approached, had no interest in abandoning his search for an African route. Moving next to Spain, Columbus had no difficulty in convincing the rulers that his plan was theoretically possible: educated people had long known that the earth was round, not flat. But until 1492 the crown was deeply involved in the costly war against the Moors of Granada. In addition, royal advisers warned (correctly, as we too often forget) that Columbus's plan was not practical because he grossly underestimated the earth's circumference (and hence underestimated the distance from the European coast westward to the coast of China) and totally overlooked the possibility that unknown continents might block the way to Asia. The advisers also thought that Columbus wanted too much for himself.

Nevertheless, the prospect of controlling direct access to the markets of Asia was attractive, and as soon as the conquest of Granada released the necessary funds, the king and queen of Spain agreed to outfit an expedition. The famous expedition of 1492 was the high point of Columbus's career. After a frightening voyage that took them farther than anyone expected, the three Spanish ships discovered land at an island which Columbus piously named for the Savior, San Salvador (now Watling's Island in the Bahamas) and next found the coasts of Cuba (which they thought to be the Asian mainland) and Hispaniola before returning to Spain with the good news. His large and well-financed second voyage (1493) planted on Hispaniola the first permanent European colony in America, named Isabella and subsequently relocated and renamed Santo Domingo, and continued the exploration of the Caribbean islands and the adjoining mainlands, as did his subsequent expeditions of 1498 and 1502.

Although Columbus had dreamed of rich conquest and lucrative trade in the highly civilized Orient, what he had found was a group of primitive societies in a part of the world previously unknown to Europeans (except for marginal contacts by the Viking seafarers). Columbus himself never gave up the idea that in some way the lands he had found were outlying portions of the civilized East. Others who went to the new lands were quicker to realize that these were entirely new regions far from Asia.

Colonization and Conquest. The earliest center of colonization was the larger islands of the Caribbean, with Santo Domingo on the island of Hispaniola being the administrative center. New settlements soon reached the islands of Cuba, Jamaica, and Puerto Rico. By 1509, settlement had extended to modern Panama, and in 1513 Balboa led an expedition across the isthmus to the Pacific Ocean. Far more impressive were the conquests of the civilized Aztec empire in Mexico by Hernando Cortés (1519–21) and the empire of the Incas in Peru (1532–33) by Francisco Pizarro. The looting of the treasures of the Aztec capital at Tenochtitlán and the Inca capital at Cuzco provided a flood of American treasure for the Spanish treasury, and the establishment of Spanish control over the rich silver mines of Mexico, Peru, and Bolivia led to a steady increase in the annual shipments of bullion (some gold, but mainly silver) to Spain throughout the second half of the sixteenth century.

Despite their good fortune in finding the precious metals that other nations sought in vain, the Spaniards could not base their colonial economy on mines of gold and silver. The real economic basis of their colonies was always agriculture, and while there was some success at producing sugar and other crops not easily grown in Europe, early colonial agriculture largely duplicated the products already grown in Spain. Cattle ranching was the chief activity, with hides and tallow being almost the only exportable products.

Colonial Administration. The Spanish colonies in America were expensive to develop and administer, especially since the mercantilistic economic policies and the bureaucratic centralization that dominated government at home were at once extended to the new regions. The central government, still mindful of the dangers posed by independent landed aristocrats in recent Spanish history, briskly pushed the original conquerors—Columbus, Cortés, and the Pizarro brothers—out of power and placed government in the hands of royal appointees who were subject to control by a special administrative council back home and who were expected to make the colonies conform politically and economically to the will of the ruler.

The Indian population of the Caribbean islands shrank catastrophically in the face of economic exploitation, social disruption, and new diseases that contact with Europeans caused. Since Spanish settlers were too few, and since they were unwilling to perform the heavy labor required by farming and mining, a serious labor shortage impeded development. As the Indians of the islands became virtually extinct, the Spaniards soon began importing Africans, whose slave status had already been established among both Moslem and Christian peoples since the late Middle Ages. Thus African slaves replaced Indians as the basic labor force in the Caribbean islands.

Despite their inability to recruit enough Spaniards to do heavy labor, the colonial promoters did attract a substantial Spanish population. In 1574 a well-informed Spanish observer estimated that the colonies contained 30,500 Spanish households (probably somewhat more than 150,000 people). Over the whole sixteenth century, an average of from 1,000 to 1,500 emigrants went out each year, and almost all were Spaniards, since the home government rigorously excluded all Jews, heretics, and foreigners. Though vast areas and large groups of Indians were outside the reach of Spanish authority, Spain before the end of the sixteenth century had firmly established an offshoot of European society in the central portions of its vast American empire, complete with a developed and highly centralized set of administrative and judicial institutions and an economic life based on agriculture (and, to a lesser extent, mining) that were compelled to conform strictly to the home government's ideas of sound policy.

For all its shortcomings, this Spanish colonial empire marked an important event in world history, and the society then created still lives on in the countries of modern Latin America. Partly because of the Spanish crown's humanitarian concern for the Indians and partly because the mainland of tropical America was far more heavily populated by Indians than were the lands north of Mexico, Spanish colonial society also undertook a difficult task that its later English, French, and Dutch rivals never tried: the social and cultural assimilation of the native population, which was widely converted to Christianity and to a remarkable (though imperfect) degree hispanized in language and culture.

Colonial Rivalry

The other European nations looked enviously at the profitable Portuguese spice trade with the Orient and at the flood of precious metals Spain derived from America. The benefits of these empires, reflected in the increased power of Portugal and especially of Spain, were very obvious, and the harmful results, such as the draining away of Portugal's limited manpower and the high administrative cost of colonial government, received little attention. The English, as far back as the expeditions of the Venetian seaman John Cabot in 1497–98, and the French, as far back as the expedition led by the Florentine captain Giovanni da Verrazano in 1523, had refused to accept the Spanish and Portuguese view that the papal decision of 1493 dividing the non-European world between Spain and Portugal had legally excluded all other nations. Though neither England nor France managed to plant successful colonies in America until the seventeenth century, both nations, plus the Dutch, sought to win a share. Foreign pirates —at first chiefly French, but later also English and Dutch—began seizing Spanish treasure shipments so frequently that by mid-sixteenth century the Spanish government developed an elaborate system of naval convoys.

More respectable, but equally opposed to Spanish law, was the practice of Portuguese, French, English, and Dutch sea captains who traded with Spanish colonial ports despite the legal exclusion of all non-Spaniards from the trade. Since the Spanish government never permitted the importation of as many slaves as the colonists wanted, Portuguese traders were able to ship additional slaves illicitly to American purchasers. French, English, and Dutch interlopers soon were loading slaves in Africa and selling them to Spanish America also; and the first of the famous Elizabethan "sea dogs," John Hawkins, began his illegal trading in the Spanish colonies by entering the slave trade in the 1560s. Illegal trade, with constant exposure to attacks by Spanish fleets and garrisons, easily led these illicit traders into piratical raids on Spanish shipping and even into plundering raids on colonial settlements. The most famous such raider was the Englishman Sir Francis Drake, but there were many others, French and Dutch as well as English. The Dutch and English at the end of the sixteenth century, after Philip II had annexed Portugal, also began conducting illicit trade in the Portuguese colonial empire in the Orient.

At an even earlier date, French, Dutch, and English explorers attempted vainly to discover northeast and northwest passages to the Far East, penetrating the Arctic coastline of Russia and discovering the St. Lawrence River and Hudson's Bay in what is now Canada. Successful colonization of overseas lands was even more costly and more difficult than occasional expeditions to explore unknown regions and trade for furs, and none of the Northern European nations matched the Spanish colonial achievement until the seventeenth century.

English and French Settlements. The first lasting Northern European settlements were made in 1607 by the English at Jamestown in Virginia and in 1608 by the French at Quebec. In 1620 a second English colony was founded at Plymouth in what is now Massachusetts, though the larger and more important Massachusetts Bay Colony, centered at Boston, was not begun until 1629. During the 1630s, still other English colonies began—Connecticut, Rhode Island, and Maryland. In 1626, the Dutch founded a colony at New Amsterdam, which the English conquered later in the century and renamed New York. Unlike the tightly controlled Spanish colonies, these Northern European colonies—especially the Dutch and the

English—were controlled by privately owned trading companies chartered but not closely regulated by home government. The English colonies also provided, either from the beginning or as a result of agitation by the early settlers, some degree of participation in provincial government by the people—not so much because their people were more liberty loving as because the home governments lacked the financial resources and the administrative bureaucracy required for direct control.

All of the mainland colonies were still tiny, struggling settlements by mid-seventeenth century. Canada had perhaps 3,000 European settlers, while Virginia may have had as many as 15,000, and the various New England colonies about 20,000. Yet all of these colonies had managed to survive the near-starvation and high mortality that affected all overseas settlements during their first few years. The English colonies were already far more populous than those of the French and the Dutch, whose settlements threatened to become mere trading posts for buying furs from the Indians. The main reason for this difference was that England during the 1630s and 1640s was bitterly split by religious and political strife and, unlike the seventeenth-century French government, made no effort to prevent religious dissidents from seeking refuge in the colonies. The rapid growth of Massachusetts Bay, which was an almost independent commonwealth controlled by Puritans, was a direct result of the persecution of Puritans by the Anglican Church authorities in England.

Motives of the Emigrants. Although colonial populations, even in Spanish America, were very small, substantial numbers of people did take the remarkable step of abandoning their home communities and undertaking the hardships of an Atlantic passage and of settlement in the colonies. In English America—especially in New England—religious discontent was an important factor. But England was the only colonizing power that allowed such religious dissidents to go overseas. Elsewhere, except for the motive of converting pagans to Christianity, religion played little part in stimulating people to settle in the colonies. Dreams of sudden wealth through conquest and looting of rich empires or through the domination of profitable trade routes always played some role. But even though early colonists often neglected laborious field work in favor of prospecting for gold, the colonies were always primarily agricultural, and the hope of acquiring large amounts of cheap land was everywhere the greatest attraction for colonists in America, especially since ownership of land had always been the chief determinant of social status in Europe.

After the early period, most settlers in the American colonies knew that they would stay in their new land forever. In the populous Orient, however, where the Europeans filled only the role of administrators and merchants, settlers more commonly expected to pile up a fortune and then return to Europe to enjoy it, though in reality only a small minority ever achieved this goal.

Effects of Overseas Expansion

The long-range effects of the discovery of America and of new trade routes to the Orient were enormous, amounting to nothing less than the revolutionizing of every non-European culture and the material and cultural transformation of even such old and powerful civilizations as those of India, China, and Japan through their contact with the Europeans. In the shorter run, however, most non-Western cultures (except those of Indian America) were affected little.

For Europe itself, the immediate effects of discovery and colonization were important but limited. The Portuguese discovery of the Cape route to India, for example, made Oriental spices like pepper somewhat more plentiful and cheaper. In purely material terms, the earliest important effect of the discoveries on the life of the masses of Europeans was a great increase in the supply of salt fish from the Grand Banks fisheries of northern North America, which were regularly visited by fishermen from Portugal and Brittany from about the beginning of the sixteenth century. In the longer run, contact with America and with the Far East introduced important new foodstuffs—maize and the potato, for example—and laid the foundations for the later growth of whole new industries, such as domestic production of cotton textiles and of china, which once had been costly and exotic luxuries but by the eighteenth century were becoming common articles of everyday use. Agricultural products such as tea, coffee, sugar, and (of course) spices, which had once been the luxuries of a favored few, gradually became accessible farther and farther down on the social scale. The gradual rise in European living standards would have been impossible without the availability of non-European resources.

The age of discovery and colonization also had important political effects on sixteenth-century Europe. Both Portugal and Spain were far more important in the early modern age than they had been in the Middle Ages, and while Portugal was too small to retain a leading position, Spain emerged as the greatest political and military power in Europe from the end of the fifteenth century until nearly the end of the Thirty Years' War in 1648. The main causes of Spanish predominance were internal: the political and military reorganization carried through by Ferdinand and Isabella and by their Hapsburg descendants, Charles V and Philip II, and the high national morale and pride that marked the conduct of Spanish soldiers and statesmen (and colonists, too) throughout the period. Nevertheless, the windfall of profits from the Portuguese pepper trade and from the silver mines of Spanish America made it possible for both Iberian countries (but especially Spain) to sustain the costs of great-power status in a way that would have been impossible if they had had to finance their wars and diplomatic adventures entirely out of the yield of their own rather backward economies.

In the longer run, the new trade routes gave a natural economic advantage to all of the Atlantic countries, and the lands bordering on the Mediterranean—especially Italy—gradually lost their predominance in international trade, banking, shipping, and even industry. The great economic leaders of medieval and Renaissance Europe, the Italian cities of Venice, Genoa, Florence, and Milan, did not collapse overnight, but by the end of the sixteenth century (though not much before), the Italian mercantile cities had clearly ceased to be world economic powers and were becoming merely centers of an increasingly lethargic regional commerce. The Portuguese and the Spanish, despite their great discoveries and their leadership in the sixteenth century, did not maintain power and prosperity. Even in their age of greatness, the capitalists of Antwerp and the South German bankers skimmed off much of the profit. By the early seventeenth century, the city of Amsterdam had become the great center of world commerce, shipping, and banking, and by the late seventeenth century, the English and the French had clearly emerged as the eonomic leaders of Europe, with Spain and Portugal lagging far behind.

Inflation and Social Tension

In terms of immediate impact on the life of the common man, the major effect of the overseas expansion of Europe was the contribution it probably made to the price inflation which underlay many of the economic problems and social stresses of the sixteenth century. The fact of rising prices is indisputable: in Spain, which was the country earliest (from about 1520) and most deeply affected, prices at the end of the sixteenth century were five times what they had been at the beginning of that century; in France, the increase over the same period was less but still startling, about two and a half times; and in England, where the inflation did not become noticeable until about 1550 and continued later, prices rose about threefold during the century after 1550. Some crucially important prices were even higher: wheat, in the form of bread, which made up the basis of the European diet, increased fivefold in England, sevenfold in France, and even more in southern Spain, the region which inflation hit worst.

As twentieth-century Americans have discovered, inflation is not just a matter of cold statistics. It is a matter of ability to buy the necessities of life, and the social effects in sixteenth-century Europe, where the great masses of urban workers and the peasants lived close to the bare subsistence level even in good years, were even more drastic than in modern times. Complaints about rising prices were heard everywhere in Europe by mid-sixteenth century at the latest. Furthermore, since governments everywhere acted to prevent collective action by the lower classes, and since there is substantial evidence that wages rose more slowly than food prices, there can be little doubt that the very poorest classes suffered most.

Economists still understand so little about the causes of inflation that economic historians debate endlessly about the sources of this particular instance. Contemporaries usually blamed price-fixing conspiracies by monopolistic capitalists like the Fuggers. However, this activity was only a contributory cause. Currency manipulation by governments, which repeatedly debased their coinage by cutting its percentage of precious metals, also contributed, but only to a secondary degree. The heavy expenses of government, especially those associated with the frequent wars, were far more important. Even more fundamental was the general economic boom of the century, which both caused price rises and was further stimulated by them. Closely related was the substantial increase in population (England increased from an estimated 3 million to about 5 million inhabitants during the century, and the German Empire from 12 to 20 million). Population increases had a particularly great impact on the most important area of inflation, foodstuffs, and must be regarded as a major cause of the inflation.

Equally important, though much debated by economic historians, was the enormous influx of gold and silver bullion from Spanish America, which reached vast and almost constantly increasing amounts during the second half of the century, when inflation became most acute. Though there are some difficulties in regarding the influx of bullion as the major source of the inflation, both economic theory concerning the effect of injecting vast new supplies of bullion into an economy, and the actual chronological and geographical pattern of price rises, suggest that American treasure was a major cause.

Inflation led to an increasingly clamorous search for culprits and for remedies. Though the theological faculty at Salamanca in Spain and the brilliant French political theorist Jean Bodin saw the importance of impersonal economic forces like shipments of bullion, most contemporaries blamed price-fixing and commodity speculation by the great capitalists. There was agitation for governmental action to curb speculation and profiteering, not only from radical religious movements with working-class connections like the Anabaptists, but also from conservative social or religious reformers like the Catholic Sir Thomas More and the Protestant Martin Luther, both of whom favored legislation to curb the antisocial, profit-seeking tendencies of the great capitalists.

Governments, however, with their lack of economic understanding and their abject financial dependence on loans from the bankers, made only half-hearted attempts to find legislative remedies. Price-fixing of basic commodities and of wages was a common practice even in medieval Europe, but neither then nor in the sixteenth century did it have much success. Any attempts by peasants or workers to take matters into their own hands by forming unions and bargaining collectively were regarded (perhaps rightly) as revolutionary conspiracies and were ruthlessly suppressed. The officially approved forms of Protestantism, though they often criticized profiteering and other socially disruptive acts of the great capitalists, and though they often encouraged palliative measures such as price controls and laws against money-lending and market speculation, lined up solidly on the side of the existing social order. Indeed, about the only real remedy that governments, religious leaders, and individual theorists could suggest for the poverty of the lower classes was colonization of the "surplus" population in the empty spaces of the New World.

Growth of Cities

Probably a more significant migration during the sixteenth and early seventeenth centuries was that from rural areas to the cities. Cities and the mercantile and industrial activity that sustained most of them were nothing new, for urban growth went back to the high Middle Ages. Some cities, casualties of the changing patterns of economic life, such as Bruges in the Low Countries, even declined in numbers and wealth. But most European cities grew during the sixteenth-century boom in business and population. Furthermore, since the filthy sanitary conditions, unstable working-class family life, and prevalence of disease ensured that nearly all cities had a death rate far higher than their birth rate, immigration from rural areas was the only major source from which the increased population could have come. Some cities grew because of their political importance, notably Paris, which may have doubled in size from 100,000 to 200,000 during the sixteenth century, and Madrid, which grew rapidly from a mere village to a city of 60,000 people after Philip II made it his capital. Other cities—Lisbon, Seville, Antwerp, and Amsterdam—grew into metropolises of about 100,000 because of their commercial importance. Most sixteenth-century cities, however, were much smaller, even important ones like Vienna, Nuremberg, Augsburg, Strasbourg, Hamburg, and Danzig, all of which grew from the 20,000 class to double that size by the end of the sixteenth century. Cities of this size were metropolises in that age; indeed, any city of more than 10,000 still seemed large, while only a tiny handful of cities—Paris, Venice, and Milan—grew to near the figure of 200,000.

Oligarchical Control

Everywhere the great cities were dominated by a closed oligarchy of very rich citizens, and while the medieval cities had never been fully democratic, the scope of popular participation tended to be reduced significantly during the period of the Renaissance and Reformation. In the countries of Western Europe, where powerful monarchies had grown up, the central government intervened increasingly in city government, though there was usually a measure of self-government. The royal authority usually encouraged limiting or eliminating the role of ordinary citizens in urban affairs and confining real political power to a small group of prominent and wealthy families. In the small towns, there was a tendency for the city laws and the guild regulations to restrain aggressive and ambitious capitalists, but in the really important places (indeed, it was the secret of their growth to importance) the governments gave the great capitalists freedom to engage in the wild speculation, price-fixing, usurious money-lending and monopolistic practices that were contrary to the economic ethics of all parts of Europe but that had nevertheless become an integral part of the economic practice of all the developed parts of Europe.

The rich merchants and bankers (most great business houses combined both functions) also generally had the support of the national governments to which they regularly lent money. Where old established town regulations restricted capitalist enterprise too much, the owners of capital simply shifted their assets to other regions where they would not be hampered by restrictions. Indeed, in the textile trades, where the urban working classes had a long tradition of political and economic resistance to the rich cloth merchants who dominated the industry, the employers often abandoned the cities altogether and let out the work of spinning and weaving to rural workers, who could survive by farming during periods of unemployment in textiles, and whose isolated rural residence made it difficult for them to combine and strike against their employers as the workers of the medieval towns had done. The decline of the great medieval towns of Flanders, which had begun as far back as the fourteenth century, was largely the result of the capitalists transferring production from the radical workers of the cities to the docile part-time industrial workers of the rural districts.

Conditions of Urban Life

Life in the cities of the early modern age was much like life in the cities of the high Middle Ages. Compared to modern cities of the same size, these were very small in area, for people everywhere lived packed closely together under conditions that would strike modern people as incredibly unsanitary and dangerous. A very few townspeople lived in great luxury, and a substantial percentage lived restricted but still fairly comfortable and secure lives. But apprentices, journeyman laborers, and (above all) unskilled and casual laborers, who did the rough, heavy, and dangerous work of the cities, led harsh and usually short lives—housed in crowded, flammable hovels, exposed to plague and other diseases, and chronically undernourished. During periods of famine, war, and widespread unemployment, life for the urban poor became unbearable, a fact reflected not only in the incredible mortality and shortness of life span, but also in the wealthier classes' pathological (but often justified) fear of the poor.

The only saving grace of life in the cities was the high degree of internal morale and social cohesiveness that bound together at least the property-owning classes. The inhabitants of cities such as Florence in Italy or Nuremberg in Germany had a high degree of civic pride and local patriotism, and though government was confined to a few rich families who inevitably shaped public policy in accord with their own interests, the typical urban government of the age not only claimed but also got a high degree of individual conformity to what the government defined as the general interest of society. The rigorous Calvinist moral and social control at Geneva, for example, though noteworthy even in its own day, was not as wildly different from the practice of most European cities as one might expect. Indeed, many of the Genevan sumptuary laws regulating dress, living style, and morality had clear precedents in the town laws of pre-Reformation medieval Geneva.

Tradition and Change in Agriculture

The vast majority of sixteenth-century Europeans were not townsmen at all but peasants, just as in the Middle Ages. For the most part, these peasants clung to their traditional routine blindly and looked with suspicion on all changes, even ones (such as the shift from labor services to cash payments in lieu of labor) that in the long run were destined to benefit them. Despite their tradition-bound outlook, the peasants were experiencing a number of significant changes whether they liked it or not. The aristocratic classes, who still owned most land, were as severely pressed by inflation as any class in Europe, and everywhere they were trying to figure out ways to increase the income from their estates. Their efforts often involved abandonment of medieval methods of land management, a process that had been going on ever since the recovery of the European economy in the high Middle Ages. The reorganization of landed estates was quite important in the sixteenth century. In Tudor England, for example, some of the greatest agricultural fortunes fell into the hands of landowners who purchased monastic estates that were still being managed according to medieval tradition and then in one way or another dissolved the traditional manorial structure and reorganized production and relations with the peasants in order to make the estate more lucrative.

Decline of Serfdom

In Western Europe, most of the successful types of change involved a full or partial transformation of the peasants from unfree serfs owing labor services to free tenants owing rent. Although these changes were usually introduced by the landlord in his own interest, their effect on the well-being of the peasants was not always unfavorable. Legally, the change from labor services to payments tended to weaken the personal bondage of the peasants. In most parts of Western Europe, the sixteenth century marked the continuation of a gradual change that was making the peasants legally free. This process went on very unevenly from locality to locality, and formal abolition of serfdom was rare. Yet in fact serfdom was coming to an end, and in 1617, an English court ruled that the status of serf had no existence in the eyes of the law.

Adaptation in Western Agriculture

In the short run, at least, the material and financial effects of changes in estate management were more important than the legal effects. On the average, the peasants fared rather well in Western and Central Europe. Indeed, where landlords elected to receive rent and other payments in cash rather than in produce and did not reserve the right to adjust the rents at frequent intervals, the sixteenth-century inflation meant that peasant tenants were the principal gainers from higher prices. Many noble families, on the other hand, became impoverished as the fixed cash rents they received declined in purchasing power. Of special importance was the decision of many great landowning nobles to quit trying to manage their estates at all and instead to lease out their lands to ambitious peasants or others who paid annual rent and then hired laborers to work the soil in whatever way they thought would be most profitable. In other cases, the landlords retained control of their lands but undertook by means fair or foul to dissolve the traditional peasant community and concentrate exclusively on the production of one cash crop. The most famous such adaptation was the effort of landlords in those parts of England that were suited to sheep-ranching to abandon all attempts to raise crops, to eject the peasant communities, pull down the villages, and produce wool for the hungry looms of England and the Continent. Sheep-ranching produced a highly profitable industrial raw material (wool) and could be conducted with very little expenditure for labor.

The social results of enclosure (the name for this practice of disbanding the medieval farming system and turning cultivated land into pasture) were important. Since raising sheep required little labor, landlords commonly evicted most of the peasants. The evicted tenants, sometimes left with not even a place to live, had to eke out a living as best they could, as wage-laborers, beggars, and even robbers. The rulers of Tudor England were seriously worried by the potential of these uprooted peasants to produce disorder, and repeated acts of Parliament attempted to outlaw the practice of enclosure and the eviction of peasants. These laws, however, had little success, for enforcement depended on the rural justices of the peace, who were recruited from precisely that class of landlords who were carrying out enclosures.

The failure of the legislation against enclosure illustrates the importance of the large English landowners. Indeed, in most parts of Western Europe, ownership of large landed estates continued to be socially respectable; and the most successful members of the urban middle class generation after generation sought respectability, once they had become rich, by investing in land in hopes that in two or three generations their family's middle-class origins would be forgotten and their descendants would rank as wealthy country gentlemen or even would rise to become members of the nobility.

Decline of East European Peasantry

While peasant society in Western Europe was moving slowly toward the abolition of serfdom, which opened to the ablest peasants a chance to rise to the status of large leaseholders and farm operators or to emigrate to the cities, rural society in Eastern Europe was tending in the opposite direction. Landlords there, too, had to change their methods of estate management if they were to remain solvent in an age of rising prices. But both because of political conditions and because the most profitable produce of lands like Prussia, Poland, and Russia was grain to be shipped to the growing cities of Western Europe, the noble landlords did not abandon the direct farming of their demesne in favor of leasing it out or converting it to pasture.

East European landlords concentrated on the production of bread grains like wheat and rye for export. This kind of agriculture required large amounts of labor. The noble landowners found that the easiest way to get this labor was to compel the peasant tenants on their estates to provide it; and since the nobility had almost total control of local government, as in Poland, or at least had rulers who were willing to give them a free hand with their tenants, as in Prussia and Russia, the result was the gradual depression of the social status of the rural population. Just as the peasants of Western Europe were rising to the rank of free men, the peasants of Eastern Europe, who had been among the most free farm workers in Europe, were becoming serfs. This brutal and often violent reduction of the peasantry to servile status was already under way in some regions by the late Middle Ages, and it did not reach completion until the eighteenth century, when Catherine the Great of Russia, after usurping the throne, bought the political support of the Russian nobility by confirming the institution of serfdom and the legal authority of landowners over their serfs.

Technological Changes

The early modern age was by no means the first period in European history to experience significant improvement of life by the invention of new technology. The early Middle Ages, with such immensely practical inventions (or adaptations from other societies) as the stirrup, the horse collar, the heavy plow, the scythe, and the water-powered mill, had already advanced substantially beyond classical antiquity in the application of animal power and better design to ease the burden of human labor. The high Middle Ages introduced the windmill, the mechanical clock, the compass and other instruments of navigation, and the use of gunpowder for cannon and handguns.

The life of Europeans in the fifteenth, sixteenth, and seventeenth centuries was similarly improved by some important developments in technology. The overseas discoveries and colonization of the age would have been impossible without the striking advances that Portuguese and other Atlantic ship designers made in the shape of hulls and especially in the rigging of sailing ships, or without the refinement of navigational instruments and mapmaking. The prosperity of European mining from the late fifteenth century resulted from improved methods of timbering underground shafts and draining or pumping ground water out of mines. These new approaches, first developed in Germany, were then applied throughout Europe and even in Spanish America by migrating German miners. Firearms, which had been so crude during the late Middle Ages that they were useful only for siege warfare, were vastly improved at the beginning of the sixteenth century, when truly effective field artillery and muskets began to play a major role in warfare. Italian military engineers of the fifteenth and sixteenth centuries developed highly refined systems of fortification, water drainage, canal-building, and artillery fire control; and during the sixteenth and seventeenth centuries, the Dutch brought their methods of diking and of draining water from swampy land to such perfection that Dutch hydraulic engineers not only reclaimed great amounts of their own land from the sea but also found employment abroad. When the English began draining the swampy fenlands of their northeastern coast in the early seventeenth century, for example, Dutch engineers were brought in to direct the process.

Large-scale Industries

Most European production of manufactured goods continued to be done in the shops of artisans, who worked alone or with the aid of a few employees, or in the home workshops of rural industrial workers. Some industries, however, almost had to be conducted on a larger scale. The printing industry, for example, not only rested on a new technology created in mid-fifteenth century but also depended on a pattern of organization that was the prototype of the later factory. Printers used complex machines, mass-produced great numbers of identical objects for sale at a low cost per unit, and developed a complex (and often tense) relationship between the owners of the costly capital investment in machinery and a corps of highly skilled and class-conscious employees.

Other trades that by their very nature involved relatively large-scale production by highly organized laborers were cannon-founding, production of brass, paper, and soap, commercial brewing of beer and ale, and the production of a number of industrial chemicals, such as gunpowder and alum. The techniques and organization for such enterprises originated in Germany and Italy for the most part, but by the seventeenth century, England was becoming the leader in such enterprises, largely because while Continental countries like France managed to restrict the mass production of cheap, low-quality manufactured goods through guilds, apprenticeship requirements, and other administrative devices, the less efficient and less bureaucratic government of England failed in its efforts to regulate industrial production. Even in England, these developments were not yet sufficiently widespread to flood the country with cheap mass-produced goods, but the tradition of industrial freedom and lax governmental control was already well established so that the next great wave of technological advance, during the eighteenth century, was put to practical use in England more rapidly than in any other country.

Although the sixteenth and seventeenth centuries mark a great advance in the natural sciences, the new science had little relation to technological and industrial advance until the eighteenth or even the nineteenth century. Even in 1650, there was relatively little in the technology of Europe that would not have been comprehensible to a man from the year 1450, or even 1250. The technology of medieval Europe had been based on wood and stone as the basic construction materials and on wind and water as the basic inanimate sources of mechanical power. Despite many refinements, that basis of European technology did not change during the Renaissance and Reformation period.

Medicine and Public Health

Even in medicine, which one might have expected to benefit from the improvements in anatomy and physiology associated with the great progress of natural science, there was no dramatic change, only piecemeal improvement. The basic theories of disease and of treatment still rested on ancient notions of preserving the balance of humors (body fluids) and of closely observing astrological influences. The training of physicians in the universities changed little. It is true that the scourge of plague, which had devastated European populations since the fourteenth century, abated somewhat. But outbreaks of plague were still frequent and still uncontrollable everywhere in Europe. Not until the late seventeenth or early eighteenth century did plague disappear from the countries of Western and Central Europe. Even then, the cause was not improved medicine, but rather the gradually improving diet of the masses of European people and better administrative techniques for imposing quarantine and preventing the spread of infectious diseases. The same causes—better nutrition and better management of public health problems, plus an economic situation that made earlier marriage financially possible—were the probable sources of the population growth of the sixteenth century.

Improvement in the Quality of Life

Life remained barren and harsh for Europeans in the early modern age, but there was substantial improvement over the conditions of the later Middle Ages. The accumulation of capital and improvements in technology and public administration laid the basis not only for Europe's partial dominance over other human societies in the early modern period but also for the radical economic, social, and political transformation that all of Western society underwent in the late eighteenth and nineteenth centuries.

Chapter Ten

The Cultural Crisis of the Late Renaissance

The sixteenth and early seventeenth centuries represent the full maturity of classical humanism and of Renaissance art. The same period represents a remarkably brilliant age of accomplishment in the vernacular literature of most of the leading European nations (Shakespeare and his contemporaries in England, for example). Hence it may seem strange to talk of a significant cultural crisis in the age. Yet the educated elite which dominated European society did face severe problems of self-confidence that forced its most brilliant members toward remarkable new achievements in science and philosophy. These levels of culture, of course, were totally outside the ken of the great masses of people. Yet in the long run, the new science and new philosophy that a few individuals of supreme genius produced had a profound impact on the whole direction of Western civilization.

Triumph of Renaissance Classicism

On superficial inspection, the future course of sixteenth- and seventeenth-century civilization seemed to have been set by the culture of Renaissance humanism and by the religious developments of both Reformations, Protestant and Catholic. Humanistic scholarship reached a high degree of maturity and technical proficiency during the sixteenth and seventeenth centuries. The editorial and interpretive work of the classical scholars of the age reached a level that was not fundamentally outgrown until the late eighteenth and early nineteenth centuries, and the editions and commentaries on classical, patristic, and biblical texts then produced continued to be reprinted and directly drawn upon for two centuries.

Furthermore, while the refined world of classical scholarship was far removed from the everyday world, the enthusiasm for study of ancient languages and literature that the Renaissance had created remained the dominant influence in all but the most elementary levels of European education. Education consisted largely of learning to read and appreciate the masterpieces of Latin and Greek literature in the original languages, and the educated classes of Europe for three centuries were saturated with the influence of ancient literature, as their own vernacular literature clearly reflects. Far from shattering this concentration on classical antiquity, the religious revival of the Reformation period confirmed and institutionalized it. The educational reconstruction inspired by Luther's friend Melanchthon in Germany, by the excellent Jesuit academies in Catholic lands, and by the Genevan Academy of Calvin and Beza, was built on the classical literary curriculum first developed by the educational reformers of Renaissance Italy. Classical literary studies provided a unifying educational curriculum for the dominant classes of all European countries.

Yet this pervasive humanistic culture had its weaknesses, the most important of which was its inability to satisfy the urgent philosophical needs of the age. Although their favorite ideas and their intellectual methods may have had certain vaguely philosophical implications, the humanists were not philosophers and did not set forth any philosophy that might be labeled as typically humanistic. Instead, the humanists regarded themselves as professional rhetoricians and regarded their arts as useful for the purpose of persuading men rather than for the discovery of truth. The humanists never even attempted in a systematic way to provide a substitute for the medieval scholastic philosophy they often affected to despise, and scholasticism continued to provide the only basis for serious and systematic study of fundamental philosophical and scientific questions well into the seventeenth century. Although humanism influenced every branch of learning, the basic structure of all professional study in all fields remained largely what it had been for many centuries.

Sources of Philosophical Unrest

Both the Renaissance and the Reformation had unsettling effects on philosophy and on all forms of learning. The ever deeper probing of ancient philosophical sources made modern Europeans increasingly aware of the sharp disagreements that divided ancient thinkers. Humanistic study of the classical past had begun with a sublime confidence that deeper understanding of the ancients would resolve the many conflicts and uncertainties that bedeviled modern (that is, late medieval) philosophers, but by the sixteenth century, many students of ancient thought had concluded that the ancient schools of philosophy were so deeply split that study of the ancients was merely increasing the confusion among modern thinkers. Ancient philosophical disputes, of Platonists against Aristotelians, of Stoics against Epicureans, and of skeptics against all who claimed to have found certain truth, were reborn among modern thinkers. Both before and after the beginning of the Protestant Reformation, conservative theologians were sharply critical of attempts to incorporate rationalistic arguments into Christian theology.

The appearance of Protestantism after 1517 raised in acute form the basic philosophical issue of how either philosophers or theologians could distinguish truth from error. This question became yet more acute because of the tendency of many small Protestant sects to split off from all other Christians and to claim that they and they alone possessed true doctrine. Not only the medieval Catholic Church but also each of the major Protestant denominations came under attack from such radical sects, and extremists challenged both the philosophical and the scriptural foundations not only of each of the "true" churches but also of such basic European institutions as the family, monogamous marriage, private property, and the secular state. Nothing in human experience seemed to be immune from attack. In religion and in secular life alike, many thinkers struggled with the problem of whether any real and objective truth could be found.

This problem was made still more acute by the intellectual impact of overseas discovery. The very fact of discovering whole new undreamed of continents was itself unsettling. As vast amounts of new information accumulated about the flora, the fauna, and the peoples of non-European parts of the globe, traditional learning about plants, animals, and human society became less and less trustworthy. Europeans (like all peoples of restricted experience) had always assumed that their own customs and institutions were based on universally valid rational principles and were "natural" and "right." Now they learned from explorers about societies that practiced polygamy, cannibalism, community of property; societies where women rather than men ruled the family; and even societies where people felt no "natural" shame in their bodies and went about naked. This experience of non-Western social customs, spread by the increasingly popular genre of travel literature, made Europeans question the naturalness of many of their own customs. The traveler's report (or books claiming to be such) also became a vehicle for thinly disguised criticism directed against the churches, governments, and social customs of Europe; and in the late seventeenth and eighteenth centuries, would-be critics regularly wrote fictitious traveler's reports about "foreign" countries as a way of getting their opinions published despite the existence of religious and political censorship.

The challenge to traditional European beliefs and practices came from all sides. Even the study of Aristotle, the best established and more widely respected philosophical authority of medieval scholasticism, could lead thinkers far from the accepted norm of Christian belief. The Italian philosopher Pietro Pomponazzi (1462–1524), who began his career as a philosophical admirer of the greatest medieval Aristotelian, St. Thomas Aquinas, adopted a radically naturalistic interpretation of Aristotle that led him to deny such traditionally Christian beliefs as the personal immortality of the soul, the creation of the world, and the possibility of miracles.

No less radical in its philosophical implications, though far less openly philosophical, was the picture of the moral world presented in the writings of the two great Florentine political theorists and historians of the early sixteenth century, Niccol[Machiavelli (1469–1527) and Francesco Guicciardini (1483–1540). Machiavelli regarded the real world of political behavior as an anarchic turmoil of conflicting egotisms in which the only hope for achieving even a little bit of order and justice lay in man's using his rational powers in order to understand and influence political behavior. His younger friend, Guicciardini, having experienced the calamitous breakdown of Italian political order at an earlier and more formative age, repudiated even the few glimmerings of optimism that survived in Machiavelli's thought and drew the cynical and disenchanted conclusion that the turmoil of clashing egotisms that caused historical events was beyond the comprehension of human reason or the effective control of human prudence. This conclusion left man, even the wisest and most observant man, as little more than the observer (and the victim) of imponderable and uncontrollable forces.

The Rise of Skeptical Philosophy

These unsettling thoughts about man's political and ethical existence were seconded by some very disturbing opinions about the power of man's mind to attain truth. The unsettling effect of overseas discoveries, the tendency of many religious thinkers both before and after the Reformation to deny the ability of human reason to understand the basic doctrines of religion, and the turmoil of conflicting opinions (both ancient and modern) that humanistic and scholastic scholarship had uncovered—all led to fundamental doubts about man's ability to reach any certain and true conclusions through reason. This development toward a skeptical challenge to rationalism was aided (as happened in so many fields of human endeavor) by the rediscovery of ancient texts bearing on the problem, the works of ancient Greek skeptics.

Some knowledge about the attack on ancient Greek philosophical rationalism by the skeptics had survived through the Middle Ages. But in the early sixteenth century, a radical follower of the anti-intellectual, evangelical preacher Savonarola, Gianfrancesco Pico della Mirandola (nephew of Giovanni Pico), wrote an attack on philosophical rationalism in which he summarized in great detail the arguments of Sextus Empiricus, the only surviving author of the most extreme school of ancient skepticism, the Pyrrhonists. Other writers of the early sixteenth century, such as the German occultist writer Agrippa von Nettesheim, the great French comic author François Rabelais, and the French anti-Aristotelian philosophers Peter Ramus and Omer Talon, also showed interest in ancient skepticism. But there is no certainty that any of them except Gianfrancesco Pico knew the works of Sextus Empiricus. In 1562, however, the humanistic printer Henri Etienne published one of the works of Sextus Empiricus in a Latin translation, and in 1569 a Latin version of all of his surviving works came out.

The tendencies toward reopening the ancient Greek debate on the reliability of human reason were already well established by 1562, but the publication of Sextus Empiricus now provided an armory of arguments and examples for modern authors who had come to mistrust human reason. Although in loose modern usage the word *skepticism* commonly implies religious unbelief, real skepticism merely calls into question the ability of human reason to attain certitude. The majority of those who systematically used skeptical arguments in the sixteenth century were enthusiastic Christians who thought that by demolishing confidence in reason they would compel their contemporaries to abandon rationalistic viewpoints that undermined religion and bring modern men to a humble acknowledgment of the truth miraculously revealed by Scripture and by the Church. Indeed, French Catholics in the sixteenth century often used skeptical arguments to undermine the dogmatic confidence of the Calvinists.

Sanchez and Montaigne

By the later sixteenth century, however, two powerful thinkers had published works of far broader import, arguing on purely philosophical grounds (though still with the help of materials borrowed from ancient skeptics) that the very foundations of all human knowledge are shaky and that in the scientific sense of universally valid conclusions demonstrated by reason, "nothing can be known." Indeed, the quoted statement is the title of the chief work of the less widely known of the two, Francisco Sanchez (1552–1623).

Less systematic but far more influential was the adoption of a skeptical position in the *Essays* of the chief literary and intellectual figure of sixteenth-century France, Michel de Montaigne (1533–92). Especially in the longest and most philosophically ambitious of his *Essays*, "An Apology for Raymond Sebond," Montaigne systmatically demolished all the foundations for confidence in human reason and seriously questioned whether man could even confidently state that one opinion was more probable than another (a position which even Sanchez had been willing to concede). Montaigne himself was a conforming but unenthusiastic Catholic who had important links to the moderate Politique group in French political life. Though he has subsequently been read as a secular-minded foe of all religion who outwardly conformed to the old religion in order to conceal his lack of faith, Montaigne's actual statements on religion merely attack the dogmatic confidence with which Calvinists excused their repudiation of the old religion. His chief disciple, the priest Pierre Charron (1541–1603), directly adapted Montaigne's skepticism to the purpose of defending the Catholic faith against the Calvinists.

The practical consequences a radical skeptic like Montaigne drew from his opinions were extremely conservative: since the weakness and unreliability of reason makes it impossible for man to discover truth on his own, the only prudent course is to accept the social customs and the religious opinions and practices that prevail in the society of which one is part. These opinions and customs can no more be proved true than can their opposite, but at least they have the merit of having stood the test of human experience through the centuries.

In the early seventeenth century, a number of intellectuals in France and Italy openly upheld skeptical viewpoints on disputed questions of religion, while outwardly conforming to the officially established Catholic faith, in part because they regarded that religion as socially useful. While it is hard to prove that such individuals were hypocrites, there can be little doubt that the ruling classes throughout seventeenth-century Europe upheld the form of Christianity prevailing in their country in part because it provided an ideology and an administrative mechanism by which the semibarbarous masses of the people could be kept under control.

Efforts to Overcome Skepticism

Skepticism was by no means a popular viewpoint in the late sixteenth and early seventeenth centuries. Even those who most assiduously applied it to the defense of traditional religion might find themselves attacked by other believing Christians for undermining the rational foundations of faith. Most philosophers of the age showed little awareness that the skeptics had placed the credibility of all philosophy in doubt. Nevertheless, the most penetrating intellects of the early seventeenth century shared a general opinion that traditional learning was in jeopardy. Francis Bacon, Pierre Gassendi, Blaise Pascal, and René Descartes—the most powerful and creative philosophers of the age—were all keenly aware of the shaky foundations of traditional scientific and philosophical knowledge. Descartes, the most powerful European thinker of the first half of the seventeenth century, is important not because he rejected all traditional learning and made systematic doubt his intellectual starting point. Rather, he is important because he devised a new approach to the problem of how to regain confidence in the results of rational thought while still facing frankly the difficult issues raised by the skeptics. Descartes's skeptical starting point was traditional among thinkers of his generation. What was new was his ability to rise above it.

Growth of Witchcraft and Magic

The shattering of European confidence in scientific reason and in the moral and scientific rationality of the universe, expressed not only by skeptics and near-skeptics but also by political cynics like Machiavelli, is also reflected in the growing popularity of magic, witchcraft, and other occult pseudo sciences during the sixteenth century. The whole period was a golden age of superstition, when both the educated classes and the inarticulate masses were more easily taken in by superstitious beliefs and practices than at any time since late Antiquity. The religious uncertainties of an age of constant turmoil and inconstant belief, the great prestige of ancient Greek and Roman authors who were themselves often grossly superstitious, and the philosophical decline of confidence in an orderly and knowable world made many persons of fair intelligence as easily disposed to believe the rhapsodic fantasies of some magical treatise as to believe the logical scientific demonstrations of an Aristotelian philosopher.

Precisely because even the serious and genuine science of the age was obscured by false theories and interlarded with gross errors, the fantastic claims of alchemy, astrology, and other pseudo sciences seemed to merit belief. The lack of a viable and orderly set of commonly accepted scientific laws made it difficult for even a balanced and sensible student of nature to reject the often preposterous statements contained in magical and occultist books that seemed to be ancient and trustworthy. Religion itself seemed to endorse belief in witchcraft and in the diabolical side of magic, and religious authorities provided both the theoretical basis and the judicial mechanism for the hysterical witchcraft delusion that afflicted various parts of Europe (and of English America) throughout the sixteenth and seventeenth centuries. The decaying old philosophy and science provided few effective controls on such superstitious barbarism, or on the activities of charlatans who exploited the credulity of their fellows.

While the prosecution of witches was almost unmitigated social disaster from beginning to end, the popularity of pseudo sciences like alchemy, astrology, and magic had some beneficial effects. In particular, the magician's clearly avowed goal of gaining knowledge that would give him effective control over the material world (by making him rich or enabling him to dominate other people) provided the new natural science with a strongly practical bent that had commonly been lacking in the intellectually subtle but excessively abstract natural science of ancient and medieval times. Knowledge for the magician, as for the modern scientist, implied control over nature rather than a purely theoretical understanding. While the pure science of the seventeenth and later centuries is not identical with technology and in certain respects is highly speculative, it has always had links with practical and applied science that were lacking from ancient and medieval science but were very evident in the pseudo sciences of magic and alchemy during the sixteenth century. Sir Francis Bacon in his utopian work *The New Atlantis* (1624) set forth the very modern notion of a society whose wealth and happiness rest on understanding and control of nature through systematic scientific research.

The Search for New Philosophy

Both a new philosophy and a new kind of natural science emerged from the intellectual turmoil of the sixteenth and early seventeenth centuries. Indeed, the new science (and the scientific technology that later grew out of it) is probably the most important development of modern Western civilization. Certainly it has been the most exportable Western commodity, for the science and technology of the West have inexorably penetrated and utterly transformed even resolutely anti-Western civilizations that have easily resisted the influence of Western religion, Western philosophy, and Western artistic and literary traditions. The rise of modern science, however, was no mere accident. Its origins lay in the philosophical and scientific confusion of the sixteenth century.

Revival of Old Traditions

The skeptics were not the only thinkers of the sixteenth century who realized that the formal scholastic philosophy of the universities had come to a dead end. From mid-sixteenth century onward, deeply concerned and ingenious thinkers were attempting—usually with indifferent success—to lay the foundations of a new philosophy that would end the uncertainty and provide a certain, socially useful, and scientifically innovative basis for the ordering of society, the defense of religion, and the discovery of truths about the universe. Even within the scholastic tradition, the efforts of the Society of Jesus to revive the popularity of St. Thomas Aquinas mark an important change, for the rationalistic Aquinas had not had a very large and enthusiastic following during the fourteenth and fifteenth centuries. The major figure in this attempt to make medieval Thomism relevant to the modern world was the Spanish Jesuit Francisco Suarez (1548–1617), who is now known mainly as a political theorist but whose writings embraced every aspect of reality and had a powerful influence on the philosophical development of Europe.

There were also other widely influential efforts to remedy the confusion in philosophy by reviving some earlier philosophy. Ever since the humanist philosopher Marsilio Ficino (1433–99) had translated the whole body of Plato's surviving works from Greek into Latin, Neoplatonism had become a fashionable philosophy among those who repudiated the scholastic philosophies, which were based on Aristotle. Yet although Neoplatonism provided a superficial philosophical system for poets and for the discussion of philosophical questions in polite society, it had little of value to say on the hard questions raised by the emerging science and the skeptical criticism of the age. On moral questions, at least, another revival and adaptation of an ancient philosophy, Neostoicism, became widely popular. The writings of Justus Lipsius (1547–1606), for example, presented a moderate Christianized version of ancient stoicism that tried to help men live in a world torn by strife and uncertainty without being overwhelmed by misery. Many educated men found Neostoicism appealing. Michel de Montaigne, for example, though a skeptic on broad speculative questions, guided his own personal life by Stoic principles. But Stoicism offered few answers to the troublesome questions about the validity of reason. It merely helped men reconcile themselves to a world that offered very much misery and very little (and very brief) contentment.

More significant in the long run were the philosophies that attempted to break free from older systems of thought. The French Protestant philosopher Peter Ramus (1515–72), for example, denounced the philosophy taught in the schools as a mere intellectual game rather than a search for truth. He attacked the revered authority of Aristotle and attempted to work out a new system of logic that would make fresh philosophical advance possible. But Ramus was more successful at pointing out the inadequacies of Aristotle and other past authorities than at working out a really original philosophy. His fame and popularity suggest that he was trying to fill a very real need, but he left little of lasting value to later thinkers. A number of philosophers in the late sixteenth century realized that a successful new philosophy would have to face the intellectual problems involved in scientific discovery, though the two most famous of these, Tommaso Campanella (1568–1639) and Giordano Bruno (1548–1600), are famous chiefly on account of the troubles that some of their speculative nonscientific theories caused with conservative Church authorities.

Philosophical Breakthrough: Bacon and Descartes

The breakthrough to a new kind of philosophy that could transcend the problems raised by the skeptics and could serve as a guide for real scientific thinking was the work of two men who shared the prevailing disenchantment with traditional learning but who managed to escape from the intellectual dead-end of skepticism. These philosophers were the Englishman Sir Francis Bacon (1561–1626) and the French philosophical and mathematical genius René Descartes (1596–1650). Although their philosophies were radically different from each other, the two men were substantially agreed on several important points. First, all past philosophies were worthless because (as the skeptics had shown) they could not attain certainty. Second, hence the traditional concern for opinions of past authorities should be abandoned, and all questions should be investigated as if they had never been studied before. Third, the basic error of past philosophies is that they have wasted their time on broad speculative questions, for which the human mind is unsuited, and have neglected the study of the phenomena of nature, which man's mind is able to comprehend. Fourth, some new method or procedure of scientific inquiry must be developed because (as anti-Aristotelians like Ramus had already shown) the traditional philosophical methods are good only for explaining what we already know and have no usefulness in the discovery of new knowledge.

Though they agreed on the need for a "new philosophy," Bacon and Descartes had very different ideas of what it should be like. Bacon was the less profound thinker of the two, but he saw more clearly than Descartes that the new "natural philosophy" (or "science," as we would call it) would have to be experimental and that scientific conclusions would have to be supported by observations of natural phenomena as well as by logically demonstrated theories. Though his own discussion of the subject is rather confused and superficial, Bacon realized that the logic of science would have to direct the mind in proceeding from observed phenomena (experimental data) to broad generalizations. Descartes, on the other hand, who was a mathematical genius of the first rank and who invented the science of analytical geometry during a few inspired months of his young manhood, realized more clearly than Bacon that natural science would have to become more like mathematics than it ever had been in the past.

The mature science of the late seventeenth century and after would have to combine the respect for experiment that dominated Bacon's thought with the rigorous mathematical logic that characterized the system of Descartes. In any case, both philosophers had outgrown their early skeptical tendencies and had restored confidence that the human mind, if rightly used, could attain scientific truths that would be both certain and useful. Both thinkers clearly stated that the long-term goal of scientific advance was to enrich human life. While neither one provided a fully satisfactory basis for scientific advance, both of them gave their followers a renewed sense of direction. Within the limits imposed by its method, science could again be expected to attain conclusions that were sufficiently certain that men could confidently use them for the needs of human life.

The price that the philosophy of the new age paid was that the scope of real science was greatly narrowed. Only in dealing with things that could be counted, weighed, and measured, and then treated quantitatively and mathematically, could there be a real science. Aspects of human experience that could not be readily treated in this way, such as ethics, aesthetics, natural theology—indeed, all branches of experience that dealt with value and quality rather than with material objects and quantity—ceased to be regarded as truly scientific. To the present day, people living after the time of Bacon and Descartes find it difficult to comprehend the medieval scholastic belief that nonmaterialistic subjects like ethics and aesthetics can also be seriously regarded as sciences.

The Scientific Revolution

The growth of a philosophy suitable for natural science was no accident, for the sixteenth and seventeenth centuries also experienced an advance in natural science so dramatic that the term "scientific revolution" has long been applied to it. This period certainly does not mark the beginning of serious scientific study, for that activity goes back at least as far as the ancient Greeks. But most branches of modern natural science in their present form can trace their beginnings back no farther than the sixteenth and seventeenth centuries.

Weaknesses of Traditional Science

The general philosophical mood of uncertainty, which tended to cast doubt on all traditional learning, provides the background for the scientific revolution, and most of the great scientific pioneers, just like the philosophers, sharply repudiated past learning and consciously set out to reform and reconstruct a science which they no longer found credible. In each specific case, furthermore, certain specific shortcomings of traditional science troubled scientific investigators so deeply that sooner or later someone was bound to propose a set of new theories that were totally opposed to the old science. In astronomy, for instance, the growth of transoceanic navigation in the late fifteenth century made navigators demand from the astronomers better charts of the heavens. The increasingly obvious shortcomings of the Julian calendar also generated a demand for calendar reform, another practical undertaking for which improvements in astronomy were helpful.

There were also theoretical considerations that made astronomers dissatisfied with traditional astronomy. The prevailing philosophies, both the Aristotelian tradition of the scholastics and the Neoplatonism popularized by many humanists, taught that the universe is constructed in an orderly and intelligent way. Hence they made people inclined to think that of two possible scientific explanations of an observed fact, the simpler and neater must be the correct one. But as centuries of astronomers had tried to fit observational data into the geocentric (earth-centered) astronomical system that medieval scientists took from the Greek astronomer Ptolemy (second century A.D.), the mechanism of orbits had grown increasingly complex. Many astronomers found the prevailing map of planetary and stellar positions offensively complicated, and hence many in the late fifteenth and early sixteenth centuries were trying to combine the known movements of the heavenly bodies into new patterns that would be simpler and more intellectually satisfying. Although astronomy was destined to be the key science in the emergence of the modern approach to scientific questions, other fields of science—notably certain branches of physics—also faced both theoretical and practical problems that created pressure for reform and reorganization.

Philosophy played an important part in the movement of thought away from the traditional natural science. One of the most important developments was advance in understanding the logic of scientific investigation. Here the crucial work was not done by one of the new breed of philosophers but by a long line of scholastic professors of logic and natural philosophy in the universities of Northern Italy, which (largely because of the international fame of their medical schools) had become the principal European centers for the study of natural science, a distinction which they retained from the fourteenth until well into the seventeenth century. The philosophers at Padua and other Italian universities transformed scholastic logic from a system that was effective chiefly in the logical demonstration of accepted truths into a system that guided thinkers in the effective incorporation of experimental data into their search for conclusions and, hence, into a system focused on the discovery of new truths. In a more general sense, the spread of skeptical attitudes, by discrediting traditional learning, opened men's minds to the search for new systems of science. The new philosophical direction illustrated by the works of Bacon and Descartes, while sharply limiting the powers of the mind in certain respects, taught that the human mind is well suited to the investigation of scientific phenomena.

Copernicus

All of these influences were at work in the thought of the first great innovator in the history of modern astronomy, Nicolaus Copernicus (1473–1543), a Polish priest who (like most of the great scientific pioneers) was educated in Italy, where he studied both law and medicine and also developed a keen interest in astronomy. Copernicus found the complexity of the existing astronomy unappealing and searched for many years for a better way to account for the observed motions of the celestial bodies. He was not particularly active as an experimenter, for his skill was mainly in the mathematical treatment of data. When his major astronomical work, *On the Revolutions of the Celestial Orbs*, came out in the last year of his life (1543), it rested on the traditional astronomical data rather than on new observations—probably an advantage, for no one could accuse the author of having dreamed up new data to fit his far-fetched theories.

What Copernicus had realized was that many of the complications in traditional astronomy stemmed from the erroneous assumption that the point of observation, the earth, was a fixed point rather than a moving object. What his famous treatise proposed was the revolutionary idea that if one assumes that the sun, rather than the earth, stands at the center of the universe, that the earth is just another planet, and that all the planets revolve around the sun rather than the earth, then the mathematical calculation of planetary orbits would be vastly simplified.

Such startling theories—particularly the notion that the earth was not the center of the universe and that it was a moving object—naturally aroused considerable opposition. Copernicus's new astronomy was attacked as contrary to both Aristotle and the Bible. Yet the main grounds for opposition to his theories were not religious. His idea that the earth moved seems to fly in the face of common sense, for the earth certainly seems to stand still, and the various heavenly bodies seem to circle around it. There were also serious scientific objections which *On the Revolutions* did not resolve. If, as he proposed, the earth is a great ball rushing through space, why are not objects on its surface hurled off and left behind? If it rotates on its axis every twenty-four hours, why does an object thrown straight up into the air still come down at the point of origin? Would not a rotating earth move out from under the object while the object is in the air, so that it would land a perceptible distance to the west of the point from which it was thrown? Finally, if the earth is whirling around a planetary orbit, why do not the fixed stars give the optical illusion of moving when viewed by an observer on the earth's surface—the phenomenon known as parallax?

All of these were serious and fully scientific objections. To the first two, Copernicus had no answer since the physical science of his day did not understand the principles of gravitation and inertia that form the basis of a modern scientist's reply. To the absence of parallax in the apparent position of the fixed stars, Copernicus could only give an answer that seemed preposterous though in fact it was true: that the stars are such a vast distance from the earth that the whole vast diameter of the earth's orbit can be treated mathematically as a point, and hence can simply be ignored, so far as any effect on the apparent position of the stars is concerned. Furthermore, since Copernicus held firm to the traditional (and incorrect) notion that all planetary orbits are perfect circles, in actual practice his calculation of the planetary orbits was no more accurate than that offered by the highly refined astronomical books of the old Ptolemaic tradition.

The only undeniable advantage that Copernicus's contemporaries could find in his theory was that he accomplished his mapping of the orbits with a simpler mechanism of celestial wheels than did the followers of the Ptolemaic or geocentric theory. This advantage was small compensation for his inability to provide convincing answers to the scientific objections. Hence his theory was widely studied but usually rejected, for while he had advanced an impressive proposal, he had not provided definitive proof of anything except its mathematical simplicity. In fact, his new astronomy could not be conclusively established until a whole new kind of physical science had been developed, and that was precisely what the next generation of great scientific pioneers accomplished.

The Work of Brahe and Kepler

Many astronomers in the late sixteenth and early seventeenth centuries continued the efforts of Copernicus's generation to improve and simplify astronomy, but most of these tried to preserve the traditional opinion that the earth stood immobile at the center of the universe. Copernicus certainly had made an impression, and several astronomers tried to work out compromise systems, of which the most famous was the "tychonic" system of the Danish astronomer Tycho Brahe (1546–1601). Brahe accepted from Copernicus the idea that all the other planets revolve around the sun, but he left the earth immobile at the center, with the sun and its collection of planets revolving around the earth once every twenty-four hours. Brahe was a great astronomical observer. With the anti-Copernican Brahe, not with Copernicus himself, modern astronomy received its first great influx of significant new experimental data.

Yet an even greater service of Brahe was that he took into his service a young astronomer far greater than himself, the German Johannes Kepler (1571–1630). Kepler at a very early age accepted the correctness of Copernicus's heliocentric system, but he worked with Brahe because he realized that he needed the vastly improved experimental material that Brahe was gathering. After inheriting Brahe's notebooks, Kepler was able to apply his supreme mathematical genius to the new data and so to discover significant new principles.

Kepler was an ardent Neoplatonist, eager to recognize the hand of an intelligent and orderly Creator in the world of nature. This enthusiasm made him grope for all discoverable mathematical harmonies, and he found hundreds of these. But the quasi-religious joy he found in the mathematical discovery of harmony in the world was always tempered by a sober resolution to accept no theory, no matter how intellectually satisfying, unless reliable experimental data confirmed that theory precisely. Kepler is quite important in the growth of modern scientific method because of the clarity with which he allowed experimental data to control his conclusions and the intense intellectual honesty which he showed in abandoning attractive and mathematically consistent theories when his observations did not provide the expected confirmation.

Among the hundreds of mathematical relationships that he showed to exist among celestial bodies, the vast majority were of no interest to anyone but a semimystical Neoplatonist. Three of his discoveries, however, are still known as Kepler's laws of planetary motion. The crucial one was his first law, which stated that the planetary orbits are ellipses, with the sun at one of the two foci of the ellipse. This abandonment of the idea that planetary orbits are perfect circles was a decisive step forward in astronomy, since for the first time, the data coming from observation conformed to the orbits postulated by astronomical theory. It was, however, a difficult step for other scientists to take, for circular motion seemed the perfect, even the inevitable, form of motion for perfect, celestial bodies. Kepler's planetary laws vastly simplified the mathematical mapping of the heavens, but they had little immediate effect, since they were so contrary to prevailing ways of thought. Galileo, for example, possessed copies of Kepler's books but never gave up the theory of circular orbits.

Galileo's World Machine

The Italian astronomer Galileo Galilei (1564–1642) was a gigantic figure in the birth of modern science. He provided nothing less than the main outlines of a whole new science of physics, which explained how the celestial mechanism of Copernicus and Kepler actually worked. Galileo was the intellectual and professional descendant of the scholastic scientists of North Italian universities. He began with, but passed beyond, the logic of scientific inquiry his predecessors had taught, arriving at a clear conception of how the natural scientist must devise experiments to confirm the truth of scientific generalizations to which his reason led him.

From an early date Galileo had inclined to think Copernicus right, and he was especially impressed by Brahe's experimental findings that undermined the traditional belief that the heavens were unchanging and that the visible celestial bodies were attached to a series of concentric and invisible spheres made of some clear substance like crystal. In 1609, after reading a description of a telescope someone had built in Holland, he constructed one of his own and employed it to make further experimental discoveries (such as the discovery of sunspots and of mountains and craters on the moon), which further undermined the traditional belief that the celestial bodies were quite different in composition from the changeable, corruptible, and malformed materials which made up the earth. He published a little book, *The Sidereal Messenger*, in 1610, and his findings soon caused him to be attacked both by traditional scientists and by politically minded churchmen who saw in the conclusions he drew from his findings a force that might disturb the faith of the people.

Although admonished by the Inquisition in 1616 to quit teaching these dangerous opinions, Galileo continued his studies in the fields of astronomy, physics, and scientific logic. Galileo's epoch-making astronomical discovery was that the universe is a great machine consisting of particles driven by forces whose workings can be calculated by the new physical laws that he himself had discovered. Gone was the notion of a celestial world unutterably perfect, totally distinct from the terrestrial world, and guided by spiritual forces such as angels and demons. The heavens now became a great mechanical structure of subtly balanced physical forces. In the field of physical science, Galileo's greatest work was in the field of dynamics, the study of moving bodies.

Galileo realized that the task of the physical scientist consisted of the twofold process of measuring forces through experimentation and calculating their mathematical relationships. Nature, he said, is a book written in the mathematical language. His most famous specific discoveries were the laws governing the acceleration of freely falling bodies and (greatest of all) a close approach (though not a full statement, which came only with Newton) to the principle of inertia, a conception totally inconsistent with the traditional Aristotelian science of moving bodies. In the field of scientific logic, Galileo is important in two areas: (1) his clear realization that fruitful experimentation must be conducted not at random but for the answering of specific questions and (2) his distinction between those qualities which can be measured and handled mathematically, such as motion or weight, and those qualities which cannot be measured in the object of study but which (he thought) have their real existence in the perceiving mind of the observer, such as tastes, colors, and smells. Only the mathematically manageable qualities, he concluded, could become the object of truly scientific investigation.

Conflict with Religious Authorities. Galileo always regarded himself as a good Catholic and took great pains to show that his teachings were not in conflict with Scripture or with the teachings of the Church. But the very attempt to demonstrate the religious propriety of his views got him into the business (very dangerous for a layman in the Italy of his day) of trying to show what the Church really taught. The warning he had already received in 1616 put him in a vulnerable position, and when in 1632 he brought out his brilliantly written *Dialogue Concerning the Two Principal Systems of the World*, he soon came under renewed attack even though the pope had personally authorized him to publish his views as long as he presented them as mere mathematical hypotheses rather than as established scientific truth.

The Roman Inquisition in 1633 ruled that the preface in which he presented his views as mere hypotheses was patently insincere (which in fact was true) and determined that this publication was a deliberate violation of the limits imposed on him in 1616. The *Dialogue* was banned, and he was compelled to make a formal public recantation of his opinion that Copernicus's theory was correct and that the earth moves. Further, he was compelled to live (quite comfortably, in fact) for the rest of his life at his country home near Florence. He continued his work in physics, though avoiding astronomy, and in 1638 published his most important work on dynamics—though he prudently had it published in Protestant Holland rather than in Italy. The most terrible ordeal for him was not his personal inconvenience or even his personal humiliation, but his anguish at seeing the authorities of the Church (in whose religious truth he firmly believed) place the whole institution in opposition to scientific conclusions he knew to be true.

The condemnation of Galileo did not kill the growth of science in Catholic lands, but it did suggest that certain topics were to be avoided and certain others handled only with extreme caution. On learning of the condemnation, the French philosopher-scientist Descartes at once delayed publication of a work in which he also accepted the truth of Copernicus's thesis. When he did publish his cosmological opinions a few years later, he did so only after adding a caution that his opinions were mere hypothesis and might be quite wrong. Although the Catholic Church never declared the Copernican hypothesis heretical, there can be no doubt that the heavy-handed way in which its administrators handled the views of Copernicus and Galileo damaged respect for the Church among scientists then and for long afterwards—precisely the situation that Galileo struggled in vain to prevent.

Advance in Biological Science

The main triumphs of the new science were in physics, and the whole mentality of natural science until at least the end of the nineteenth century was dominated by methodological concepts created by the physicists and astronomers of the seventeenth century. With the work of Sir Isaac Newton late in that century, the lines of development represented by such brilliant and creative figures as Copernicus, Kepler, and Galileo converged into a scientific synthesis of overwhelming power. Yet there were important advances in other fields. In biological science, especially botany, the preparation of annotated humanistic editions of Roman and Greek scientific writers produced efforts to identify the flora and fauna described in the ancient texts with the plant and animal life known to the editors' own times. The flood of new and exotic specimens from Africa, the Americas, and Asia made this task of integrating ancient with modern knowledge even more difficult, and a number of authors from the middle of the sixteenth century onward attempted to create and to publish complete descriptive catalogs of botanical specimens, of which the most famous was the *Pinax* (1623) by Caspar Bauhin (1560–1624) of Basel.

Even more striking than the descriptive natural histories were the discoveries made by anatomists, for these works at their best echoed the clash found in the physical sciences between traditional learning based on ancient and medieval books and the challenge posed by new theories and new discoveries. In the fields of anatomical illustration (and also in the illustration of animals, plants, and mineral specimens) the artists of Renaissance Italy and their Northern disciples made significant advances. The most famous such artistic anatomist, though not the first, was Leonardo da Vinci (1452–1519), who practiced dissection even more assiduously than other master painters, though the most interesting results of his anatomical sketches and other scientific studies remained in his unpublished notebooks and had little if any influence.

Vesalius on Anatomy. Far more important for science was the Belgian anatomist and physician Andreas Vesalius, whose *On the Structure of the Human Body* (published in Latin in 1543) is important in two respects. First, though traditional in many respects, the book challenged the reliability of the standard medieval textbook on anatomy, the ancient Greek author Galen (second century A.D.), because Galen had based some of his teachings on dissection of animal rather than human specimens. Far more challenging to tradition (at least implicitly) were the excellent woodcut illustrations of dissected cadavers printed with Vesalius's text. These illustrations are clearly based on accurate and searching dissection. Their precise origin is not certain, but they seem to have been done by several artists in the workshop of the Venetian painter Titian. Vesalius himself may have been one of the illustrators.

Harvey: Physics Applied to Physiology. Late Renaissance work in biological science reached its most brilliant achievement early in the seventeenth century with the work of the English physician William Harvey (1578–1657). Like Vesalius, who prepared his chief work while teaching at the University of Padua, and also like Copernicus and Galileo, Harvey was a product of the flourishing North Italian universities. Harvey is most famous for his treatise *On the Movement of the Heart and the Blood* (in Latin, 1628), in which he set forth and demonstrated his theory of the circulation of the blood, a theory that eventually changed medical practice and that from the beginning posed a serious challenge to the prevailing theories in physiology. As befits a man who studied at Padua while Galileo was teaching there, Harvey proved his theory by a purely mathematical and mechanical demonstration that the vast amount of blood pumped by the heart in a given time could be accounted for only by the theory that the same blood somehow was circulated and recirculated through the veins and arteries. What is particularly striking about Harvey is that he confidently believed his mathematical demonstrations even though the anatomy of his time knew of no actual connection between the veinous and arterial systems. Not until the introduction of effective microscopes in the second half of the seventeenth century did the Italian scientist Malpighi provide complete experimental verification of Harvey's theory by discovering the capillaries in the lungs of a frog.

The State of Science about 1650

The full maturity of the new mechanical science did not come until after the work of Newton in the late seventeenth century. Even the spectacular genius of men like Kepler and Galileo had not resolved all the unanswered questions that the new astronomy raised and the new physics struggled to answer. Although it is hard to respect the institutional bureaucrats who troubled and partially silenced a creative genius like Galileo, there was still substantial reason for learned and intelligent students of nature to remain unconvinced by the "new science." More important than the particular scientific conclusions which innovators like Kepler, Galileo, and Harvey had reached was their success in surmounting the skeptical crisis of late sixteenth-century thought and restoring confidence that if the mind kept within the narrow limits of the measurable and mathematically calculable, it could reach clear, reliable, and useful conclusions. In the following age, this trust in the new intellectual method of natural science led to a dramatic shift from the pessimism and uncertainty of late Renaissance culture to the exultant confidence in the orderliness of the world and in the power of human reason which produced the optimism of the Enlightenment.

Accomplishments in Literature and the Arts

Although the culture of the sixteenth and early seventeenth centuries was dominated more by its doubts and fears than by optimism, the age was one of brilliant achievement in many fields of human endeavor. The philosophical and scientific work already discussed was the most historically decisive of these achievements, for it laid the intellectual and material foundations for the temporary dominance of European society over all other existing forms of civilization and for the permanent transformation of all non-European cultures under the impact of this Western challenge. For most Europeans in the age itself, however, the scientific and philosophical advance must have seemed far less important than the achievements in fields like the visual arts, music, and literature.

Art: The Mannerist Style

In the field of art, the full maturing of the High Renaissance style was a brief and transient moment. The death of Pope Leo X in 1521, coinciding as it did not only with the Reformation challenge to the popes, the chief patrons of art, but also with the death of two of the three greatest Italian Renaissance masters (Leonardo da Vinci in 1519 and Raphael in 1520) conveniently marks the end of an age. Although the third great master, Michelangelo, lived on until 1564, his style underwent a marked transformation during the 1520s. All later artists of the sixteenth century (and for long afterwards) were not only influenced but almost overwhelmed by the work of the Renaissance masters.

Yet the style had clearly changed. The High Renaissance painters had long since outgrown the unreflective realism of some quattrocento art and had achieved a poised balance and an idealization of form that are the true characteristics of the style. In the later works of Michelangelo, such as his *Last Judgment* (1534–41), the sense of repose and the idealization of form were deliberately destroyed as the artist sought to express the overpowering emotionalism of the judgment scene.

The actual origin of these new directions is not in Michelangelo but in the work of a number of young Florentine painters who repudiated the classical balance of their elders and sought to express their emotions by a deliberate introduction of discord. This new style, commonly known as "Mannerism," displayed many diverse tendencies, and a refined elegance or a concentration on technical tricks are also typical of artists commonly classed as "mannerist." None of these early mannerists—Rosso Fiorentino, Portormo, Parmigianino and Bronzino—achieved success comparable to that of the great Renaissance masters. Later, however, at least two major figures are associated with the Mannerist style, the Venetian painter Tintoretto (1518–94) and—by far the greatest exponent of the style—the Greek-born and Venetian-trained Domenikos Theotocopoulos (1541–1614), commonly known as El Greco. Although he settled in Spain, El Greco painted in the Italian tradition. His works show the vivid emotionalism, the visual elegance, and the deliberate exaggeration and distortion of forms that cause Mannerism to be regarded as a distinct style and not just as a later and less successful version of the Renaissance style.

The Baroque Style in Art

The mannerist style, however, was too esoteric to appeal broadly beyond an educated and artistically trained elite, and too unstable and idiosyncratic to dominate the arts for long. The future belonged to a later style that would consciously continue the High Renaissance heritage but would emphasize overwhelming effects and an earth-bound realism that resembled Renaissance work but cast aside its idealized vision of man. This style, commonly called Baroque, can be found very early in the paintings of Correggio (d.1534), whose works are voluptuous and overpowering, and in the more prosaic work of Paolo Veronese (1528–88). The Baroque style emerged fully and became dominant because of the success of several painters active at Rome in the late sixteenth century. Caravaggio (1573–1610) achieved realism by introducing everyday persons and scenes into his religious paintings, but the richness of design and the skillful blending of classical elements with a lush naturalism achieved by Annibale Carracci (1560–1609) made him a more popular figure.

Because of its emphasis on overpowering emotional effect, the Baroque style was most successful in architecture, since the viewer could be overwhelmed by an entire artistic environment. Although Michelangelo's modifications of the style of St. Peter's Cathedral at Rome in mid-sixteenth century can be seen as tending toward Baroque (especially the enormous dome), the architectural shape of the future emerged in another Roman church, the Gesù, mother church of the Jesuit order, designed by Giacomo Vignola and Giacomo della Porta and built in 1575–84. The gorgeous ornateness, the skilled use of the interplay of light and shadow to focus attention on the altar and to increase emotional intensity, and the remarkable unity of the facade point toward the Baroque style of the future. This elegant and showy style reached its maturity in the work of the sculptor and architect Gianlorenzo Bernini (1598–1680), best known for the ornate *baldachino*, or tabernacle, for the main altar of St. Peter's, and for the vast colonnade which still defines and dominates St. Peter's Square.

The Baroque style did not long remain confined to Rome or even to the Counter-Reformation religious spirit that helped to inspire it. By the late sixteenth century, all serious students of art in North Europe longed to study the Renaissance masters in Venice, Florence, and Rome. Peter Paul Rubens (1577–1640), a Flemish Catholic, developed his own Baroque style during eight years of study in Italy. His work has the lush richness, the vivid emotionalism, and the visual tension of the greatest Italian Baroque painters.

Rubens had a spectacularly successful career. While he was the only first-rate Baroque painter of the Spanish Netherlands, the rebel provinces of the North developed an art that reflected the solid comfort of Dutch life and that (no doubt because of Protestant strictures against idolatry) depicted secular topics or narrative biblical scenes. Although there were many Dutch painters of great talent, one name eclipses all the others, Rembrandt van Rijn (1606–69), who acutely captured the humanity of both the biblical scenes and of the pictures he painted of contemporary life, not least of all in the several striking self-portraits. Spanish Baroque painting produced its greatest native figure in Diego Velásquez (1559–1660), whose career as a court painter produced not just ordinary portraits but masterpieces of character portrayal. French Baroque art produced its greatest achievements in architecture rather than in painting, and only after the personal rule of Louis XIV began in 1660.

Venice and Baroque Music

The Baroque age also produced a musical literature that was ornate and impressive. The Reformation contributed the tradition of the chorale or congregational hymn, a tradition that took its rise from Luther's own love of music but did not reach its maturity until the eighteenth century with the work of Bach. Catholic Italy dominated most other branches of music. The religious music of Palestrina (1524–94), papal organist and choirmaster, continued the earlier Flemish tradition in music but, in the spirit of Catholic

Reform, purged Church music of the many secular elements that had intruded into it during the late Middle Ages.

Whereas Rome was conservative and traditional, Venice became the center of a progressive musical tradition that produced in Giovanni Gabrieli (1557–1612) a great composer who foreshadowed the later divorce of instrumental from vocal music. He produced religious motets that, being free from a specific setting in worship services, could disregard tradition. Gabrieli had been organist at St. Mark's cathedral in Venice. His successor, Claudio Monteverdi (1567–1643), produced an even more tradition-free music and created in his *Orfeo* (1607) the first full-length work of a new Baroque genre, the opera, which combined music and drama. In 1637 Venice founded the first public opera house. The creative Venetian style of the early seventeenth century eventually exerted its influence in France and in Germany, and in the late seventeenth and early eighteenth century, court music, especially the ballet and the opera of the French court and its many German imitators, provided a major cultural expression of the splendor and power of the absolute monarchies.

An Age of Literary Genius

The sixteenth and early seventeenth centuries were also a creative age in most of the vernacular literatures, and an age of absolutely unequaled greatness in two of them. Germany seems to have been drained of literary creativity by the struggles of the Reformation, though Martin Luther himself was a literary giant as well as a religious leader. Italy continued to produce important literature despite its political disasters. France produced several important writers, and England and Spain achieved a literary eminence they have never surpassed. Although these vernacular literatures were deeply influenced by classical humanism—borrowing many themes, motifs, and verse forms directly from ancient literature—and although they are conventionally classed as "Renaissance" literature, the greatest authors used the classical heritage freely and independently and were not slavishly bound by the ancient past.

Italian Vernacular Literature. The literature closest to Renaissance humanism was the Italian. An earlier chapter has discussed the work of the most influential sixteenth-century writers, the poets Ariosto and Tasso and the prose writers Castiglione, Machiavelli, and Guicciardini, all of whom well illustrate the blending of ancient and modern elements. Italy also produced the most overrefined and artificial literary form, the pastoral. The *Arcadia* of Jacopo Sannazzaro, published in 1502, hardly ranks as great literature, but its highly artificial picture of the life of incredibly refined and intellectual shepherds and shepherdesses set the style for the work of many authors in many lands, with Sir Philip Sidney's *Arcadia* (1590) being perhaps the most effective example.

The historical interest of Machiavelli and Guicciardini continued with the *Lives of the Most Eminent Painters, Sculptors, and Architects* (1550) by Giorgio Vasari, whose well-informed (and sometimes distorted) ideas have influenced the interpretation of art ever since. Far more intellectually profound was the work of Paolo Sarpi on the *History of the Council of Trent* (1610–18). It presented a sharply antipapal account of recent Church history that could have been published nowhere in Italy except in independent-minded Venice. Two of the Italian philosophers of the period, Giordano Bruno (1548–1600) and Tommaso Campanella (1568–1639), possessed a striking literary style. The greatest of the Italian scientists, Galileo, was also an important literary figure, for he consciously adopted the dialogue form and the vernacular language in order to popularize scientific theories that most other scientists would have hidden away in dull and unreadable Latin treatises. Indeed, his dazzling literary skill may explain part of the determination of his scientific and theological enemies to silence him. All in all, Italian literature continued to flourish even if it produced its greatest works in utilitarian genres like history, philosophy, and natural science. All other European nations consciously borrowed themes and forms from the Italians.

France: From Rabelais to Classicism. France was one of the earliest nations to feel the powerful Italian influence. A group of poets in the mid-sixteenth century, known as the Pléiade and led by Pierre Ronsard (1524–85) and Joachim du Bellay (1522–60), deliberately set out to remodel French-language poetry on the model of the classical poets and their modern Italian disciples. Even earlier, the Italian influence was strong in the poems of Clement Marot (1497–1544) and of his royal patroness (and poet), Marguerite de Navarre, sister of King Francis I. The greatest sixteenth-century figures, however, were more free in their reaction to Italian influences. The humorous prose tales *Gargantua* and *Pantagruel* of François Rabelais (1490–1553) are dominated by a rollicking wit that makes no pretense of conforming to the smooth and elegant literary style of the Italians. In fact, while reflections of humanistic learning abound in his prose tales, Rabelais deliberately rejected all the literary conventions and let his sense of humor and his sharp satirical judgment play freely upon all aspects of contemporary life, including the humanist as well as the scholastics.

More obviously classical in spirit, but equally free in his approach to the ancient heritage, was Michel de Montaigne (1533–92), whose *Essays* have been discussed earlier. Montaigne as a boy was taught to speak Latin as fluently as French, and the spare elegance and clarity of his writing could only have been achieved under the influence of classical prose and could only be rivaled in his century by one other great master of French expository prose, the reformer John Calvin (1509–64). The classical influence became far stronger in seventeenth-century France in literature as well as in art, and both the literary theory of the age and the dramatic works of the most influential playwrights of the century, Pierre Corneille (1606–84) and Jean Racine (1634–99), produced the highly formal and intensely intellectual classical style that spread from the court of Louis XIV to the rest of Europe during the period after 1660.

Spain's Golden Age. Spain and England produced literatures which were less refined and classical, and hence more popular and powerful, than the French. The novel *Don Quixote* by Miguel de Cervantes (1547–1616) is a satirical attack on the medieval tradition of chivalric romances, but the author's standpoint is plain common sense and a sense of real life, not the austere standards of a classicist. The work stands in the old Spanish tradition of the picaresque tale of roguish adventures, but the profound characterization of the deranged hero, Don Quixote, and of his prosaic but equally ineffectual squire, Sancho Panza, gives the work a permanent place among the masterpieces of world literature.

Spain also had an active and highly popular dramatic tradition with several playwrights of talent and one of real genius, Felipe Lope de Vega (1562–1635). The productivity of Lope de Vega is almost beyond belief: he produced some 1,800 plays, of which nearly 500 survive. These plays were popular entertainments, reflecting the religious intensity and patriotism of the nation, and were not designed to be read as literature. Yet only the great English playwrights of the age achieved anything of comparable excellence. Patriotic fervor also produced at least one poetic work of high quality, the epic *Os Lusiadas* (1572) by the Portuguese poet Luiz de Camões, who celebrated the heroism of the explorer Vasco da Gama.

The Elizabethan Age in Literature. Except for a few works of the humanists (notably Sir Thomas More), Renaissance England has a rather sparse literary record until the reign of Queen Elizabeth I (1558–1603), but the nation more than made up for its earlier backwardness during this period. Part of the inspiration for English literature came from the Italian Renaissance authors, studied both at first hand and through their French imitators. As early as the reign of Henry VIII, the Earl of Surrey and Sir Thomas Wyatt had adopted themes and verse forms from Italy, with the sonnet being their most successful form. A long generation later, Sir Philip Sidney (1554–86) did much to popularize the new literary style with his treatise *A Defence of Poesie*, his sonnets, and his widely read pastoral, *Arcadia*. The Puritanical poet Edmund Spenser (1552–99) in his *Shephearde's Calendar* (1579) adopted the artificial pastoral theme of Renaissance Italy, and in his masterpiece, the *Faerie Queene*, followed the chivalric themes and the complex allegories of the medieval tradition. Yet the subtlety of his verse forms and the profundity and vividness of his poetic imagery made his writings achieve something quite beyond the medieval or the Renaissance tradition.

The Italian, the medieval, and the classical influences continued to stimulate talented poets in the reign of King Charles I (1625–49) and helped to shape the work of one of the greatest of all poets, John Milton (1608–74), whose works constitute the last great achievement of Renaissance literature in England.

Drama: The Age of Shakespeare. Even more powerful than the poetic tradition, however, was the remarkable development of English drama during the lifetime of its greatest figure, William Shakespeare (1564–1616). Regular professional theaters developed in London during the 1570s just about the same time as in Madrid. Although the Middle Ages had produced a native folk drama associated with religious festivals, and the humanists of the earlier sixteenth century had produced a learned drama influenced by Italian playwrights and by ancient models, the new English dramatists attained the profundity of classical plays without losing touch with their mass audience. A group of pioneers active during the 1570s and 1580s failed to achieve anything of first quality, but their works created the audience and established the traditions within which Christopher Marlowe (1564–93) and the even greater Shakespeare brought English dramatic art to its fulfillment.

Shakespeare was never formally learned, but he mastered not only the literary and theatrical conventions of his day but also enough classical and historical information that he could meet the popular taste for plays on ancient themes and also for plays based on England's own history. Most of all, however, Shakespeare developed great insight into the workings of the human soul. His great tragedies, such as *Hamlet*, *Macbeth*, and *King Lear*, remain vital parts of dramatic literature because of their author's sensitivity to human character. Shakespeare was also successful with his many comedies and with a third genre, the history play, which dealt with episodes from England's unstable medieval past that still had immediate political relevance for Elizabethans.

The most influential London playwright after Shakespeare's retirement, Ben Jonson (1573–1637), had far more classical learning. Able though he was, however, neither Jonson nor anyone else in the next generation could match Shakespeare's genius; and English drama became less and less powerful until the triumph of Puritanism in the 1640s virtually destroyed it for nearly a generation. The new drama of the Restoration period after 1660 was a very different and far less significant literary form.

Greatness of Late Renaissance Culture

The greatness of both English and Spanish drama at their height was their success in appealing to an audience of extremely diverse social and intellectual background. The classical French drama that was just beginning to win the upper hand and push aside the unsophisticated popular drama never, even at its most appealing, extended its popularity so far outside the restricted circle of courtiers and intellectuals. When it reached its full development under Louis XIV, this drama, like the classical art and literature that also came under royal patronage (and control), was part of an official cultural program that systematically fostered proper social, political, cultural, and religious attitudes.

But rigid classicism was a distinctly post-Renaissance phenomenon. The culture of the Renaissance and Reformation period no doubt also reinforced prevailing social attitudes, but if only because the period before 1648 was more afflicted with internal doubts and conflicts, the age left greater freedom for spontaneous creation in literature and the other arts. Whether in spite of its doubts and conflicts or because of them, the age of Montaigne, Cervantes, and Shakespeare; of Palestrina, Gabrieli, and Monteverdi; of Caravaggio, Rubens, and Rembrandt; and of Kepler, Galileo, and Descartes was one of the most creative periods in the whole history of mankind. Late in the seventeenth century, Sir Isaac Newton, the scientific genius who pulled together all the diverse elements of the new physical science into a synthesis that dominated Western thought until the beginning of the nineteenth century, acknowledged his indebtedness to earlier figures like Kepler, Descartes, and Galileo by admitting, "If I have seen farther [than other men], it is because I have stood on the shoulders of giants." At least until the cultural revolution that marked the beginning of the twentieth century, any author, composer, or artist might have said as much about his debt to his great precursors of the sixteenth and early seventeenth centuries.

Chapter Eleven
The Struggle for Stability, 1600–1648

The brilliant cultural achievements of the age, the apparent power of the authoritarian monarchies of Western Europe, and the incredible luxury in which the upper classes (but only they) lived are striking characteristics of European society in the late sixteenth century. An observer who looks only at the glittering art of the Baroque age, at the extravagant pageantry of the royal courts, and at the vast colonial empires and worldwide political schemes of the major powers might conclude that European society about 1600 was stable and secure. Yet all this outward splendor and power barely covered over an inherent tension and instability in social, economic, and political life that are strikingly reminiscent of the tension and instability of the Baroque art of the age.

An Age of Political Turmoil

Instability was especially marked in the political field. In the history of Continental Europe, the Thirty Years' War (1618–48), though focused in Germany, involved nearly every major country in Europe; it was the result of political and religious breakdown in Central Europe produced by defects in the political and religious settlements of the sixteenth century. In the history of England, likewise, the English Civil Wars (1642–46 and 1648) cut a permanent swath through the continuity of English history and led to the first political execution of a European monarch by his rebellious subjects (1649). This war, too, was the result of fatal flaws in the apparently successful religious and constitutional system inherited from the Tudor age. Indeed, major Renaissance monarchies had already failed when put to the test during the late sixteenth century. The resplendent French monarchy which contemporaries generally thought to be the most powerful political organism in Europe collapsed utterly during the Wars of Religion (1562–98) in the face of aristocratic factionalism, religious disunity, and weak royal leadership. Likewise, Hapsburg Spain, the dominant political and military power of the sixteenth century, was unable to prevent its king from losing control of the northern half of his rebellious Netherlandish provinces.

The crisis of political authority grew deeper in the new century. Almost simultaneously in the early 1640s, frantic efforts at political reform intended to arrest the decline of Spanish power stirred up major revolts in two provinces that had been largely exempt from the heavy burdens of Spanish empire building, Catalonia and Portugal. Catalonia in northeastern Spain rose in rebellion in 1640 against royal efforts to reduce its special privileges, and it took twelve years before the province was fully pacified. Portugal, which had been claimed and occupied by Philip II of Spain in 1580, also revolted in 1640 against the Spanish government's attempt to make it pay a larger share of the costs of Spanish world leadership. In this case the revolt succeeded and the Portuguese nation reestablished its independence. The Spanish government also faced unrest that threatened to produce revolution in the southern province of Andalusia in 1641.

At about the same time, in 1639, Scotland rose up in the national resistance against King Charles I that led directly to the first English Civil War beginning in 1642. The deteriorating political situation in England was further aggravated in 1641 by a bloody massacre of their English Protestant oppressors by the native Catholic Irish in the province of Ulster.

Again at the end of the 1640s, there was a series of revolts and widespread unrest: (1) revolution in the most important of the Spanish possessions in Italy, the Kingdom of Naples, in 1647; (2) two extremely complex political uprisings (the Fronde) led by the well-to-do judicial bureaucrats and the higher nobility of France in the period of 1648–51, and severe popular rioting at Paris; (3) political agitation in the army of the new republican Commonwealth of England, as the rank-and-file soldiers, led by radical Congregationalist and Baptist preachers, argued for a fully democratic political system but were successfully opposed by their generals; and (4) great political tension between the semimonarchical prince of Orange and the dominant republican oligarchy in the Netherlands, a condition which produced a coup d'état by the prince and then a total collapse of the antirepublican Orange faction when Prince William II suddenly died of smallpox, leaving as his successor an infant son.

Explanations of the Breakdown

Historians of the various countries involved in these political disorders have found plenty of "causes" of a purely local or national character to explain them. Yet the fact that these disturbances were clustered closely around a few years—1618 for the disturbances in Bohemia and the emergence of war in Germany, 1639–41 for a whole host of revolutions, and 1649–51 for the final series—suggests that certain general forces were at work almost everywhere in Europe. For the later revolutions, the strains of the Thirty Years' War offer a plausible explanation, but there is the difficulty that the greatest and most radical revolution occurred in England, which (to the disgust of many ardent Protestants) had remained neutral, while war-torn Germany itself was unaffected by domestic revolutions. Besides, lengthy and exhausting international wars had also occurred in the sixteenth century without setting off a series of revolutions. General climatic conditions often had precipitated social unrest by causing crop failures, and the resultant food shortages and high prices drove to desperation a lower class which always lived near the margin of starvation. But the early 1640s, the most disturbed period, do not seem to have experienced the kind of widespread famine that might explain revolutions that were scattered across the map of Europe.

Effects of Economic Depression. The general causes of the political turmoil must be sought, therefore, in two factors that operated everywhere: fundamental defects in the traditional organization of government and society, which made governments too weak and inflexible to resolve crises peacefully, and a widespread economic depression, which subjected social and political structures to pressure they could not bear. There is ample evidence that shortly before 1620, a general economic depression began, accompanied (and perhaps in part caused) by a slowdown in the rapid population growth that had helped to make the sixteenth century an age of prosperity. Some regions (Spain, for instance) experienced declines in population so severe that even firmly Catholic governments became alarmed about the large number of men and women leading celibate lives in monastic communities. The few figures we have for industrial production, and the substantially more numerous and more reliable figures for international trade clearly demonstrate the onset of hard times that in many places lasted until the second half of the century.

The Instability of Renaissance Monarchies. The effects of this economic situation in politics were not always immediate. But they were drastic. The financial basis for the impressive but incredibly wasteful and inefficient governments of sixteenth-century Europe was extremely shaky. Only the soaring prosperity of the age, plus certain temporary windfalls like the influx of American treasure into Spain and the profits from the confiscation of monastic lands in England, allowed the European governments to conduct their overambitious foreign policies and their costly wars and to meet the expenses of their profligate royal courts. The size and expense (and social uselessness) of a king's entourage in the sixteenth century were almost beyond belief. For a nobleman to receive a visit from Queen Elizabeth of England and her entire court may have been an honor, but it was also a financial disaster, for he would have to feed and house not only several hundred people but also all the hundreds of horses that transported the royal court. At least on great state occasions, monarchs and the great nobles wore not only the most elegant textiles that skilled weavers could produce but also vast amounts of jewelry draped about them or sewn to their clothing—pearls and diamonds and other gems so numerous that contemporary accounts often reckon their weight by pounds rather than by their numbers. For example, the suit of a French nobleman attending a royal baptism in 1606 was studded with fifty pounds of pearls.

Each of the great nobles maintained his own smaller version of the royal household, with somewhere between thirty and a hundred personal servants: secretaries, chaplains, cooks, footmen, coachmen, pages, and valets whose sole function was to wait on him and his family. In properly bred noble circles, the last questions anyone asked were how much something cost and how the cost was to be paid, and the noble parasites who clustered at court in search of gifts and pensions were themselves surrounded by other parasites who lived off them—not only their hordes of retainers but a whole host of tradesmen who offered goods and services: artisans producing luxury goods, priests, sorcerers, prostitutes, armorers, gunsmiths, poets, musicians, artists, and countless others. The industry of serving the creature comforts of a royal court became a major source of wealth for capital cities like Paris, London, and Madrid.

Such utterly thoughtless extravagance was financially ruinous even in times of prosperity: the English fleet in the Armada crisis of 1588 was short-rationed on gunpowder, while Queen Elizabeth continued to purchase the gem-encrusted gowns that suited her station. Even the relatively parsimonious Tudor queen met the expenses of her household and her wars only by selling off blocks of land from the royal estates, thus leaving her Stuart successors faced with depleted financial resources that forced them into many of the fiscal policies that alienated their subjects and so helped produce the disastrous political crisis of seventeenth-century England. Like rulers in all countries, Elizabeth I shifted most of the burden of paying the salaries of royal officials (such as collectors of revenues, judges, and secretaries of state) from the royal treasury to the public by forcing private individuals who used the services of these officials to pay fees. With remarkable short-sightedness, many of the royal governments—the French, for example—raised current revenues by selling lucrative government positions (as judges, for instance) to the highest bidder, even though it would obviously be harder to direct and to discipline an officeholder who had bought his office.

The rate of expenditure by the monarchs and their nobles could not have gone on forever even if prosperity had continued. With the onset of depression about 1620, the whole showy system began collapsing. The gap between expenditure and income, which had always been hard to manage, now reached critical proportions. Just at this time, the outbreak of war in

Bohemia in 1618 and the spreading involvement of all the great powers made expenditures increase dramatically. Not only the royal governments but also the payers of taxes and fees—and the suppliers of merchandise to the court, who went unpaid even longer than usual—found the situation unbearable. Governments everywhere suddenly began trying to cut expenditures and increase revenues, a complex process that was absolutely necessary but politically and financially unacceptable to nobles whose pensions were cut or discontinued, to public officials who found their salaries and income from fees reduced, and especially to taxpayers who found not only that new taxes were being demanded but also that many of the tricks they had used to escape old taxes were no longer being allowed.

Attempted Reforms Arouse Opposition. In each major country, an administration devoted to retrenchment and to fiscal reform came to power—the count-duke Olivares in Spain, the cardinals Richelieu and Mazarin in France, and archbishop Laud and the earl of Strafford in England. But the policies they carried out, while often rational and necessary, aroused opposition not only among the common people but also (and most important) among highly privileged groups whose vested interests the reforms threatened.

In Spain, for example, Olivares was faced with a fiscal crisis so deep that further pressure on the kingdom of Castile, which bore most of the costs of supporting the extravagant court and the country's wars, seemed impossible. Hence Olivares adopted the perfectly sensible policy of trying to abolish the exemptions that privileged regions like Catalonia and Portugal had enjoyed. This attempt evoked charges of tyranny and unconstitutional acts that produced the revolutions of 1640 in both Catalonia and Portugal.

In France, the sin of the two great cardinals who headed the royal administration was chiefly that they tried to restrict the political influence of the great nobles and to compel both the nobles and the privileged corporations of judges (the Parlements) to conform to the royal will and to accept fiscal measures, such as the creation and sale of new judgeships, which reduced the revenues of the privileged orders. The result, between 1648 and 1651, was the two Frondes.

In England, finally, the government of King Charles I relied on the doctrine of inherent royal powers (prerogative) to impose taxes and other burdens the Parliament had rejected and followed a cautious policy of neutrality in the Thirty Years' War, which the more zealous Protestants of the country attributed to an ill-concealed favoritism for the Catholic religion. Such foreign and domestic policies may have been wise and even constitutional, but they generated a bitter antagonism over constitutional and religious questions that burst forth into demands for radical political reform and a new religious policy when the crown's desperate financial situation forced it to call Parliament into session in 1640.

Ideological Divisions and the Political Crisis

The economic upheaval of the period from about 1620 was the main reason why the top-heavy, extravagant, and inefficient royal governments of Western Europe ran into severe political crises. But there were also ideological divisions on religious questions that made political problems more difficult to manage. In Catholic countries, by the early seventeenth century, a politically and socially useful type of piety, largely the work of Jesuit religious thinkers and reformers, had made the old religion magnificent and powerful once again and in countries like France and the southern parts of Germany had permanently checked the growth of Protestantism. But precisely because of its formalism and its ties to the political and social "establishment," this type of Catholic religiosity impressed many devout persons as too morally lax and too spiritually superficial and formalistic.

Jansenism

A group of ardent Catholics, centered around the abbey of Port-Royal near Paris and influenced by the writings of the Belgian bishop and theologian Cornelius Jansen (1585–1638), rebelled against the moral and spiritual laxity of popular Catholicism and reemphasized man's dependence on divine grace and the need for morally rigorous standards of Christian living. Since Jansen's emphasis on grace extended to an affirmation of predestination, the "Jansenists" were quickly accused of having fallen into the Calvinist heresy. In 1653 the pope condemned Jansen's heresies. But in the meantime, Jansenism had won the loyalty of many of the most brilliant minds and most devout spirits. Though condemned also by the Sorbonne and persecuted by th administration of Cardinal Mazarin and later by Louis XIV, Jansenism survived as a barely underground form of austere Catholicism, associated historically and socially with the noble and bureaucratic leaders of the Fronde rebellions and later with the malaise that many of the finest spirits of seventeenth-century France felt concerning the brutal state building and the crass materialism of the monarchy as administered by Richelieu, Mazarin, and Louis XIV. Jansenists found especially offensive the way in which the monarchy systematically used the official Catholic Church in pursuit of its political goals.

Arminianism

A similar blend of religious tension with social and political conflict afflicted the Calvinist parts of Europe, especially the Netherlands. Early in the seventeenth century, an influential professor of theology at Leyden, Jacobus Arminius (1560–1609) began publicly to question the emphasis on absolute predestination and on moral rigorism that had prevailed in Dutch

Calvinism. A rival professor at Leyden, Franciscus Gomarus (1563–1641), charged that Arminius and his followers were subverting the true Reformed faith. This theological dispute between Arminians and Gomarists became involved in a bitter political and social struggle between Jan van Oldenbarnevelt (1547–1619), the leader of the upper middle-class elite of Holland, and Maurice of Nassau (1567–1625), who as governor of all seven provinces and as commander of the armed forces (and leader of the highest-ranking noble family, the house of Orange) represented a monarchist tendency. The poor resented the rich, unwarlike, and freethinking urban patriciate of the Dutch towns and tended to favor both the monarchical ambitions of the prince of Orange and the defense of strict Calvinism.

Because the Gomarists, or ultra-Calvinists, had the support of his political clientele, Maurice of Nassau came out on the side of true Calvinism, staged a military coup which allowed him to execute Oldenbarnevelt, and helped the Calvinist clergy call a religious conference, the Synod of Dort, which adopted an extreme Calvinist confession of faith. After the death of Maurice in 1625, however, the moderate Arminian and politically republican factions reasserted themselves, and the Netherlands grew into the most intellectually and religiously tolerant country in seventeenth-century Europe.

English Puritanism

The most striking ideological division of the early seventeenth century, however, occurred in England. Although the Anglican Church reestablished after the accession of Queen Elizabeth I in 1558 had been constructed largely along lines of political expediency, it proved a remarkably effective device for uniting the country in religion and for winning the great majority of Englishmen over to a basically Protestant religious standpoint. From the very first, however, some Protestants (even some of Elizabeth's bishops) felt that the Church had retained too many remnants of "popery." Although the theology of most Anglican theologians was Calvinistic, the Church was not fully Calvinist in its credal statements, and it never accepted the radically simplified Reformed worship practices or the Calvinist system of governing the Church through boards of elders and a series of representative assemblies.

Least of all was the Calvinist ideal of a self-governing church, free from political control, acceptable in Elizabethan England: the queen not only had the title of supreme governor of the Church in England, but actually did govern the Church with a firm and sometimes heavy hand. Those Protestants, usually Calvinists, who wished to purify the Church of its "popish" and unscriptural characteristics came to be called "Puritans." Under Elizabeth they were never more than a small minority, though they had some aggressive spokesmen in the House of Commons. Most Puritans rejected the efforts of radicals like Thomas Browne to organize schismatic reformed congregations in opposition to the lawfully established Church, but they kept up a constant agitation for further reform.

Growing Influence of Puritanism. Unfortunately for the stability of the national Church, the great appeal of Calvinist theology, discipline, and organization among the educated classes caused Puritanism to win a spiritual mastery among the ablest and most devout people of the age. In the early seventeenth century, in addition to the spread of Puritan beliefs and practices among wealthy and educated people, two other developments made many Englishmen desire further reforms.

First, within Anglicanism a new "High Church" movement grew up and, with its emphasis on the apostolic succession of bishops and on the spiritual value of the elaborate ceremonial which the Puritans disliked, not only offended many Puritans but also seemed to be undermining the fundamental Protestant doctrine of salvation by faith alone. The High Church faction was quickly accused of sharing the unsound views of Arminius and other Dutch critics of Calvinist orthodoxy. Many English Protestants who had never been Puritans began to fear that the High Churchmen must be secret Catholics trying to undermine the Church from within.

Second, a series of political developments under James I and Charles I made many Englishmen worry about "papists" and traitors high in court circles. James I's insistence on ending the war against Spain because he realized that the nation was unwilling to pay the taxes required for effective military effort, the conversion of his Danish-born queen to Catholicism, the presence of a number of known Catholics at the royal court, and his unwillingness to intervene in the Thirty Years' War in Germany—all these developments stimulated suspicion of the religious views and political loyalty of royal advisers. Under Charles I, the humiliating failures in the military campaigns against France in the later 1620s and the Catholic chapel allowed to the queen, a French princess, further deepened these suspicions.

To make matters worse, royal religious policy changed. James I had been hostile to the Puritans and at the Hampton Court Conference in 1604 had rejected their demands that he transform the Anglican Church into something closer to the Presbyterian Church of Scotland. But he fully intended to preserve the Church as it had developed under Queen Elizabeth I, and his opposition to Puritan demands was not unpopular. But whereas James had held the High Church faction at arm's length, his son Charles I had become a devout High Church Anglican and showed his favor for this group by naming William Laud (1573–1645), one of the most extreme High Church clergymen, to the highest position in the Church, archbishop of Canterbury.

The policies of Archbishop Laud caused the great Puritan emigration of the 1630s, which founded and populated the colony of Massachusetts Bay.

But those Puritans who stayed in England became increasingly hostile to both the political and the religious line of the Stuart monarchy. A substantial minority of them resolved to use the first opportunity they might have to make Parliament resist royal religious policy and ultimately to destroy the Elizabethan religious system and replace it with a national Presbyterian Church. There were many purely political and constitutional causes of the English Civil Wars, but the rise of a politically influential and increasingly revolutionary minority of Puritans who intended to take control of the Church away from the king was one of the most important.

Absolutism on the Continent

The Continental countries in the early seventeenth century all experienced a strong tendency toward absolute monarchy, but with varying results. In France, the new Bourbon dynasty had in Henry IV (1589–1610) a brilliant ruler who ended the Wars of Religion, brought the aristocracy firmly under royal control and skillfully used royal power to stimulate the prosperity and the national solidarity of the French people. Henry's mastery of French politics enhanced the prestige of the monarchy. His unexpected death at the hand of a religious fanatic in 1610, however, demonstrated how much the monarchy's authority depended on the personal qualities of the king. During the long minority of King Louis XIII (1610–43), the queen mother, Marie de' Medici, could not hold the high nobles in check.

Louis XIII himself lacked the intelligence and force of character needed to dominate the country, and no doubt the political drift of the government in the years after 1610 would have produced serious political turmoil if the king had not honestly faced his own limitations and delegated his own authority to a loyal and extremely able man, Cardinal Richelieu. Thanks to the unfailing support he got from the king, Richelieu from 1624 to his death in 1642 was able to compel all other high officials to report directly to himself and to impose his own ideas of domestic and foreign policy despite the constant conspiracies of the king's mother and the king's dull-witted but ambitious brother to force him from office. Although Richelieu's administration had many flaws, it kept the country internally stable and opened the period of French political and military domination of Europe.

French monarchy functioned far less successfully after the death of Richelieu in 1642 and of Louis XIII in 1643. Cardinal Mazarin, Richelieu's hand-picked successor, was unpopular because of his foreign nationality, his low social origins, and his blatant corruption. But his main troubles occurred because the new king, Louis XIV, was a small child and could not back up his chief minister the way his father had done. The long and costly war against Spain pushed this unpopularity past the point of peaceful complaint, and France experienced the Parlementary Fronde of 1648–49 and the Fronde of the Princes in 1650–51. The movements failed chiefly because the rebels were so bitterly divided among themselves and so selfish in their pursuit of power and in maintenance of their obsolete caste privileges that they were unable to drive the sharp-witted Mazarin from power permanently.

The Spanish government, like the French, was highly authoritarian. But the personal incompetence of Philip III (1598–1621) and Philip IV (1621–65) and the limited talents of the men they put in high office meant that the government could not cope with the obvious decline of Spanish power and wealth. The main cause of this decline was not royal or ministerial incompetence but the inability of the primitive economy to continue bearing the burdens of world empire, especially after the unearned bonanza of American treasure shipments began to dwindle in the early seventeenth century. The rulers knew that the country was in trouble, but their clumsy though well-intentioned efforts at reform were a major cause of the revolutions in Catalonia and Portugal. Spain's Golden Age had come to an end. Well before 1648, it had become clear that France on the Continent and both England and the Netherlands at sea had ended Spain's century and a half of military and political predominance.

Germany: The Thirty-Years' War, 1618–48

The sorry fate of Germany during the Thirty Years' War was no novelty, for the political structure of the old Holy Roman Empire had been decrepit since the thirteenth century, and the determined effort of the Emperor Charles V to restore the Catholic faith and to reconstruct the political authority of the monarchy had definitively failed by the time of the Religious Peace of Augsburg in 1555. The collapse of that peaceful settlement between Catholic and Lutheran princes had been impending since the end of the sixteenth century. This collapse stemmed directly from two basic weaknesses of the 1555 settlement. First, by failing to give explicit legal status to the third and newest of Germany's major religious groups, the Calvinists, the Augsburg treaty ensured that the rapid spread of Calvinism would breed political and religious unrest. Second, by failing to provide a clear and enforceable procedure for cases where a Catholic ecclesiastical prince—a prince-bishop or abbot who ruled a political state in addition to his religious function—turned Protestant, married, and attempted to secularize his state and transform it into a hereditary principality, the Augsburg treaty guaranteed that each such secularization would precipitate a crisis. The Protestant character of most of northwestern Germany, well established by 1600, rested largely on such secularizations.

Revival of Catholics and Hapsburgs

Both the problem of Calvinism and the problem of secularization were made far more dangerous by two other factors. One was the resurgence of German Catholicism, led by the Jesuit order and by a number of pious and able secular princes, such as the dukes of Bavaria. Taking advantage of their rights under the 1555 treaty, such Catholic rulers vigorously acted to wipe out heresy in their lands. They also firmly upheld the rights of their religion in Germany, attempting to compel the restoration of lands secularized by ecclesiastical princes and firmly insisting that Calvinist princes had no right to establish their faith.

The second disturbing element was the reemergence of the Austrian branch of the Hapsburg family as leaders of the Catholic cause. After two generations of relative weakness and passivity, the Hapsburgs rearranged their dynastic affairs to ensure that all of their Austrian and Bohemian lands would eventually be inherited by Archduke Ferdinand of Styria. Ferdinand was an able and ambitious ruler, determined to reassert the imperial authority to which he would in due course be elected. He also was determined to use his political authority to destroy Protestantism wherever he had the legal right and the actual power to do so, as in Styria, and to limit very narrowly the rights of Protestants in regions where he lacked the legal right or the power to attack heresy directly.

The spread of Calvinism (mainly in southwestern Germany) and the resurgence of Catholicism bred an atmosphere of instability and fear in which all sides prepared for war. The emergence of Ferdinand of Styria as a major influence on Hapsburg policy, and the certainty that he would inherit all the lands of the Austrian Hapsburgs deepened the fears of Protestants. As tension grew, many of the more insecure Protestant rulers organized an Evangelical Union (1608) to resist Catholic encroachments; the Catholic states formed a rival Catholic League headed by Duke Maximilian of Bavaria.

The Interests of Foreign Powers. These tensions in Germany also aroused the fears and ambitions of foreign powers. Although the king of France, Henry IV, was now a Catholic, he was concerned about Hapsburg efforts to reassert authority in western Germany. Henry watched with alarm every advance of the Catholic party in western Germany. When the Hapsburgs attempted to adjudicate a succession dispute in the strategic west German principalities of Cleves and Jülich and occupied those states in 1609, Henry IV was ready to fight to keep these territories out of pro-Spanish hands, since the Spanish in case of war would use all friendly provinces in the Rhine valley as channels for the movement of men and munitions from their bases in northern Italy to the Low Countries. Only the murder of the French king by a Catholic fanatic in 1610 prevented war from breaking out over the Cleves-Jülich question.

Spain, of course, was also interested in German politics, not only out of a desire to support the Catholic faith and to help the king's Austrian cousins but also in order to improve its Rhineland supply lines to the southern Netherlands in case of future wars with France and the Dutch. The Evangelical League had signed a military alliance with France, and the Catholic League with Spain, so that any religious war in Germany would quickly involve the two outside powers.

Revolt in Bohemia and War in Germany. The war that almost came in 1610 actually did begin in 1618 in what seemed to be a far less explosive area. The Protestant-dominated Estates of Bohemia had agreed to accept Ferdinand of Styria as their next king when his cousin the Emperor Matthias (1612–19) should die, even though Ferdinand's promises to uphold the constitutional privileges of the Protestants were evasive. When Matthias and Ferdinand tried to keep the Protestant Estates from assembling to protest against certain royal policies in 1618, the dominant Protestant nobles seized control of the government. Then in order to get both leadership and outside aid, the rebels elected as their new king the leader of the Evangelical Union in Germany, the Elector Frederick of the Rhenish Palatinate, who was a Calvinist.

The involvement of the elector Palatine in the Bohemian rebellion ensured that the war not only would spread into Germany but also would involve the foreign powers. Ferdinand of Styria, who managed to secure election to the emperorship in 1619, obtained military aid from Spain and from the duke of Bavaria to suppress the Bohemian uprising. Then, in order to punish Frederick of the Palatinate for his attempt to take the Bohemian throne and also in order to reward his Bavarian ally, the new emperor helped Bavarian and Spanish armies occupy the Palatinate. The ruthless suppression of Calvinism in the conquered province alarmed even the anti-Calvinist Lutheran princes; and even more important, the appearance of a Spanish army on the Rhine alarmed the French and the Dutch.

Foreign Defenders of German Protestantism. Although the fighting seemed to be nearly over by 1623, the French, the Dutch, and even the English (who felt compelled to help the expelled Palatine elector, a son-in-law of King James I) persuaded King Christian IV of Denmark to intervene in behalf of the German Protestants (and in pursuit of his own territorial ambitions in northern Germany) by promising him financial support. When King Christian's forces proved no match for the imperial and Bavarian armies, France and the Netherlands next subsidized the intervention of a far more formidable Protestant champion, King Gustavus Adolphus of Sweden. The victories of Gustavus Adolphus marked a decisive turn of the tide of military operations, and Sweden remained a major participant in the war down to its end in 1648. By 1635 the German princes on both sides were ready to accept a compromise settlement of the religious issues.

Unfortunately for the Germans, the Thirty Years' War had long since ceased to be a religious war over issues left over from the preceding century. Instead, it had become a political struggle among the intervening foreign powers, who had no intention of ending the war in Germany until their own interests had been protected. Indeed, the war even expanded, as Cardinal Richelieu, alarmed by a series of Swedish reverses, in 1635 brought France openly into the war on the side of the Protestant princes. So for thirteen more years Germany had to endure being a battlefield for all of Europe.

When peace finally came (Treaty of Westphalia, 1648) after lengthy negotiations, the settlement clearly showed that the age of dynastic politics had arrived. The religious questions of the rights of Calvinist princes and the control of secularized ecclesiastical principalities by the Protestants were settled in favor of the Protestant side on terms that could have been achieved as early as 1635. What really had to be negotiated was the price the Germans would pay to be left in peace by the foreign powers. All the foreign powers quickly agreed to make peace in Germany if they were given the German lands they coveted. Sweden received control of nearly the whole north German coast. France made a significant gain of formerly German lands along its eastern frontier, including at the town of Breisach its first toehold on the Rhine River. The Swiss received recognition of their complete independence from the old German empire, and in a separate treaty, Spain recognized Dutch independence.

Effects of the War. The effects of this long and bloody war on Germany have long been debated. The physical destruction and loss of life were very great, although some districts escaped untouched. The striking decline of Germany in cultural importance and in wealth, though often blamed on the war, had begun long before 1618, partly because of the political fragmentation of the country and partly because of changing trade routes. The one evil effect that clearly can be attributed to the war is the almost total destruction of the political authority of the imperial government; and even this collapse was the continuation of a series of political disasters which went back to the thirteenth century. Although the Holy Roman Empire survived in name until 1806, it was now little more than a dual league of the Catholic and the Protestant German states. The Hapsburg successors of Ferdinand II, though they carefully retained control of the imperial title, now concentrated their energies not on attempts to restore imperial control over the German princes but on attempts to build a powerful and well-organized state in their hereditary Austrian lands. The self-governing German states, more than three hundred in number, henceforth acted openly like independent nations, conducting their own foreign policies and seeking their own territorial aggrandizement.

The only sign of hope for a better future for Germany was the success of a few of the larger states in becoming fairly important middle-sized monarchies. Prussia emerged from the 1648 settlement with increased territory and population and with the first beginnings of those military and bureaucratic traditions that a century later allowed it to emerge as a major European power. At an even earlier date, Austria under the Hapsburg emperors began acting as a major power quite independently of its ruler's status as titular head of all of Germany. The war of 1618–48 had burned out the last remnants of solidarity left over from the old Germany of the Middle Ages, and the dynamic new Germany of modern times had barely begun to emerge. In the European politics of the next century, Germany became a bundle of weak and loosely held territories which the great powers used as a reservoir of land and people who could be passed back and forth as political pawns in the game of power politics.

England: The Puritan Revolution

The eventual rival of France for leadership in Europe, England passed through a bloody political crisis of its own that was far more surprising than the continued decline of the Holy Roman Empire. England had been the best ruled and most unified of the medieval feudal monarchies, and after sharing the decline of all Western European states during the fourteenth and fifteenth centuries, it had developed a strong and generally popular government under the talented Tudor dynasty (1485–1603). Nevertheless, the apparent solidity of its political institutions concealed serious defects that led to a rapid political decline under the first king from the Scottish-born dynasty of Stuart, James I (1603–25), and to open civil war under his son Charles I (1625–49).

Some of these defects were financial. Despite its apparent power and popularity, the Tudor monarchy had never established the principle that taxes formed a regular part of government revenue rather than only a temporary expedient in times of war. Despite his real talent as a fiscal administrator (or because of it), the first Tudor, Henry VII, financed his government chiefly from the royal estates, from the customs revenues (which were not regarded as a tax), and from the fines and confiscations he imposed on wealthy rebels. This pattern of revenue persisted throughout the Tudor period and on into the Stuart age, and in a period of price inflation, of increased demands for government services, and of costly wars and extravagant royal courts, it was never adequate. The Tudor monarchy survived financially only because of the drastic confiscation of the accumulated wealth of the Church conducted by Henry VIII. By the middle of the sixteenth century even much of this windfall of valuable lands had been squandered on war and on royal extravagance.

Queen Elizabeth I improved the condition of the royal treasury. Yet during the Spanish war that filled the last two decades of her reign, though the great queen received annual grants of taxes, she and her ministers never had the political courage to demand that Parliament vote enough money to cover the costs of the war. The Elizabethan government got by through a policy of allowing unpaid bills to accumulate and through regular sale of royal lands to make up the difference between income and expenditure. The Stuart dynasty in 1603 thus inherited a monarchy with depleted capital resources. During his first decade in England, James I tried repeatedly to negotiate a deal whereby Parliament would pay off his predecessor's bills and guarantee him an adequate annual revenue. But Parliament, habituated by centuries of precedent to regard taxes as a temporary expedient rather than as a regular basis of government finance, refused to come to terms with James I's ministers.

Results of Royal Poverty

The political results of this abortive negotiation were very serious. First, Parliament quickly realized that the poverty of the crown left the royal government exposed to pressure by Parliament, which might gain unprecedented control over royal policy by doling out money only in return for concessions in areas like foreign policy, religion, and appointment to high office, which the Tudors had jealously preserved as matters determined by the king alone. Second, having failed in its efforts to gain adequate revenues through cooperation with Parliament, the crown began systematically to exploit many extra-Parliamentary sources of revenue, such as impositions (additions to customs duties), fines on members of the powerful landowning classes who avoided many payments traditionally due under the feudal system, ruthless exploitation of the crown's right to take feudal estates into custody (and pocket the annual revenues) when the heir was a minor, forced loans from wealthy merchants, and special levies for important national purposes like building ships for the navy. Although there was good constitutional precedent for nearly every one of these extra-Parliamentary levies, the unprecedented firmness with which the government of James I and Charles I imposed them caused bitter opposition and charges of unconstitutional government.

Other Sources of Conflict

Several other issues also generated conflict between crown and Parliament. By their very success in using Parliament to endorse their religious and political measures, the Tudor monarchs had created an increasing sense of self-importance and an increasing maturity of procedure in Parliament. Even Elizabeth I experienced some difficulties with Parliament. But Elizabeth was an able political manipulator and had always managed to keep control of business in the House of Commons by identifying the natural leaders of the House and bringing them into her service. James I and Charles I were far less competent in dealing with Parliament, and their neglect of the political and financial ambitions of able English politicians led to the rise of a disgruntled political leadership that soon began to block official legislation and to push legislative programs of their own.

Many issues that always had been solely concerns of the crown now became subjects of bitter debate: royal hostility to the Puritans (who were especially numerous among the wealthy class represented in the House of Commons) and royal favor to the High Church faction after Charles I became king; dissatisfaction with James I's refusal to plunge headlong into the Thirty Years' War in defense of the Protestant side; personal antagonism toward many of the royal favorites whom the Stuarts put into high office despite their incompetence.

Friction between Crown and Parliament

The inability of crown and Parliament to work together became increasingly clear. As early as 1614, Parliament was so fully out of control that it did not pass a single law (or grant a single penny of tax money). In 1621, when Parliament openly challenged the crown's traditional right to forbid debate of foreign policy, James I came in person to the House of Commons and struck from their journal a resolution that he thought unconstitutional. In 1628 and 1629, under Charles I, Parliament attempted to impeach unpopular officials and forced the king to endorse a Petition of Right, which defined as illegal the use of forced loans, arbitrary arrests, and trial of civilians by court-martial. Finally, at the end of the 1629 session, the House of Commons physically resisted the king's order to dissolve Parliament by locking its doors and having members hold the Speaker bodily in his chair until the House had shouted through resolutions attacking the continued use of extra-Parliamentary taxes and the favor shown to the High Church clergymen.

The breakdown of the political system had become so acute that from 1629 to 1640 Charles I governed without calling a Parliament. At the cost of adopting a policy of careful economizing and of abstention from war, the royal government managed to get by on its nontax revenues. But the attempt of Charles I and his High Church archbishop, William Laud, to extend the Anglican Church system into strongly Presbyterian Scotland precipitated a rebellion that forced the king to call the English Parliament to raise money. The English opposition, which itself sympathized with the Scots, quickly became vocal in the "Short Parliament" held in the spring of 1640. Foolishly, the king dissolved this Parliament and tried to suppress the Scottish rebels with wholly inadequate forces. The result was a military disaster that left the Scots in control of the northern part of England. Thus Charles I had to summon another Parliament in the autumn of 1640 in an attempt to get the money required by his desperate financial and military situation.

The Long Parliament. This "Long Parliament," which was not legally dissolved until 1660, quickly came under the leadership of a group of radical politicians headed by John Pym. The vast majority of the members wanted to defend the Protestant religion against High Church policies that they thought of as "popish," to abolish all extra-Parliamentary taxes and many of the executive and judicial agencies used to enforce them, and to compel King Charles to dismiss royal officials, such as the Earl of Strafford and Archbishop Laud, who had carried out the objectionable policies. Between 1640 and 1642, the Parliament passed, and the king reluctantly signed, legislation to accomplish these goals. But Pym and his closest associates were not satisfied with limited reforms. Their ultimate goals involved the destruction of the Anglican Church, its replacement by a national Presbyterian Church, and the establishment of Parliamentary control over the naming of high officials and the determination of policy. Being a brilliant politician, Pym advanced cautiously toward these revolutionary goals by exploiting the religious hysteria and the political suspicions of the rank-and-file members. Even so, by late 1641 there was a swing away from radicalism. When Pym tried to revive Parliamentry antagonisms by having Commons pass a Grand Remonstrance restating all the old grievances against the king, it passed by only eleven votes.

The emergence of a moderate royalist group which did not approve the radical religious and political programs of Pym might well have split the Parliament and allowed a skillful king to regain control. But the bloody massacre of English Protestants by the oppressed Catholics of Ireland in 1641 not only renewed religious hysteria but also raised the question of whether Parliament could trust the king to command the army. The attempts by Parliament to deny the king his constitutional right to command the army deepened the political divisions. Finally, early in January of 1642, the king heard a rumor that Pym intended to impeach the queen (who was mistrusted as a French Catholic princess) and reacted by personally trying to arrest the radical leaders on the floor of Commons on charges of treasonable correspondence with the Scots. This bungled attempt so enraged Parliament and the masses of strongly Puritan London that a few days later the king and his court moved to the royalist city of Oxford. After a few uneasy months during which the Parliamentary majority and the king (joined by a large minority from Parliament) negotiated while each side recruited troops, open civil war broke out in August 1642.

The English Civil Wars. The appeal to armed force represented the final breakdown of the traditional constitution. Two savage periods of civil war, in 1642–46 and in 1648, involved not only England but also Scotland and Ireland, and both times ended in the victory of the Parliamentary armies and the captivity of the king. What tipped the balance of power against the royalist armies was the rise of a true military genius, Oliver Cromwell, to control of the Parliamentary forces. But whereas the Parliamentary majority (now that the moderate royalists were subtracted) wished to maintain the monarchy as a figurehead behind which the wealthier classes represented in Parliament would rule, and also intended to establish a highly intolerant Presbyterian Church like that of their Scottish allies, Cromwell and his army had concluded that the king could never be trusted, and they were dominated by anti-Presbyterian Independents (Congregationalists and Baptists) who insisted on a policy of religious toleration that Parliament had no intention of granting. After a long period of uneasy negotiations, Parliament and its own army fell out. The result was a seizure of power by Cromwell and his army, who decided to execute the king (January 1649), to abolish the monarchy and the House of Lords, and to set up a republican government headed by Cromwell as Lord Protector.

Oliver Cromwell had no personal ambition to be a military dictator, but that is what the inexorable logic of events had made him. Between 1649 and his own death in 1658, he experimented constantly with various ways to give his rule a legal and constitutional basis. Repeatedly, however, he found that his Parliaments thwarted his desire for religious toleration and refused to support his government with the necessary taxes and legislation. Hence repeatedly he had to send in his troops to purge or to dissolve the Parliament. In spite of his earnest desire for a return to normal political life, he ruled not as a constitutional executive but as the leader of the military high command. After his death in 1658 and the resignation of his less talented son, Richard, the generals of the army opened negotiations with the exiled son of the martyred king and in 1660 restored the monarchy.

What this act meant, however, was not that England had turned its back on the Parliamentary cause, but that the nation had learned that orderly and constitutional government could be restored only by a return to the old ideal of a political authority shared by crown and Parliament. The Restoration did not mean a return to the authoritarian monarchy of the Tudors, but a return to the far more limited monarchy desired by the moderate royalists in the Parliament of 1640–42, a monarchy stripped of its powers of arbitrary taxation and arbitrary arrest, and constrained by its financial limitations to rule with the consent of Parliament and not against it.

Stabilization of Political Life

England's return to the monarchy (but a monarchy clearly limited by the claims of Parliament) set it on a political course that eventually resolved its political instability but also made it sharply distinct from all Continental monarchies. After mid-century, France's exaltation of royal power under King Louis XIV (1643–1715) set it on the authoritarian path foreshadowed by the policies of Henry IV and Cardinal Richelieu. Spain, after surviving its revolutionary crisis of the 1640s, developed along similar lines of royal absolutism, and in Germany, the medium-sized principalities, which had been the real beneficiaries of the Protestant Reformation and also of the Peace of Westphalia, aped both the political structure and outward trappings of the great French monarchy that now replaced Spain as the dominant European power. These absolute monarchies had many defects that led to the great revolutionary upheaval of the late eighteenth century, but their emergence in the decades just after 1648 clearly ended the instability and violence that characterized European political life in the first half of the seventeenth century. A new age of absolute monarchy, dynastic politics, and relative internal political stability had opened.

Suggestions for Further Reading

Introduction

1. General Accounts and Interpretations.

Breisach, Ernst. *Renaissance Europe, 1300–1517.* New York, 1973.
Cheyney, Edward P. *The Dawn of a New Era, 1250–1453.* New York, 1936.
Gilmore, Myron P. *The World of Humanism, 1453–1517.* New York, 1952.
Ferguson, Wallace K. *Europe in Transition, 1300–1520.* Boston, 1962.
Grimm, Harold J. *The Reformation Era, 1500–1650.* 2d ed. New York, 1973.
Hay, Denys. *Europe in the Fourteenth and Fifteenth Centuries.* New York, 1966.
———. *The Italian Renaissance in Its Historical Background.* Cambridge, England, 1961.
Hillerbrand, Hans J. *The World of the Reformation.* New York, 1973.
Kingdon, Robert M., ed. *Transition and Revolution: Problems and Issues of European Renaissance and Reformation History.* Minneapolis, 1974.
Koenigsberger, H. G., and George L. Mosse. *Europe in the Sixteenth Century.* New York, 1968.
Lucas, Henry S. *The Renaissance and the Reformation.* 2d ed. New York, 1960.
Rice, Eugene F., Jr. *The Foundations of Early Modern Europe, 1460–1559.* New York, 1970.
Sellery, George Clarke. *The Renaissance: Its Nature and Origins.* Madison, Wis., 1950.
Spitz, Lewis W. *The Renaissance and Reformation Movements.* 2 vols. Chicago, 1971.
Wilcox, Donald J. *In Search of God and Self: Renaissance and Reformation Thought.* Boston, 1975.

2. Collections of Readings

Bainton, Roland G., ed. *The Age of the Reformation.* Princeton, N.J., 1956.
Cassirer, Ernst, Paul Oskar Kristeller, and John Herman Randall, Jr., eds. *The Renaissance Philosophy of Man.* Chicago, 1948.

Gundersheimer, Werner L., ed. *The Italian Renaissance.* Englewood Cliffs, N.J., 1965.
Ross, James Bruce, and Mary Martin McLaughlin, eds. *The Portable Renaissance Reader.* New York, 1953.
Spitz, Lewis W., ed. *The Northern Renaissance.* Englewood Cliffs, N.J., 1972.
_____. *The Protestant Reformation.* Englewood Cliffs, N.J., 1966.
Ziegler, Donald J., ed. *Great Debates of the Reformation.* New York, 1969.

3. The Renaissance Problem

Bouwsma, William J. *The Interpretation of Renaissance Humanism.* Washington, D.C., 1959.
Burckhardt, Jacob. *The Civilization of the Renaissance in Italy.* Trans. by S. G. C. Middlemore (many editions).
Chabod, Federico. *Machiavelli and the Renaissance.* Trans. by David Moore. New York, 1958.
Dannenfeldt, Karl H., ed. *The Renaissance: Basic Interpretations.* 2d ed. Lexington, Mass., 1974.
Ferguson, Wallace K. *The Renaissance in Historical Thought.* Boston, 1948.

Chapter 1

Bean, J. M. W. *The Decline of English Feudalism, 1215–1590.* New York, 1968.
Bloch, Marc. *French Rural History*, trans. Janet Sondheimer. Berkeley, 1966.
Cambridge Economic History of Europe, vols. I (2nd ed.), II, and III.
De Roover, Raymond. *The Rise and Decline of the Medici Bank, 1397–1494. Cambridge, Mass., 1963.*
Dollinger, Philippe. *The German Hansa*, trans. D. S. Ault and S. H. Steinberg. Stanford, Cal., 1970.
Lane, Frederic C. *Venice: A Maritime Republic.* Baltimore, 1973.
Lopez, Robert S. *The Commercial Revolution of the Middle Ages, 950–1350.* New York, 1971.
_____. "Hard Times and Investment in Culture," in *The Renaissance: Six Essays.* Rev. ed.; New York, 1962.
_____. and Irving W. Raymond, eds., *Medieval Trade in the Mediterranean World*". New York, 1955.
Luzzato, Gino. *An Economic History of Italy from the Fall of Rome to the Beginning of the Sixteenth Century*, trans. Philip Jones. New York, 1961.
Martin, Alfred von. *Sociology of the Renaissance.* London, 1944.
Miskimin, Harry A. *The Economy of Early Renaissance Europe, 1300–1460.* New York, 1969.
Slicher van Bath. B. H. *The Agrarian History of Western Europe*, trans. Olive Ordish. New York, 1963.
Thrupp, Sylvia. *The Merchant Class of Medieval London.* Chicago, 1948.

Chapter 2

Brucker, Gene A. *Renaissance Florence.* New York, 1969.
Goldthwaite, Richard A. *Private Wealth in Renaissance Florence: A Study of Four Families.* Princeton, N.J., 1968.
Gundersheimer, Werner L. *Ferrara: The Style of a Renaissance Despotism.* Princeton, N.J., 1973.
Herlihy, David. *Pisa in the Early Renaissance: A Study of Urban Growth.* New Haven, Conn., 1958.
Martines, Lauro. *Lawyers and Statecraft in Renaissance Florence.* Princeton, N.J., 1968.
Perroy, Edouard. *The Hundred Years War.* Trans. by David C. Douglas. New York, 1951.
Pullan, Brian. *Rich and Poor in Renaissance Venice.* Cambridge, Mass., 1971.
Schevill, Ferdinand. *History of Florence.* New York, 1936.
______. *Siena: The History of a Medieval Commune.* New York, 1909.
Strayer, Joseph R. *On the Medieval Origins of the Modern State.* Princeton, N.J., 1970.

Chapter 3

Cohn, Norman. *The Pursuit of the Millennium: Revolutionary Messianism in Medieval and Reformation Europe and Its Bearing on Modern Totalitarian Movements.* 2d ed. New York, 1961.
Flick, Alexander C. *The Decline of the Medieval Church.* 2 vols. New York, 1930.
Huizinga, Johan. *The Waning of the Middle Ages.* London, 1924.
Hyma, Albert. *The Christian Renaissance: A History of the "Devotio Moderna."* Grand Rapids, Mich., 1924.
Jacob, E. F. *Essays in the Conciliar Epoch.* Rev. ed. South Bend, Ind., 1963.
Jedin, Hubert. *A History of the Council of Trent.* Vol. I. Trans. by Ernest Graf. New York, 1957. (Also Vol. II for the Reformation period.)
Kaminsky, Howard. *A History of the Hussite Revolution.* Berkeley, Calif., 1967.
Leff, Gordon. *Heresy in the Later Middle Ages: The Relation of Heterodoxy to Dissent, c. 1250–c. 1450.* 2 vols. New York, 1967.
Oberman, Heiko Augustinus. *The Harvest of Medieval Theology.* Cambridge, Mass., 1963.
Pastor, Ludwig von. *History of the Popes from the Close of the Middle Ages.* Trans. by F. I. Antrobus et al. 40 vols. London, 1891–1953.
Post, R. R. *The Modern Devotion.* Leiden, 1968.
Reeves, Marjorie. *The Influence of Prophecy in the Later Middle Ages: A Study in Joachinism.* Oxford, 1969.
Ridolfi, Roberto. *The Life of Girolamo Savonarola.* Trans. by Cecil Grayson. New York, 1959.
Ullmann, Walter. *The Origins of the Great Schism.* London, 1948.
Tierney, Brian. *Foundations of the Conciliar Theory.* Cambridge, England, 1955.

Weinstein, Donald. *Savonarola and Florence: Prophecy and Patriotism in the Renaissance*. Princeton, N.J., 1970.

Chapter 4

Baron, Hans. *The Crisis of the Early Italian Renaissance: Civic Humanism and Republican Liberty in an Age of Classicism and Tyranny*. 2d ed. Princton, N.J., 1966.
Cassirer, Ernst. *The Individual and the Cosmos in Renaissance Philosophy*. Trans. by Mario Domandi. Oxford, 1963.
Garin, Eugenio. *Italian Humanism: Philosophy and Civic Life in the Renaissance*. Trans. by Peter Munz. New York, 1965.
Gray, Hanna. "Renaissance Humanism: The Pursuit of Eloquence," *Journal of the History of Ideas* 24 (1963): 497–514.
Holmes, George. *The Florentine Enlightenment, 1400–50*. New York, 1969.
Kristeller, Paul Oskar. *The Philosophy of Marsilio Ficino*. New York, 1943.
______. *Renaissance Thought: The Classic, Scholastic, and Humanist Strains*. New York, 1961.
Larner, John. *Culture and Society in Italy, 1290–1420*. New York, 1971.
Martines, Lauro. *The Social World of the Florentine Humanists, 1390–1460*. Princeton, N.J., 1963.
Mommsen, Theodor E. "Petrarch's Conception of the 'Dark Ages,'" *Speculum* 17 (1942): 226–42.
Panofsky, Erwin. *Renaissance and Renascences in Western Art*. Stockholm, 1960.
______. *Studies in Iconology: Humanistic Themes in the Art of the Renaissance*. New York, 1939.
Rice, Eugene F., Jr. *The Renaissance Idea of Wisdom*. Cambridge, Mass., 1958.
Seigel, Jerrold E. *Rhetoric and Philosophy in Renaissance Humanism: The Union of Eloquence and Wisdom, Petrarch to Valla*. Princeton, N.J. 1968.
Trinkaus, Charles. *In Our Image and Likeness: Humanity and Divinity in Italian Humanist Thought*. 2 vols. Chicago, 1970.
Weiss, Roberto. *The Dawn of Humanism in Italy*. London, 1947.
Wilcox, Donald J. *The Development of Florentine Humanist Historiography in the Fifteenth Century*. Cambridge, Mass., 1969.
Wilkins, Ernest Hatch. *Life of Petrarch*. Chicago, 1961.
Wölfflin, Heinrich. *Classic Art: An Introduction to the Italian Renaissance*. Trans. by Peter and Linda Murray. London, 1952.
Woodward, William Harrison. *Vittorino da Feltre and Other Humanist Educators*. Cambridge, England, 1897.

Chapter 5

Bainton, Roland H. *Erasmus of Christendom*. New York, 1969.
Benesch, Otto. *The Art of the Renaissance in Northern Europe: Its Relation to the Contemporary Spiritual and Intellectual Movements*. Cambridge, Mass., 1947.
Bush, Douglas. *The Renaissance and English Humanism*. Toronto, 1939.

Caspari, Fritz. *Humanism and the Social Order in Tudor England.* Chicago, 1954.
Chambers, R. W. *Thomas More.* London, 1935.
Gundersheimer, Werner L., ed. *French Humanism, 1470–1600.* New York, 1969.
Huizinga, Johan. *Erasmus of Rotterdam.* New York, 1924.
Jayne, Sears. *John Colet and Marsilio Ficino.* Oxford, 1963.
McConica, James K. *English Humanists and Reformation Politics under Henry VIII and Edward VI.* Oxford, 1965.
Panofsky, Erwin. *Albrecht Dürer.* 2 vols. Princeton, N.J., 1943.
Phillips, Margaret Mann. *Erasmus and the Northern Renaissance.* London, 1949.
Spitz, Lewis W. *The Religious Renaissance of the German Humanists.* Cambridge, Mass., 1963.
Strauss, Gerald E. *Pre-Reformation Germany.* New York, 1973.
Tracy, James D. *Erasmus: The Growth of a Mind.* Geneva, 1972.
Wadsworth, James B. *Lyons, 1473–1503: The Beginnings of Cosmopolitanism.* Cambridge, Mass., 1962.
Weiss, Roberto. *The Spread of Italian Humanism.* London, 1964.

Chapter 6

Atkinson, James. *Martin Luther and the Birth of Protestantism.* London, 1968.
Bainton, Roland H. *Here I Stand: A Life of Martin Luther.* Nashville, Tenn., 1950.
Bax, E. Belfort. *The Peasants' War in Germany, 1525–1526.* London, 1899.
Boehmer, Heinrich. *Martin Luther: Road to Reformation.* Trans. by John W. Doberstein and Theodore G. Tappert. Philadelphia, 1946.
Chrisman, Miriam Usher. *Strasbourg and the Reform: A Study in the Process of Change.* New Haven, Conn., 1967.
Ells, Hastings. *Martin Bucer.* New Haven, Conn., 1931.
Erikson, Erik. *Young Man Luther: A Study in Psychoanalysis and History.* New York, 1958.
Gritsch, Eric W. *Reformer Without a Church: The Life and Thought of Thomas Müntzer.* Philadelphia, 1967.
Harbison, E. Harris. *The Christian Scholar in the Age of the Reformation.* New York, 1956.
Holborn, Hajo. *Ulrich von Hutten and the German Reformation.* Trans. by Roland H. Bainton. New Haven, Conn., 1937.
Iserloh, Erwin. *The Theses Were Not Posted: Luther between Reform and Reformation.* Trans. by Jared Wicks. Boston, 1968.
Kirchner, Hubert. *Luther and the Peasants' War.* Trans. by Darrell Jodock. Philadelphia, 1972.
Lecler, Joseph. *Toleration and the Reformation.* Trans. by T. L. Westow. 2 vols. New York, 1960.
Manschreck, Clyde L. *Melanchthon: The Quiet Reformer.* New York, 1958.
Moeller, Bernd. *Imperial Cities and the Reformation: Three Essays.* Trans. by H. C. Erik Midelfort and Mark U. Edwards, Jr. Philadelphia, 1972.
Ozment, Steven E. *The Reformation in the Cities: The Appeal of Protestantism to Sixteenth-Century Germany and Switzerland.* New Haven, 1975.

Schapiro, J. Salwyn. *Social Reform and the Reformation.* New York, 1909.
Schwiebert, E. G. *Luther and His Times: The Reformation from a New Perspective.* St. Louis, 1950.
Strauss, Gerald. *Nuremberg in the Sixteenth Century.* New York, 1966.

Chapter 7

Bainton, Roland H. *The Travail of Religious Liberty.* Philadelphia, 1951.
Boehmer, Heinrich. *The Jesuits.* Trans. by P. Strodach. Philadelphia, 1928.
Clasen, Claus-Peter. *Anabaptism, A Social History, 1525–1618: Switzerland, Austria, Moravia, South and Central Germany.* Ithaca, N.Y., 1972.
Dickens, A. G. *The Counter-Reformation.* New York, 1969.
______. *The English Reformation.* London, 1964.
Dudon, Paul. *St. Ignatius of Loyola.* Trans. by W. J. Young. Milwaukee, 1949.
Elton, G. R. *Policy and Police: The Enforcement of the Reformation in the Age of Thomas Cromwell.* Cambridge, England, 1972.
Evennet, H. Outram. *The Spirit of the Counter-Reformation.* Cambridge, England, 1968.
Farner, Oskar. *Zwingli the Reformer: His Life and Work.* Trans. by D. G. Sear. New York, 1952.
Fülöp-Miller, René. *The Jesuits: A History of the Society of Jesus.* Trans. F. S. Flint and D. F. Tait. New York, 1963.
Jackson, Samuel M. *Huldreich Zwingli: The Reformer of German Switzerland, 1484–1531.* New York, 1901.
Kingdon, Robert M. *Geneva and the Coming of the Wars of Religion in France, 1555–1563.* Geneva, 1956.
Knappen, M. M. *Tudor Puritanism: A Chapter in the History of Idealism.* Chicago, 1939.
Littell, Franklin H. *The Origins of Sectarian Protestantism: A Study of the Anabaptist View of the Church.* New York, 1964.
McNeill, John T. *The History and Character of Calvinism.* New York, 1954.
Monter, E. William. *Calvin's Geneva.* New York, 1967.
O'Connell, Marvin R. *The Counter Reformation, 1559–1610.* New York, 1974.
Walker, Williston. *John Calvin, the Organiser of Reformed Protestantism, 1509–1564.* New York, 1906.
Wendel, François. *Calvin: The Origins and Development of His Religious Thought.* Trans. by P. Mairet. New York, 1963.
Williams, George Huntston. *The Radical Reformation.* Philadelphia, 1962.

Chapter 8

Allen, J. W. *A History of Political Thought in the Sixteenth Century.* London, 1928.
Black, J. B. *The Reign of Elizabeth.* 2d ed. Oxford, 1959.
Braudel, Fernand. *The Mediterranean and the Mediterranean World in the Age of Philip II.* Trans. by Siân Reynolds. 2 vols. New York, 1972.

Church, William F. *Constitutional Thought in Sixteenth-Century France.* Cambridge, Mass., 1941.

Davies, R. Trevor. *The Golden Century of Spain, 1501–1621.* London, 1937.

Elliott, J. H. *Imperial Spain, 1469–1716.* New York, 1964.

Elton, G. R. *The Tudor Revolution in Government: Administrative Changes in the Reign of Henry VIII.* Cambridge, England, 1973.

Geyl, Pieter. *The Revolt of the Netherlands, 1555–1609.* 2d ed. London, 1958.

Gilbert, Felix. *Machiavelli and Guicciardini: Politics and History in Sixteenth Century Florence.* Princeton, N.J., 1965.

Hexter, J. H. *Reappraisals in History: New Views on History and Society in Early Modern Europe.* London, 1961.

Koenigsberger, H. G. "The Organization of Revolutionary Parties in France and the Netherlands during the 16th Century," *Journal of Modern History* 27 (1955): 335–51.

Major, J. Russell. "The French Renaissance Monarchy as Seen through the Estates General," *Studies in the Renaissance* 9 (1962): 113–25.

Mattingly, Garrett. *The Armada.* Boston, 1959.

______. *Renaissance Diplomacy.* Boston, 1955.

Neale, John E. *The Age of Catherine de Medici.* London, 1943.

______. *Elizabeth I and Her Parliaments.* 2 vols. London, 1953–1957.

______. *The Elizabethan House of Commons.* London, 1949.

______. *Queen Elizabeth.* New York, 1934.

Ridolfi, Roberto. *The Life of Niccol[Machiavelli.* Trans. by Cecil Grayson. London, 1963.

Slavin, Arthur J., ed. *The "New Monarchies" and Representative Assemblies: Medieval Constitutionalism or Modern Absolutism?* Lexington, Mass., 1964.

Chapter 9

Boxer, C. R. *The Portuguese Seaborne Empire, 1415–1825.* New York, 1969.

Braudel, Fernand. *Capitalism and Material Life, 1400–1800.* Trans. by Miriam Kochan. London, 1973.

Burke, Peter, ed. *Economy and Society in Early Modern Europe: Essays from Annales.* London, 1972.

Elliott, J. H. *The Old World and the New, 1492–1650.* Cambridge, England, 1970.

Green, Robert W., ed. *Protestantism and Capitalism: The Weber Thesis and Its Critics.* Boston, 1859.

Kamen, Henry. *The Iron Century: Social Change in Europe, 1550–1660.* New York, 1971.

Morison, Samuel Eliot. *Admiral of the Ocean Sea* (a life of Christopher Columbus). 2 vols. Boston, 1942.

Nef, John U. *Industry and Government in France and England, 1540–1640.* Ithaca, N.Y., 1957.

Parry, J. H. *The Establishment of the European Hegemony, 1415–1715: Trade and Exploration in the Age of the Renaissance.* London, 1949.

Penrose, Boies. *Travel and Discovery in the Renaissance, 1420–1620.* Cambridge, Mass., 1952.
Tawney, R. H. *The Agraran Problem in the Sixteenth Century.* London, 1912.
_____. *Religion and the Rise of Capitalism.* New York, 1926.
Weber, Max. *The Protestant Ethic and the Spirit of Capitalism.* Trans. by Talcott Parsons. New York, 1958.

Chapter 10

Boas, Marie. *The Scientific Renaissance, 1450–1630.* London, 1962.
Bouwsma, William J. *Venice and the Defense of Republican Liberty: Renaissance Values in the Age of the Counter Reformation.* Berkeley, Calif., 1968.
Butterfield, Herbert. *The Origins of Modern Science, 1300–1800.* London, 1957.
Cochrane, Eric, ed. *The Late Italian Renaissance, 1525–1630.* New York, 1970.
Crombie, A. C. *Medieval and Early Modern Science.* 2 vols. New York, 1959.
Curtis, Mark H. *Oxford and Cambridge in Transition, 1558–1642: An Essay on Changing Relations between the English Universities and English Society.* Oxford, 1959.
Evans, R. J. W. *Rudolf II and His World: A Study in Intellectual History, 1576–1612.* Oxford, 1973.
Hall, A. R. *The Scientific Revolution, 1300–1800.* Boston, 1954.
Haydn, Hiram. *The Counter-Renaissance.* New York, 1950.
Kelley, Donald R. *Foundations of Modern Historical Scholarship: Language, Law, and History in the French Renaissance.* New York, 1970.
Koyré, Alexandre. *From the Closed World to the Infinite Universe.* New York, 1958.
Macfarlane, Alan. *Witchcraft in Tudor and Stuart England.* New York, 1970.
Monter, E. William, ed. *European Witchcraft.* New York, 1969.
Munz, Peter. *The Place of Hooker in the History of Thought.* London, 1952.
Popkin, Richard H. *The History of Scepticism from Erasmus to Descartes.* Assen, the Netherlands, 1960.
Rossi, Paolo. *Francis Bacon: From Magic to Science.* Trans. by Sacha Rabinovitch. London, 1968.
Santillana, Giorgio de. *The Crime of Galileo.* Chicago, 1955.
Thomas, Keith. *Religion and the Decline of Magic.* London, 1971.
Walker, D. P. *The Ancient Theology: Studies in Christian Platonism from the Fifteenth to the Eighteenth Century.* Ithaca, N.Y., 1972.
Yates, Frances A. *Giordano Bruno and the Hermetic Tradition.* Chicago, 1964

Chapter 11

Aston, Trevor, ed. *Crisis in Europe, 1560–1660.* London, 1965.
Aylmer, G. E. *The King's Servants: The Civil Service of Charles I, 1625–1642.* New York, 1961.
Foster, Robert, and Jack P. Greene, eds. *Preconditions of Revolution in Early Modern Europe.* Baltimore, 1970.

Haller, William. *The Rise of Puritanism.* New York, 1938.
Huizinga, J. H. *Dutch Civilisation in the Seventeenth Century and Other Essays.* Trans. by Arnold J. Pomerans. London, 1968.
Pearl, Valerie. *London and the Outbreak of the Puritan Revolution: City Government and National Politics, 1625–43.* London, 1961.
Ruigh, Robert E. *The Parliament of 1624.* Cambridge, Mass., 1971.
Stone, Lawrence. *The Crisis of the Aristocracy, 1558–1641.* Oxford, 1967.
Walzer, Michael. *The Revolution of the Saints: A Study in the Origins of Radical Politics.* Cambridge, Mass., 1965.
Wedgwood, C. V. *Richelieu and the French Monarchy.* London, 1949.
———. *The Thirty Years' War.* London, 1938.

Index